FREE Test Taking Tips DVD Offer

To help us better serve you, we have developed a Test Taking Tips DVD that we would like to give you for FREE. **This DVD covers world-class test taking tips that you can use to be even more successful when you are taking your test.**

All that we ask is that you email us your feedback about your study guide. Please let us know what you thought about it – whether that is good, bad or indifferent.

To get your **FREE Test Taking Tips DVD**, email freedvd@studyguideteam.com with "FREE DVD" in the subject line and the following information in the body of the email:

   a. The title of your study guide.

   b. Your product rating on a scale of 1-5, with 5 being the highest rating.

   c. Your feedback about the study guide. What did you think of it?

   d. Your full name and shipping address to send your free DVD.

If you have any questions or concerns, please don't hesitate to contact us at freedvd@studyguideteam.com.

Thanks again!

AP Psychology 2020 & 2021

Test Prep AP Psychology Review Book &
Practice Test Questions for the
Advanced Placement Psych Exam
[Updated for the Latest Exam Description]

Table of Contents

Quick Overview

As you draw closer to taking your exam, effective preparation becomes more and more important. Thankfully, you have this study guide to help you get ready. Use this guide to help keep your studying on track and refer to it often.

This study guide contains several key sections that will help you be successful on your exam. The guide contains tips for what you should do the night before and the day of the test. Also included are test-taking tips. Knowing the right information is not always enough. Many well-prepared test takers struggle with exams. These tips will help equip you to accurately read, assess, and answer test questions.

A large part of the guide is devoted to showing you what content to expect on the exam and to helping you better understand that content. In this guide are practice test questions so that you can see how well you have grasped the content. Then, answer explanations are provided so that you can understand why you missed certain questions.

Don't try to cram the night before you take your exam. This is not a wise strategy for a few reasons. First, your retention of the information will be low. Your time would be better used by reviewing information you already know rather than trying to learn a lot of new information. Second, you will likely become stressed as you try to gain a large amount of knowledge in a short amount of time. Third, you will be depriving yourself of sleep. So be sure to go to bed at a reasonable time the night before. Being well-rested helps you focus and remain calm.

Be sure to eat a substantial breakfast the morning of the exam. If you are taking the exam in the afternoon, be sure to have a good lunch as well. Being hungry is distracting and can make it difficult to focus. You have hopefully spent lots of time preparing for the exam. Don't let an empty stomach get in the way of success!

When travelling to the testing center, leave earlier than needed. That way, you have a buffer in case you experience any delays. This will help you remain calm and will keep you from missing your appointment time at the testing center.

Be sure to pace yourself during the exam. Don't try to rush through the exam. There is no need to risk performing poorly on the exam just so you can leave the testing center early. Allow yourself to use all of the allotted time if needed.

Remain positive while taking the exam even if you feel like you are performing poorly. Thinking about the content you should have mastered will not help you perform better on the exam.

Once the exam is complete, take some time to relax. Even if you feel that you need to take the exam again, you will be well served by some down time before you begin studying again. It's often easier to convince yourself to study if you know that it will come with a reward!

Test-Taking Strategies

1. Predicting the Answer

When you feel confident in your preparation for a multiple-choice test, try predicting the answer before reading the answer choices. This is especially useful on questions that test objective factual knowledge. By predicting the answer before reading the available choices, you eliminate the possibility that you will be distracted or led astray by an incorrect answer choice. You will feel more confident in your selection if you read the question, predict the answer, and then find your prediction among the answer choices. After using this strategy, be sure to still read all of the answer choices carefully and completely. If you feel unprepared, you should not attempt to predict the answers. This would be a waste of time and an opportunity for your mind to wander in the wrong direction.

2. Reading the Whole Question

Too often, test takers scan a multiple-choice question, recognize a few familiar words, and immediately jump to the answer choices. Test authors are aware of this common impatience, and they will sometimes prey upon it. For instance, a test author might subtly turn the question into a negative, or he or she might redirect the focus of the question right at the end. The only way to avoid falling into these traps is to read the entirety of the question carefully before reading the answer choices.

3. Looking for Wrong Answers

Long and complicated multiple-choice questions can be intimidating. One way to simplify a difficult multiple-choice question is to eliminate all of the answer choices that are clearly wrong. In most sets of answers, there will be at least one selection that can be dismissed right away. If the test is administered on paper, the test taker could draw a line through it to indicate that it may be ignored; otherwise, the test taker will have to perform this operation mentally or on scratch paper. In either case, once the obviously incorrect answers have been eliminated, the remaining choices may be considered. Sometimes identifying the clearly wrong answers will give the test taker some information about the correct answer. For instance, if one of the remaining answer choices is a direct opposite of one of the eliminated answer choices, it may well be the correct answer. The opposite of obviously wrong is obviously right! Of course, this is not always the case. Some answers are obviously incorrect simply because they are irrelevant to the question being asked. Still, identifying and eliminating some incorrect answer choices is a good way to simplify a multiple-choice question.

4. Don't Overanalyze

Anxious test takers often overanalyze questions. When you are nervous, your brain will often run wild, causing you to make associations and discover clues that don't actually exist. If you feel that this may be a problem for you, do whatever you can to slow down during the test. Try taking a deep breath or counting to ten. As you read and consider the question, restrict yourself to the particular words used by the author. Avoid thought tangents about what the author *really* meant, or what he or she was *trying* to say. The only things that matter on a multiple-choice test are the words that are actually in the question. You must avoid reading too much into a multiple-choice question, or supposing that the writer meant something other than what he or she wrote.

5. No Need for Panic

It is wise to learn as many strategies as possible before taking a multiple-choice test, but it is likely that you will come across a few questions for which you simply don't know the answer. In this situation, avoid panicking. Because most multiple-choice tests include dozens of questions, the relative value of a single wrong answer is small. As much as possible, you should compartmentalize each question on a multiple-choice test. In other words, you should not allow your feelings about one question to affect your success on the others. When you find a question that you either don't understand or don't know how to answer, just take a deep breath and do your best. Read the entire question slowly and carefully. Try rephrasing the question a couple of different ways. Then, read all of the answer choices carefully. After eliminating obviously wrong answers, make a selection and move on to the next question.

6. Confusing Answer Choices

When working on a difficult multiple-choice question, there may be a tendency to focus on the answer choices that are the easiest to understand. Many people, whether consciously or not, gravitate to the answer choices that require the least concentration, knowledge, and memory. This is a mistake. When you come across an answer choice that is confusing, you should give it extra attention. A question might be confusing because you do not know the subject matter to which it refers. If this is the case, don't eliminate the answer before you have affirmatively settled on another. When you come across an answer choice of this type, set it aside as you look at the remaining choices. If you can confidently assert that one of the other choices is correct, you can leave the confusing answer aside. Otherwise, you will need to take a moment to try to better understand the confusing answer choice. Rephrasing is one way to tease out the sense of a confusing answer choice.

7. Your First Instinct

Many people struggle with multiple-choice tests because they overthink the questions. If you have studied sufficiently for the test, you should be prepared to trust your first instinct once you have carefully and completely read the question and all of the answer choices. There is a great deal of research suggesting that the mind can come to the correct conclusion very quickly once it has obtained all of the relevant information. At times, it may seem to you as if your intuition is working faster even than your reasoning mind. This may in fact be true. The knowledge you obtain while studying may be retrieved from your subconscious before you have a chance to work out the associations that support it. Verify your instinct by working out the reasons that it should be trusted.

8. Key Words

Many test takers struggle with multiple-choice questions because they have poor reading comprehension skills. Quickly reading and understanding a multiple-choice question requires a mixture of skill and experience. To help with this, try jotting down a few key words and phrases on a piece of scrap paper. Doing this concentrates the process of reading and forces the mind to weigh the relative importance of the question's parts. In selecting words and phrases to write down, the test taker thinks about the question more deeply and carefully. This is especially true for multiple-choice questions that are preceded by a long prompt.

9. Subtle Negatives

One of the oldest tricks in the multiple-choice test writer's book is to subtly reverse the meaning of a question with a word like *not* or *except*. If you are not paying attention to each word in the question, you can easily be led astray by this trick. For instance, a common question format is, "Which of the following is…?" Obviously, if the question instead is, "Which of the following is not…?," then the answer will be quite different. Even worse, the test makers are aware of the potential for this mistake and will include one answer choice that would be correct if the question were not negated or reversed. A test taker who misses the reversal will find what he or she believes to be a correct answer and will be so confident that he or she will fail to reread the question and discover the original error. The only way to avoid this is to practice a wide variety of multiple-choice questions and to pay close attention to each and every word.

10. Reading Every Answer Choice

It may seem obvious, but you should always read every one of the answer choices! Too many test takers fall into the habit of scanning the question and assuming that they understand the question because they recognize a few key words. From there, they pick the first answer choice that answers the question they believe they have read. Test takers who read all of the answer choices might discover that one of the latter answer choices is actually *more* correct. Moreover, reading all of the answer choices can remind you of facts related to the question that can help you arrive at the correct answer. Sometimes, a misstatement or incorrect detail in one of the latter answer choices will trigger your memory of the subject and will enable you to find the right answer. Failing to read all of the answer choices is like not reading all of the items on a restaurant menu: you might miss out on the perfect choice.

11. Spot the Hedges

One of the keys to success on multiple-choice tests is paying close attention to every word. This is never truer than with words like almost, most, some, and sometimes. These words are called "hedges" because they indicate that a statement is not totally true or not true in every place and time. An absolute statement will contain no hedges, but in many subjects, the answers are not always straightforward or absolute. There are always exceptions to the rules in these subjects. For this reason, you should favor those multiple-choice questions that contain hedging language. The presence of qualifying words indicates that the author is taking special care with his or her words, which is certainly important when composing the right answer. After all, there are many ways to be wrong, but there is only one way to be right! For this reason, it is wise to avoid answers that are absolute when taking a multiple-choice test. An absolute answer is one that says things are either all one way or all another. They often include words like *every*, *always*, *best*, and *never*. If you are taking a multiple-choice test in a subject that doesn't lend itself to absolute answers, be on your guard if you see any of these words.

12. Long Answers

In many subject areas, the answers are not simple. As already mentioned, the right answer often requires hedges. Another common feature of the answers to a complex or subjective question are qualifying clauses, which are groups of words that subtly modify the meaning of the sentence. If the question or answer choice describes a rule to which there are exceptions or the subject matter is complicated, ambiguous, or confusing, the correct answer will require many words in order to be expressed clearly and accurately. In essence, you should not be deterred by answer choices that seem excessively long. Oftentimes, the author of the text will not be able to write the correct answer without

offering some qualifications and modifications. Your job is to read the answer choices thoroughly and completely and to select the one that most accurately and precisely answers the question.

13. Restating to Understand

Sometimes, a question on a multiple-choice test is difficult not because of what it asks but because of how it is written. If this is the case, restate the question or answer choice in different words. This process serves a couple of important purposes. First, it forces you to concentrate on the core of the question. In order to rephrase the question accurately, you have to understand it well. Rephrasing the question will concentrate your mind on the key words and ideas. Second, it will present the information to your mind in a fresh way. This process may trigger your memory and render some useful scrap of information picked up while studying.

14. True Statements

Sometimes an answer choice will be true in itself, but it does not answer the question. This is one of the main reasons why it is essential to read the question carefully and completely before proceeding to the answer choices. Too often, test takers skip ahead to the answer choices and look for true statements. Having found one of these, they are content to select it without reference to the question above. Obviously, this provides an easy way for test makers to play tricks. The savvy test taker will always read the entire question before turning to the answer choices. Then, having settled on a correct answer choice, he or she will refer to the original question and ensure that the selected answer is relevant. The mistake of choosing a correct-but-irrelevant answer choice is especially common on questions related to specific pieces of objective knowledge. A prepared test taker will have a wealth of factual knowledge at his or her disposal, and should not be careless in its application.

15. No Patterns

One of the more dangerous ideas that circulates about multiple-choice tests is that the correct answers tend to fall into patterns. These erroneous ideas range from a belief that B and C are the most common right answers, to the idea that an unprepared test-taker should answer "A-B-A-C-A-D-A-B-A." It cannot be emphasized enough that pattern-seeking of this type is exactly the WRONG way to approach a multiple-choice test. To begin with, it is highly unlikely that the test maker will plot the correct answers according to some predetermined pattern. The questions are scrambled and delivered in a random order. Furthermore, even if the test maker was following a pattern in the assignation of correct answers, there is no reason why the test taker would know which pattern he or she was using. Any attempt to discern a pattern in the answer choices is a waste of time and a distraction from the real work of taking the test. A test taker would be much better served by extra preparation before the test than by reliance on a pattern in the answers.

FREE DVD OFFER

Don't forget that doing well on your exam includes both understanding the test content and understanding how to use what you know to do well on the test. We offer a completely FREE Test Taking Tips DVD that covers world class test taking tips that you can use to be even more successful when you are taking your test.

All that we ask is that you email us your feedback about your study guide. To get your **FREE Test Taking Tips DVD**, email freedvd@studyguideteam.com with "FREE DVD" in the subject line and the following information in the body of the email:

- The title of your study guide.
- Your product rating on a scale of 1-5, with 5 being the highest rating.
- Your feedback about the study guide. What did you think of it?
- Your full name and shipping address to send your free DVD.

Introduction to the AP Psychology Exam

Function of the Test

The Advanced Placement (AP) Psychology exam is part of the College Board's Advanced Placement Program, which affords high school students the opportunity to pursue college-level coursework while in high school. Like every other exam in this program, the AP Psychology exam is the culminating final exam for its respective course. Although students can register for and take an AP test without completing the related AP course, most test takers attempt the exam at the culmination of the AP course in the given AP subject, which typically lasts the duration of the academic year. Taking the AP Psychology course and scoring well on the exam demonstrates to prospective colleges that a high school student has attempted the hardest course level available to them, and can even earn the student college credit or advanced placement.

New in the fall of 2019, the AP Psychology course and exam are structured in nine major units that are further subdivided into numerous topics. The course is designed to explore the concepts of psychology including the ideas, methods of study, and theories involved in human behavior and mental processes. The exam evaluates students' understanding and application of these concepts.

Test Administration

The AP Psychology exam is offered on a certain date in May each year and is mostly administered by schools that offer an AP Psychology course. However, students can make arrangements with a school to take an AP exam even if they did not take the course at that particular school. All AP exams cost the same amount of money, with an additional fee added for exams administered outside of the U.S. and Canada. Schools can also add fees to cover their costs of administering the exams if they wish, but most offer the exams at the standard base rate.

Accommodations for students with documented disabilities include time extensions, large-type exams, large-block answer sheets, Braille devices, question readers, response writers, and more. Students seeking accommodations should contact the Disabilities Office of College Board Services.

Students may take an AP exam every time it is offered (i.e., once a year). Scores from all attempts will be reported in the score report after each test.

Test Format

The AP Psychology exam contains two sections and lasts 2 hours. The first section contains 100 multiple-choice questions, lasts 70 minutes, and contributes 66.7% to a test taker's overall score. Each question contains five answer choices and test takers select the single best response. The multiple-choice questions address three skill categories: Concept Understanding, Data Analysis, and Scientific Investigation. Of the 100 multiple-choice questions, 75-80% are Concept Understanding, 8-12% are Data Analysis, and 12-15% are Scientific Investigation questions. The second section contains two free-response questions, lasts 50 minutes, and contributes 33.3% to a test taker's overall score. The first free-response question is a Concept Application question, which addresses the first skill category (Concept Understanding). This question assesses a test taker's ability to coherently explain human behavior and apply psychological theories and perspectives to real-life contexts. It is worth 7 points. The second free-response question is a Research Design question, which is also worth 7 points. This question measures

all three skill categories, though the third category (Scientific Investigation) is the primary focus. Test takers are presented with a scenario or exercise that assesses their ability to analyze a research study aimed at some aspect of human psychology. Quantitative data will need to be interpreted and analyzed.

The exam, like the course, is designed to cover nine major units, each which is further subdivided into numerous topics. The nine units and their approximate weight in the exam are listed in the table below:

Content Unit	Approximate Share of Questions
Unit 1: Scientific Foundations of Psychology	10-14%
Unit 2: Biological Bases of Behavior	8-10%
Unit 3: Sensation and Perception	6-8%
Unit 4: Learning	7-9%
Unit 5: Cognitive Psychology	13-17%
Unit 6: Developmental Psychology	7-9%
Unit 7: Motivation, Emotion, and Personality	11-15%
Unit 8: Clinical Psychology	12-16%
Unit 9: Social Psychology	8-10%

Scoring

Answers to the multiple-choice questions are scored by a machine, and students receive a raw score of one point for each correct answer. Answers to the free-response questions are scored by thousands of experts, trained AP teachers and college professors; these questions are scored on a scale that varies between three and ten points, depending on the length and complexity of the question. The free-response scores are weighted and then added to the multiple-choice scores. This raw score is then scaled to a composite AP score, which ranges from 1 to 5, with 5 being the maximal score. While there is no set passing score, most colleges and universities require a score of at least 3 to place out of a class, and a 4 or 5 to earn college credit. The AP score interpretation guide, which gives meaning to the scores such that they signify how qualified a student is to receive advanced placement or college credit, assigns the following recommendations for the possible AP scores: a score of 1 is assigned "no recommendation," 2 is "possibly qualified," 3 is "qualified," 4 is "well qualified," and a student who earns a score of 5 is considered "extremely well qualified."

In 2018, the passing rate (score of 3 or above) was 64.5%. 20.5% of the students who took the AP Psychology exam earned a 5, 25.3% earned a 4, 18.7% earned a 3, 13.5% earned a 2, and 22.0% earned a 1.

Recent Updates

Along with most AP courses and exams, the AP Psychology course and exam was revamped for fall 2019. It is now structured to have nine major units rather than six big ideas. There are still four big ideas that

underlie the content of the course and exam, but the College Board has shifted the emphasis and format to one they feel better meets their goals for students attempting the course.

Unit 1: Scientific Foundations of Psychology

Introducing Psychology

How Philosophical and Physiological Perspectives Shaped the Development of Psychological Thought

People have been studying the human thoughts, behavior, and the mind for thousands of years in a broad sense. The empirical basis of psychology has its roots in the work of philosophers in Ancient Greece. Socrates and Plato, two of the most well-known Ancient Greek philosophers shared the perspective of **dualism,** which posited that the body and mind were separate entities, and after death, only the mind survived. They also contended that ideas are innate, in that humans are born with them. On the other hand, thought Socrates and Plato were mentors for Aristotle, he disagreed with them and was a proponent of **monism,** which posited that the body and mind were united as one inseparable entity. Moreover, rather than believing ideas are innate or products of nature, Aristotle believe ideas were a product of nurture, in that they were brought about by experiences.

Records of interest in psychological thought are then sparse until the Renaissance. In the 1600s, Rene Descartes studied the body-mind connection by dissecting animals to visualize their brains and nervous systems. Like Socrates and Plato, Descartes was curious about how the physical body worked with the conceptual mind. John Locke was the father of **empiricism,** which contends that knowledge is derived from experiences. He believed that our minds are *tabula rasa* at birth, which means that they are "blank slates." It is through lived experiences that the mind starts forming ideas and connections.

Locke, along with his contemporary Frances Bacon, started trying to investigate the mind in a scientific way, using the scientific method instead of just casual observations and anecdotes. The work of these early philosophers and physicians lay the groundwork for what would become the official discipline of psychology in 1879. Additionally, it can be seen that even thousands of years ago, the nature versus nurture debate was one of the most central questions pertaining to human behavior and thought.

The Research Contributions of Major Historical Figures in Psychology

Mary Whiton Calkins
Mary Whiton Calkins (1863–1930) was the first female president of the American Psychological Association. She attended Harvard and earned a doctoral degree, but it was not awarded because of her gender. Calkins proposed the concept of **paired association**, which is a learning technique that involves the coupling of two things—typically words—in the form of a stimulus and response.

Charles Darwin
Charles Darwin (1809–1882) was a biologist and naturalist best known for his work in evolution; however, his work indirectly contributed to the field of psychology as well. Darwin theorized that humans and animals had a common ancestor and therefore, emotional and behavioral traits of animals could be used to better understand human behavior. Darwin's theories paved the way for future **comparative psychology**, which is the study animals to help understand human behavior, emotions, and actions. Another of Darwin's notable contributions to the field of psychology involved examining the influence of biological phenomena, like evolution and natural selection, on human behavior. The **theory of evolution** explains that a species evolves and adapts over time in order to better the chances of the

survival of that species. The concept of **natural selection** states that the traits within a species that are most likely to contribute to the longevity of that species will survive and be passed on to future offspring. For example, according to evolutionary psychologists, characteristics like advanced memory and speech have been biologically selected over time because they were more advantageous to human survival. These concepts have become the foundation of evolutionary psychology.

Dorothea Dix

Dorothea Dix (1802–1887) was an activist for the humane treatment of the mentally ill during the 1800s in the United States, Canada, and Europe. Dix led reform movements, which included the creation of the first public hospital for the mentally ill in Pennsylvania and asylums in several other states. She also fought for legislation to provide funding for large scale reform across the United States and the establishment of national asylums, but the bill was defeated. Dix championed reform for the mentally ill Great Britain and Scotland as well.

Sigmund Freud

Sigmund Freud (1856–1839) introduced **psychoanalytic theory**, which proposed three components of the mind including the conscious, preconscious, and unconscious minds. The conscious mind contains thoughts and feelings that a person is aware of. The preconscious mind contains information that a person can retrieve if needed. The unconscious mind stores thoughts and urges a person is not aware of; however, the unconscious mind still affects the individual's personality, feelings, and actions. Intimately died to these divisions, Freud also proposed three distinct personality components including the id, ego, and the superego. The impulsive motivation of the **id** is to seek pleasure. The **superego** develops as a result of societal influence and provides a framework for morality. The function of the **ego** is to manage the conflict between the id and the superego.

Freud also proposed several stages of human development that occur before the age of 5. According to his theory, a disruption at any of the stages affects an individual's personality development. Freud's psychosexual development stages include oral, anal, phallic, latency, and genital.

Another major contribution by Freud is the concept of **defense mechanisms**. These protective mechanisms occur at unconscious levels and reduce anxiety and stress in an individual. One of the more well-known defense mechanisms is **repression,** or the stifling of uncomfortable thoughts and feelings from reaching consciousness. Another defense mechanism is **projection**, which is when an individual projects or assigns his or her own feelings on to another person to avoid sitting as directly with those feelings.

G. Stanley Hall

G. Stanley Hall (1846–1924) founded child and educational psychology and had significant influence in psychological trends of that time. Hall created the first journal in child and educational psychology called *Pedagogical Seminary*. He was the American Psychological Association's first president.

William James

William James (1842–1910), often dubbed "the father of American psychology," offered one of the first courses in psychology in the United States and introduced several influential concepts to the field. He is known for the development of **functionalism**, which studies the correlation between internal feelings, external actions, and the environment and considers the whole cognitive, environmental, and emotional experience of people, rather than just the internal experience addressed via introspection. James also introduced **pragmatism**, which argued that a concept could not actually be proven and therefore, the focus should be on the functionality and practicality of the concept. One of James' most significant contributions was the multivolume and widely-used text called *The Principles of Psychology*. Another concept that James contributed to is the James-Lang theory of emotion. James believed that a situation causes a person to have a physical response and a related interpretation of the event, which then leads to an emotional reaction. In other words, the individual's interpretation of the event and reaction lead to the emotional response, not the event itself.

Ivan Pavlov

Ivan Pavlov (1849–1936) was a Russian physiologist who introduced the concept of **classical conditioning** in 1906. Classical conditioning is a form of learning that pairs two non-related stimuli. In Pavlov's famous experiment, he presented a dog with food (the stimulus), which caused the dog to produce saliva (the automatic biological response). He then paired the food presentation with a bell (the neutral stimulus). After repeated exposure, the dog became conditioned to produce saliva when presented with the bell, even in the absence of food.

Jean Piaget

Jean Piaget (1896–1980) proposed a theory of **cognitive development.** Cognitive development considers how a child's mind develops and perceives the world. Piaget's cognitive development work was the first to argue that children and adults differ in their styles and ways of thinking. Piaget's stages demonstrate how he believed children's cognitive abilities change and develop overtime, acquiring new skills at every stage. He also argued that intelligence was not set; rather, intelligence develops as a result of both biological and environmental factors. Piaget's theory included the concept of **schemas**—frameworks or pattern of behaviors in response to a specific stimulus or piece of information.

Carl Rogers

Carl Rogers (1902–1987) was considered a leader in the development of humanism. Rogers introduced the person-centered approach to therapy. This approach was influenced by Maslow's concept of self-actualization, but expanded on it by adding that having a supportive and encouraging environment is crucial for a person to achieve growth and self-actualization.

B.F. Skinner

B.F. Skinner (1904–1990) continued work on behaviorism—initiated by John Watson—and introduced the concept of operant conditioning. Skinner theorized that not only could behavior result from external stimulus, but it also could be impacted by consequences following the behavior. **Positive reinforcement** (receiving a pleasant consequence or eliminating a unpleasant consequence) following a behavior resulted in an increase in the desired behavior. Receiving **negative consequences** or punishment resulted in a decrease in a behavior. **Behaviorism** uses scientific methodology and focuses only on observable behavior and how it is affected by external factors. Some limitations of this perspective are that it does not account for other aspects of humans, like their biology, genetics, and internal thoughts and feelings.

Margaret Floy Washburn

Margaret Floy Washburn (1871–1931) was the first female to be awarded a PhD in psychology. Washburn's work focused on animal behavior and physical movement with one of her most significant contributions being a text called *The Animal Mind: A Textbook of Comparative Psychology.* Washburn argued that all cognitive functions, in particular those related to learning and emotions, manifest physically and can be studied.

John Watson

John Watson (1847–1939), influenced by Pavlov's concept of classical conditioning, believed that all behavior could be explained by reactions to external stimuli. This resulted in the development of the behaviorism school of thought. Watson disagreed with previous theories that attributed human behavior to internal drives. Watson expanded on Pavlov's conditioning experiment with animals and demonstrated that human behavior could be impacted by conditioning.

Wilhelm Wundt

Wilhelm Wundt (1832–1920) is considered the founder of modern psychology. In 1879, Wundt opened the first psychological laboratory called the Institute for Experimental Psychology in Germany. Wundt contributed significantly to the field by formally separating psychology from philosophy and other disciplines. He introduced the concept of introspection. Wundt conducted experiments and provided specific training to participants so that he could uniformly examine and record their internal reactions and sensations after exposure to an objective stimulus. Wundt's work demonstrated the validity of psychology as an experimental science and he is consequently known as the father of experimental psychology. He coined the term **voluntarism**, which can be defined as using the power or will of the mind to organize thoughts and processes.

Wundt also wrote the first psychology text called *Principles of Physiological Psychology*. Edward Titchener, a student of Wundt, further developed his work and introduced **structuralism**, which sought to classify the components of the human mind. Titchener developed "A Textbook of Psychology," where he proposed three elements of the conscious mind including sensations/perceptions, ideas, and affections/emotions.

The Different Theoretical Approaches in Explaining Behavior

There are several different theoretical perspectives or views of human psychology. These psychological schools of thought explain human personality, development, and behavior. Psychological theories and approaches fall into one or more of these perspectives.

Structuralism

Structuralism is focused on the structure of the mind. The first structuralist, Edward Bradford Titchener, encouraged introspection as the means to figure out the mind's structure. Structuralism considered sensations that someone experienced after perceiving something, like after smelling a rose. However, the high degree of introspection central to structuralism lends itself to issues such as a lack of reliability and objectivity.

Functionalism

Functionalism was pioneered by William James. James was mostly focused on the function of the brain and what it does and why it does those things. He was influenced by Darwin's theory of evolution and felt that structures like the nose, for example, adapted to smell because doing so aided human survival.

Early Behaviorism

Behaviorism focuses solely on observable behaviors as compared to internal feelings, responses, or thoughts. Behaviorists study how behaviors are reinforced or decreased in response to external stimuli.

Gestalt

Max Wertheimer, along with Kurt Koffka and Wolfgang Kohler, are considered to be the pioneers of the school of gestalt psychology. This perspective, in contrast to introspective psychology, looks at the mind and behavior together as a whole. Gestalt psychology examines how individuals view and perceive the world in terms of entire experiences. A central concept is that the whole is greater than the sum of its parts. Human perception is also a significant concept in this approach to studying human behavior. People perceive information based on beliefs and what they expect to see, not just on what they see, and the brain cognitively supplies missing information. An example would be seeing movement when looking at a string of lights that are blinking in sequence. Perception is further explained by gestalt theory with principles called **perceptual organization laws,** which describe common ways the mind tends to group items together. The following are some of these laws:

Similarity: The tendency to group like things together, like silverware in a drawer.

Pragnanz: The tendency to see and interpret Items in the simplest form, like seeing a smiley face instead of a group of random punctuation symbols.

Proximity: The tendency to group things that are in close proximity together. An example would be assuming several people standing close to each other are together.

Continuity: The tendency for our eyes to create connections with lines or points that are grouped together.

Closure: The tendency for the mind to fill in missing information to provide a completed picture when there are gaps in information, like seeing recognizable pictures in clouds or constellations.

Psychoanalytic/Psychodynamic

The psychodynamic perspective explores the psychology of personality and asserts that personality is developed as a result of unconscious drives, or an individual's inner motivations and childhood experiences. This perspective was developed as a result of the work of Sigmund Freud.

Humanistic

The humanistic approach focuses on individuals reaching their full potential and viewing a person as a whole, not as a being solely governed by internal drives or external forces. The humanist approach views human behavior in terms of choices that are influenced by a combination of things including the environment, biology, and emotional factors. Humanistic theories focus on people's subjective views and experiences, not on objective and measurable experimentation. Due to this subjectivity, the humanistic theory and its interventions are not as reliably tested with the scientific method as some other perspectives, such as behaviorism. Abraham Maslow is one of the major contributors to humanism. Maslow developed the hierarchy of needs and suggested that individuals work towards achieving basic needs (like food and shelter) first before they can work toward achieving less critical needs like social acceptance and prestige.

Evolutionary Approach

Evolutionary approach views human behavior as a direct result of biological influences that have been passed down and inherited. Based on the initial work of Charles Darwin, this approach to investigating human psychology asserts that behavior is internally driven by mechanisms meant to protect survival and reproduction and that those traits and behavior patterns that increased reproductive success have been passed down. The ideas of natural selection and evolution are central to this approach.

Biological Approach

The biological approach considers how human physiology and biology including hormones, genetics, and the neurology affect human psychology. This perspective asserts that cognitive processes are genetic, and behavior is driven by biology. For instance, a biological psychologist would look for biological influences for the causes of depression, such as brain chemistry or injury as well as a person's genetic predisposition and endocrine health and function.

Cognitive Approach

The cognitive approach focuses on mental functions like memory, problem solving, and language. A central focus is how one's thoughts influence their behavior, and how humans interpret, process, and recall information.

Biopsychosocial Approaches

The biopsychosocial approach to studying human behavior and psychology was first developed by George Engel in 1977, and is used frequently in modern psychology. It utilizes multiple schools of thought and elements that influence a person including biology, social, environmental, and psychological factors.

Sociocultural

The sociocultural approach to studying human behavior came about as more people in the field traveled and noted how there were differences in spoken language, body language, gestures, and behaviors in different cultures. In the sociocultural approach, the impact that cultural differences have on thoughts and behaviors is studied and used to help understand and predict behavior.

The Strengths and Limitations of Applying Theories to Explain Behavior

Psychologists and researchers in the field of psychology develop and utilize theories to explain human behavior, specifically how and/or why certain behaviors or behavioral patterns occur. There are strengths and limitations to the practice of applying theories to explain human behavior. They provide a framework or model to help study, understand, and predict behavior. However, a major limitation is that most theories cannot be proven true unless there is a way to experimentally test them using the rigorous scientific method. This is not possible for many psychological and behavioral theories because each individual might react in his or her own way, which means that there could be any number of reasons for observable behaviors. Additionally, theories that try to explain behaviors are not always applicable to all the multitudes of situations, or they might not hold true for certain situations. For example, a theory might only pertain to a small subset of population like toddlers of single, working dads.

The Different Domains of Psychology

There are several different domains of human psychology. These psychological schools of thought or specialty explain human personality, development, and behavior from different focused perspectives. Depending on the domain of focus, the site or environment in which the psychologist typically works may vary.

Biological Domain

Biological psychologists perform research on brain function and injuries as they relate to psychopathology and mental illness. This field of psychology utilizes biological theory, which seeks to understand how hormones, genetics, and brain functioning affect behavior. Biological psychologists typically work as researchers for hospitals, mental health and substance abuse treatment centers, pharmaceutical companies, and government agencies.

Clinical Domain

Clinical psychology assists people with issues ranging from minor emotional and psychosocial challenges to major mental health diagnoses. Clinical psychologists provide assessment and intervention services to those individuals. As with its counselling counterpart, clinical psychology helps individuals improve their overall emotional and social functioning; however, this discipline is more likely to include treatment of persons with more severe psychopathologies like personality disorders, depression, or anxiety.

Cognitive Domain

Psychologists in the field of cognitive psychology study all of the processes of the mind. These may include problem solving, learning, and memory. They may help patients improve their metacognitive skills, or their ability to think about their thinking and learning. Cognitive psychologists may work as researchers, utilizing the scientific method to study cognitive processes, or they may also work directly with clients to treat cognitive deficiencies or problems like the effects of brain injury, language disorders, dementia, or learning disabilities.

Cross-Cultural Domain

Cross-cultural psychology looks at human behavior through a cultural lens, taking into account an individual's cultural influence and its effect on that person's thoughts, feelings, and actions. This specialty area focuses on similarities and variances between behaviors as a result of culture across societies. Cross-cultural psychologists may be found working as researchers, in businesses, in direct practice, or in a public policy capacity.

Counseling Domain

Counseling psychologists help individuals improve interpersonal functioning related to emotional, social, and mental health factors. Counseling psychologists use therapeutic treatments and interventions like those based on cognitive, behavioral, or psychodynamic theories to treat individuals with a variety of challenges like job-related stress, marital problems, or other issues that negatively affect one's quality of life. Counseling psychology tends to focus more on helping clients that are rather emotionally or psychologically functional. For example, a counseling psychologist may treat those that have interpersonal or relationship problems as opposed to a person with a more disruptive psychological diagnosis like dissociative identity disorder or a personality disorder.

Developmental Domain

Developmental psychologists study the stages of growth and development that individuals experience throughout their lives. Those development stages could include physical, social, emotional, and cognitive changes. Psychologists in this field may work with patients with developmental disabilities or language deficiencies and/or their families. One may find developmental psychologists in clinics, hospitals, or private practices directly treating individuals, or in educational institutions performing developmentally-centered research.

Educational Domain

Educational psychologists study all aspects of learning with a variety of populations from children to adults. These psychologists focus more on larger-scale evaluation, assessment, data analysis, and recommendations as opposed to individual test administration. Educational psychology also utilizes

cognitive behavioral schools of thought to research variability in intelligence development and learning. They may also consider the best ways to motivate students and ways to create an optimal learning environment for students at large.

School psychologists—a branch of educational psychology—utilize theories of developmental and social psychology to assist in learning and teaching. School psychologists work directly with families, school systems, teachers, and students to help create an effective learning environment. They also utilize standardized tests to evaluate children's developmental, cognitive, intellectual, or socioeconomic functioning in order to make recommendations for any required specialized interventions. School psychologists can be found in many levels of schools from elementary to colleges.

Experimental Domain
This discipline of psychology focuses on exploring and finding the answers about behavior using the scientific method. These psychologists typically select a hypothesis, perform research, collect data, and come to a conclusion by performing experiments. Experimental psychologists can be found as researchers in academia and in the private and public sectors.

Human Factors Psychology
This discipline of psychology focuses on a variety of areas that affect people like workplace challenges, ergonomics, product design, human-computer relations, etc. For example, a human factors psychologist, using a knowledge of human cognitive processes, can help to design a computer terminal that is user-friendly based on human psychological or behavioral needs or tendencies. Another example may involve collaborating with engineers to design a phone that would be more intuitive for a person to use based on cognitive processes, not just technical specifications. Human factor psychologists work on real-world practice issues that affect human performance and use psychological knowledge of human behavior to build a more effective bridge between humans and the products and/or systems that they use.

Industrial–Organizational Domain (I/O)
This field of psychology is focused on human behavior in occupational settings. This could include research, training, employee development, and performance assessment in the workplace. I/O psychologists may participate in training development or worker motivation, research consumer trends, improve structure and efficiency, or assist with recruitment and retention of employees, helping employers create a productive, positive, satisfying workplace for their employees.

Personality Domain
A personality psychologist looks at how an individual's patterns of thoughts, behaviors, and actions affect their interactions with others and their environment. They may also help people with personality disorders to manage difficulties with interpersonal functioning and life management. A psychologist in this concentration may use tests to assess, diagnose, and treat personality disorders. These psychologists view personality as a result of a combination of individual and environmental influences and may work in private practices, schools, health care centers, or social service organizations.

Psychometric Domain
Psychometric psychology focuses specifically on psychological testing and measurement and the differences in people's personality traits, knowledge, intelligence, and competencies. The types of tests could include personality, intelligence, or career testing, among others. Examples of assessments that might be administered by a psychometric psychologist are the Myers-Briggs assessment (a personality test) and the Stanford-Binet IQ test. This field focuses on all aspects of psychological assessment from

development, administration, methodology, to the analysis of the results and testing procedures themselves. Psychologists in this discipline can either work directly with individuals to administer tests and provide results or in research and test development.

Social Domain

Social psychology examines people's interaction with other individuals or groups and how those interactions impact actions, thoughts, or feelings. For example, from a social psychology perspective, an individual's likes or dislikes are learned and developed from his or her social interactions. **Self-concept**, or what a person thinks and believes about himself, is also a consideration in social psychology. This perspective argues that an individual develops a sense of self by interactions, feedback, and comparison with those around him or her. As an example, if a man believes he is intelligent, when using a social psychology lens, he may have come to that belief about himself because his IQ is higher than the average or because he has been told that he is more intelligent than others.

Positive Domain

Positive psychology is a relatively new domain, beginning around 1998 by then president of the American Psychological Association, Martin Seligman. It focuses on the positive aspects of one's life or what makes life "most worth living." The domain addresses all aspects of one's life, like physiology, relationships, culture, spirituality, occupations, cognition, etc., but with a specific lens honed in on the positive elements of such aspects. Positive psychology is a direct reaction against the domains of behaviorism and psychoanalysis, both of which focus on "mental illness," negative thinking, and maladaptive behaviors. Instead, positive psychology seeks to foster happiness and contentment.

Research Methods in Psychology

The Purpose, Strengths, and Weaknesses of Different Types of Research

Simply defined, **research** involves systematically investigating an experience or observed phenomenon, either to understand what causes it, what influences it, or to develop a theory about how that experience or occurrence can cause a future event. Systematic investigation can occur through a number of different scientific methods. **Deductive research** focuses on a specific theory, and then establishes a hypothesis to methodically test the theory in order to support or discredit it. Deductive research often involves setting up experiments, trials, or data collection surveys to gather information related to the theory. **Inductive research** examines information that's already available (such as in established datasets like the U.S. Census Report) to highlight data trends and make inferences and/or projections from those patterns.

Research designs determine how to structure a study based on factors such as the variables being tested, the level to which the researcher is manipulating a variable in the study, the types of subjects in the study, what the study is testing or looking for, the frequency and duration of data collection, and whether the data collected is qualitative or quantitative in nature. These concepts will be examined further in the following sections.

Quantitative research utilizes logical, empirical methods of collecting information. This information is called **data** and is often analyzed using statistics. Non-experimental quantitative research includes forms of data collection where the researcher collects data that's already available in some form. They then analyze this dataset to describe the relationship between pre-determined variables. The researcher does not set up a novel system of trials to produce new data, and they can't randomize any data collected.

The researcher has no part in manipulating any variables or establishing a separate control group to which they can compare collected data. The lack of a control group, researcher-controlled variable manipulation, and randomization are often seen as weaknesses in non-experimental quantitative research studies.

Qualitative research is commonly employed in social sciences, including the field of counseling. It typically focuses on the analysis of a group of people (which is sometimes biased) to understand different aspects of human behavior, relationships, and social interactions. The researcher does not manipulate variables when conducting qualitative research. Qualitative research is primarily conducted without rigid structures in place.

Experiments

Experimental quantitative research employs highly controlled processes, with the hope of determining a causal relationship between one or more input (**independent**) variables and one or more outcome (**dependent**) variables. It uses random sampling and assignment methods to make inferences for larger populations. Typically, it compares a control group (serving as a baseline) to a test group. Ideally, experimental studies or experiments should be able to be replicated numerous times with the same results. The ultimate goal of a well-designed experiment is to declare that a particular variable is responsible for a particular outcome, and that, without that variable, the associated outcome wouldn't occur.

Quasi-experimental quantitative research employs many of these same qualities, but it often doesn't use random sampling or assignment in its studies or experiments. Consequently, quasi-experimental research produces results that often don't apply to the population at large. They do, however, often provide meaningful results for certain subgroups of the population.

Correlational Studies

These analyze the strength of the relationship between two variables in one group. One unique type of correlational design is found in **ex post facto studies**, in which the researcher examines two existing groups and analyzes the correlation between the variables of interest. Another unique type of correlational design is found in **prediction studies**, where the researcher determines a correlation between variables, and then uses it to predict other correlations, related events, or future events. The strength and description of the correlation is indicated by the **correlation coefficient (r),** which falls between -1 and 1. If r = 0, it indicates there's no relationship between the two variables, while r = 1 indicates a direct, perfect correlation. If *r* equals a negative value, it indicates an inverse relationship between the two variables. If *r* equals a positive value, it indicates a direct relationship between the two variables. Regardless of how strong the correlation is between two variables, it doesn't indicate that one causes the other. It simply indicates that these two variables tend to occur (or not occur) together to some degree.

Survey Research

Surveys can be conducted through telephone or face-to-face interviews. They can also be conducted through paper or electronic questionnaires (either at an external facility or at the study participant's home). Survey designs are generally used when research about a particular topic is limited, so that more information can be gathered to better shape the research question or topic. Surveys are easy (and usually cost-efficient) to administer, but they can also result in low or biased participant response rates.

Interviews

These are typically more personal in nature. Interviews can be conducted in person, over the telephone, or via e-mail or regular mail. The interviewer asks the individual or group a series of meaningful questions related to the research topic. The interview can be structured with the interviewer having pre-set questions to ask, or it can be unstructured with the interviewer asking questions based on the flow of conversation and the answers given by the interviewee(s).

Naturalistic Observations

In an observation, the researcher simply watches the individual or group of interest. However, a number of additional factors usually shape the development of the observation study. The researcher can observe the participant(s) in a specific situation or highly controlled context, or the researcher can observe the participant(s) in their day-to-day routine. The participant(s) may or may not know that they are being observed for specific behaviors. The researcher can involve themselves in the context and become part of the observation study. The researcher can also freely write down data from the observations, or use a pre-made scale or data sheet to document specific behaviors.

Case Studies

These are detailed and documented examples of the topic of interest. They can be real or hypothetical situations. Case studies often record data over a period of time to examine a specific variable of interest. They can examine a situation involving one individual, a family, a larger community of people, or an organization. Case studies frequently look at how people relate to one another, and/or to their physical or emotional environment.

Focus Groups

These bring together a relatively small group of individuals. The group can be diverse in nature or have many similar interests. A facilitator guides a discussion within the group to discern information about individual or collective viewpoints about a specific issue.

Longitudinal Studies

A **longitudinal study** describes a research design in which information is repeatedly collected for the same research participants over an extended period of time, which can span several years or even decades. Because longitudinal studies involve observing the same individuals over the course of their lives, any differences observed in them are less likely to be due to cultural variations across generations. Longitudinal studies can be **retrospective**, which is when researchers use existing data such as medical records, or **prospective**, which entails researchers collecting new information. Though this type of research method can be structured as a randomized experiment, longitudinal studies often serve as an **observational study**.

When longitudinal studies are observational, researchers observe daily life in the real world without any efforts to control or manipulate it, as opposed to in a lab setting where more control could be exerted, thus making this research design a type of naturalistic study. Longitudinal studies are common in psychology. In social-personality and clinical psychology, longitudinal studies are typically used to observe rapid fluctuations in one's behavior, cognition, and emotions on a daily basis. And in developmental psychology, longitudinal studies observe trends pertaining to one's growth and development that occur throughout their lifespan.

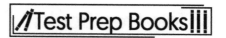

Cross-Sectional Studies

Also referred to as a **transverse** or **prevalence study**, or a **cross-sectional analysis**, a **cross-sectional study** describes a research method that involves evaluating variable information gathered at a specific point in time across a sample population. This sample population includes different people with similar features being compared. Like longitudinal studies, cross-sectional studies are also **observational studies**, with researchers recording information in a population but not controlling or manipulating variables. Cross-sectional studies are also known as **descriptive research**, as opposed to being causal or relational, meaning that researchers wouldn't use this type of study to determine causality. In other words, cross-sectional studies are used to describe traits that exist within a certain group, not to determine cause-and-effect relationships between variables. This approach tends to obtain initial data and make inferences about potential relationships as a means of supporting more research.

Cross-sectional studies are often used by developmental psychologists. In developmental research, this method examines people of various age ranges at the same time, as opposed to observing individuals over many years or several decades. However, the challenge with this approach is that any differences observed in a group of people are more likely to be related to cultural differences across generations.

The Value of Reliance on Operational Definitions and Measurement in Behavioral Research

In research, an **operational definition** describes procedures used to outline a set of tests necessary to determine the nature of a phenomenon and its underlying properties. Researchers use these operational definitions to measure the variables of a study. A **variable** is anything that can be measured. When operational definitions are clear enough, researchers can later replicate a study and obtain the same results. **Replication** refers to the repetition of research, generally with different conditions and different participants, to find out if the results in the original study are applicable to the other conditions and participants, which in turn enables researchers to learn whether or not those original results are valid and reliable. The scientific process consists of making an observation, forming a prediction, conducting a test, interpreting the data, and communicating the results.

When studying a specific variable in the testing phase, it's important to first operationally define the variable before evaluating and analyzing that variable. The two main variables in an experiment consist of an independent variable and a dependent variable. An **independent variable** is anything that can be altered or manipulated in a study to test its effects on the dependent variable. Its alteration isn't affected by any other variable in the study, thus being independent of everything else. A **dependent variable** is what researchers test and measure in a research study, with any changes made to it depending on any changes made to the independent variable. For instance, if a researcher was interested in studying whether caffeine affects one's appetite, the presence or absence of caffeine would serve as the independent variable, whereas the effect on that person's appetite would be the dependent variable.

Measurement is important in research. Without measurement, it would be difficult for researchers to perform experiments or devise theories. Also, when using a measurement, it should measure the construct it's purported to measure. For instance, if the construct being studied is depression, researchers would most likely use a measure such as the Beck Depression Inventory, because it measures that specific construct.

The Experimental Method

Identifying Independent, Dependent, Confounding, and Control Variables in Experimental Designs

A **variable** is one factor in a study or experiment. An **independent variable** is controlled by the researcher and usually influences the dependent variable (the factor that's typically measured and recorded by the researcher).

In experiments, the researcher declares a hypothesis that a relationship doesn't exist between two variables, groups, or tangible instances. This hypothesis is referred to as the **null hypothesis**. Errors can be made in accepting or rejecting the null hypothesis based on the outcomes of the experiment. If the researcher rejects the null hypothesis when it's actually true, it is known as a **type I error**. A type I error indicates that a relationship between two variable exists when, in reality, it doesn't. If the researcher fails to reject the null hypothesis when it's actually false, it is known as a **type II error**. A type II error indicates that a relationship between two variables doesn't exist when, in reality, it does. These errors typically result when the experiment or study has weak internal validity.

How Research Design Drives the Reasonable Conclusions That Can Be Drawn

Experiments

The primary method of data collection in psychology is experimental research. In this type of study, psychologists directly manipulate the variables to determine causation. In this way, experiments help identify and understand cause-and-effect relationships. Experiments fall into three categories. The first type is a **controlled experiment**, which takes place in an environment under the control of the researchers. This could be a laboratory or another location. Another type is called a **field experiment**, where researchers conduct experiments outside of a laboratory or other controlled clinical space. Variables are still manipulated by the researchers; however, the environment can be more unpredictable. The third type is called a **natural experiment** and takes place in non-clinical environments and the researchers are not able to manipulate the variables.

Correlational Research

Correlational research allows researchers to find relationships between variables, but researchers are not able to manipulate either of the variables nor are they able to determine causation. For instance, in the summer, there may be an increase of children riding bikes and simultaneously, the rate of children contracting the flu may decrease. If that were the case, there might be a relationship between those variables, but using correlational research methods one would not be able to support the theory that one of those variables *caused* the change in the other.

There are three types of correlations. **Positive correlations** refer to variables both decreasing or increasing in relation to the other. **Negative correlations** refer to one or more variables increasing while the other decreases. **No correlation** means that there does not appear to be a relationship between variables. The example of more children riding bikes and contracting the flu less in the summer would be a negative correlation. Examples of correlation methods include natural observation and surveys.

Natural observation is a method frequently used in this type of research. Researchers using this technique will evaluate subjects in natural or non-clinical environments. Researchers also typically attempt to be as inconspicuous as possible when performing natural observation. One challenge of this

type of observation is sampling, because obtaining a representative sample would be difficult with the real-life circumstances of a natural observation. Other challenges of this method are limited control over the environment and the participants. A type of practice a psychologist can utilize to increase the validity and reliability of natural observation is by very clearly operationalizing the variables.

Another common method of correlational research is survey administration. During this process, researchers will ask participants to share their responses to predetermined questions in writing, digitally, or orally. Advantages of the survey method are low costs, and its ease of distribution, administration, and processing of data. Disadvantages are low return rate and subjectivity of participant responses.

Random Assignment of Participants Versus Random Selection of Participants

Sampling is the method of collecting participants for a study. It's a crucial component of the research design and study process. There are a number of different ways to select samples, and each method has pros, cons, and situations where it's the most appropriate one to use.

Simple Random Sampling

For this type of probability sampling, the participants are taken directly from a larger population with the characteristics of interest. Each individual in the larger population has the same chance of being selected for the sample.

Pros: closely represents the target population, thus allowing for results that are the highest in validity

Cons: obtaining the sample can be time consuming

Use When: a highly controlled experiment setting is necessary

Stratified Random Sampling

For this type of probability sampling, the researchers first examine the traits of the larger population. Traits are often demographic or social in nature like age, education status, marital status, and household income. Researchers then divide the population into groups (or strata) based on these traits. Members of the population are only included in one stratum. Researchers then randomly sample across each stratum to create the final sample set for the study.

Pros: closely represents the target population, which allows for results that are highest in validity. Since the sampling method is so specific, researchers are able to use smaller samples.

Cons: obtaining the sample can be tedious. Researchers may first need to compile and become acutely knowledgeable about the demographic characteristics of the target population before selecting a representative sample.

Use When: a highly-controlled experiment setting is necessary; demographic, social, and/or economic characteristics of the target population are of special interest in the study; or researchers are studying relationships or interactions between two subsets within the larger population

Systematic Random Sampling

For this type of probability sampling, researchers pick a random integer (n), and then select every *n*th person from the target population for the research sample.

> Pros: a simple, cost-effective sampling technique that generally provides a random sample for the researchers. It ensures that sampling occurs evenly throughout an entire target population.

> Cons: researchers need to ensure that their original target population (from which the sample is selected) is randomized and that every individual has an equal probability of being selected. Researchers need to be familiar with the demographics of the target population to ensure that certain trends don't appear across the selected participants and skew the results.

> Use When: a highly controlled experiment setting is necessary; researchers are short on time or funding and need a quick, cost-efficient method to create a random sample.

Convenience Sampling

This is a type of non-probability sampling where researchers select participants who are easily accessible due to factors like location, expense, or volunteer recruitment.

> Pros: saves time and is cost-effective since researchers can create their sample based on what permits the easiest and fastest recruiting of participants

> Cons: highly prone to bias. It is difficult to generalize the results for the population at large since the sample selection is not random.

> Use When: conducting initial trials of a new study, when researchers are simply looking for basic information about the larger population (i.e., to create a more detailed hypothesis for future research)

Ad Hoc Sampling

For this type of non-probability sampling, researchers must meet a set quota for a certain characteristic and can recruit any participant as long as they have the desired characteristics.

> Pros: allows for greater inclusion of a population that might not otherwise be represented

> Cons: results won't be indicative of the actual population in an area

> Use When: it's necessary that a group within the larger population needs a set level of representation within the study

Purposive Sampling

Another non-probability sampling method used when researchers have a precise purpose or target population in mind.

> Pros: helps increase recruitment numbers in otherwise hard-to-access populations

> Cons: usually unable to generalize the results to larger populations beyond the sample's specific subset

> Use When: researchers have a precise purpose for the study, or a specific group of participants is required that isn't easy to select through probability sampling methods

Selecting a Research Method

Predicting the Validity of Behavioral Explanations Based on the Quality of Research Design

External Validity

External validity illustrates how well inferences from a sample set can predict similar inferences in a larger population (i.e., can results in a controlled lab setting hold true when replicated in the real world). A sample set with strong external validity allows the researcher to generalize or, in other words, to make strongly supported assumptions about a larger group. For a sample to have strong external validity, it needs to have similar characteristics and context to the larger population about which the researcher is hoping to make inferences. A researcher typically wants to generalize three areas:

Population: Can inferences from the sample set hold true to a larger group of people, beyond the specific people in the sample?

Environment: Can inferences from the sample set hold true in settings beyond the specific one used in the study?

Time: Can inferences from the sample set hold true in any season or temporal period?

If results from the sample set can't hold true across these three areas, the external validity of the study is considered threatened or weak. External validity is strengthened by the number of study replications the researcher is able to successfully complete for multiple settings, groups, and contexts. External validity can also be strengthened by ensuring the sample set is as randomized as possible.

Internal Validity

Internal validity illustrates the integrity of the results obtained from a sample set, and indicates how reliably a specific study or intervention was conducted. Strong internal validity allows the researcher to confidently link a specific variable or process of the study to the results or outcomes. The strength of a study's internal validity can be threatened by the presence of many independent variables. This can result in confounding, where it's difficult to pinpoint exactly what is causing the changes in the dependent variables. The internal validity can also be threatened by biases (sampling bias, researcher bias, or participant bias) as well as historical, personal, and/or contextual influences outside the researcher's control (natural disasters, political unrest, participant death, or relocation). Internal validity can be strengthened by designing highly controlled studies or experiment settings that limit these threats.

Confounding Variables

Researchers will attempt to identify and account for any **confounding variables**, which can be defined as one or more variables that can also have an unintended cause-and-effect relationship with the dependent and independent variables. Confounding variables are troublesome because they affect the results of the experiment; moreover, that change is related to the confounding variable instead of the variables being tested. In the planning stages of an experiment, the variables must be **operationalized**. This involves explaining, defining and specifying each variable in measurable terms. For instance, in the school/test scores example, does home schooling mean any type of learning in the home or will community home school groups be included? Are there certain tests to be examined? Operationalizing the variables is crucial to the credibility of the research. Validity and reliability of research also

contribute to the credibility of the study. **Validity** can be explained as the degree to which the research is accurately measuring what is intended to measure. The **reliability** describes whether the study can be duplicated and whether similar results would occur if it were to be duplicated. These concepts are significant in all psychological research studies.

Statistical Analysis in Psychology

Basic Descriptive Statistical Concepts

Measures of Central Tendency
Comparing data sets within statistics can mean many things. The first way to compare data sets is by looking at the center and spread of each set. The center of a data set is measured by mean, median, and mode. These are sometimes referred to as **measures of central tendency**.

Mean
The first property that can be defined for this set of data is the **mean**. This is the same as average. To find the mean, add up all the data points, then divide by the total number of data points. For example, suppose that in a class of 10 students, the scores on a test were 50, 60, 65, 65, 75, 80, 85, 85, 90, 100. Therefore, the average test score will be:

$$\frac{50 + 60 + 65 + 65 + 75 + 80 + 85 + 85 + 90 + 100}{10} = 75.5$$

The mean is a useful number if the distribution of data is normal (more on this later), which roughly means that the frequency of different outcomes has a single peak and is roughly equally distributed on both sides of that peak. However, it is less useful in some cases where the data might be split or where there are some outliers. **Outliers** are data points that are far from the rest of the data. For example, suppose there are 10 executives and 90 employees at a company. The executives make $1000 per hour, and the employees make $10 per hour.

Therefore, the average pay rate will be:

$$\frac{\$1000 \times 10 + \$10 \times 90}{100} = \$109 \ per \ hour$$

In this case, this average is not very descriptive since it's not close to the actual pay of the executives *or* the employees.

Median
Another useful measurement is the **median**. In a data set arranged in numerical order, the median is the point in the middle. The middle refers to the point where half the data comes before it and half comes after, when the data is recorded in numerical order. For instance, these are the speeds of the fastball of a pitcher threw (in mph) during the last inning that he pitched (in order from least to greatest):

90, 92, 93, 93, 95, 96, 97, 97, 97

There are nine total numbers, so the middle or median number is the fifth one, which is 95.

In cases where the number of data points is an even number, then the average of the two middle points is taken. In the previous example of test scores, the two middle points are 75 and 80. Since there is no single point, the average of these two scores needs to be found. The average is:

$$\frac{75 + 80}{2} = 77.5 \ mph$$

The median is generally a good value to use if there are a few outliers in the data. It prevents those outliers from affecting the "middle" value as much as when using the mean.

Since an outlier is a data point that is far from most of the other data points in a data set, an outlier is necessarily far from the median of the data set. The outliers can have a substantial effect on the mean of a data set, but usually do not change the median or mode, or do not change them by a large quantity. For example, consider the data set (3, 5, 6, 6, 6, 8), which has a median of 6 and a mode of 6, and a mean of $\frac{34}{6} \approx 5.67$. Now, suppose a new data point of 1000 is added so that the data set is now (3, 5, 6, 6, 6, 8, 1000). This does not change the median or mode, which are both still 6. However, the average is now $\frac{1034}{7}$, which is approximately 147.7. In this case, the median and mode will be better descriptors for most of the data points.

The reason for outliers in a given data set is a complicated problem. It is sometimes the result of an error by the experimenter, but often they are perfectly valid data points that must be taken into consideration.

Mode
One additional measure to define for X is the **mode**. This is the data point that appears most frequently. If two or more data points all tie for the most frequent appearance, then each of them is considered a mode. In the case of the test scores, where the numbers were 50, 60, 65, 65, 75, 80, 85, 85, 90, 100, there are two modes: 65 and 85.

Variation

Spread
Methods for determining the **spread** of the sample include calculating the range and standard deviation for the data. The **range** is calculated by subtracting the lowest value from the highest value in the set. Given a data set X consisting of data points $(x_1, x_2, x_3, \ldots x_n)$, the **variance** of X is defined to be:

$$\frac{\sum_{i=1}^{n}(x_i - \bar{X})^2}{n}$$

This means that the variance of X is the average of the squares of the differences between each data point and the mean of X.

Given a data set X consisting of data points $(x_1, x_2, x_3, \ldots x_n)$, the **standard deviation** of X is defined to be:

$$s_x = \sqrt{\frac{\sum_{i=1}^{n}(x_i - \bar{X})^2}{n}}$$

In other words, the standard deviation is the square root of the variance.

Both the variance and the standard deviation are measures of how much the data tend to be spread out. When the standard deviation is low, the data points are mostly clustered around the mean. When the standard deviation is high, the data are generally quite spread out, or else that there are a few substantial outliers.

As a simple example, compute the standard deviation for the data set (1, 3, 3, 5). First, compute the mean, which is $\frac{1+3+3+5}{4} = \frac{12}{4} = 3$. Now, find the variance of X with the formula:

$$\sum_{i=1}^{4}(x_i - \bar{X})^2 = (1-3)^2 + (3-3)^2 + (3-3)^2 + (5-3)^2 = -2^2 + 0^2 + 0^2 + 2^2 = 8$$

Therefore, the variance is $\frac{8}{4} = 2$. Taking the square root, the standard deviation is $\sqrt{2}$.

Note that the standard deviation only depends upon the mean, not upon the median or mode(s). Generally, if there are multiple modes that are far apart from one another, the standard deviation will be high. A high standard deviation does not always mean there are multiple modes, however.

Quartiles and Percentiles

The **first quartile** of a set of data X refers to the largest value from the first ¼ of the data points. In practice, there are sometimes slightly different definitions that can be used, such as the median of the first half of the data points (excluding the median itself if there are an odd number of data points). The term also has a slightly different use: when it is said that a data point lies *in the first quartile*, it means it is less than or equal to the median of the first half of the data points. Conversely, if it lies *at* the first quartile, then it is equal to the first quartile.

When it is said that a data point lies in the **second quartile**, it means it is between the first quartile and the median.

The **third quartile** refers to data that lies between ½ and ¾ of the way through the data set. Again, there are various methods for defining this precisely, but the simplest way is to include all of the data that lie between the median and the median of the top half of the data.

Data that lies in the **fourth quartile** refers to all of the data above the third quartile.

Percentiles may be defined in a similar manner to quartiles. Generally, this is defined in the following manner:

If a data point lies **in the n-th percentile**, this means it lies in the range of the first $n\%$ of the data.

If a data point lies **at the n-th percentile**, then it means that $n\%$ of the data lies below this data point.

Correlation Coefficient

As mentioned previously, the **correlation coefficient (r)** measures the association between two variables. Its value is between -1 and 1, where -1 represents a perfect negative linear relationship, 0 represents no relationship, and 1 represents a perfect positive linear relationship. A **negative linear relationship** means that as x values increase, y values decrease. A **positive linear relationship** means that as x values increase, y values increase.

The formula for computing the correlation coefficient is (n is the number of data points):

$$r = \frac{n(\sum xy) - (\sum x)(\sum y)}{\sqrt{n(\sum x^2) - (\sum x)^2}\sqrt{n(\sum y^2) - (\sum y)^2}}$$

Both Microsoft Excel® and a graphing calculator can evaluate this easily once the data points are entered. A correlation greater than 0.8 or less than -0.8 is classified as "strong" while a correlation between -0.5 and 0.5 is classified as "weak."

Frequency Distribution

A set of data can be described in terms of its center, spread, shape and any unusual features. The center of a data set can be measured by its mean, median, or mode. The spread of a data set refers to how far the data points are from the center (mean or median). A data set with data points clustered around the center will have a small spread. A data set covering a wide range will have a large spread.

When a data set is displayed as a graph like the one below, the shape indicates if a sample is normally distributed, symmetrical, or has measures of skewness. When graphed, a data set with a normal distribution will resemble a bell curve.

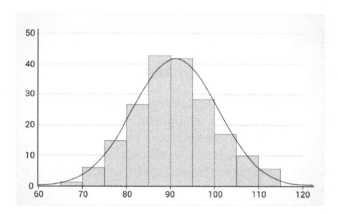

If the data set is **symmetrical**, each half of the graph when divided at the center is a mirror image of the other. If the graph has fewer data points to the right, the data is **skewed right**. If it has fewer data points to the left, the data is **skewed left**.

Right-Skewed   Symmetric   Left-Skewed

A description of a data set should include any unusual features such as gaps or outliers. A **gap** is a span within the range of the data set containing no data points. An **outlier** is a data point with a value either extremely large or extremely small when compared to the other values in the set.

The previous graphs can be referred to as **unimodal** since they all have a single peak. This is contrast to **bimodal** graph that have multiple peaks.

Descriptive Statistics and Inferential Statistics

The field of statistics describes relationships between quantities that are related, but not necessarily in a deterministic manner. For example, a graduating student's salary will often be higher when the student graduates with a higher GPA, but this is not always the case. Likewise, people who smoke tobacco are more likely to develop lung cancer, but, in fact, it is possible for non-smokers to develop the disease as well. **Statistics** describes these kinds of situations, where the likelihood of some outcome depends on the starting data.

Descriptive statistics involves analyzing a collection of data to describe its broad properties such average (or mean), what percent of the data falls within a given range, and other such properties. An example of this would be taking all of the test scores from a given class and calculating the average test score. **Inferential statistics** attempts to use data about a subset of some population to make inferences about the rest of the population. An example of this would be taking a collection of students who received tutoring and comparing their results to a collection of students who did not receive tutoring, then using that comparison to try to predict whether the tutoring program in question is beneficial.

Ethical Guidelines in Psychology

How Ethical Issues Inform and Constrain Research Practices

Researchers should strive not to harm any population when conducting studies or experiments. All biomedical and behavioral research requires the approval of an independent institutional review board (IRB) to begin. In addition, the IRB monitors the research study for its duration to ensure that populations aren't experiencing any harm. Typically, IRB-approved studies require a participant consent form, the guarantee of anonymity and/or confidentiality for all participants and associated data, and strict monitoring and evaluation processes.

Researchers should also be mindful of producing, collecting, and publishing accurate, authentic, and non-biased data. Failure to collect or publish data that does not support the researchers' hypotheses or motives—or that inadvertently brings awareness to another sensitive issue—can also be grounds for ethical concern.

Accountability is an important aspect in conducting research. Researchers typically need to have a purpose for conducting their studies. This purpose should be beneficial to the target population, fair, timely, cost-efficient, and should not harm any groups in the process. Funding sources, as well as internal and external auditing groups, may regularly evaluate research operations and outcomes. This is done to ensure that the funds are used appropriately, the research process is ethical, and useful results are obtained. Typically, structured evaluation processes (such as benchmarks and reporting practices) are established and documented during the study's planning and proposal periods.

How Ethical and Legal Guidelines Protect Research Participants and Promote Sound Ethical Practice

American Psychological Association's Guidelines

The American Psychological Association (APA), which is the professional organization that oversees the psychology profession, has established guidelines to ensure all psychologists practice in an ethical manner. Additionally, these standards help to protect the confidentiality and psychological and physical health of clients and research participants. The APA developed the Ethical Principles of Psychologists and Code of Conduct that include guidelines for psychologists related to confidentiality, human interactions, record keeping, training, publication, and research. In particular, when conducting research with human participants, there are standards psychologist must adhere to in order to protect the rights and safety of participants.

Federal Regulations

All psychological research must abide by federal and state regulations governing research on human subjects. The following are some of the mandatory regulations for psychologists conducting research with human subjects:

Informed consent: Researchers must obtain consent from the participants in the study or experiment. Informed consent means that the participants must understand the study's purpose and expectations and they have the right to refuse to participate as well as withdraw at any time during the process.

Confidentiality: Steps must be taken to protect participants' confidentiality and ensure identifying information is kept private. Researchers must also comply with government requirements related to reporting abuse to vulnerable populations like children or the elderly. They must inform subjects when, as in those situations, confidentiality will not be kept.

Deception: At times, it may be necessary to withhold some information about a study from participants. Guidelines allow researchers to do this if it is vital or justified for the benefit of the project. Psychologists must explain any deception to the participants as early as possible, but no later than at the end of the data collection stage. Additionally, the guidelines require that psychologists not withhold information about any pain or distress that may be caused to the participants during the study.

Debriefing: Researchers must provide study participants with an opportunity following the study to be informed about the purpose and results of the study.

Local Institutional Review Board (IRB)

Researchers must have permission and approval from the institution or school that is sponsoring the research. Most organizations or institutions have an institutional review board that will review the request and approve the research study.

Institutional Animal Care and Use Committee (IACUC)

Animals are used in psychological experiments when necessary and when it would not be feasible or safe to use human subjects. The use of animals allows psychological researchers to better understand human behavior and cognitive functions. The American Psychological Association (APA) also makes provisions for the ethical treatment of animals used in research.

As with human research there are several areas covered under guidelines for ethical use of animal testing:

Justification: The purpose of the study and the need to use animals must be clearly defined. Additionally, the benefits to the species or humans must be identified and the research must address a significant scientific purpose.

Personnel: All researchers involved in testing with animals must be appropriately trained and aware of all animal care guidelines.

Housing and care: Animals should be housed and cared for in a humane manner, that is appropriate to the type of animal being utilized. Housing should also meet state and federal guidelines. Care should be taken to minimize pain or discomfort to the animal as much as possible.

Unit 2: Biological Bases of Behavior

Interaction of Heredity and Environment

How Heredity, Environment, and Evolution Work Together to Shape Behavior

For many years, psychology has held an abiding and invested interest in studying the various factors that shape our behavior. One of the oldest issues in psychology related to this interest is the **nature versus nurture debate**, which consists of people debating whether biological traits or environmental elements exert the most influence over one's behavior. While this debate still rages, research shows that genes and environment each play a vital role in an individual's growth and development. Behavior is shaped through a complex interaction between heredity, environment, and evolution. **Epigenetics** is a framework in psychology used to gain a better understanding of how gene expression is influenced by one's experiences and environments to help shape their behavior. Behavioral traits are usually controlled by the interaction of multiple genes, which is referred to as **polygenic inheritance**. Originally, researchers posited that one's behaviors and other traits were determined by a genetic blueprint fixed from birth. However, further research has shown that our genes are more like a switchboard than a blueprint.

Genes are more active and subject to change than previously thought, and are capable of being either expressed or silenced, depending on certain environmental factors. When these epigenetic alterations are heritable, they are able to influence evolution in numerous organisms, which include plants and animals. Epigenetics plays an important role in the evolutionary process. When organisms produce offspring that are best suited to survive in their environment, environmental stressors alter genetic expression, which in turn is passed down to their own offspring to ensure that they will not only survive, but flourish in their environment. Stress offers a chance for adaption to newly arising selection pressures. In other words, evolution focuses on those physical and psychological traits that will enable an organism to survive and flourish in it respective environment.

Key Research Contributions of Scientists in the Area of Heredity and Environment

Charles Darwin
As mentioned previously, Charles Darwin was a biologist and naturalist best known for his work in evolution, although his work indirectly contributed to the field of psychology as well. Because Darwin theorized that humans and animals had shared common ancestry, he believed that the emotional and behavioral traits of animals could be used to better understand human behavior. This idea set the foundation for comparative psychology. Darwin's theories of natural selection and evolution also are applicable to human psychology.

Predicting How Traits and Behavior Can Be Selected For Their Adaptive Value

Behavior consists of all the ways one interacts with other organisms and their environment. Some behaviors are biologically hardwired, whereas others are shaped through experience. In the vast majority of cases, behaviors tend to have both a genetic and environmental component. Among other traits, behavior is influenced by the process of natural selection. Many of these selected behaviors increase an organism's **fitness**, which ensures that organism's chances of both survival and reproduction. These naturally-selected behaviors can vary from one organism to another. Some examples include the mating rituals of birds, the wiggle dance of bees, the camouflage capacity of the katydid, and a human being's ability to learn languages. If certain heritable features increase or decrease an organism's prospect of survival and reproduction, then it stands to reason that those features that manage to improve survival and reproduction will increase in frequency over subsequent generations. This is what's referred to as **evolution by natural selection**. However, if the features leading to successful reproduction aren't heritable, then no meaningful evolution actually takes place.

English scientist **Herbert Spencer** coined the term **survival of the fittest** as a means of describing **Charles Darwin**'s evolutionary process of natural selection. **Natural selection** enables an organism to adapt to changes that occur across generations; however, it doesn't help a species cope with rapid environmental changes; therefore, an organism needs to modify their behaviors and practices to be able to cope with these types of changes. Evolution is influenced by natural selection and these adaptive behaviors. An organism needs to learn to cope with environmental changes; otherwise, that organism wouldn't be able to survive and reproduce. To better understand a behavior, there are four elements to study. It's important to determine 1) what causes a specific behavior, 2) how that behavior develops, 3) the adaptive value of the behavior, and 4) how the behavior itself evolved. Evolutionary biology, behavioral biology, genetics, anatomy, physiology, ethology, comparative psychology, and neurobiology are examples of fields that endeavor to trace the circuitry underlying behavior in order to better understand it.

The Endocrine System

The Effect of the Endocrine System on Behavior

Behavioral endocrinology is the study of how the endocrine system impacts behavior. More specifically, this field examines how hormones affect behavior and how behavior can also affect hormones. The hypothalamus is located in the brain and provides communication between the endocrine and nervous systems to regulate hormones and keep the body's functions in balance with the release of those hormones. Hormones are chemicals that are released into the blood stream by the endocrine system and drives bodily functions. The endocrine system's primary job is to make these hormones for the body and is made up of all of a body's glands. **Hormones** can be thought of as messengers that alert the body to perform in different ways. They can be transported and accepted by any cells that have the appropriate receptor for that hormone. Hormones play a part in the body's growth, the development of sexual characteristics and metabolism, and some also affect behavior.

The **endocrine system** is made of the ductless tissues and glands that secrete hormones into the interstitial fluids of the body. **Interstitial fluid** is the solution that surrounds tissue cells within the body. This system works closely with the nervous system to regulate the physiological activities of the other systems of the body to maintain homeostasis. While the nervous system provides quick, short-term responses to stimuli, the endocrine system acts by releasing hormones into the bloodstream that get distributed to the whole body. The response is slow but long-lasting, ranging from a few hours to a few weeks.

Hormones are chemical substances that change the metabolic activity of tissues and organs. While regular metabolic reactions are controlled by enzymes, hormones can change the type, activity, or quantity of the enzymes involved in the reaction. They bind to specific cells and start a biochemical chain of events that changes the enzymatic activity. Hormones can regulate development and growth, digestion and metabolism, mood, and body temperature, among other things. Often small amounts of a hormone will lead to significant changes in the body.

Major Endocrine Glands

Hypothalamus: A part of the brain, the hypothalamus connects the nervous system to the endocrine system via the pituitary gland. Although it is considered part of the nervous system, the hypothalamus plays a dual role in regulating endocrine organs.

Pituitary Gland: A pea-sized gland found at the bottom of the hypothalamus with two lobes, called the anterior and posterior lobes. The pituitary gland plays an important role in regulating the function of other endocrine glands. The hormones it releases control growth, blood pressure, certain functions of the sex organs, salt concentration of the kidneys, internal temperature regulation, and pain responses.

Thyroid Gland: This gland releases hormones, such as thyroxine, which are important for metabolism, growth and development, temperature regulation, and brain development during infancy and childhood. Thyroid hormones also monitor the amount of circulating calcium in the body.

Parathyroid Glands: These are four pea-sized glands located on the posterior surface of the thyroid. The main hormone secreted is called **parathyroid hormone** (PTH), which helps with the thyroid's regulation of calcium in the body.

Thymus Gland: The thymus is in the chest cavity, embedded in connective tissue. It produces several hormones important for development and maintenance of normal immunological defenses. One hormone promotes the development and maturation of **lymphocytes**, which strengthens the immune system.

Adrenal Gland: One adrenal gland is attached to the top of each kidney. Each adrenal gland produces **epinephrine**, which is responsible for the "fight or flight" reactions in the face of danger or stress. The hormones epinephrine and **norepinephrine** (which is responsible for the "rest and digest functions") cooperate to regulate states of arousal.

Pancreas: The pancreas is an organ that has both endocrine and exocrine functions. The endocrine functions are controlled by the pancreatic **islets of Langerhans**, which are groups of beta cells scattered throughout the gland that secrete insulin to lower blood sugar levels in the body. Neighboring alpha cells secrete glucagon to raise blood sugar.

Pineal Gland: The pineal gland secretes **melatonin**, a hormone derived from the neurotransmitter **serotonin**. Melatonin can slow the maturation of sperm, oocytes, and reproductive organs. It also regulates the body's **circadian rhythm**, which is the natural awake/asleep cycle. It also serves an important role in protecting the CNS tissues from neural toxins.

Testes and **Ovaries:** These glands secrete testosterone and estrogen, respectively, and are responsible for secondary sex characteristics, as well as reproduction.

Overview of the Nervous System and the Neuron

Biopsychology, also known as **psychobiology,** examines how the brain and other biological factors like hormones, neurotransmitters, and genetics affect human behavior, emotions, and thoughts. A foundation of biopsychology is study of the **central nervous system**, which is made up of the spinal cord and brain. The central nervous system makes it possible for different parts of the body to connect and

communicate with one other. The brain is responsible for controlling the functions of the body, which includes cognitive processes, perceptions, and life-sustaining bodily processes and movement. The brain is composed of nerve cells called **neurons**. These neurons pass information back and forth between one other to facilitate all physiological processes. These neurons are not actually connected to each other; in between neurons is a space called a **synapse**.

The Nervous System and its Subdivisions and Functions

The human **nervous system** coordinates the body's response to stimuli from inside and outside the body. There are two major types of nervous system cells: neurons and neuroglia. **Neurons** are the workhorses of the nervous system and form a complex communication network that transmits electrical impulses termed **action potentials**, while **neuroglia** connect and support the neurons.

Although some neurons monitor the senses, some control muscles, and some connect the brain to other neurons, all neurons have four common characteristics:

Dendrites: These receive electrical signals from other neurons across small gaps called **synapses**.

Nerve cell body: This is the hub of processing and protein manufacturing for the neuron.

Axon: This transmits the signal from the cell body to other neurons.

Terminals: These bridge the neuron's axon to dendrites of other neurons and are involved with delivering the nervous signal via chemical messengers called **neurotransmitters**.

Here is an illustration of a typical nerve cell:

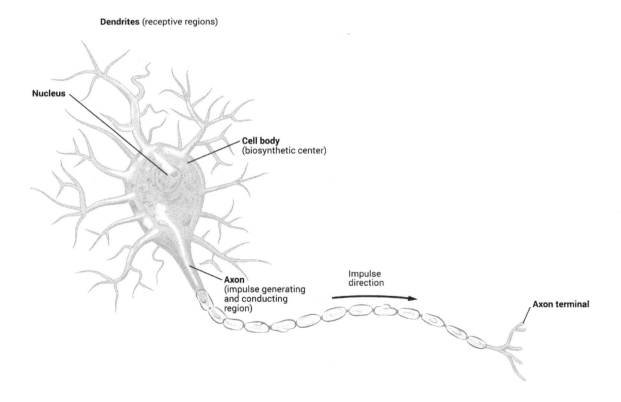

36

There are two major divisions of the nervous system: central and peripheral.

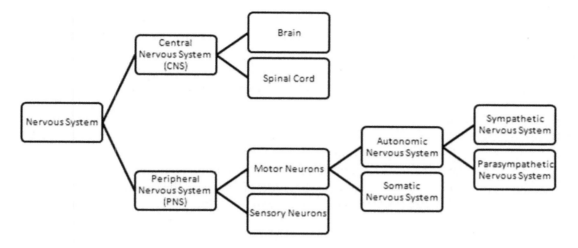

Central Nervous System

The **central nervous system** (CNS) consists of the brain and spinal cord. Three layers of membranes, called the **meninges**, cover and separate the CNS from the rest of the body.

Peripheral Nervous System

The **peripheral nervous system** (PNS) includes all nervous tissue besides the brain and spinal cord. The PNS consists of the sets of **cranial** and **spinal nerves** and relays information between the CNS and the rest of the body. The PNS has two divisions: the autonomic nervous system and the somatic nervous system.

Autonomic Nervous System

The **autonomic nervous system** (ANS) governs involuntary, or reflexive, body functions. Ultimately, the autonomic nervous system controls functions such as breathing, heart rate, digestion, body temperature, and blood pressure.

The ANS is split between **parasympathetic** nerves and **sympathetic** nerves. These two nerve types are antagonistic, so they have opposite effects on the body. Parasympathetic nerves typically are useful when resting or during "safe" conditions; they decrease heart rate, decrease inhalation speed, prepare digestion, and allow urination and excretion. Sympathetic nerves, on the other hand, become active when a person is under stress or excited, and they increase heart rate, increase breathing rates, and inhibit digestion, urination, and excretion.

Somatic Nervous System and the Reflex Arc

The **somatic** nervous system (SNS) governs the conscious, or voluntary, control of skeletal muscles and their corresponding body movements. The SNS contains afferent and efferent neurons. Afferent neurons carry sensory messages from the skeletal muscles, skin, or sensory organs to the CNS. Efferent neurons relay motor messages from the CNS to skeletal muscles, skin, or sensory organs.

The SNS also has a role in involuntary movements called **reflexes**. A reflex is defined as an involuntary response to a stimulus. Reflexes are transmitted via what is termed a **reflex arc**, where a stimulus is sensed by a receptor and its afferent neuron, interpreted and rerouted by an **interneuron**, and delivered to effector muscles by an efferent neuron to respond to the initial stimulus. A reflex can bypass the brain by being rerouted through the spinal cord; the interneuron decides the proper course of action, rather than the brain. The reflex arc results in an instantaneous, involuntary response. For example, a physician tapping on the knee produces an involuntary knee jerk referred to as the **patellar tendon reflex.**

Basic Processes and Systems in the Biological Bases of Behavior

The nervous and endocrine systems are the primary physiologic systems involved in behavior. Communication between neurons occurs through electrochemical processes and plays a major role in human behavior, as it is the structure of communication throughout the nervous system. Neuronal communication within the nervous system plays a major role in human behavior as it allows communication from the body to the brain, between different parts of the brain, and from the brain to the rest of the body. The primary way in which neural communication influences behavior is through mood fluctuations, which, in turn, influence a person's behaviors. Certain behaviors will also trigger the release of particular neurotransmitters, such as dopamine, leading to a pleasurable feeling which encouraging the repetition of those behaviors. Although neuronal communication influences behavior, it does not dictate behavior and is only one factor involved in how humans act.

Influence of Neurotransmitters on Behavior

Neurotransmitters are active in the process of communication between neurons. Different types of neurotransmitters are released by various types of cells, and all have an impact on behavior in different ways. Some neurotransmitters, such as norepinephrine and serotonin, can directly impact one's mood. Others have a role in motor movement, such as acetylcholine. Endorphins are a natural painkiller and glutamate is involved in memory. Some neurotransmitters are considered **inhibitory** and others are **excitatory**. The release of more excitatory neurotransmitters is likely to lead to an action potential in the post-synaptic neuron, whereas the release of inhibitory neurotransmitters serves to prevent an action potential. Many mental health medications and treatments for other diseases function by mimicking, blocking, or changing the levels of certain neurotransmitters. Depression, schizophrenia, Alzheimer's, and Parkinson's are just a few examples of conditions or diseases that are directly connected to high or low levels of certain neurotransmitters. Recreational drugs have a similar effect to medications, often increasing or mimicking mood-enhancing neurotransmitters.

Some of the more significant neurotransmitters and their functions include the following:

Dopamine: feelings of happiness, pleasure and movement

Endorphins: assists with pain relief and feelings of pleasure

Epinephrine/adrenaline: related to stress, or the flight-or-fight mechanism

Norepinephrine: energy and feelings of excitement

Serotonin: helps stabilize and modulate mood

GABA (Gamma Aminobutyric Acid): allows neurons to activate less. It is believed to improve mood or calm the nervous system.

Glutamate: important in memory and learning

Neural Firing

The Basic Process of Transmission of a Signal Between Neurons

Communication between neurons begins when the dendrites at the end of one neuron receive neurotransmitters into receptor sites, causing the neuron to depolarize and send an electrical charge down the axon to the other end of the neuron. This is called the **action potential** and follows the **all-or-none** principle. A neuron either fires or does not fire; there can be no weak or partial action potential. **Neurotransmitters**, the chemical messengers of the brain, are then released from the synaptic vesicles within the axon terminal at the end of the neuron into the synaptic gap between the first neuron and the next one. If enough neurotransmitters bind to receptor sites on the post-synaptic neuron, then the action potential will be set off again and the process will continue to the next neuron.

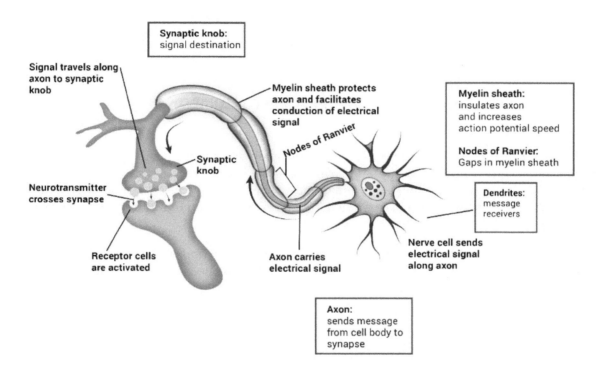

Influence of Drugs on Neural Firing

The Influence of Drugs on Neurotransmitters

Drugs work directly to affect neurotransmitters by either making it more **or less** difficult for them to deliver their messages.

Reuptake Mechanisms

Neurotransmitters transport information from one neuron to another across the synapse. After the neurotransmitter is released to deliver information to the destination neuron, it is then sent back to the originating neuron, and that process is called **reuptake**. Neurotransmitters can be excitatory and make the destination neuron fire, or inhibitory and stop the next neuron from firing.

Depressant drugs, like alcohol, inhibit neurotransmitters GABA and glutamates from exciting the nervous system and creates a sedating effect. Stimulants mostly effect dopamine by increasing the amount released and delaying the reuptake. This will create feelings of increased alertness and energy. Some stimulants may also affect serotonin and norepinephrine. Opioids, cannabinoids, and hallucinogens affect serotonin, dopamine, and endorphins.

Agonists

Some drugs are **agonistic**, which means they increase the communication being carried by the neurotransmitter. When an enhanced neurotransmitter is released, the reuptake process is not as efficient.

Antagonists

Some substances can be **antagonistic**, which means that they inhibit the ability of the neurotransmitter to transport its message. This interference can happen in two ways by blocking the neurotransmitter from attaching to the destination neuron or preventing the neurotransmitter from being released.

The Brain

The Nervous System and its Subdivisions and Functions in the Brain

Major Brain Regions

The major divisions of the brain are the forebrain, the midbrain, and the hindbrain. The **forebrain** consists of the cerebrum, the thalamus, and hypothalamus, and the rest of the limbic system. The **cerebrum** is the largest part of the brain, and its most well-researched part is the outer cerebral cortex. The cerebrum is divided into right and left hemispheres, and each cerebral cortex hemisphere has four discrete areas, or **lobes**: frontal, temporal, parietal, and occipital.

The **hypothalamus** controls the endocrine system and all of the hormones that govern long-term effects on the body. Each hemisphere of the **limbic system** includes a **hippocampus** (which plays a vital role in

memory), an **amygdala** (which is involved with emotional responses like fear and anger), and other small bodies and nuclei associated with memory and pleasure.

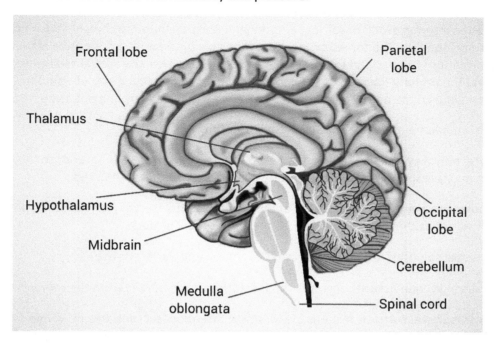

The **midbrain** oversees alertness, sleep/wake cycles, and temperature regulation, and it includes the **substantia nigra**, which produces **melatonin** to regulate sleep patterns. The notable components of the **hindbrain** include the medulla oblongata and cerebellum. The **medulla oblongata** is located just above the spinal cord and is responsible for crucial involuntary functions such as breathing, heart rate, swallowing, and the regulation of blood pressure. Together with other parts of the hindbrain, the midbrain and medulla oblongata form the **brain stem**. The brain stem connects the spinal cord to the rest of the brain. To the rear of the brain stem sits the **cerebellum**, which plays key roles in posture, balance, and muscular coordination. The spinal cord itself carries sensory information to the brain and motor information to the body. It is encapsulated by its protective bony spinal column.

Lobes
As mentioned, the cerebrum is divided into discrete lobes. The **frontal lobe** governs duties such as voluntary movement, judgment, problem solving, and planning, while the other lobes have more sensory involvement. The **temporal lobe** integrates hearing and language comprehension, the **parietal lobe** processes sensory input from the skin, and the **occipital lobe** functions to process visual input from the eyes. For completeness, the other two senses, smell and taste, are processed via the olfactory bulbs. The **thalamus** helps organize and coordinate all of this sensory input in a meaningful way for the brain to interpret.

Cortical Areas
The brain is a vast, intricately interconnected neural network composed of various structures performing numerous functions. Various structures of the brain are ripe with gyri, sulci, and fissures. A **gyrus** describes a ridge or cortical fold between crevices on the brain's cerebral surface. A **sulcus** consists of a shallow groove on the brain's surface. A **fissure** describes a deep furrow in the brain.

The **cerebrum** is the largest division of the brain. The cerebrum is divided by the **longitudinal fissure** into the left and right hemisphere, each of which is divided into four lobes, which include the frontal lobe, temporal lobe, parietal lobe, and occipital lobe. The **frontal lobe** is responsible for functions such as planning, decision making, problem solving, emotional regulation, impulse control, reasoning, memory formation, and personality. The **temporal lobe** is responsible for hearing, information retrieval, and language organization. The **parietal lobe** controls sensory integration and spatial awareness and perception, and the primary function of the **occipital lobe** is tending to aspects of visual stimuli. Each of these cortical regions of the brain contains a wide array of structures carrying out a variety of functions.

The cerebrum is made up of several notable, distinct features:

- The **precentral gyrus** (also referred to as the **primary motor area**) is anterior to the central sulcus and is responsible for the voluntary movements of skeletal muscles.

- The **postcentral gyrus** is the location of the primary somatosensory cortex of the parietal lobe, which serves as the main receptive area for one's sense of touch.

- The **central sulcus of Rolando** separates the frontal and parietal lobe.

- The **lateral Sylvian fissure** separates the frontal and parietal lobe from the temporal lobe.

- The **intraparietal sulcus** is responsible for visual attention, saccadic eye movements, visual control of pointing and reaching, grasping and manipulating hand movements, depth perception, finger movements, and understanding numbers.

- The **superior frontal gyrus** contributes to working memory (short-term information processing) and other higher cognitive functions.

- The **middle frontal gyrus** is responsible for semantic processing, target detection, working memory, cognitive control, and functional connectivity.

- The **inferior frontal gyrus** is the location of **Broca's area**, which is involved in language processing and speech production.

- The **superior temporal gyrus** is the location of **Wernicke's area**, which is responsible for language comprehension.

- The **middle temporal gyrus** is involved in cognitive processes such as facial recognition, distance contemplation, and understanding word meaning.

- The **inferior temporal gyrus** is responsible for visual object recognition.

- The **supramarginal gyrus** is part of the somatosensory cortex in the parietal lobe that interprets tactile data, space and limb location, and the identification of gestures and postures.

- The **angular gyrus** is located in the parietal lobe that plays a role in a number of functions that include language, spatial cognition, number processing, attention, memory retrieval, and theory of mind (attributing mental states to oneself and others and understanding that others perceive things differently than oneself).

- The **superior parietal lobe** is responsible for spatial orientation, visual input, and sensory data from one's hand.

- The **inferior parietal lobe** is responsible for perceiving emotions, interpreting sensory information, language, mathematical skills, and body image.

- The **olfactory bulb** is one of the oldest structures in the brain, located in the forebrain, and is responsible for the detection of odors.

- The **occipital lobe** contains different areas related to visual communication, which include the **visual receiving area** that receives visual images of language and the **visual association area**, which is important for reading comprehension.

- The **cerebellum** is responsible for managing voluntary motions such as balance, coordination, posture, and speech.

Brain Lateralization and Hemispheric Specialization

The concept of brain lateralization theorizes that one side, or hemisphere of the brain, is responsible for certain functions, as well as the opposing side of the body. For example, the left hemisphere is responsible tasks related to math and rationality or logic, as well as controlling the right side of the body. The right brain hemisphere is responsible for creative functions like art, music, and imaginative tasks, as well as controlling the left side of the body.

Roger Sperry and Michael Gazzaniga studied patients whose nerve connections (corpus callosum) between the right and left hemispheres of their brains were surgically severed. This type of operation was done to treat severe epilepsy after all other treatments failed. Sperry and Gazzaniga found that the patients that had this procedure had what they called **split-brain syndrome**. The right and left hemispheres of their brains were no longer able to effectively communicate. In some cases, subjects in the study could not identify an object being held in their hand. Others had developed a dual personality where they received conflicting demands from the rational left side of their brains and the right imaginative side that was more driven by urges and instinct. Others provided one answer when the right hemisphere received a question and gave a different answer to the same question when the left side received it. Sperry and Gazzaniga's work offered significant contributions to the study of brain laterization.

The Contributions of Key Researchers to the Study of the Brain

Paul Broca
Paul Broca (1824–1880) was a French surgeon and physical anthropologist. He was the first to propose that each of the hemispheres of the brain was responsible for certain functions. Broca studied and was a significant contributor to learning more about the causes of losing the ability to form words. He theorized that speech originated in the left front region of the brain. This became known as the "convolution of Broca," or Broca's area.

Carl Wernicke
Carl Wernicke (1848–1905), a German neuropsychiatrist, made important contributions to the study of brain anatomy and function. Wernicke was one of the first to theorize that the brain was made up of pathways and regions each with its own function and purpose. He also contributed to evidence that there was hemisphere specialization. In studying a stroke patient, Wernicke found that the individual

43

was able to speak, but could not understand when he was being spoken to. After the patient's death, Wernicke discovered a lesion on the rear of the left side of his brain. This area would become known as **Wernicke's area**. He coined the term **fluent aphasia**, which is the ability to speak, but not necessarily comprehend words or use them appropriately. This area is located close in proximity to Broca's area and with similar language function; however, Broca's area is related to speech development not comprehension. Another one of Wernicke's significant contributions is his work in a "Textbook of Brain Disorders," where he connected each known neurological disorder to a related area of the brain.

Tools for Examining Brain Structure and Function

Historic and Contemporary Research Strategies and Technologies that Support Research

Case Studies
In psychology, a **case study** consists of a thorough investigation of a single individual, group, community, or a particular event. Researchers obtain data through various methods such as observations, interviews, or reconstructing the case histories of those involved. Most information collected and analyzed during a case study can be either **qualitative**, which entails verbal outlines rather than measurements, or **quantitative**, which consists of numerical data. In most case studies, details gathered about the research participants tend to be biographical, retrospective, and focused on immediate events in their daily lives.

Because this research can continue for an extended timeframe, researchers can study certain processes or developments as they occur. Also, due to the relatively smaller number of participants in a case study, researchers can investigate a subject matter of interest in a more detailed fashion than they could with a larger group. The strengths of a case study include the ability to provide detailed information, yield insight for future research, and allow for research into otherwise impractical situations. However, the limitations of a case study include the difficulty to replicate, lack of generalizability to a larger population, susceptibility to researcher bias, and that they tend to be time consuming.

Split-Brain Research
As briefly introduced previously, the **split-brain technique** (also called a **corpus calloscotomy**) consists of patients undergoing a surgical procedure that entails cutting through the bundle of nerve fibers (corpus callosum) connecting the left and right hemispheres of their brain. This procedure has typically been performed to help patients decrease their symptoms of severe epilepsy—a condition that involves erratic electrical outbursts in the brain. A goal of split-brain research has involved examining certain specialized functions of each hemisphere. Research shows that the left hemisphere is dominant in language and speech, whereas the right hemisphere is dominant in visual-motor skills.

However, after split-brain surgery has been performed, interhemispheric communication usually doesn't function as effectively. This particular impairment can lead to a condition known as **split-brain syndrome**, which describes how the separation of the left and right hemisphere affects agency and behavior. In split-brain syndrome, the right hemisphere behaves independently of the left hemisphere and affects the patient's ability to engage in rational decision making, resulting in a sort of split personality arising in the patient. The left hemisphere conveys orders indicating the patient's rational ambitions, while the right hemisphere delivers contradictory directives exposing originally concealed desires. Nevertheless, noninvasive measures can now be used to study hemispheric interaction.

Imaging Techniques

Since the advent of noninvasive imaging capabilities, researchers have used neuroimaging techniques to scan the brain. Neuroimaging incorporates several methods that either directly or indirectly study the brain's structures, functions, and pharmacological activities. These scanning techniques fall under two categories: structural imaging and functional imaging. **Structural imaging** explores the structure of the brain and helps to diagnose disease or injury. **Functional imaging** diagnoses metabolic diseases and lesions and is also used in neurological and cognitive research.

Examples of scanning techniques researchers typically use include the electroencephalogram (EEG), magnetic resonance imaging (MRI), functional magnetic resonance imaging (fMRI), and positron emission topography (PET). The **EEG** shows brain activity occurring during certain psychological states, such as wakefulness and sleepiness, and is also useful in helping to diagnose seizure activity and other medical issues, including either overactivity or underactivity, in certain regions of the brain. The **MRI** is used to discern among grey matter, white matter, and cerebrospinal fluid. The **fMRI** measures brain functioning through a computer's combination of various images taken a fraction of a second apart. And the **PET scan** uses the brain's glucose (its fuel) to illustrate where neurons are firing.

Lesioning

Also known as an **ablation experiment**, **lesioning** is a research technique in which certain brain regions are either disabled or completely removed as a means of determining their specific functions. The term **ablation** describes this removal through the use of lasers, surgery, or vaporization. Lesioning has been used as part of the study of cognitive neuroscience, particularly with regard to **declarative memory**, which describes the memory of facts and events, and information that can be consciously recalled. This research method involves studying different brain lesions that occurred as a result of injury, illness, or damage inflicted by the researcher.

The two brain structures researchers most often use in this type of study consist of the amygdala and the hippocampus. The **amygdala** is an almond-shaped set of neurons in the temporal lobe shown to play a key role in emotional processing, and the **hippocampus** is a curved structure also located in the temporal lobe that is involved with learning, memory formation, and emotion. Typically performed on lab rats, lesioning studies measure the capacity for learning a new set of skills and applying that learning to different situations. Lesioning has played an important role in helping researchers better understand brain functions.

Autopsy

An **autopsy** is a surgical procedure typically used for research or educational purposes. This procedure consists of an extensive examination via dissection of a corpse to determine the cause of death, as well as the mode and manner of death, or to evaluate the extent of any underlying disease or injury that may be present. Autopsies are typically undertaken by pathologists, while the coroner helps determine the cause of death. Only a small portion of most deaths require an autopsy, particularly when the death is either sudden or the result of an unnatural cause. In clinical medicine, autopsies can help identify medical errors, a previously undetected infectious disease, or exposure to hazardous materials. Sometimes autopsies can be conducted virtually via the use of medical imaging technologies.

In psychology, there's also a type of study referred to as a psychological autopsy, which is a valuable tool used in cases of a completed suicide. A **psychological autopsy** entails obtaining all available details on the deceased individual through the use of structured interviews with people close to the victim, as well

as any attending healthcare personnel. And with nonhuman animals, procedures such as a **necropsy** are performed to determine their cause of death.

The Contributions of Key Researchers to the Development of Tools for Examining the Brain

Roger Sperry

American neuropsychologist Roger Sperry (1913–1994) is most known for his work with split-brain research. Along with researcher Michael Gazzaniga, Sperry was the first to study split brains in humans. Their study found that numerous patients who underwent the split-brain procedure suffered from **split-brain syndrome**, which is when the left and right hemisphere work independently of each other to the extent that it can result in the sufferer experiencing a sort of split personality, although the phenomenon of split personality is rare. However, in some cases, impaired interhemispheric communication could result in personality remaining intact while still allowing patients to use each hemisphere to perform independent intellectual tasks. Aside from his work with split brains, Sperry is also known for his **chemoaffinity hypothesis**, which states that neurons form connections with their targets based on their interactions with distinct molecular markers during development, and that an organism's genotype determines their initial wiring diagram.

The Adaptable Brain

The Role of Neuroplasticity in Traumatic Brain Injury

Neuroplasticity describes the brain's ability to reorganize itself in response to behavior, environmental cues, learning, exposure to repeated stimuli, thought, emotion, and experience. This kind of activity-dependent plasticity can have positive implications for learning, memory, healthy development, and recovery from a **traumatic brain injury (TBI)**. These brain changes happen on various levels, ranging from small cellular alterations that stem from learning to larger cortical remapping resulting from injury.

Although neuroplasticity can persist throughout an individual's life, research shows that the adult brain exhibits a lower degree of plasticity than the developing brain of children. Two types of brain changes include structural plasticity and functional plasticity. **Structural plasticity** occurs when the brain actually alters its physical structure to accommodate learning. **Functional plasticity** involves the brain transferring certain functions from a damaged brain region to other undamaged regions, essentially helping the brain to compensate for a certain functional deficit. While this surprising consequence of neuroplasticity can result from normal experiences, it has also been noted to play an important role in one's recovery from TBI, thus serving as the scientific basis for the treatment of acquired brain injuries.

Evidence suggests that neuroplasticity helps explain improvements in functionality by showing how cortical reorganization acts as the mechanism of change during efforts at rehabilitation from TBI. For instance, consider a man who suffers an injury that paralyzes his right arm. Research shows that, with enough rehabilitation, the paralyzed arm could eventually relearn how to move and perform functions such as wiping tables, playing sports, and even writing. This example demonstrates that damaged brain functions are able to recover by transferring over to healthy, undamaged brain regions after generating new connections between intact neurons.

From both an investigative and treatment standpoint, TBIs can prove to be challenging. In general, a TBI entails structural injuries or physiological alterations in brain function. Even though brain injuries account for a substantial portion of trauma, the seriousness of a TBI ranges from mild, which usually

involves a momentary shift in consciousness, to severe, which consists of chronic intervals of unconsciousness and/or even amnesia. Fortunately, most TBI cases that are treated medically are typically regarded as mild, with most patients being able to recover from these types of injuries.

The Contributions of Key Researchers to the Study of Neuroplasticity

Michael Gazzaniga

Aside from other notable contributions, American psychologist Michael Gazzaniga (1939–) is known for his work with split-brain patients. Alongside Roger Sperry, Gazzaniga was among one of the first to study split brains in humans. He helped advance our knowledge of interhemispheric communication and functional lateralization in the brain. After split-brain surgery, the left and right hemispheres become out of sync. The right hemisphere ceases to properly convey information to the left hemisphere. The right hemisphere is unable to reach the language capabilities of the left hemisphere, where the conscious mind works to interpret the reasons for its actions. After finding that the mind isn't cognizant of information it doesn't receive, Gazzaniga devised a theory of consciousness, which is backed by neuroscientific research. Gazzaniga is considered among the leading researchers in the field of cognitive neuroscience, studying the neural basis of mind. Over several years, he has written extensively on this subject.

States of Consciousness and Their Impact on Behavior

The mind has three main states of consciousness: conscious, subliminal, and unconscious. Each state is produced by a different wavelength in the brain and responsible for a different level of understanding and information processing. **Beta waves** operate at around 13-30 Hz and are associated with learning, worry, and activities that involve mental focus. For this reason, these wavelengths are involved in the conscious mind. **Alpha waves** are 8-13 Hz and are the wavelengths that predominate during relaxing or daydreaming, which are functions that are considered part of the subliminal mind. **Theta waves** are 4-8 Hz and involved in deeper relaxation, dreams, and the REM phase of sleep. They are also part of the subliminal, and somewhat unconscious, mind. Lastly, **delta waves** are up to 4 Hz. They are involved in deep sleep and the unconscious mind. **Alertness** is a heightened sense of awareness. It is an active state of attention in which a person is quick to react to stimuli.

The Major Psychoactive Drug Categories

Consciousness-altering drugs, or **psychoactive drugs**, are pharmaceutical substances that produce changes in mood, perception, and consciousness.

Types of Consciousness-Altering Drugs and Their Effects on the Nervous System and Behavior

1. **Anxiolytics:** Decrease anxiety; used to sedate the central nervous system

2. **Euphoriants:** Induce a state of intense elation and alter perception; increase the activity of certain neurotransmitters

3. **Stimulants:** Stimulate the mind and cause a person to wake up; enhance the activity of certain neurotransmitters in the brain

4. **Depressants:** Induce a calm state of mind, reduce anxiety, and can alter perception; can induce sleep

5. **Hallucinogens:** Produce distinct alterations in perception, time, and emotional states; disrupt the interaction of nerve cells and serotonin, which helps regulate behavior and perception

Drug Dependence, Addiction, Tolerance, and Withdrawal

The reward pathway in the brain is responsible for the feeling of pleasure in response to an enjoyable experience. It engages all five senses and then motivates a person to repeat the enjoyable activity to feel pleasure again. Drugs, such as psychoactive substances, bypass the senses and start the pathway directly in the brain, causing a large release of dopamine and an abnormally intense feeling of pleasure. The brain then adjusts for this overabundance of dopamine by reducing the number of dopamine receptors, causing a low feeling to follow the immense high. Addiction causes the person to crave the feeling of intense pleasure again and the cycle of drug use to continue.

Addiction is a complex process involving biological, social, cultural and genetic factors. There is some disagreement in the addiction treatment community about the causes and best treatments for substance abuse disorders. There are several models of addiction.

The earliest theory of addiction is called the **Moral Model**. This model implies that the person abuses substances because they are morally weak. The addict is viewed as a sinner or criminal and one who does not have the intestinal fortitude to change negative behaviors, therefore choosing to wallow in the misery of their sins.

The **disease model** or **medical model** of addiction, upon which the twelve-step program of Alcoholics Anonymous (AA) is based, specifies that the addict suffers from an illness that will never be cured and is progressive in its development. Even if the individual ceases alcohol intake, the disease remains. AA literature indicates that when one relapses, even after years of sobriety, the addict picks up not where they left off, but where the disease would have taken them if the drinking had continued. It is seen as a medical disorder and, at times, referred to in the *Big Book of AA* as having an allergy, with alcohol as the identified allergen. This theory is accepted and understood by many successful AA participants who have maintained sobriety throughout this program for years and who have shared their experience of strength and hope to help others struggling with addiction.

The **bio-psychosocial model** of addiction focuses on the role of the environment. Cultural and social factors influence one's beliefs and attitudes about substance use. In certain religions, it is unacceptable to use alcohol. In others, it may be encouraged—such as the huge sale and consumption of beer at Catholic picnics and fish fries. An addict's observation of others and their patterns of alcohol ingestion influences their attraction to drug or alcohol use as a means for tension relief or a form of celebration.

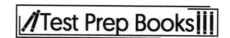

Exposure to family or community members who use large quantities of intoxicants may serve to normalize dysfunctional patterns of use. Some youth observing parents consuming a quart of vodka each night may believe their family members are just normal drinkers, whereas other youth are raised in environments where alcohol is unacceptable or served only on rare occasions.

The **learning theory** of addiction is based on concepts related to positive reinforcement. The assumption underpinning this model is that addiction is a learned behavior through operant conditioning, classical conditioning, and social learning. Social learning takes place through observation. Learning theory posits that the interplay between these three factors contribute to the initiation, maintenance, and relapse of addictive behaviors. The intoxicant serves as an immediate reinforcement in the form of increased euphoria or relaxation. In some cases, it also deters withdrawal symptoms. Both of these forms of reinforcement increase the likelihood that the behavior will be repeated in an effort to recreate the sensation of feeling better.

Genetic theory is based on research indicating that biological children of parents who struggle with addiction or alcoholics are more prone to addiction than children of non-alcoholics. According to genetic therapy, this genetic predisposition towards addiction accounts for about half of one's susceptibility to becoming an addict. Theorists of this model agree that other factors, such as social experiences, have an impact upon the formation of an addiction.

The Contributions of Major Figures in Consciousness Research

William James
As mentioned previously, William James (1842–1910) offered one of the first psychology courses in the United States and authored the influential text *Principles of Psychology*. He also developed functionalism and pragmatism. Another notable contribution to the field of psychology was his James-Lang theory of emotion, which posits that a situation causes a person to have a physical response and a related interpretation of the event, which in turn, leads to an emotional reaction. In other words, it is not the event itself, but the individual's interpretation of the event and reaction that lead to the emotional response.

Sigmund Freud
Along with establishing psychoanalysis, Austrian doctor Sigmund Freud (1856–1939) made several contributions to the field of psychology. Freud devised a set of therapeutic strategies centered around talk therapy that involved concepts such as transference, countertransference, free association, and dream interpretation. He regarded dreams as "the royal road to the unconscious." He developed a personality theory composed of three fundamental structures of the human mind, which include the **id (instinct)**, **ego (reality)**, and **superego (morality)**. His **psychosexual theory of development** outlined how people are born with an instinctual libido, which he divided up into five stages, including the oral, anal, phallic, latent, and genital stages. But perhaps the most important contribution Freud made was his conception of the **unconscious**, which proposed that our awareness existed below the surface and that we often don't act in accordance with our conscious thoughts. Freud used psychoanalysis as a means of making the unconscious conscious.

Sleep and Dreaming

Aspects of Sleep and Dreaming

Neural and Behavioral Characteristics of the Stages of the Sleep Cycle

Sleep is an unconscious state of the mind. It is a time for the brain to process information and experiences that were learned during the day. It also helps transfer information to the long-term memory.

Stages of Sleep: There are four stages of non-**rapid eye movement** (REM) sleep that occur before REM sleep. Stage 1 involves the transition from being awake to being asleep. Stage 2 involves a slowing of the heart rate and breathing. Stage 3 is a deep sleep. Stage 4 is a very deep sleep with a transition to mostly delta brain waves. REM sleep is where dreams occur and heart rate and breathing actually quicken.

Sleep Cycles and Changes to Cycles: On average, sleep cycles last from 90 to 110 minutes in adults. They begin with Stage 1 and then progress to REM sleep after about ninety minutes. The first REM sleep lasts about ten minutes and increases in length with each subsequent sleep cycle, with the final one lasting up to one hour.

Sleep and Circadian Rhythms: Although the pattern of sleep cycles is consistent from childhood through adulthood, the timing of sleep changes. A **circadian rhythm** is a biological process that follows a twenty-four-hour cycle. Humans have an internal circadian pacemaker that makes them aware of the time of the day and when they should go to sleep and wake up. As a person develops and ages, the preferred time to go to sleep and wake up changes. Children tend to go to sleep early in the evening, adolescents tend to stay up late into the night, and adults tend to go to sleep at the end of the evening or early in the night.

Dreaming: **Dreams** are a series of thoughts and images that occur in a person's mind while they are asleep. They mostly occur during the REM stage of sleep. There are several theories as to why people dream including memory consolidation, emotional regulation, and threat simulation.

Theories of Sleep and Dreaming

The function of sleep has served as a source of interest for centuries, dating as far back as the days of ancient Greece, but it's only in the past century that modern researchers have investigated sleep in ways both objective and systematic. However, while we are now capable of studying sleep and its associated processes, researchers still don't seem to have a clear consensus on exactly why we sleep. It's well-established that sleep plays an important role in our health and wellness, and follows a relatively predictable pattern, but much is still being learned. Researchers have proposed numerous theories that endeavor to explain our need for sleep.

Some of these theories include the repair and restoration theory, evolutionary theory, information consolidation theory, and the clean-up theory of sleep. The **repair and restoration theory** outlines how NREM sleep restores physiological functions while REM sleep restores mental functions. The **evolutionary theory** proposes that sleep serves as a means of energy conversation, allowing all species to sleep during those times of wakefulness that would prove most dangerous. The **information consolidation theory** suggests that sleep allows for the processing of information attained throughout the day. The **clean-up theory** posits that sleep acts as a way for the brain to do some "spring cleaning" of toxins and waste products generated during the day. Dreaming exists within this same realm of mystery.

Even though much time and effort has been dedicated to studying this process, researchers still do not seem to have a solid consensus on why exactly we dream either. Several theories have been proposed to explain the function of dreams. Some theories include the psychoanalytic theory, activation-synthesis model, and information processing theory of dreaming. The **psychoanalytic theory** suggests that dreams are representative of our unconscious thoughts, desires, and motivations; they are composed of **latent content** (hidden psychological meaning) and **manifest content** (actual content of the dream). The **activation-synthesis model** describes how dreams are the result of brain circuits that become activated during REM sleep. The **information processing theory** explains that sleep enables us to consolidate and process all the information accumulated throughout the day and that dreams are simply the result of this activity. Various other theories are still being further developed to understand the reason for dreaming.

Symptoms and Treatments of Sleep Disorders

Sleep disorders describe a group of conditions resulting in one's inability to receive an optimal amount of sleep. They affect a third of the American population between the ages of twenty to sixty. While troublesome external factors are known to occasionally disturb one's sleep patterns, when difficulties with sleep start occurring frequently, it may be indicative of a sleep disorder. There are many different types of sleeping disorders, ranging in both severity and category, so each set of symptoms can vary. However, some general symptoms commonly associated with sleep disorders include anxiety, irritability, inability to focus, difficulty falling or remaining asleep, fatigue, recurring naps during the day, and depression.

Some examples of the many different types of sleep disorders include insomnia, aberrant behaviors or movements during sleep (parasomnias), restless leg syndrome, narcolepsy, and sleep apnea. A lack of sleep can also negatively affect one's energy levels, physical health, relationships, and task performance. The cause of sleep disorders is multifactorial. Some factors that can serve as potential causes of a sleep disorder include allergies and respiratory problems, chronic pain, frequent urination, and stress.

Once a sleep disorder is diagnosed, there are certain courses of treatment one can pursue, ranging from medical to lifestyle changes. Because there are several different causes and types of sleeping disorders, treatments for this condition can also vary. Medical approaches can include allergy or cold medications, melatonin supplements, sleeping pills, treatments for any other underlying health conditions, a dental guard to wear at night to prevent bruxism (teeth grinding), or a breathing apparatus (CPAP machine) or surgery for those suffering from sleep apnea. Lifestyle changes that could also be incorporated into one's daily life include undertaking a healthier diet, exercising regularly, adhering to a sleep schedule, reducing use of alcohol and tobacco, restricting caffeine intake, and consuming less water before bed.

Sleep–Wake Disorders: Sleep is essential for restoration and repair of the body as well as for processing of the information received during the waking hours. There are many different types of sleep-wake disorders that are disruptive to getting a proper night of sleep, such as insomnia, restless leg syndrome, narcolepsy, and breathing-related sleep disorders.

Unit 3: Sensation and Perception

Principles of Sensation

General Principles of Organizing and Integrating Sensation

Perception is the interpretation of sensory information in order to understand the environment. It begins with an object stimulating one or more of the sensory organs in the body. For example, light stimulates the retina in the eye and odor molecules stimulate the receptors in the nasal cavity. In a process called **transduction**, this stimulation information is transformed into neural activity. These neural signals are then transmitted to the brain and processed there. The brain then creates a memory of this stimulus. When an unfamiliar object is encountered, the brain tries to collect as much information about the object as possible. When a familiar object is encountered again, the brain uses the senses to confirm that the object is indeed the familiar one.

Sensory organs help resolve different facets about an object. Depth perception is how a person judges their distance from an object. Each eye has a slightly different view on the same object, which can help distinguish where an object is located and what it fully looks like. The relative size of two objects can be distinguished by the differently sized images that are projected onto the retina. **Relative motion** can be determined by detecting that objects closer than the visual point of focus are moving in the opposite direction of the viewer's moving head and vice versa. **Perceptual constancy** is the idea that objects are stable and unchanging despite changes in sensory stimulation. The brain can identify familiar objects at any distance, from any angle, and with any illumination. Shape, color, and brightness are all perceived the same as they were originally. For example, a woman standing one hundred feet away appears small, but the brain knows what her actual height is and processes it as such.

Gestalt's Principles

Gestalt's principles are a set of principles that help explain perceptual organization. They are based on the idea that a whole is different than the sum of its parts. There are five parts to this set of principles:

1. **Law of Similarity:** Similar things tend to appear grouped together in both visual and auditory settings.

2. **Law of Pragnanz:** Objects in the environment are seen in a way that makes them appear as simple as possible. For example, the Olympics ring symbol is seen as five intertwined circles as opposed to a collection of curved and connected lines.

3. **Law of Proximity:** Objects that are near to each other tend to appear grouped together.

4. **Law of Continuity:** Points that are connected by a straight or curved line are seen in a way that follows the smoothest path.

5. **Law of Closure:** The brain often fills in the gap between separate objects to make a complete whole.

Depth Perception

Depth perception illustrates one's ability to view the world in three dimensions, which in turn allows for discerning proximity or distance. Increased space between one's eyes amounts to better depth perception. Depth perception stems from various depth cues classified as monocular or binocular.

Monocular cues provide depth information when a scene is viewed with one eye. These cues include motion parallax, perspective, aerial perspective, interposition, and texture gradient. **Motion parallax** describes how closer objects appear to pass rapidly while farther objects look stationary. **Perspective** involves watching a scene narrow as it trails off into the distance. **Aerial perspective** describes how images become blurrier as their distance increases. **Interposition** describes how an object appears closer if one object partially blocks the view of another. **Texture gradient** involves an object's texture being clearer to see when viewed up close compared to at a distance.

Binocular cues involve depth information from both eyes. These cues include retinal disparity and convergence. **Retinal disparity** (or **stereopsis**) involves the brain assessing depth in a scene via the use of two images of the same scene gathered from relatively different angles. **Convergence** describes the concurrently inward movement of both eyes toward one another when perceiving an object.

Bottom-up and Top-down Processing

Bottom-up and **top-down** processing are two different methods of information processing. Sensory input is considered bottom-up processing, while top-down processing involves the organization of information from many different sources and is considered a more complex process. Bottom-up processing can be described as a progression from individual elements to a complete picture. A stimulus is seen clearly, and the brain can make sense of the object using only the senses. Top-down processing involves the receipt of vague sensory information followed by the resolution of it using internal hypotheses and expectation interactions. The brain uses more than just the sensory areas to figure out what the stimulus is.

Basic Principles of Sensory Transduction

Sensation

Humans understand the world around them through sensory processing. The human body has receptors that sense or detect different types of energy or stimuli and then process that information through the nervous system. This is the simplified process of sensation, such as that involved in touch and smell. The energy is converted to electrical signals and then transmitted to the brain through a series of action potentials travelling along the axons of millions of neural cells.

Thresholds

The **sensory threshold** is the amount or level of stimulus that is required for an individual to register a sensation. The absolute threshold refers to the smallest detectable level of any kind of sensory stimulus that an individual can detect 50% of the time during a given test. The **difference threshold** is the smallest difference between two stimuli that an individual can actually detect as being different 50% of the time during a given test.

Weber's Law

Ernst Weber was a German physician who observed that in order for the difference between two stimuli to be detected, the stimuli must differ by a constant proportion. This idea was then formulated into **Weber's Law**, which is written as $k = \Delta R/R$, where k is a different constant for each sensation, R is the

amount of existing stimulation, and ΔR is the amount of stimulation that needs to be added for a **Just Noticeable Difference (JND)**.

Signal Detection Theory

The process of **signal detection** occurs when someone detects a stimulus and must distinguish it from background noise. Signal detection theory states that how an individual perceives a stimulus depends on the individual's physical and psychological state, as well as the intensity of the stimulus. For example, in a crowded parking lot, an individual may not notice the rustling of leaves on the ground, but on a quiet day, the sound of the rustling leaves would be more apparent and the individual may pay more attention to it, since there are fewer background noises.

Sensory Adaptation

Sensory adaptation occurs when there is constant exposure to a stimulus. Over time, an individual becomes less sensitive and more adaptable to that stimulus.

Psychophysics

Psychophysics is a field that studies an individual's relationship between physical stimuli and their psychological experience. Experiments are done that can be objectively measured and have quantitative outcomes, such as with threshold measurements.

Sensory Receptors

Different types of sensory receptors recognize different types of energy. For example, light receptors, which are located in the eyes, and sound receptors, which are located in the ears, convert their respective energy stimuli to neural activity through different specialized pathways.

Sensory Pathways

Each type of stimuli, such as touch, hearing, and vision, follows a different sensory pathway from the receptor to the brain. However, generally, all pathways have three long neurons called the primary, secondary, and tertiary neurons. The **primary neuron** has its cell body in the dorsal root ganglion of the spinal nerve. The **secondary neuron** has its cell body either in the spinal cord or in the brain stem. The **tertiary neuron** has its cell body in the thalamus. The pathway includes many breakpoints, or stations, each of which plays a different role in information processing. For example, if a painful sensation is felt on the finger, one station may cause the hand to withdraw from the stimuli and another station may cause the head to turn towards the source of the pain.

Types of Sensory Receptors

Different types of sensations are processed by different sensory receptors. Below is a list of the main sensory receptors found in the human body.

Mechanoreceptors: Detect touch through contact with the body surface and detect sound through vibrations in the air or water. They are located in the skin, hair follicles, and ligaments.

Photoreceptors: Detect vision through visible radiant energy

Thermoreceptors: Detect warmth and cold through changes in skin temperature

Chemoreceptors: Detect smell through substances dissolved in the air or water through the nasal cavity, and taste through substances that come in contact with the tongue

The Research Contributions of Major Historical Figures in Sensation and Perception

Gustav Fechner

German psychologist Gustav Fechner (1801–1887) is responsible for developing the field of **psychophysics**, which helped establish the groundwork for experimental psychology. Fechner's primary goal was to create a set of scientific methods used to measure the connection between the body's physical behavior and the mind's mental activity, both of which he believed exist on the same level playing field. He posited that if numbers ever came to represent sensations, then it would open up psychology to mathematical treatment and make it an exact science.

One of the most well-known results of his postulations is known as the **Weber-Fechner law**, named after Fechner and his professor Ernst Weber. Each of these laws relate to human perception, particularly the relationship between the actual change occurring in a physical stimulus and the perception of change. While some of his work was highly controversial and met with criticism and rejection, Fechner secured a place in history by having mental activity be a serious subject of objective study, paving the way for psychology to become a formal scientific discipline. Fechner's work started a revolution in psychology, inspiring figures like German psychologist Wilhelm Wundt to open the first formal laboratory for psychological research.

David Hubel

Alongside fellow researcher Torsten Wiesel, Canadian-American neurophysiologist David Hubel (1926–2013) studied the structure and function of the visual cortex. He was a co-recipient of the Nobel Prize in Physiology or Medicine for their work concerning the brain's ability to process visual information. Hubel's work revealed how the patterned organization of neural cells engage in visual processing and how the connections formed between nerve cells both filter and transduce sensory information travelling from the retina of the eye to the brain's cerebral cortex, as well as how experience changes the cortex during development.

This research helped establish the notion of critical periods in one's development and revealed that if an animal didn't receive a sufficient amount of visual experiences, their visual system would start suffering a decline in its performance. One of the practical applications inspired by his work has involved improved therapies for children born with vision problems such as cataracts or strabismus (crossed eyes). His work has also led to the modern study of the cerebral cortex and has been important in cortical plasticity research. This understanding of sensory processing in animals has also inspired the development of a descriptor used in computer vision for object recognition and baseline matching.

Ernst Weber

German physiologist Ernst Weber (1795–1878) is among one of the founders of experimental psychology. Weber is best known for his research on sensory response to pressure, temperature, and weight. He discovered a rule referred to as the **just-noticeable difference** (or **JND**), which describes the amount by which something must be altered for any difference to be noticed. This rule is included in what's referred to as **Weber's law**, which involves measuring the perception of change in a stimulus. His work with Gustav Fechner has been helpful in the areas of vision and hearing and has also affected the ability to measure attitude objectively (**attitude scaling**) and other developments.

Another of Weber's contributions involved determining the accuracy of tactile sensations, specifically between different points on the skin, hence discovering what is known as the **two-point threshold**, which describes the smallest separation where two points applied concurrently to one's skin can be distinguished from each other. Weber also helped discover that electrical stimulation of certain brain regions, or the peripheral part of the vagus nerve, slows the heart's activity and brings it to a halt. This discovery in physiology is important because it shed light on an unknown yet indispensable nerve action.

Torsten Wiesel

Alongside fellow researcher David Hubel, Swedish neurophysiologist Torsten Wiesel (1924–) studied the visual cortex, and was a recipient of the Nobel Prize in Physiology or Medicine for their work concerning how visual information is processed in the brain. Their experiments significantly expanded on the scientific understanding of the processing of sensory information.

Wiesel investigated the brain's visual cortex by keeping track of the difference in activity occurring between its cortical cells and discovered that the key difference occurring between these cells is the amount of information that each one can process. He distinguished between simple cells and complex cells in the primary visual cortex. **Simple cells** are those that tend to prefer the stimulus orientation that generates the strongest response, whereas **complex cells** are most responsive to lines moving in one direction. This research showed that the process by which an image is produced involves simple stimuli being constructed into more complex representations. His work also showed that ocular dominance forms early on in childhood development, which has paved the way for therapies aimed at improving vision problems such as cataracts and strabismus. Later in his life, Wiesel also became known for his extensive work as a global human rights activist.

Principles of Perception

How Experience and Culture Can Influence Perceptual Processes

Perceptual Set

In psychology, a **perceptual set** describes how we observe or perceive certain types of sensory information while ignoring other types, basically serving as a kind of bias or predisposition. This theory posits that perception is an active process drawing on selection, inferences, and interpretation. Perceptual set involves the perceiver having expectations and selecting certain features of sensory information on which to focus, as well as understanding and categorizing information and making inferences from that inflow of data. Our perception is influenced by this perceptual set, which, in turn, is influenced by several factors that include culture, emotion, expectations, and motivation.

Culture plays a vital role in shaping who people will become through ways of thinking, feeling, acting, and believing that are shared with others in the same cultural setting, each of which in turn influences how they will come to perceive the world around them. For instance, physical standards of attractiveness are more culture-based, meaning they tend to vary from one culture to another, so to use an example, Americans would be more likely than Kenyans to stigmatize obesity.

Emotions trigger perceptual expectations, which, in turn, causes us to grow accustomed to perceiving situations in accordance with our emotional state. For example, research has shown that feelings of loneliness or acceptance affect how we perceive temperature. When we feel lonely, our environment feels cold, whereas when we feel accepted, we perceive our environment as feeling warm. Expectations are derived from a scene's context, our previous experiences, and essentially any events that occurred recently and repeatedly. The brain evaluates various probable events that are happening, and when an expected event has been chosen, then the brain will start perceiving that particular image.

For example, if a person wakes up in the morning to the sweet aroma of coffee, then they might expect that their roommate or housemate is already awake brewing some, and in this instance, chances are that their perception of the situation will prove accurate, especially if it has happened more than once or twice. An example of how motivation can affect our perception is through motivated reasoning. **Motivated reasoning** describes how our judgments can be biased by self-serving impetuses, hence causing us to start becoming biased toward those conclusions that confirm our preconceived beliefs. For example, a climate change denier is more likely to deny or discredit scientific evidence that points to global warming while favoring data that they believe indicates the contrary to be true, hence keeping in line with their beliefs. To concisely summarize, we tend to become sensitive to certain information over others.

Context Effects

In cognitive psychology, the **context effect** describes how environmental factors surrounding a particular event affect how people both perceive and remember the event. For instance, an event is perceived and remembered more favorably if the surrounding context was pleasant in nature. An example involves someone who goes shopping. If they feel comfortable enough in that store, then not only are they more likely to make a purchase but are also more likely to return to that setting at a later date. However, the opposite is also true, in that a setting is perceived and recalled less favorably if the experience was more unpleasant. As a result, the context effect has an extensive impact on marketing and consumer decisions, thus making this effect a predominant area of focus in marketing research. The context effect can also affect various cognitive domains such as learning skills, memory, and object and word recognition.

When analyzing data, the context effect employs the use of a **top-down design**, which uses previous knowledge and experiences to enhance one's understanding of an image and help with interpreting a stimulus; however, a **bottom-up design**, which is contingent on processing sensory data, can also be used for analysis of a particular stimulus. Making use of both sensory data and previous knowledge to reach a conclusion is a feature of **optimal probabilistic reasoning** (or **Bayesian inference**), which describes a statistical method used to revise a hypothesis's probability as more data become readily available. In other words, when context effects happen, people use environmental cues perceived while analyzing the stimuli and then make decisions influenced by the environment or prior exposure to objects.

Schema

In psychology and cognitive science, a **schema** serves as a cognitive framework that helps people both organize and interpret information gathered from the world around them. British psychologist **Frederic Bartlett** was the first to use schemas as a basic concept in his theory of learning. He posited that one's understanding of the world is generated through a system of abstract mental constructs. Swiss developmental psychologist **Jean Piaget** also popularized the use of schemas in his theory of cognitive development. According to his cognitive theory, children go through various stages of intellectual growth and development. He viewed schema as an organization of knowledge and the process one goes through in order to attain that knowledge. We are constantly adapting to everchanging environments by absorbing and subsequently learning new information, and in turn, existing schemas are modified to help assimilate and accommodate all this new incoming information.

Schemas can be used to organize our present knowledge about the world and provide a context for future insights. Some examples of a schema include archetypes, rubrics, scripts, and social roles.

Archetypes describe innate tendencies that play an important role in influencing human behavior and personality. One example of an archetype includes that of the Caregiver, which is also referred to as the Helper, who is motivated by compassion, generosity, and committed assistance.

Rubrics are guides containing evaluative criteria, definitions for that particular criteria, and a scoring method. An example of a rubric consists of what an educator uses to set up a grading criterion for students working on a specific assignment.

Scripts consist of a sequence of behaviors expected in any given scenario. A common example of a script in psychology consists of a hungry customer wanting to dine at a restaurant, surrounded by other people and props, who enters the restaurant, orders, eats their meal, pays, and then exits the restaurant. This example shows the customer following a series of behaviors attained through habit, practice, and routine.

Social roles describe a set of connected and conceptualized behaviors and actions undertaken in a certain social situation. An example of this consists of a classroom, where a teacher assumes the role of a leader who has nearly complete control over the social dynamics occurring in that classroom.

This schematic processing also acts as a sort of heuristic strategy that allows people to both encode and retrieve their memories without a lot of strenuous mental effort. However, while schematic processing is certainly useful, it isn't without its drawbacks. Schemas can also give way to stereotypes and bias and prejudice in certain circumstances, such as when someone recalls an event that never happened because it proves consistent with their schema, making it more believable to them. However, despite these drawbacks, schemas are still useful guides to perception.

The Role of Attention in Behavior

Attention is the process of selectively focusing on particular information while ignoring other information that is present.

Selective Attention

Selective attention is the process by which the brain filters out large amounts of sensory information in order to focus on one single message. For example, someone who is filtering out a person talking to them while paying attention to the television would be using selective attention. When the brain becomes overloaded with sensory information, it begins to filter out the information that is unimportant and concentrate on what is needed and wanted.

There are several models that have been used to understand selective attention. One of the oldest models is the **spotlight model**. The idea behind this theory is that the visual field has an area of focus in the middle, an area of fringe around that, and a margin around the outer edge. Objects in the focus area are seen in high resolution while the objects located in the fringe area are a much lower resolution and are seen much more crudely. The cut off of the fringe area is referred to as the margin. Another model that builds on the spotlight model is called the **zoom-lens model**. This enhanced model incorporates the idea that if attention is being directed to a smaller focus area, the information being processed becomes sharper, or clearer, and can be processed faster.

Another theory of selective attention is the **bottleneck model**. This model explains how when the brain is overloaded with information, it has to find a way to choose what information to process first. This information is allowed through the bottleneck while the other information must wait to be processed. While some psychologists have hypothesized that the information that is waiting to get processed is

completely ignored, others have proposed that it is actually just attenuated and if something important, like the person's name, were part of the message, the brain would begin to process that information.

Divided Attention

Divided attention is when a person is processing more than one piece of information at a time. This process occurs frequently, such as when driving and paying attention to speed, traffic, and traffic signals or when listening to music while doing homework. It is an important part of everyday life. Attention resources are limited, so the more resources that are devoted to one task, the less that are available for another simultaneous task.

Visual Anatomy

The Vision Process

Vision Process
Structure and Function of the Eye
The **eye** is an elaborate organ that allows individuals to transduce light into neural signals and process their surrounding environment. Depending on their level of focus and concentration on an image, humans can see more or less detail on that object. The eye has many features that are similar to those of a camera. The **lens** allows the eye to focus light. The **ciliary muscles** bend the lens to change its shape and adjust the focus. The **cornea** is curved and bends the light rays so that they can form an image on the **retina** in the back if the eye. The amount of light that enters the eye is controlled by the **pupil**. The **optic nerve**, which is made up of the axons from the ganglion cells in the eye, then conveys the visual information to the brain.

Diagram of the Eye

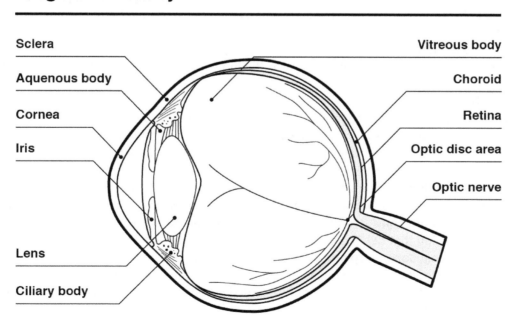

Visual Processing

Visual processing begins in the retina. Images that are taken in through the cornea and lens are transmitted upside down onto the retina. The two types of photoreceptors in the retina are called rods and cones. **Rods** are part of the scotopic system and can be stimulated with low light intensity. **Cones** are part of the photopic system and need strong light intensity to be stimulated. The **photopic system** is responsible for color vision. The signals that are produced from the processing that occurs in the retina are then transferred to ganglion cells, whose axons make up the optic nerve. Signals travel along these axons to the brain, where the visual information is processed, and the images are returned to their proper orientation.

Visual Pathways in the Brain

An individual's visual field is the entire area that they can see without moving their head. The visual cortex in the right hemisphere of the brain receives its input from the left half of the visual field and the visual cortex in the left hemisphere of the brain receives its input from the right half of the visual field. Some retinal ganglion cells have axons that lead to the superior colliculus in the brain, which helps coordinate the rapid movements of the eye towards a target. Others have axons that lead to the nuclei of the hypothalamus that control **circadian rhythms**, or the daily cycles of human behavior, or to the midbrain nuclei to control the size of the pupil and coordinate movement of the eyes or to map the visual space.

Parallel Processing

Parallel processing is the method by which the brain distinguishes incoming stimuli of differing quality. When processing visual stimuli, the brain divides what it sees into the categories of color, motion, shape, and depth. Each quality is analyzed individually, but simultaneously, and then combined together for comprehension of the object.

Feature Detection

Feature detection is a process that starts gradually when an individual begins looking at an object. At first, the individual may look at the overall object, but as the neurons in the brain become more focused on the object, smaller details become more apparent. Feature detection allows the brain to become more selective in what it focuses on. For example, from a picture of a woman's face, the brain begins to see the curves, angles, and small lines of the face as the individual looks at the picture for a longer time.

Visual Perception

Visual perception is one of the most extensively studied topics in psychology. The human eye is a fascinating organ. Light enters through the **cornea**, which helps focus that light onto the photoreceptors in the retina to translate it into an image, and then passes this sensory information along to the visual cortex in the brain. Our retina contains two types of receptor cells called rods and cones, each of which are sensitive to light. **Rods** process vision at lower light levels (also called **scotopic vision**) and spatial acuities, and don't facilitate color vision, whereas **cones** are responsible for vision at higher light levels (also called **photopic vision**) and spatial acuities, and are able to process color vision. Two types of processes related to vision that depend on the directionality of visual information include bottom-up and top-down processing. **Bottom-up processing** is data-based in that the representation of a viewed object is gradually constructed from an image processed by the retina of the eye, while **top-down processing** is more knowledge-based in that objects are identified using one's pre-existing knowledge to help mediate the processing of the visual information.

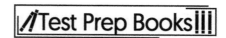

As it currently stands, there are different theories of visual perception that have been proposed in psychology. A few examples of them include the Gestalt theory, Gibson theory, and empirical theory of perception. The **Gestalt theory** is based on perceiving reality in its simplest form by understanding the entire structure of an object rather than just the sum of its parts. The **Gibson theory** posits that the mind perceives environmental stimuli directly and without any additional cognitive processing. The **empirical theory** suggests that an object of perception is determined by individual and evolutionary experience with sense impressions and the objects from which they arise.

Theories of Color Vision

Currently, there are two major theories that outline and guide research on the subject of color vision. One is called the **trichromatic theory** (also called the **Young-Helmholtz theory**), and the other is called the **opponent-process theory**. The two theories are complementary and help explain processes that function at differing levels of the visual processing system. Based on the work of **Thomas Young** and **Herman von Helmholtz**, the **trichromatic theory of color** describes how the visual system can lend itself to the subjective experience of color. There are three receptors in the retina of the eye that process the perception of color; one receptor has a peak sensitivity to the color green, another to blue, and another one to red. According to this theory, the combination of these colors generates all the colors that we can perceive. The **opponent process theory** posits that our ability to perceive color is governed by three receptor complexes, each with opposing actions; one is the red-green complex, another is the blue-yellow complex, and the third one is the black-white complex. According to this theory, these cells are only able to detect one color at a time because each of the two colors oppose one another.

Common Sensory Conditions

Visual and Hearing impairments

Sensory impairment can describe the loss of any of our senses. Out of all our senses, vision and hearing loss tend to be the most common types of sensory impairments. **Vision loss** can describe either partial or complete loss of vision. Some examples of vision impairment include myopia, hyperopia, astigmatism, and presbyopia. **Myopia** (or nearsightedness) describes individuals with difficulty seeing things clearly at a distance. **Hyperopia** (or farsightedness) describes individuals who, as they grow older, have trouble reading things up close. **Astigmatism** involves light being focused unevenly in the eye, which in turn causes images to appear blurry or shadowed. **Presbyopia** describes a condition in older adults where the lens loses its ability to sufficiently focus on near or distant objects.

Hearing loss can describe either partial or complete loss of hearing. Some examples of hearing impairment include conductive hearing loss, sensorineural hearing loss, neural hearing loss, and mixed hearing loss. **Conductive hearing loss** consists of any problem affecting the outer or middle ear that prevents sound from being properly directed to the inner ear. **Sensorineural hearing loss** occurs when there are missing or damaged hair cells in the cochlea of the ear. **Neural hearing loss** occurs when the auditory nerve loses the ability to transmit signals to the brain. **Mixed hearing** loss describes a combined loss of conductive and sensorineural hearing loss. While these types of sensory-related issues are typically common in most people, there is another phenomenon that only some people will ever develop that affects the senses--synesthesia.

Synesthesia

Synesthesia describes a perceptual phenomenon that occurs when the stimulation of one sensory pathway automatically activates a secondary sensory pathway. People with synesthesia are commonly referred to as **synesthetes**. Only a small percentage of the population naturally develops synesthesia, while many others can temporarily experience this phenomenon when using psychedelic drugs. There are various forms of synesthesia and awareness of these types of perceptions varies in each case. Some of the different kinds of synesthesia include:

- **Grapheme-color synesthesia** is one of the most common forms of synesthesia. It involves letters and numbers (together known as **graphemes**) being tinted with a color, though not everyone sees each of these graphemes in the same color scheme.

- **Chromesthesia** is another common form of synesthesia that describes the association of sounds with colors. Sounds heard on a daily basis can trigger the perception of color in synesthetes.

- **Spatial sequence synesthesia** describes the ability to see number sequences as points in space.

- **Number form synesthesia** involves numbers that spontaneously appear whenever a synesthete thinks about numbers.

- **Auditory-tactile synesthesia** describes how synesthetes experience sensations in the body induced by certain sounds, such as feeling touched after hearing a certain word despite not being physically touched.

- **Ordinal linguistic personification describes** how numbers and letters are each associated with genders or personalities.

- **Misophonia** is a neurological disorder where specific sounds trigger negative emotions such as anger, fear, and disgust.

- **Mirror-touch synesthesia** is a rarer form of synesthesia where synesthetes experience the same sensations that others experience. This has been associated with the brain's mirror neurons, which are related to empathy.

- **Lexical-gustatory synesthesia** is another rare form of synesthesia describing how synesthetes experience certain tastes whenever certain words are heard.

While some synesthetes have reported previously concealing their experiences with synesthesia, others have reported not even being aware that their experiences were at all uncommon before realizing other people didn't have them.

Visual Perception

The Role of Top-Down Processing in Producing Vulnerability to Illusion

As mentioned, **top-down processing** is a knowledge-based process in that objects are recognized using one's pre-existing knowledge to help facilitate how visual information is processed. This type of processing basically describes a progression from the whole to its components, or the general to the individual. For example, a person engages in top-down processing when they're able to perceive an entire word before its specific letters.

Visual illusions consist of images perceived in a manner differing from objective reality. There is a contradiction between what the eye sees and how the brain interprets an image. The eye receives visual information, which is then transmitted to the brain's visual cortex for further processing. A major source

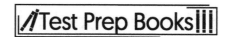

of contention among psychologists involves the extent to which one's perception is contingent on information in their environment. Some psychologists contend that the process of perception depends more on the perceiver's prior knowledge and experiences, as well as the information present in the stimulus.

Copious amounts of information are lost while being transmitted to the brain. As a result, the brain ends up having to venture a guess as to what exactly it's perceiving. After the sense receptors obtain this information, it merges with our past experiences and other previously stored information about the surrounding world, which in turn influences our perception of reality. However, a consequence of this top-down perceptual process is that it makes us more vulnerable to visual illusions. A common example of this type of visual illusion is the **Rubin vase**, which is an image that can be perceived as either two black faces looking at each other in front of a white backdrop or a white vase in front of a black backdrop. The brain then has to interpret these patterns based on previously stored information about faces and vases.

Auditory Sensation and Perception

The Hearing Process

Diagram of the Ear

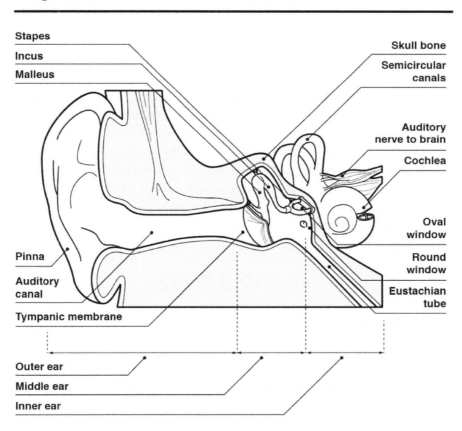

Structure and Function of the Ear

Each part of the ear plays a specific role in hearing. The **external ear** captures sound waves and sends them down the ear canal to the **eardrum**, or **tympanic membrane**. The shape of the external ear is important because it increases the efficiency of sounds within a certain frequency, especially those within the range important for speech perception, and helps with sound localization, so that individuals can identify where a sound is coming from. The **middle ear** consists of a chain of three small bones called **ossicles** that connect the tympanic membrane to the **oval window**, which is the opening of the inner ear. The ossicles are responsible for transferring and concentrating the mechanical stimuli of the tympanic membrane through the fluid of the middle ear to the auditory portion of the inner ear, which is called the **cochlea.** The inner ear has a structure called the **organ of Corti** that then converts the sound energy into neural activity. The organ of Corti has hairs on it that either convey messages to the brain or receive messages back from the brain.

Auditory Processing

Once a sound reaches the organ of Corti, it then travels as an electrical signal through the auditory ganglion cells and afferent nerves to the cochlear nuclei in the brainstem. There is a cochlear nucleus on each side of the brainstem, one for each ear. The signal then reaches *the superior olivary nuclei*, which is the first location to receive signals from both ears. This helps greatly with auditory localization. Signals then travel to the inferior colliculus, the medial geniculate nucleus, and then to the auditory cortex. The neurons on this pathway are arranged in a very organized manner, dependent on the stimuli that they process. For example, cells that respond to high frequency sounds are at a distance from those that respond to low frequency sounds.

Sensory Reception by Hair Cells

Each ear contains about 3500 inner hair cells (IHCs) and 12,000 outer hair cells (OHCs). IHCs cannot regenerate, so damage to them causes a permanent decrease in hearing sensitivity. The IHC and OHC each have about 50 to 200 **stereocilia**, which are even smaller, stiff hairs protruding from them. Approximately 16 to 20 auditory nerve fibers come in contact with each IHC. The organ of Corti has two **afferent** nerve fibers, whose job is to convey messages from the hair cells to the brain, and two **efferent** nerve fibers, whose job is to convey messages from the brain to the hair cells. When fluid moves in the cochlea, the hair cells inside the organ of Corti start to bend in response to the vibrations that the fluid influx produces. The small movements then cause excitation of the hair cells and of the afferent axons. The sound stimulus is translated into electrical signals that are sent to the auditory brainstem and auditory cortex of the brain.

Chemical Senses

Taste and Smell Processes

Taste

Humans can detect four basic tastes with gustatory (taste nerve) cells: sweet, salty, sour, and bitter. The human tongue has small projections, called **papillae**, that contain most of the taste receptor cells, or taste buds. Each papilla has one or more cluster of 50 to 150 taste buds. In addition to the taste buds, the papillae also contain pain receptors, which can sense spice for example, and touch receptors.

Taste buds are specific for one of the four taste sensations and are activated through different mechanisms. Below are descriptions of how each taste is sensed by the brain.

Salty
Salt-sensing taste buds are activated when sodium ions are transported across the membrane of the taste bud through sodium ion channels. The taste buds get partially depolarized, causing a release of neurotransmitters. This stimulates afferent neurons, which relay the stimulation information to the brain.

Sour
Sour tastes are sensed when sour foods or drinks release a hydrogen ion, which blocks the potassium channels of the taste bud membranes. The build-up of potassium in the cell leads to depolarization, neurotransmitter release, and stimulation information gets sent to the brain.

Sweet
The taste buds that sense sweetness have a more complicated stimulation pathway than those of the salty and sour taste buds. When sweet molecules bind to the receptors on their taste buds, a conformational change occurs in the molecule, which then activates a G-protein called **gustducin.** Several other proteins are activated along the pathway, which eventually leads to a blockage of potassium ion channels and an opening of a calcium ion channel. The influx of calcium to the cell causes a greater depolarization of the cell, release of neurotransmitters, and afferent neurons transmit the stimulation information to the brain.

Bitter
The bitter taste sensation has an even more complex pathway than that of sweetness. Bitterness is thought to the be the most sensitive of the tastes and is often perceived as sharp and unpleasant. In a similar pathway to the sweet taste, taste receptors are coupled to the G-protein gustducin. When a bitter substance is sensed, the gustducin breaks apart. Potassium ion channels are closed, calcium ion channels are opened, and the taste cell is depolarized. Neurotransmitters are released, and afferent neurons transmit stimulation information to the brain.

Smell
Olfactory cells/chemoreceptors that detect specific chemicals
The dorsal portion of the nasal cavities is lined with an **olfactory epithelium**. This epithelium contains the receptor neurons that sense smell. If the olfactory epithelium is ever damaged, it has the capability to regenerate itself, including replacement of the receptor neurons. The chemical nature of odors is important for distinguishing between them because odors bind to olfactory receptors that are specific for a certain functional group of the odorant.

Pheromones
In addition to the main olfactory epithelium, the olfactory system has a **vomeronasal organ (VNO)**. Both organs are responsible for detecting pheromones, which are secreted chemicals that trigger a social reaction from members of the same species.

Olfactory Pathways in the Brain
The axons of the olfactory nerves terminate at the anterior end of the brain in a structure called the **olfactory bulb**. The olfactory bulb is organized into **glomeruli,** which are spherically-shaped neural

circuits. The output from the bulb goes to the prepyriform area, the amygdala, and the hypothalamus within the brain for information processing.

Body Senses

Sensory Processes, Relevant Anatomical Structures, and Specialized Pathways in the Brain for the Body Senses

Somatosensation is the reception and interpretation of sensory information that comes from specialized organs in the joints, ligaments, muscles, and skin. The somatosensory system consists of nerve cells, or sensory receptors, that respond to changes in these organs, including pressure, texture, temperature, and pain. Signals are sent along a chain of nerve cells to the spinal cord and then to the brain for information processing. Nociceptors are sensory receptors that detect pain in a range from acute and tolerable to chronic and intolerable. The skin is the largest organ in the somatosensory system. It contains three types of touch receptors: mechanoreceptors, thermoreceptors, and nociceptors. Muscles and joints contain mostly **proprioceptors**, which detect joint position and movement, as well as the direction and velocity of the movement.

Touch
The sensation of **touch** involves a collection of numerous senses that encompass feelings of pain and pleasure, pressures such as itching and tickling, and temperatures such as cold and warmth. In general, when we experience a sensation, sensory signals are transduced (or converted) into a neural impulse to be processed in a specialized region of the brain. The system responsible for sensing touch is referred to as the **somatosensory cortex**, which is distributed throughout all the major parts of the body and includes sense receptors in the periphery—consisting of one's muscles, organs, and skin—as well as neurons located in the central nervous system. Touch receptors become stimulated by chemical, mechanical, and thermal energy.

Neurons are divided into primary, secondary, and tertiary neurons. Receptors located in the dorsal root ganglia transmit the information to secondary neurons that then crossover to specific brain areas. Touch signals travel from the spinal cord to the brain's **thalamus**, which serves as a sort of relay station for our senses, before being transmitted for processing in the brain's parietal cortex, specifically the postcentral gyrus, where there is a neurological map of the anatomical classifications of the body known as the **cortical homunculus**. This neurological map is a distorted representation of the human body based on the proportions of the human brain dedicated to processing sensory or motor functions for different bodily areas.

For instance, nerves transmitted from the hands cover large brain regions, whereas nerves arriving from the arms or torso tend to terminate over much smaller cortical areas, so rather than representing the actual size of a body part, the size of a brain region associated with a bodily area actually indicates the complexity of the activity being performed.

Pain
The experience of **pain** is a signal in our nervous system alerting us to the prospect of something being wrong. It's an unpleasant sensation that can range from aching, tingling, stinging, and burning. Pain can be dull or intense, acute or chronic, and can occur either intermittently or continuously. The term that describes how the brain processes and perceives this pain is referred to as **nociception**. Transduction of this pain sensation occurs when A-delta and C fibers are depolarized by chemical, mechanical, and

thermal energy, which are then converted into an action potential. Then after going through the subsequent process of conduction, the skin's sensory receptors transmit a message through these nerve fibers to the spinal cord and brainstem, and then after the process of modulation, these impulses travel to the brain, which helps process this sensation of pain. The thalamus acts to decode and then relay this information throughout the sensorimotor cortex, insular cortex, and the anterior cingulate, to be perceived as an unpleasant feeling that can be localized to a certain area of the body. The different types of pain we experience each come from one of these nerve fibers.

For instance, pain that is acute and intermittent emanates from the stimulation and transmission of impulses over A-delta nerve fibers, while chronic and continuous pain derives from the stimulation and transmission of C fibers. So, as can likely be gathered, the process through which the brain receives pain information from the body is by no means passive.

Vestibular

Vestibular sense includes the sense of balance and spatial orientation. Combining these two things allows for the coordination of movement and balance. The receptors for the vestibular system are also found within the inner ear. This system allows the brain to understand how the body is moving and accelerating at each moment.

Kinesthesis

Kinesthetic sense is the sensation of movement and orientation. This sense is composed of information that comes from the sensory receptors in the inner ear regarding motion and orientation as well as in the stretch receptors that are in the muscles and ligaments, which provide information about stance. When the brain receives information regarding these movements, it can help to control and coordinate the body's actions, such as simultaneous walking and talking.

Unit 4: Learning

Introduction to Learning

The Contributions of Key Researchers in the Psychology of Learning

Albert Bandura

Albert Bandura (1925–) developed Social Learning Theory (which has now been renamed Social Cognitive Theory). The basic premise of this theory is that personality is largely driven by one's social environment, including parental influence and nurturing, relationships with other caregivers, and factors within one's socioeconomic status (such as environmental safety and stressors). Bandura also developed the idea of self-efficacy, which is an individual's belief in their own ability to achieve their goals. Finally, using the Bobo Doll experiment, he showed observational learning, or modeling, in full effect. Children who observed adults acting violently toward a blow-up doll were more likely to act violently in the same way.

Ivan Pavlov

Ivan Pavlov (1849–1936) was a Russian physiologist who developed the theory of classical conditioning. **Classical conditioning** describes the process of pairing an unconditioned biological stimulus with a conditioned neutral stimulus. An example of this is the well-known case of Pavlov's dog, which consisted of pairing meat (unconditioned stimulus) with the sound of a bell (conditioned stimulus) in order to elicit the response of salivation, indicating that conditioning has occurred.

Robert Rescorla

American psychologist Robert Rescorla (1940–) specializes in studying the role that cognitive processes play in classical conditioning, focusing on behavior and learning in animals. In the past, researchers viewed conditioning as simply an automatic process. However, researchers now believe that some information processing does occur in conditioning. Rescorla demonstrated that the pairing of two different stimuli doesn't always result in the same degree of conditioning. Along with fellow researcher Allan Wagner, Rescorla created the **Rescorla-Wagner model of conditioning**. This model increased our knowledge of the processes associated with learning. According to the model, if the signal of the conditioned stimulus serves as a reliable predictor of the appearance of an unconditioned stimulus, then conditioning tends to be even more effective. This model has paved the way for various theoretical developments and new experimental findings.

Throughout his career, Rescorla has also devised research on both instrumental training and Pavlovian conditioning. Rescorla used numerous methods as a means of conducting tests on associative learning, which includes fear conditioning, reward training, and autoshaping. **Fear conditioning** is a type of learning where aversive stimuli in the form of electrical shocks are associated with an otherwise neutral stimulus until a fear response is eventually produced. An example of fear training would consist of showing a research participant pictures of certain objects while administering an electric shock, which in turn would induce fear by the participant eventually starting to associate the pictures with the shocks. **Reward training** is a method of training used as a means of reinforcing desired behaviors through the introduction of some kind of reward. A parent giving their child an allowance for doing chores serves as an example of reward training. **Autoshaping** uses successive trials to gradually change an existing

response toward a more desired behavior via reinforcement of precise behavioral segments. Getting a rat to press a lever via introduction of a reward serves as an example of shaping.

B. F. Skinner

B.F. Skinner (1904–1990) was an American psychologist who developed the theory of behaviorism and the term **operant conditioning**. The basic concept of operant conditioning is that behavior that is reinforced will increase, and behavior that is punished will decrease.

Edward Thorndike

Edward Thorndike (1874–1979) was American behavioral psychologist who developed the operant conditioning theory that influenced Skinner. Thorndike is famous for experiments with cats learning puzzle boxes. He also had a significant impact on educational psychology and created the **law of effect,** which is the basic premise behind operant conditioning.

Edward Tolman

Edward Tolman (1886–1959) was an American psychologist who founded purposive behaviorism. Tolman is also known for promoting **latent learning**, which is a form of observational learning wherein information is retained on a subconscious level, but behavior is changed later on, only when sufficient motivation is present.

John B. Watson

American psychologist John B. Watson (1878–1958) played a key role in setting the stage for behaviorism, which at one point dominated the field of psychology. **Behaviorism** is the theory that conditioning can explain animal and human behavior, without placing much emphasis on how cognition, feelings, introspection, and other types of internal consciousness might impact them. The goal of behaviorism was to base its theoretical assumptions and experimental findings on purely observable data and understand how behavior was a natural consequence of being conditioned to external stimuli. Watson believed it was a foolish endeavor to interpret the mind's inner workings and thought that a psychologist should concern themselves solely with behaviors that they could observe.

He also applied his behavioral theory to language and memory and believed that language was taught (conditioned) via imitation and learned by manipulating the habit of making sounds with the larynx. He believed emotions such as fear could be learned. His well-known yet controversial "Little Albert" experiment was geared toward understanding how fear could be conditioned. He used loud noises to condition baby Albert to start fearing white rats, or anything even remotely resembling a white rat. However, the reason this experiment is mired in controversy is because baby Albert was withdrawn from the study and was never deconditioned of his fear, which persisted well into his adult years. Nevertheless, the principles of behaviorism have been used by many therapists, including Aaron Beck, who developed **cognitive-behavioral therapy (CBT)**, which is used to help clients better understand how their thoughts and feelings can impact their behavior. CBT is now one of the most widely researched therapeutic modalities used by therapists today.

John Garcia

American psychologist John Garcia (1917–2012) is most known for his research into the phenomenon of taste aversion. **Taste aversion** describes how animals come to relate the taste of certain foods with symptoms such as sickness, nausea, and vomiting, which can be caused by substances that are either spoiled, toxic, or poisonous. Garcia's studies into taste aversion involved irradiated rats. He noticed that, even before being irradiated, rats had already developed an aversion to certain substances. Rats were given sweet water that varied from having no radiation to strong amounts of radiation. He found that those rats exposed to the most radiation consumed a much lesser amount of sweetened water than the other rats. To validate these original findings, Garcia replicated this study various times, and each time demonstrated that the stimulus used does indeed matter. Because of his discovery, this phenomenon has also been dubbed the "Garcia effect." Taste aversion is viewed as an adaptive trait, or a type of survival mechanism, that informs the body to steer clear of potentially harmful substances, which in turn decreases the prospect of consuming the same substance, or something akin to it, yet again in the future. This type of association serves as another example of classical conditioning.

William Perry

William Perry (1913–1998) examined the development of college students during his professorship at the Harvard Graduate School of Education. He developed a scheme that focused on learning and the retention of information, the act and experience of knowing something, and how mental functions, like thinking and reasoning, develop in relation to knowledge. In this scheme, Perry lists four categories of development that college students will progress sequentially through most, and sometimes all, of these categories:

Dualism: Students view knowledge in binary categories—right answers versus wrong answers. They believe teachers hold the "right" answers, and the student's job is to learn and retain these answers.

Multiplicity: Students begin to realize that gray areas can be found in knowledge and that people may have differences of opinion in unproven matters.

Relativism: Students begin to examine opinions systematically, to validate or debunk them in various contexts of knowledge.

Commitment in relativism: Students choose to commit to certain beliefs based on personal opinions, beliefs, interests, needs, and goals. Typically, they realize that they should remain flexible in their commitments, since new information can be presented at any time that could impact their beliefs.

Interpreting Graphs that Exhibit the Results of Learning Experiments

Graphing is an essential element in mathematics and scientific research. In regard to experiments, being able to interpret graphs enables an individual to understand the variables tested and the results gathered, especially as they pertain to the shape of a curve being representative of situations in the real world.

A **slope** describes the rate of the vertical change between two points to the horizontal change between those same two points. The **X-axis** (or run) represents the horizontal change, whereas the **Y-axis** (or rise) represents the vertical change. A **positive slope** moves upward on a graph from left to right, whereas a **negative slope** goes downward on a graph from left to right.

Also called **trendlines**, the **lines of best fit** refer to the general directions that points on a graph are taking. The shape observed on a graph is called a **trend**, and these lines help make the pattern clearer. These graphs would be used to indicate a **correlation**, or relationship, between two variables. A **positive correlation** involves two variables moving in the same direction, whereas a **negative correlation** describes variables moving in opposite directions. For example, research showing that an extended timeframe increases one's rate of learning would indicate a positive correlation, because as the amount

of time allotted increases, so does one's ability to learn. However, it's important to differentiate correlation from causation. Correlation simply indicates that a relationship between two variables exists, whereas **causation** describes how one event occurs as a result of another event, which in turn indicates a causal relationship between the two events. Hence, correlation does not imply causation. In other words, a correlation that has been observed to exist between two variables doesn't necessarily indicate a cause-and-effect relationship between those variables.

An **intercept** describes a point on a graph where a straight line crosses either the X-axis, which is called the **X-intercept**, or the Y-axis, which is called the **Y-intercept**. The latter is also referred to as an initial value. The **initial value** indicates the output value when a linear function's input is zero. In other words, the initial value is Y when X is zero. The intercept has a significant meaning in the particular context of a problem being investigated in research. For instance, in an experiment, the initial value would indicate when someone has either started a task or began keeping track of that task, as well as any related changes.

The Essential Characteristics of Insight Learning, Latent Learning, and Social Learning.

Behavioral psychology is known for its emphasis on different types of learning, which include insight learning, latent learning, and social learning. **Insight learning** involves how someone finds a solution to a problem through a sudden realization and without the need of continuous trials. An individual can draw upon their prior experiences while also using novel and logical ways of perceiving causality. However, insight isn't an unprompted occurrence, but actually requires a pre-solution period involving research into a particular domain, as well as some idle time before an idea or concept is spontaneously formulated. An example of this phenomenon includes a monkey in a cage unsuccessfully reaching for a nearby banana before finally poking it with a stick and devising a method of using the stick to successfully acquire the banana, and then doing the same thing the following day.

Latent learning involves an unconscious learning and retention of certain information without reinforcement or any particular type of motivation. An example of this type of learning includes a child observing proper table manners but not exhibiting any knowledge of them until a situation arises that prompts them to put those manners to use. **Social learning** proposes how new behavior can be attained by simply observing and imitating others performing that behavior, and then become motivated to recreate that learned behavior. According to social learning theory, learning is a cognitive process in social environments, whether through observation or direct instruction, even if there's an absence of any direct reinforcement. Along with observation, learning can take place in the presence of vicarious reinforcement, where reward and punishment are merely observed and thus experienced more indirectly.

One of the most famous experiments demonstrating social learning is psychologist Albert Bandura's Bobo Doll experiment. Children watched adults hit a blow-up doll that looked like a clown, and afterwards, results showed that the children modeled the adults by engaging in that same aggressive behavior with the doll. Social learning starts with paying attention in order to learn, followed by retaining the information that has been observed, reproduction of the learned behavior via its implementation, and being motivated to reproduce the behavior, or in some cases refraining from reproducing it. Principles of social learning have been applied in the fields of criminology and developmental psychology, and have been used to investigate the impact of media violence on aggression and how media can be used to encourage positive social change.

Observational Learning

Observational learning takes place when someone's behaviors are adjusted or changed in response to watching someone else.

Modeling

Modeling happens when behaviors are displayed by one person and imitated by another. This most powerfully shows itself in the case of children, who emulate the behaviors of adults or their peers. Modeling was clearly displayed in Albert Bandura's Bobo Doll Experiment. As just mentioned, children who observed adults acting violently toward a blow-up doll were more likely to act violently in the same way.

Biological Processes that Affect Observational Learning

Mirror neurons are a specific type of neuron in the frontal and parietal lobes of the brain that are involved in imitating the behavior of others and in feeling what others are feeling. First observed in monkeys, mirror neurons fire both when observing someone else perform a behavior and when engaging in that behavior oneself. These neurons help explain observational learning and the capacity for imitation, as well as the phenomenon of empathy.

Vicarious emotions are an aspect of empathy, in which people feel the same emotions another person is experiencing. When one observes someone else in a particular situation, it stimulates the parts of the brain that would activate the emotions that a person would feel if they were in that situation themselves.

Applications of Observational Learning to Explain Individual Behavior

Children, in particular, learn to adopt the behaviors that they observe around them. Thus, the modeling set by parents and others will impact how they speak and act toward others, their work ethic, their levels of aggression, and countless other areas. Observational learning also impacts the individual behaviors of adults. For example, the kinds of television programs and movies that people watch will influence their behaviors.

Applying Learning Principles to Explain Emotional Learning, Taste Aversion, Superstitious Behavior, and Learned Helplessness

As it pertains to behaviorism, some of the principles of learning outlined so far have included how association is the key to learning; and behavior is mostly a product of environment, is strengthened or weakened by outcomes, responds better to reward than punishment, and that the course a behavior takes in the future is contingent on whether it has been reinforced or punished. These principles can be applied to concepts such as emotional learning, taste aversion, superstitious behavior, and learned helplessness.

Emotional learning consists of using recognizable skills to manage our emotions and identifying emotions in others, which is important for developing the processes of self-awareness, self-control, and interpersonal skills. Educators can help their students practice assuming the perspectives of others, such as encouraging them to consider how a literary character felt. Focusing on reinforcing the positive behavior of this perspective-taking that occurs with emotional learning can increase the prospect of this behavior happening again.

Taste aversion describes how animals come to relate the taste of certain foods with symptoms of illness induced by substances that are potentially dangerous to ingest. Association serves as the means through

which we learn information, such as when an unconditioned stimulus is repeatedly paired with a conditioned stimulus to the point where the conditioned stimulus gradually generates the same response as the unconditioned stimulus. In this instance, the animals repeatedly exposed to dangerous substances learned to avoid them by associating them with the symptoms they induced.

Superstitious behavior consists of the presence of a reinforcer or punisher arising in close proximity with an independent behavior, along with a misunderstanding of science and causality and a positive belief in the irrational, which in turn can affect the likelihood of that behavior occurring again. Walking under a ladder bringing us bad luck is an example of this concept. **Learned helplessness** occurs when someone suffers from feelings of powerlessness after experiencing a traumatic event, which can consist of exposure to repeated aversive stimuli outside of their control. This concept demonstrates that previous learning can lead to an extreme behavioral alteration and help explain why some individuals may just accept a negative situation and remain passive in them, even if they do in fact have the ability to change them. For example, a child who performs poorly on science exams and other assignments will quickly start feeling that nothing they do will have any effect on their performance in that subject.

Habituation and Dishabituation

When a person or animal shows a decreased response to a stimulus over time, it is considered habituation. Something that may at first provoke a response will, after time and repeated exposure to the stimulus, cease to yield the same response. A person who moves to a new city with lots of traffic may at first have trouble sleeping but will after time adjust to the new stimulus and resume old patterns of sleep. **Dishabituation** occurs when there is again an increase in responsiveness to the same stimulus as prior to the habituation. This happens when a similar and stronger stimulus is presented and then the old stimulus is presented again. A person who has adjusted to the noise of traffic in a new house may experience dishabituation if one night many emergency vehicles with sirens drive by. The sound of normal traffic again may then disrupt sleep patterns.

Examples of How Biological Constraints Create Learning Predispositions

Researchers Ivan Pavlov and John Watson posited that learning was similar for all types of animals. However, behaviorists later indicated that an animal's biology can constrain their learning abilities. **Biological constraints** describe how the ability to learn new tasks is limited by an organism's cognitive, physical, response, or sensory capabilities. In classical conditioning, a response to a stimulus is automatic and involuntary. Humans and nonhumans alike are able to learn how to associate a pair of situations and react to the first while anticipating the second. In operant conditioning, an organism voluntarily acts on their environment before a consequence occurs. Animals can learn a certain stimulus's predictability, indicating an expectancy of the stimulus, which in turn demonstrates that cognitive processes are taking place. Biological constraints make an organism more inclined to learn associations that are naturally adaptive.

Organisms tend to drift toward their instinctive, biologically predisposed behaviors, particularly if they previously behaved in any way that would otherwise be unnatural for them. An organism's natural predispositions restrain the stimuli and responses that the animal is able to associate. Some examples of these constraints include chimps or gorillas learning how to use sign language to communicate, but being somehow biologically constrained from learning how to speak or read written language. In John Garcia's experiment on taste aversions, animals can learn to avoid a substance that will cause them to become sick, but not when other stimuli, such as light or noise, are used to indicate it. Raccoons can be trained to put a coin in a box by using food as a positive reinforcer; however, due to their biological

constraints, they can't be trained to put more than one coin in a box. And humans are likelier to fear predators than plants because predators pose more of a threat to them.

Classical Conditioning

Basic Classical Conditioning Phenomena

An important concept of development has to do with learning and the way in which humans learn new behaviors. A famous psychologist, Ivan Pavlov, conducted research with dogs that proved to be ground-breaking in the field of classical conditioning. In his experiment, a ringing bell was paired with the presentation of food, which produced salivation in the dog. The ringing sound eventually produced salivation from the dog even in the absence of food. Salivation then became the conditioned response to hearing a bell, and thus, the theory of classical conditioning was developed. The important finding of this research is that humans learn by association.

Acquisition

Acquisition is the initial learning phase after a response has already been established and eventually strengthened. During this stage of classical conditioning, an unconditioned stimulus is repeatedly paired with a neutral stimulus. An **unconditioned stimulus** describes anything that automatically and naturally elicits a response without the need for learning. Anything elicited naturally is called an **unconditioned response**. Once a subject makes an association, they generate a behavior in response to the previously neutral stimulus, which in turn becomes a **conditioned stimulus**. At this point, a response has been acquired. This learned response is called a **conditioned response**. For example, let's return to Pavlov's dog. A dog is being conditioned to salivate in response to the sound of a ringing bell, which initially serves as a neutral stimulus before becoming a conditioned stimulus. Then the sound of the bell is repeatedly paired with the presentation of food, which serves as the unconditioned stimulus.

When the dog salivates to the sound of the bell, as it would to food, acquisition has taken place, because the dog now associates the ringing bell with food. Once this conditioned response is established, the salivation response is gradually reinforced to ensure the behavior remains solidified. Salience plays an important role in this process. If a conditioned stimulus is too subtle, an association may not occur. For instance, the sound of a bell should be loud and unexpected, which will increase the likelihood that the dog will hear it and an association will be made. Timing is also a factor. If there is too much of a delay between when an unconditioned stimulus and a conditioned stimulus are presented, an association takes longer to form.

Extinction

In classical conditioning, **extinction** describes when an unconditioned stimulus and a conditioned stimulus are no longer paired together, which results in a decrease or disappearance of a conditioned response. For example, in the Pavlov experiment, if the scent of food (unconditioned stimulus) was paired with a loud whistle (the conditioned stimulus) instead of a ringing bell, it would gradually start eliciting the conditioned response of hunger. However, if that same unconditioned stimulus was no longer paired with that conditioned stimulus, then that conditioned response would eventually cease. Conditioned taste aversions serve as another example of a phenomenon that can be affected by extinction.

Imagine eating a piece of candy and then getting sick and vomiting. As a result, you form a taste aversion to this particular candy and avoid eating it again, even though it had once been one of your

favorite snacks. But there is a way of overcoming this avoidance. Little by little, if you expose yourself to this particular piece of candy, regardless of its tendency to make you feel unsettled, as you continue eating it without experiencing regurgitation once again, your conditioned aversion will eventually decrease. However, also bear in mind that extinction isn't always necessarily permanent.

Spontaneous Recovery

Spontaneous recovery describes how a conditioned response can potentially reemerge after a rest period, or at least a reduced response, associated with extinction. However, extinction could reappear soon after spontaneous recovery if the unconditioned stimulus and the conditioned stimulus are no longer associated. This phenomenon is applicable to those responses that have been shaped through both classical conditioning and operant conditioning.

For example, if you trained a dog to salivate to the sound of a bell (conditioned stimulus), and then ceased to reinforce the behavior, the response would gradually become extinct. Then after a rest period, where you don't present this conditioned stimulus at all, you suddenly start ringing the bell again and find that the dog spontaneously recovered the previously learned response. In Pavlov's experiment, he associated a tone with food in order to encourage a salivatory response to the tone, indicating the dog had successfully associated the tone with food. He later noticed that when the tone was no longer paired with the presentation of food, extinction occurred. Then, after a two-hour rest period, he reintroduced the same tone, and the dog's salivation response returned, which demonstrated that the previously extinct response had been spontaneously recovered in the dog.

Generalization

Stimulus generalization describes how a conditioned stimulus can elicit similar responses once the response has already been conditioned. An example of this in Pavlov's experiment is having something similar to the sound of a bell being able to evoke the same salivatory response in dogs, even if it hasn't been previously paired with food. In Watson's controversial "Little Albert" experiment, a baby was conditioned to fear a white rat by pairing it with loud noises. Along with fearing the rat in question, the baby exhibited generalization by becoming fearful of any other objects that even remotely resembled the original stimulus (white rat). In other words, the group of stimuli doesn't need to be identical to the original stimulus but can in fact be similar to it.

It's important to understand how stimulus generalization can affect an individual's responses to a conditioned stimulus. Once this generalization occurs, it can end up proving particularly problematic, especially in such instances when it's imperative that this person can distinguish between different stimuli and in turn only respond to a specific type of stimulus. Imagine you are training your dog to obey a specific command using conditioning. You are using a treat to generate an association between hearing the command and receiving a treat, and you find that it works. However, this could cause your dog to respond upon hearing similar commands, which can make this training process even more arduous, so it's important you also train your dog to discern different types of commands.

Stimulus Discrimination

Stimulus discrimination refers to being able to differentiate between a conditioned stimulus and other stimuli that have not been paired with an unconditioned stimulus. In other words, responding to certain stimuli and not to others, indicating that discrimination has occurred. An example of discrimination would be training a dog to obey a command and doing this often enough where the dog can eventually distinguish between this command and other commands. Another example would be if, in an experiment, a ringing bell served as the conditioned stimulus, discrimination would consist of the ability to discern the difference between the sound of the ringing bell and other similar sounds, and because the subject could differentiate these stimuli, they would only respond upon being presented with that conditioned stimulus. Let's refer back to Pavlov's dog once more. If Pavlov were to use a bullhorn as a substitute for his ringing bell, and the dog didn't produce a salivatory response, then it would mean that the dog had learned to distinguish between the sound of the bell and the bullhorn, hence indicating that the conditioned response would not be produced by just any noise. As a result, stimulus discrimination would allow the dog to generate a conditioned response only upon hearing a very particular sound instead of just any sound at all.

Higher-Order Learning

Also referred to as **second-order conditioning**, **higher-order learning** describes how a previously neutral stimulus is paired with a conditioned stimulus to generate the same conditioned response as the already conditioned stimulus. When a neutral stimulus is paired with an unconditioned stimulus, and eventually elicits the same response as the unconditioned stimulus, the neutral stimulus then becomes a conditioned stimulus. This concept of higher-order learning is essentially just extending this type of conditioning to another level. While first-order conditioning involves the conditioned stimulus simply being paired with an unconditioned stimulus in order to generate a response, this second-order conditioning entails pairing a conditioned stimulus with another stimulus that has been conditioned to produce a response.

For example, in first-order conditioning, a dog learns to associate the sound of a bell (conditioned stimulus) with the presence of food (unconditioned stimulus), but in second-order conditioning, this dog will then learn how to associate the sound of the bell with the presence of light, which serves as another conditioned stimulus. Thus, if you were to then undertake third-order conditioning, it can follow with a further stimulus being added to elicit a response. This concept of higher-order learning can also be applied to fear conditioning.

Unconditioned Stimulus

An **unconditioned stimulus** involves anything that automatically and naturally evokes a response without the need for learning. In Pavlov's experiment with dogs, the presence of food served as the unconditioned stimulus, because the dog will instinctively respond to the smell and sight of food without any need for conditioning to take place. However, this concept isn't applicable only to dogs. If a human smells one of their favorite foods being cooked for dinner, they will automatically begin craving the meal and feeling very hungry in the process. Because the food on its own naturally elicits this hungry response, it would serve as the unconditioned stimulus.

Other examples of an unconditioned stimulus can involve a loud noise causing an organism to flinch, an onion making your eyes tear, and pepper making you sneeze. As it relates to each of these examples, the unconditioned stimulus automatically triggers a reflexive response. No learning needs to occur with an unconditioned stimulus because it just occurs naturally on its own. No additional stimulus needs to be presented with this stimulus in order for a response to be elicited. However, if you want conditioning to take place, then an unconditioned stimulus would need to be paired with an otherwise neutral stimulus.

Unconditioned Response

An **unconditioned response** generally refers to something that is naturally elicited from an unconditioned stimulus. In Pavlov's experiments with dogs, salivation in response to the presence of food would serve as the unconditioned stimulus, as this response will be instinctive and not require any

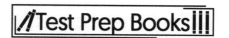

conditioning at all. However, this phenomenon doesn't apply to dogs only. If a human smells one of their favorite snacks being baked for dessert, they will instinctively begin craving the snack and feeling very hungry as a result. Because the craved hungry response is automatically evoked by the snack in question, it would serve as the unconditioned response.

There are various other examples that can demonstrate an unconditioned response. Some of these other examples include the reflexive response of twitching your leg when you receive a tap on your kneecap, jerking your hand back when touching something hot out of the oven, pulling your foot away after stepping on a giant anthill, and moving away from a beehive. As it pertains to these examples, the response occurs naturally and instinctively, hence we see how an unconditioned response is innate and something that doesn't require any prior learning. This is one of the ways an unconditioned response is differentiated from a conditioned response.

Neutral/Conditioned Stimulus

Once an association is made with a stimulus, it generates a behavior from the subject in response to the previously neutral stimulus. This is what's known as a **conditioned stimulus**. Before this stimulus is paired with an unconditioned stimulus, it's referred to as a **neutral stimulus**, because on its own it's just that: neutral. However, upon being paired with an unconditioned stimulus, the neutral stimulus becomes a conditioned stimulus once it generates the same type of response that the unconditioned stimulus would evoke on its own.

In Pavlov's experiment with dogs, the neutral stimulus is the sound of a bell, which on its own wouldn't elicit any type of salivatory response, but once the bell is paired with the presence of food (unconditioned stimulus) and eventually elicits the same salivatory response, it becomes a conditioned stimulus. Once this conditioned stimulus is successfully paired and later associated with the unconditioned stimulus, we would know that an association has been formed between these two stimuli. The goal of classical conditioning is to repeatedly pair two stimuli together in order to elicit a new learned response in either a human or nonhuman subject. This is how a conditioned stimulus is differentiated from an unconditioned stimulus.

Conditioned Response

A **conditioned response** describes a response that has been learned, which is one of the ways it is differentiated from an unconditioned response. Whereas an unconditioned response is elicited naturally and without any prompting or prior learning whatsoever, a conditioned response is something that occurs as a result of a conditioned stimulus being paired with an unconditioned stimulus, hence necessitating the need for prior learning in order for an association to be made.

In Pavlov's experiment with dogs, the conditioned response is the salivation that occurs in response to the sound of the bell, which acts as the neutral/conditioned stimulus, after it is paired with the presence of food, which acts as the unconditioned stimulus. For instance, a dog that salivates to the smell and sight of food would be an unconditioned response to an unconditioned stimulus, because the response was automatically elicited from a natural stimulus and didn't require learning. However, if the dog salivates to the sound of the bell, it would indicate a conditioned response to a conditioned stimulus because prior learning needed to occur before this response could be generated from an otherwise neutral stimulus. For a conditioned response to occur, a conditioned stimulus and an unconditioned stimulus must first be paired together.

Differences Between Principles of Classical Conditioning, Operant Conditioning, and Observational Learning

Classical conditioning involves repeatedly pairing an unconditioned stimulus with a conditioned stimulus to the point where the conditioned (learned) stimulus eventually produces the same type of response as the unconditioned (natural) stimulus. Recall that in Pavlov's dog experiment, he paired an unconditioned stimulus (the presence of food) with a neutral stimulus (the sound of a bell) in order to elicit a salivatory response from dogs. In the presence of food, a salivatory response would serve as an unconditioned response, whereas a salivatory response that is generated when a bell is rung would be a conditioned response. The goal was to elicit the same salivatory response from the sound of the bell as would be generated from the smell and sight of food by presenting both these stimuli together, which in turn would indicate that an association has been successfully made between the two. A conditioned response can only occur when an unconditioned stimulus and a conditioned stimulus are paired.

Operant conditioning entails a subject's behavior being modified by either positive or negative reinforcement or punishment. Through operant conditioning, the subject forms an association between a certain behavior and a particular consequence.

- **Positive reinforcement** involves adding a reward in order to increase the occurrence of a desired behavior. An example of this would involve a parent giving their child an allowance for doing chores around the house so they're more likely to keep doing them.

- **Negative reinforcement** entails taking something unpleasant away in order to reinforce a desired behavior. For instance, most cars today will produce an obnoxious beeping noise until you put on your seatbelt. The removal of this unpleasant noise would act as a form of negative reinforcement, as it is encouraging you to wear your seatbelt.

- **Positive punishment** involves the introduction of an unpleasant stimulus in order to reduce an unwanted behavior. An example of this would involve a student receiving a ticket for parking in the faculty lot. The ticket would serve as the positive punishment discouraging the student from making the same mistake again.

- **Negative punishment** entails taking away something considered pleasant in order to decrease an unwanted behavior. An example of this would consist of a parent taking away a child's television privileges for misbehaving. The removal of television serves as the negative punishment because the goal of it is to discourage the child from misbehaving again.

Observational learning describes learning that occurs by watching how others behave. For example, a young child is less likely to take a cookie from the jar without permission after observing their older sibling being reprimanded for engaging in that same behavior.

Operant Conditioning

Predicting the Effects of Operant Conditioning

Skinner also did important research in the field of learning, specifically **operant conditioning**. Operant conditioning theory focuses on behavioral changes that can be seen or measured. The basic concept is

that behavior that is reinforced will increase, and behavior that is punished will decrease. There are several key concepts integral to an understanding of this form of learning:

Positive Reinforcement: Anything that serves as a form of reward, including food, money, praise, or attention

Negative reinforcement: An unpleasant stimulus that is removed when behavior is elicited, such as a man finally cutting the grass to stop his wife from nagging him about it

Punishment: An unpleasant response from the environment—e.g., a slap, an unkind word, or a speeding ticket—that, when encountered, increases the likelihood that a behavior will cease. Two problems arise with using punishment. Once the negative stimulus is removed, the behavior is likely to continue. Punishment can also cause humiliation, anger, resentment, and aggression.

Superstition: An incorrect perception that one stimulus is connected to another. Skinner found that when teaching a rat to press a lever for food, if the rat chases its tail before pressing the lever, it will mistakenly believe that the tail chase is required and will do both behaviors each time it wants food.

Shaping: The process of changing behavior gradually by rewarding approximations of the desired behavior (for example, first rewarding a rat for moving closer to the lever).

Predicting How Different Factors Will Influence the Quality of Learning

Skinner found that there are different schedules of reinforcement and that some work better than others. These include the following:

Continuous rate: Person or animal is rewarded every time a behavior is demonstrated

Fixed ratio: Reward is given after a fixed number of attempts

Variable ratio: Reward is forthcoming at unpredictable rates, like a slot machine

Fixed interval: Reward is given only after a specific length of time has passed

Variable interval: Reward is given after an unpredictable amount of time has passed

Extinction: Occurs when a behavior disappears or is extinguished because it is no longer being reinforced. To stop tantrum behavior in toddlers, ignoring the behavior will decrease or stop the tantrum, if the desired reward is parental attention or parental aggravation.

Social and Cognitive Factors in Learning

How Behavior Modification, Biofeedback, Coping Strategies, and Self-Control Can Be Used To Address Behavioral Problems

Behavior modification can involve positive reinforcement, negative reinforcement, positive punishment, and negative punishment. Each approach is used as a means of modifying some aspect of one's behavior. To review again, positive reinforcement adds a reward to help reinforce a desired behavior, negative reinforcement removes something unpleasant to reinforce a desired behavior,

79

positive punishment involves adding something unpleasant to decrease an unwanted behavior, and negative punishment entails removing a pleasant stimulus in order to decrease an unwanted behavior. The outcome is contingent upon the type of behavior modification technique being employed.

Biofeedback is a method using auditory or visual feedback to improve one's performance and overall well-being. For instance, biofeedback can be used to help people control involuntary bodily functions such as blood pressure, heart rate, migraines, muscle tension, and pain perception. Because these symptoms can often serve as somatic responses to certain stressors, biofeedback can be used to address these behavioral responses to stress by alleviating the full extent of the symptoms. However, biofeedback tends to have more lasting effects when used in conjunction with psychotherapy.

Coping strategies describe certain approaches in behavior, thoughts, and feelings that can prove efficient in helping people adjust to changes in their lives. Some people have a lower stress tolerance than others, and as a result, these people are more likely to demonstrate behavioral problems in response to those stressors. Learning different methods of coping, and then applying them correctly, can effectively address behavioral problems. Some examples of these coping strategies include taking a deep breath, focusing on something positive, journaling, talking to someone, and practicing meditation.

Self-control consists of a set of skills people can use to maintain their motivation and attain personal goals. Some examples of self-control skills include designating a certain time each day to engage in a desired behavior, using visual reminders about one's daily goals, and thinking about the benefits of achieving a goal. In the case of behavioral problems, self-control techniques help enable individuals to become more aware of their own behavioral patterns so that they can develop the means of changing them for the better.

Contingencies

A **contingency** describes a relationship between two events, essentially where one event would be contingent upon—or a consequence of—another event. In behaviorism, all behaviors are a response to precursors and have consequences, and the goal is to make this relationship clear to the subject whose behavior is being addressed. **Applied Behavioral Analysis (ABA)** is a therapeutic modality aimed at changing behavior in some way, whether it involves increasing a desired behavior, replacing difficult behaviors, or decreasing, if not extinguishing, unwanted behaviors, particularly if those unwanted behaviors are dangerous.

Reinforcement must be expeditious, clear, and consistent. When any of these factors are lacking, a contingency is less likely to be successfully established with the subject of focus. Positive reinforcement, negative reinforcement, positive punishment, and negative punishment are all examples of contingencies. Each of them involves a specific approach with an equally specific goal of changing one's behavioral patterns. For instance, if the goal of an educator is to increase a desired behavior in a student, then the student needs to learn that receiving a certain type of reinforcement is contingent on how they behave. Contingencies basically help pave the way for successful behavior modification in the subject of focus.

Unit 5: Cognitive Psychology

Introduction to Memory

Comparing and Contrasting Various Cognitive Processes

There are three interconnected components of attitudes in the ABC Model: affective, behavioral, and cognitive. **Cognition** is the process of acquiring knowledge and then using thought, experience, and the senses to further understand it. Cognition is both conscious and unconscious and involves reasoning, problem solving, and decision-making skills. Cognition itself refers to a person's thought patterns, beliefs, and ideas. The affective component has to do with feelings or emotions. The behavioral element relates to a person's actions, which are usually the direct result of one's attitude. The three components of attitude are interconnected and influence each other.

Effortful Versus Automatic Processing
Effortful processing occurs when a person learns new information by paying attention and practicing. Rehearsing a play to learn the lines would be an example of effortful processing. **Automatic processing** is a way a person takes in information without consciously devoting attention to the process. Examples of automatic processing are walking and speaking.

Deep Versus Shallow Processing
The processing of memories falls on a continuum from shallow to deep. Shallow processing is simply rehearsing the information over and over with no care for the meaning (ex. memorizing a poem to recite for a grade) based on the orthographic or phonetic components. Deep processing is more involved and links information to things like pictures or information that someone already knows. It involves **semantic processing**, which is when the meaning of a new word is encoded and related to other known synonyms, and elaboration rehearsal. Deep processing leads to better information retention whereas shallow processing leads to fragile memories.

Selective Versus Divided Attention
Focused attention is also referred to as **selective attention**. As the name implies, focused attention occurs when someone focuses on a specific set of information or aspects of their surroundings and ignores the rest. **Divided attention**, however, is when one attempt to put their focus on several different areas at once, which is also considered multitasking.

Metacognition
Metacognition involves an individual thinking about their own thinking, or the way they process, learn, and assimilate new ideas.

Describing and Differentiating Psychological and Physiological Systems of Memory

Memory is the process by which information is encoded, stored, and retrieved by the brain.

Short-Term Memory
After information goes into the sensory memory, some of it will then go on to live in short-term memory. This memory system holds information for a very short amount of time (thought to be

seconds). This information is relatively difficult to manipulate and is generally task-related. Information stored here is readily available until it is either lost or transferred to long-term memory. An example of something involving short-term memory would be someone calling out a phone number to someone else who then begins dialing it.

> Working Memory: This is a part of the short-term memory where the information can be manipulated slightly. A person is using their working memory when they a small amount of information that they are using to make a decision, such as when reading a menu and deciding what to order.

> Implicit Memory

This type of memory is a part of long-term memory. Procedural memory is where one stores information about how to do things like walking and riding a bike.

Long-Term Memory
Information from short-term memory can be encoded and consolidated and then sent long-term memory, particularly if the information has remained in the short-term memory for a longer stretch of time. Information in long-term memory storage may last from a few hours to the length of the individual's life. Theoretically, there is no limit to the capacity of long-term memory storage.

Sensory Memory
This system is where the information related to senses is stored. Information stored here is very detailed but not held for very long; it's thought to be held for milliseconds to a couple seconds. Sensory memory is not under conscious control; rather, it is an automatic response. Manipulation of sensory memories does not occur, and some of the information gets transferred quickly to working memory, but much is lost because the capacity of the working memory is unable to handle the sheer volume of the sensory-related details involved in incoming sensory memory data. Types of sensory memories include:

> Iconic Memory: The storage of visual sensory input, such as data the mind gleans when one looks around a restaurant and takes in the surroundings, and then the visual memory of the flicking candles in momentarily "burned" into the person's brain.

> Echoic Memory: The storage of auditory information, which can be quite detailed, but only lasts in the brain for 3-4 seconds.

> Haptic Memory: The sensory memories of touch, involving sensors over the body that detect pain, itching, pressure, vibration, etc. For example, this type of memory is useful for automatically determining the best way to grip something when reaching for it.

Prospective Memory
Prospective memory describes a type of memory where someone recalls a planned intention or remembers to perform a specific plan of action at some point in the future. The need for prospective memory can range from moderately simplistic tasks, such as picking up paper towels at the grocery store or responding to a text message, to more complex tasks, such as performing specific safety procedures before flying a plane. Another way to describe prospective memory is "remembering to remember." Prospective memory is different from **retrospective memory**, which involves the recall of something from the past, such as a specific event at a certain point in one's life. Prospective memory can be related to an event or time and is usually triggered by a specific cue, such as remembering to

mail a letter to a relative after looking at a neighbor's mailbox or setting up a reminder of an important business meeting with a potential client.

Explicit Memory

Explicit memory, also referred to as **declarative memory**, describes another type of long-term memory process that can be consciously and intentionally recalled to attention, such as remembering what time your favorite restaurant closes. This is differentiated from procedural memory, which is a more unconscious form of memory. Explicit memory is divided into semantic memory and episodic memory, which involve the retention of facts, and previous experiences, respectively. **Semantic memory** involves processing concepts and ideas that aren't related to personal experiences. Some examples of semantic memory include remembering a state capital, the arrangement of letters in the alphabet, and the colors of the light spectrum. **Episodic memory** consists of the recollection of personal, autobiographical events that occurred at a certain time and place. Some examples of episodic memory include remembering the meal that you ate for dinner last night, your first day at a new job, or a friend's wedding ceremony.

Physiological Systems

Neural Plasticity

Neural plasticity is the ability of the brain to change throughout a person's lifetime. The neural synapses in the brain that are important for learning and memories are constantly changing size and shape and making new connections to accommodate the new information.

The Contributions of Key Researchers in Cognitive Psychology

Noam Chomsky

Noam Chomsky (1928–) felt that language had a very important role in cognitive psychology. Chomsky felt that people are born with a pre-determined tool for language that exists in their brains. The world around them ignites that tool. The concept of this natural tool for language being brought to life by one's environment is known as **universal grammar**. Chomsky's views about language and language development were different than others in the field in that he felt that people were pre-disposed to language. He pointed to the fact that young children learn language at a rapid rate and often use words that they've never encountered.

Hermann Ebbinghaus

Hermann Ebbinghaus (1850–1909) wanted to study memory and how it works, but to do so, he needed to be able to have subjects memorize something that would not relate to anything they might have prior knowledge of. To conduct his research, he came up with "nonsense syllables" and used these in experiments regarding memory. Ebbinghaus made several key contributions. The first is the idea of the forgetting curve. The **forgetting curve** defines how we lose information after we've learned it and how quickly. The second is the learning curve, which defines how quickly one learns information. Lastly, the spacing effect showed that when someone spaces learning out over time, the effect is greater than when learning occurs in a single instance.

Wolfgang Köhler

Wolfgang Köhler (1887–1967) discovered insight learning through his research with primates. **Insight learning** is the sudden learning of information. With insight learning, the person responds to the entire situation. At first there are trial and error scenarios and then the solution comes about all at once. It is also referred to as the "a-ha moment."

Elizabeth Loftus

Elizabeth Loftus (1944–) made several key findings in the area of cognitive psychology. One such finding was the **misinformation effect**. The basic premise of the misinformation effect is that post-memory events can change a person's memory of an event. This was important because it led to discovering the issue of suggestibility with memories. Her research also focused on eyewitness memory, which experts have found to be non-reliable especially when related to criminal proceedings. The reason why eyewitness memory can be flawed is because of confounding, simultaneous events or situations when these memories are being encoded, such as high emotional arousal, etc. Loftus has also been a key researcher in **false memories**, which are common especially in sexual abuse scenarios. False memories occur when someone remembers something that has not happened or remembers something differently than it occurred.

George A. Miller

George A. Miller (1920–2012) was one of the founders of cognitive psychology. He specifically studied how linguistics and psychology are married. He did extensive research on memory including working memory, which is an active state of short-term memory. He helped to develop WordNet, which was a database that linked words together and was used by computer programs.

Encoding

The Principles that Underlie Constructing and Encoding Memories

Process of Encoding Information

Encoding begins with perception of stimuli through the senses. From these sensations, a short-term memory is created. The information is sent to the sensory area of the cortex and then to the hippocampus in the brain. The hippocampus analyzes the information and decides whether to store it in the long-term memory.

Processes that Aid in Encoding Memories

New memories can be encoded easier if they can be associated with memories that are already stored in the brain. **Elaboration** is a strategy of organization that allows new information to associate with long-term memories. The use of mnemonics, rhymes, acronyms, and acrostics are all examples of mnemonics that make remembering information easier. The association of images with words also aids in memory encoding.

Storing

The Principles that Underlie Effective Storage of Memories

When new memories are made or new behavior is learned, the brain stores the information by changing the strength of some of its synapses. The memories are encoded within these synapses. Different types of memories are stored in different types of neurons.

Types of Memory Storage

As previously mentioned, the **sensory memory** is responsible for holding sensory information about objects that a person encounters. It can recall that information very quickly, even after observing the object for a very short length of time. The sensory memory is an automatic response and is out of conscious control. The **working**, or **short-term**, **memory** has a limited amount of storage. It is

responsible for holding, processing, and manipulating information when it first reaches the brain for just a few minutes at longest. This memory aids in reasoning and decision-making tasks. The **long-term memory** holds information indefinitely and has a very large capacity. It is generally outside of a person's awareness, but the memories stored here can be recalled to the working memory when needed.

Long-Term Potentiation
Long-term potentiation is an enhancement in the signal transmission between two neurons that results from the repeated pairing and stimulation of the neurons. The strength of the action potential is boosted, there is an increase in the number of receptors on the dendrite, and sometimes the amount of neurotransmitter available is increased as well.

Retrieving

Strategies for Retrieving Memories

Semantic networks are formed when a piece of knowledge is better understood by linking together several different concepts. **Spreading activation** is a method for searching a semantic network to retrieve a specific piece of information.

Recall, Recognition, and Relearning
There are two main methods of accessing memories: recall and recognition. **Recall** is the retrieval of information that had been previously encoded and stored in the brain. **Recognition** is mostly an unconscious process in which an event or object is associated with a previously stored memory. Relearning involves learning information again that has been previously learned. This process can make retrieving information in the future easier and can improve the strength of memories.

Retrieval Cues
Retrieval cues are stimuli that aid in memory retrieval from the long-term memory. They can be external, like the smell of a candle that reminds you of a childhood memory, or internal, like a feeling of sadness that reminds you of a death in the family.

The Role of Emotion in Retrieving Memories
Memories that are emotionally charged are usually easier to recall. Memories associated with strong emotions, pleasant or unpleasant, are remembered better than less emotional events that occurred at the same time. Positive memories often contain more details, which aids in retrieval.

Processes that Aid Retrieval
Exercising can help increase a person's heart rate and get the blood flowing to the brain, which in turn enlarges the hippocampus, a vital part of the brain for memory.

Forgetting and Memory Distortion

Strategies for Memory Improvement and Typical Memory Errors

Studies have shown that doing certain things can improve memory. The following are some examples of activities or strategies that can improve memory:

Exercise: Even as little as 10-15 minutes of physical activity a day can improve memory, and some research has shown that information gleaned while exercising may be remembered more easily.

Repetition: Studies have found that repeating information out loud will increase retention of the information. Repeating the information to someone else (or verbally aloud instead of silently in one's head) is an even better way to increase the memory.

Sleep: Getting enough sleep is invaluable in optimizing one's memory and helping one remember new information. Getting at least seven hours of sleep a night is recommended to avoid compromising recall and memory retention.

Focusing Attention: When learning new information, if attention is solely focused on the information trying to be retained, retrieval later on will be augmented.

Spacing Out Bouts of Studying: When learning information for a test or other such need, studying over a period of time instead of waiting until the night before will help give the brain time to process the information and store it more permanently so that it can be recalled when needed.

Organizing Information: Studies have shown that when someone groups like information together, it's easier to recall at a later date.

Mnemonic Devices: Remember ROYGBIV from grade school? This classic way of remembering the colors of the rainbow uses a mnemonic device. There are different types of mnemonic devices, including abbreviations and rhymes.

Visual Cues: Using visual cues (photographs, charts, graphs, etc.) can help encode information to assist with memory.

Linking New Information: When learning new information, if one can establish a connection between the new information and things they already know, then they can greatly increase the chance of remembering it later.

Reading Aloud: Similarly to repeating information previously learned, when studying new information, reading it aloud has been proven to increase the learning capacity for the information being retained.

Variety: Varying the things one does to learn information will help one stay fresh and keep their memory constantly improving. For example, if someone is trying to learn all the muscles in the body, if they read about them, use flashcards, watch a movie, take part in a dissection, make a model, etc., they can increase their ability to learn and remember the information.

Foods & Supplements: The following supplements are thought to aid in memory retention and retrieval: folic acid, vitamin B6, and vitamin B12, vitamin C, vitamin E, and coenzyme Q10. The following foods are thought to aid in memory: fatty fish, coffee, blueberries, turmeric, broccoli, pumpkin seeds, dark chocolate, nuts, oranges, eggs, and green tea.

Aging and Memory

Normal aging causes a decline in memory abilities and cognitive tasks. The brain is slower to encode new memories as well as to recall previously-stored memories.

Memory Dysfunctions

Memory dysfunction occurs when there is damage to the neurological structures of the brain that work towards the storage, retention, and recollection of memories. They can be progressive, like Alzheimer's disease and Korsakoff's syndrome, or immediate, such as in the case of a head injury. Alzheimer's disease is a neurodegenerative disease that starts with short-term memory loss and advances to disorientation and behavioral issues. Korsakoff's syndrome is a result of a deficiency of thiamine in the brain, most often caused by alcoholism, that results in severe memory loss as well an inability to create new memories.

Alzheimer's disease is the most common form of dementia and is associated with a deficit in the neurotransmitter acetylcholine. Alzheimer's is a progressive disease of the brain that is caused by the development of plaques and tangles, both parts of proteins, in and around nerve cells. Early-onset Alzheimer's is strongly genetic and inherited from parents. Late-onset Alzheimer's is most likely the result of a combination of genetic and environmental factors.

Decay

The **theory of decay** proposes that memories fade from the brain over time. It becomes harder to retrieve them as the strength of the memory wears away.

Interference

Retroactive interference theory proposes that when a person learns something new and there is an overlap or interaction with a past learned behavior, it becomes harder to retrieve the old knowledge. **Proactive interference theory** proposes that past memories inhibit a person's full ability to retain new memories.

Memory Construction and Source Monitoring

Since the brain has a limited capacity for storage of memories, there is a theory that proposes memories are not stored as whole entities, but rather, as pieces of data that can be pieced together to create the whole memory. Every time a memory is recalled, it is newly reconstructed. Unfortunately, this allows room for error with each memory. **Source-monitoring errors** occur when a memory is attributed to the wrong source, such as learning new information from a friend but later stating that a person read about it in the newspaper. It can be due to limited encoding of source information or by a disruption in the judgement process when deciding on the source.

Biological Bases of Memory

Psychological and Physiological Systems of Short- and Long-Term Memory

Short-term memory describes small chunks of information that can be held, but not really manipulated, in one's mind for a short timeframe. Areas such as the frontal lobe and hippocampus—located in the temporal lobe—are each associated with short-term memory. A person is able to increase their capacity for short-term memory through a process known as chunking. **Chunking** consists of the ability to organize material into shorter, meaningful chunks as a means of making the retained information more manageable. Some examples of short-term memories include remembering the seven digits of someone's phone number, recalling the lot where you parked your car, remembering the place where you left off in a book, or recalling what you ate for breakfast this morning. This information is either stored or forgotten.

Long-term memory involves information being held in the mind for an indefinite period of time. The hippocampus plays an integral role in transforming short-term memories into long-term memories. Some examples of long-term memories include one's high school or college graduation ceremony, skills an individual learns from their place of employment, an event one attended several years ago, or the date of a spouse's birthday.

Procedural memory can be thought of as a subtype of or component of long-term memory. This type of memory consists of the retention of motor skills such as talking, walking, riding a bike, driving a car, and playing an instrument.

Memory undergoes four stages of processing. The order of these four stages includes encoding, consolidation, storage, and retrieval. **Encoding** involves breaking down information and converting it into a construct to be stored in the brain. An example of this includes repeating a phone number to yourself to increase the likelihood of retention. This is also known as **rehearsal**. **Consolidation** is the process of stabilizing information after it has already been encoded. An example of this entails a student who devises a habit of studying for an exam two days in advance in order to properly file the information come the time of the exam. **Storage** describes placing newly attained information into memory for later retrieval. An example of this process is a person storing a word read in a book by changing it into a sound or a specific meaning. **Retrieval** refers to getting information out of storage. An example of this consists of organizing information in sequences such as by size or time, or alphabetically, so that an association is formed, which increases the chances of memory retrieval.

Introduction to Thinking and Problem Solving

Problem-Solving Strategies

Types of Problem Solving

Problem solving is the mental process of reaching a goal using complex logic to fill in the missing information that stands between a person's present condition and the goal. There are several different ways of attempting to solve a problem. Using the **problem-solving cycle**, a person would define the problem, develop a strategy to fix the problem, find the resources available for implementing the strategy, monitor progress, and then evaluate the solution for accuracy. Another method is the **GROW method**, in which *G* stands for goal, *R* stands for reality or the current situation, *O* stands for obstacles and options, and *W* stands for way forward or the path that the person would take to reach their goal. **PDCA** is another four-step approach that stands for planning, doing, checking, and acting.

Approaches to Problem Solving

There are many different strategies that can be used to solve a problem once it has been identified. The table below describes some of these options.

Technique	Description
Abstraction	Solving the problem in a model of the system before applying it to the real system
Analogy	Using a solution that solves an analogous problem
Brainstorming	Suggesting many solutions or ideas and combining and developing them until an optimum solution is found
Divide and Conquer	Breaking down a large, complex problem into smaller, solvable problems

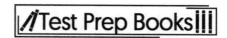

Hypothesis Testing	Assuming a possible explanation to the problem and trying to prove (or, in some contexts, disprove) the assumption
Means-ends Analysis	Choosing an action at each step to move closer to the goal
Reduction	Transforming the problem into another problem for which solutions exist
Research	Employing existing ideas or adapting existing solutions to similar problems
Root Cause Analysis	Identifying the cause of a problem
Trial-and-Error	Testing possible solutions until the right one is found

The Characteristics of Creative Thought and Creative Thinkers

Creative thinkers typically possess specific characteristics. Some of these characteristics are as follows:

Curiosity: A creative thinker asks questions and is curious about the world around them. They want to find out about what they do not know.

"Zero-Based Thinking": This type of thinking involves thinking of a starting point where one previously made a decision, but trying to determine if they could go back to that point with the current information to consider whether they would make the same decision or what would they differently.

Change: Creative thinkers are not rigid nor afraid of change. They understand that change is necessary and inevitable and they embrace it, allowing themselves to be more open to experiences.

Admitting Mistakes: Creative thinkers are open to admitting their mistakes or when they may have made a bad decision in the past.

Learning: Those who have fully embraced and achieved the ability to think creatively understand the important concept that no one can know everything. There is always something to learn. When faced with a situation that they don't know the answer, to a creative thinker will often try to reach out to someone who has dealt with the situation before and see how that person approached it. Creative thinkers understand that learning through others is invaluable.

Goals: Having and working toward goals is a quality that is at the forefront of most creative thinker's minds. Not only do creative thinkers usually have goals and dreams, but they have roadmaps or plans to achieve them and practice visualizing achieving them.

Ego: Intimately tied to being comfortable admitting mistakes and learning from them is the concept that a creative person's ego doesn't get in the way of their actions or thinking.

Biases and Errors in Thinking

Problem-Solving Strategies and Factors that Create Bias and Errors in Thinking

There are five main barriers to effective problem-solving: confirmation bias, mental set, functional fixedness, unnecessary constraints, and irrelevant information. **Confirmation bias** includes preconceived notions that make a person more willing to favor studies that align with their beliefs. **Mental set** describes a person's bias towards attempting to solve a problem in a way that has worked previously, even though a different method may be more efficient. **Functional fixedness** is a type of mental set in which a person will not use an object for any other purpose than its original function. **Unnecessary**

constraints are when a person subconsciously places boundaries on a task at hand. **Irrelevant information** is information that is present along with a problem that is unrelated to the problem and will not help in solving the task.

Heuristics are approaches to problem-solving that are practical but not necessarily optimal or perfect. They help people to form judgements about a situation and then make a decision. Biases occur when the heuristics deviate from logic and probability. Two examples of common biases are overconfidence and belief perseverance. **Overconfidence** occurs when a person has greater confidence in a piece of information than the actual objective accuracy of that information. **Belief perseverance** occurs when a person continues to maintain their belief despite the appearance of contradictory new information.

Introduction to Intelligence

Intelligence and Measuring Intelligence

Intelligence describes the ability of an individual to learn and retain information, to think critically about information, and to apply that information to theoretical or real-world problems. It typically focuses on an individual's ability to absorb and work with abstract concepts and concrete information. The Intelligence Quotient (IQ) index describes an individual's intellectual ability.

Abstract Versus Verbal Measures
Intelligence quotient (IQ) tests consist of an assorted combination of questions that encourage the use of skills pertaining to abstract reasoning. The purpose of using these types of tests is to measure intellectual ability rather than how much factual information someone knows, but in actuality, both are indicated. **Abstract measures** are used to test one's aptitude for logical reasoning and nonverbal skills by assessing one's capacity for obtaining analogies, rules, and structures from logical and abstract reasoning. This ability is subsequently used to figure out the right response from a set of various possible options. These types of tests are typically used as a part of job assessment.

Verbal measures are used to test one's ability to utilize language-based reasoning to analyze information, ranging from acquired knowledge, attention to verbal details, and general verbal reasoning. This type of reasoning entails listening to or reading words, having a conversation, thinking, and writing. Verbal tasks can consist of abstract or concrete ideas. The Stanford-Binet IQ test, the Wechsler Adult Intelligence Scale (WAIS), and the Wechsler Intelligence Scale for Children (WISC) are all commonly used standardized tests designed to measure intelligence. However, a criticism of these tests is that they tend to focus more on cognitive ability rather than examine the contributions of other factors such as emotion, level of motivation, morality, and social skills.

Speed of Processing
Processing speed is defined as the amount of time it takes for an individual to complete a mental task. It's an important basis in the assessment of cognitive abilities in domains such as academic performance, intellectual development, learning, and reasoning. Processing speed can be used when identifying visual patterns, completing exams warranting simple decisions, performing basic quantitative calculations, or completing a reasoning task under pressure. However, while processing speed can help in making intelligence run more efficiently, intelligence and processing speed are actually mutually exclusive concepts, meaning that one doesn't necessarily serve as a consistent or reliable predictor of the other. For instance, if someone's processing speed is slow, it just means that some tasks will be more difficult to complete than others, such as math skills, reading comprehension, note-taking,

planning, decision making, problem solving, or even paying attention. Processing speed simply indicates a more efficient ability to learn and think and finish straightforward tasks. In other words, processing speed describes the timeframe that occurs between understanding information and responding to it. Some examples of processing speed include taking either thirty or sixty minutes to complete a task, or how easy or difficult it is to follow a set of instructions.

Fluid Intelligence

Fluid intelligence describes one's ability to engage in flexible thinking, reasoning, and problem solving in new and unique situations. When using fluid intelligence, we don't rely on any pre-existing knowledge or experience but instead make use of abstract thinking, logic, and pattern recognition skills when solving a novel problem. This type of intelligence often relates to nonverbal tasks such as puzzles or quantitative problems, and can even play a role in creative processes such as art or music, regardless of any previous training. Research indicates that fluid intelligence usually starts decreasing as we age, sometimes before we even reach our thirties.

While psychologist Charles Spearman was technically the first to divide intelligence, it was another psychologist by the name of Raymond Cattell who first coined the term fluid intelligence. An example of fluid intelligence is observing a series of numbers and identifying a pattern between them in order to obtain the correct response. Fluid intelligence involves learning how to think outside the box and then applying that skill before finally arriving at an answer. In other words, fluid intelligence starts with observing a problem, recognizing and interpreting patterns and understanding the relationship between them, and reaching a logical conclusion.

Crystallized Intelligence

Crystallized intelligence consists of how knowledge is acquired through learning and experience. Unlike fluid intelligence, crystallized intelligence relies on pre-existing knowledge of facts and skills in a specific domain, whether learned in school or from past experiences, and increases as we age and attain more knowledge. Hence, the more knowledge and understanding of different subjects we pick up over the years, the stronger our crystallized intelligence becomes in the process. Vocabulary tests and reading comprehension are some examples of situations that make use of crystallized intelligence. Psychologist Raymond Cattell also identified this type of intelligence.

People with a high level of crystallized intelligence tend to be identified as "book smart," compared to those with fluid intelligence, who are commonly referred to as "street smart." Fluid intelligence usually starts first when learning something new, but upon learning that task, crystallized intelligence would then proceed to take over from there. Therefore, while fluid intelligence and crystallized intelligence depict two different abilities, they can also work in unison. For instance, when taking a test, you would first use fluid intelligence to devise a technique for completing a novel problem, but then make use of crystallized intelligence when observing and discerning different terms or symbols.

Flynn Effect

The **Flynn effect**, named for intelligence researcher James Flynn, describes a significant and extended increase in test scores pertaining to both fluid and crystallized intelligence. This effect has been measured in various countries worldwide. Some measures of intelligence, such as performances on Raven's Progressive Matrices, have been increasing for the past century. These increases in test scores have appeared linear over the years up to this point. However, some countries have actually shown a decline in IQ scores. Skepticism has been expressed over the implications of the Flynn effect. For instance, while most experts would assume that test scores in specific domains of knowledge (crystallized intelligence) would be the ones on the rise, researchers are actually finding that scores related to abstract problem solving (fluid intelligence) are the ones increasing.

Over recent years, several psychologists have accepted what has been dubbed the **multiplicity hypothesis**, which posits that the Flynn effect can be explained by a wide array of factors that include stimulating environments, progresses made in early education, increased test complexity, improved attitudes about taking tests, and sufficient nutrition. New technology could also account for this phenomenon because it can encourage abstract thinking. Flynn actually believes that this increase could represent an increase in abstract problem solving as opposed to intelligence itself.

Stereotype Threat

A **stereotype threat** occurs when there is a negative stereotype against a particular group, and a member of that group experiences anxiety about fulfilling the stereotype. Their performance will suffer, due to the anxiety of conforming to the stereotype, even though there is no legitimate reason for a poorer performance.

Savant Syndrome

Savant syndrome describes a rare condition in which an individual with substantial mental disabilities demonstrates certain abilities far exceeding the average range. While the skills at which savants are noted to excel tend to be related to memory, such as superior autobiographical memories, a wide range of areas can be affected that include the ability to perform calculations at an accelerated rate, enhanced artistic abilities and musical capabilities, and even more proficient and detailed spatial skills, especially as those that pertain to map making. However, it's typically just one particular skill that's present.

Some develop this syndrome naturally via a neurodevelopmental disorder such as autism spectrum disorder, whereas others might develop it as a result of an acquired brain injury. While half of those with savant syndrome are somewhere on the autism spectrum, others usually have some type of disease affecting their central nervous system. Some neurological studies have found that damage to the anterior temporal lobe, which helps process semantic content, can result in savant syndrome. In those with autism, it has been suggested that their tendency toward meticulous detail processing could predispose them to developing savant syndrome. There's currently no consensus accounting for this combination of both talent and deficiency.

Emotional Intelligence

The concept of emotional intelligence, measured by the Emotional Quotient (EQ) index, takes into account how an individual perceives feelings, the nonverbal and verbal communication of others, and other fluid concepts. This includes understanding group dynamics, interpersonal relationships, social norms, and self-awareness. It typically focuses on an individual's ability to understand personal motivations and feelings, and on his or her ability to interact positively with surrounding people and environment.

Here are the five components of emotional intelligence:

Five Components of Emotional Intelligence

	Definition	Characteristics
Self-Awareness	Identifying one's own emotions, motivations, and desires, and the effects they have on others	Confidence Sense of Humor Awareness of Others' Perception of Self
Self-Regulation	Being able to express oneself appropriately by controlling one's own emotions before acting	Honesty Adaptibility Disarming in Tense Situations
Motivation	Exhibiting self-motivation or the desire to better one's self; eagerness to learn	Initiative Determination
Empathy	Being able to understand others' emotions as if they were one's own	Intuition of Others' Reactions Awareness of Others' Needs
Social Skill	Being able to manage relationships and construct social networks	Leadership Communication Managing Conflict

How Culture Influences the Definition of Intelligence

Over the years, researchers have discovered that people in non-Western cultures tend to have definitions about intelligence that are vastly different from those that have influenced the development of tests in the Western world. In fact, another one of the criticisms of intelligence tests are their potential for cultural bias, largely because different cultures view intelligence differently. For instance, those living in Western cultures typically see intelligence as a means of creating specific categories and engaging in logical discourse, while people living in Eastern cultures view intelligence as a necessity for those belonging to a community, to distinguish inconsistencies and intricacies and to successfully conform to the specific social roles within that community.

Given that most Western cultures tend to be more individualistic—placing an emphasis on personal achievements and individual rights and self-reliance—and most Eastern cultures tend to be more collectivistic—emphasizing the group over the desires of individuals—these cultural variations in the definition of intelligence make sense. These and other basic differences in cognitive processing across Western and Eastern cultures alike are most likely related to these differing views concerning intelligence. However, it's important to bear in mind that a person's race, ethnicity, nationality, and particular social group doesn't automatically indicate their cultural perspective. In other words, culture is a collection of experiences that can influence one's mentality, so an individual's background doesn't necessarily reflect their personal views on intelligence, or other subjects.

Generally speaking, there are various examples of these differing cultural perspectives on intelligence. Some examples include people in central Africa viewing intelligence as an indicator of cleverness and a

sense of responsibility to society, people in China viewing intelligence as an ability to empathize with others, and most Americans viewing intelligence in terms of academic performance and cognitive skills.

Comparing and Contrasting Historic and Contemporary Theories of Intelligence

Charles Spearman

English psychologist Charles Spearman (1863–1945) is known for various contributions to the field of psychology. Some of his most notable contributions include pioneering factor analysis and devising both the rank correlation coefficient and the general intelligence factor (also known as the *g* factor). **Factor analysis** outlines a statistical technique describing any variability that exists among observable and correlated data and that is used to decrease a significant number of variables into a lesser number of factors. For example, people asked about their schooling, vocation, and income stream could all respond similarly. All of these factors are associated with the variable of socioeconomic status. The **correlation coefficient** assesses how efficiently the relationship between two variables is described using a particular function, for example, when there's an almost perfect correlation between one's pants size and waistline. The *g* **factor** is used to investigate cognitive abilities and human intelligence. Intelligence tests that assess people's different cognitive skills were influenced by this *g* factor.

Howard Gardner

American developmental psychologist Howard Gardner (1943–) is a very well-known figure in the field of psychology. While he has written numerous articles and books throughout the span of his career, his most notable contribution consists of devising what has been dubbed the theory of multiple intelligences. The **theory of multiple intelligences** distinguishes human intelligence into distinctive modalities, as opposed to viewing intelligence as a single general ability. In other words, Gardner looked at the different types of intelligence that people can possess. His theory consisted of eight different types of intelligence:

- **Musical-rhythmic intelligence** relates to good or absolute pitch. An example is a musician who can sing, play instruments, and compose music.

- **Visual-spatial intelligence** consists of the ability to solve spatial navigational problems, visualizing things from different angles, facial and scene recognition, and observation of fine details. Some examples of those likely to fall under this category would include architects, photographers, and physicists.

- **Verbal-linguistic intelligence** outlines a penchant for words and languages. For example, a person with high verbal-linguistic intelligence is typically skilled at reading, writing, storytelling, and memorizing vocabulary.

- **Logical-mathematical intelligence** describes the use of abstractions, critical thinking, logic, numbers, and reasoning. For instance, a person proficient in this skill is able to successfully apply logic and reason to assimilate and accommodate new information and generally make sense of things.

- **Bodily-kinesthetic intelligence** consists of the ability to control one's bodily movements and skillful handling of objects. Some examples include athletes, dancers, actors, and soldiers.

- **Interpersonal intelligence** involves the ability to be sensitive to how others think and feel and cooperate with others. Some examples of professions that typically rely on this type of intelligence include managers, teachers, administrators, and social workers.

- **Intrapersonal intelligence** has to do with introspection and self-reflection. Consider a person who can predict their own emotional reactions to particular events, outline their strengths and weaknesses, and has a profound understanding of themselves. Such people would likely be theologians, entrepreneurs, and counselors.

- **Naturalistic intelligence** involves cultivating and conveying details about one's natural environment. Some examples here of those relying on this type of intelligence include hunters, gatherers, farmers, and scientists.

Robert Sternberg

Along with his triarchic theory of intelligence, Sternberg (1949–) is also best known for his triangular theory of love and three-process view. The **triangular theory of love** posits that love is best understood in relation to three features that when combined can form all the points of a triangle. These three features include an intimacy component, a passion component, and a commitment component. An **intimacy component** describes feelings of attachment, closeness, and a sense of connection. The **passion component** involves the intense feelings people experience that drive both sexual and romantic attraction. The **commitment component** merges the other components together by focusing on short-term and long-term plans to stay with one another.

The **three-process view** describes three kinds of insight, which includes selective-encoding, selective-comparison, and selective-combination. In **selective-encoding**, a person is able to distinguish, or filter out, important aspects of a problem from the more irrelevant ones. In **selective-comparison**, an individual can recognize information after establishing a relationship between acquired knowledge and experience. Lastly, in **selective-combination**, a person recognizes information by gaining an understanding of all the different elements composing it and then mentally assembling it all back together.

The Contributions of Key Researchers in Intelligence Research and Testing

Alfred Binet

In the 1900s, French psychologist Alfred Binet (1857–1911), along with medical student Theodore Simon, developed the first test to determine which children would succeed in school. His initial test, the Binet-Simon, focused on the concept of mental age, and included memory, attention, and problem-solving skills. In 1916, Binet's work was brought to Stanford University and developed into the Stanford-Binet Intelligence Scale, which has since been revised multiple times and is still widely used.

Raymond Cattell

In the 1940s, Raymond Cattell (1905–1998) began developing theories on fluid and crystallized intelligence. His student, John Horn, continued this work. The Cattell-Horn Theory hypothesized that over one hundred abilities work together to create forms of intelligence. **Fluid intelligence** is the ability to think and act quickly and to solve new problems, skills that are independent of education and enculturation. **Crystallized intelligence** encompasses acquired and learned skills, and is influenced by personality, motivation, education, and culture. In 1949, Catell and his wife, Alberta Karen Cattell, founded the Institute for Personality and Ability Testing at the University of Illinois. Cattell developed several assessments, including the 16 Personality Factor Questionnaire and the Culture Fair Intelligence Test.

John Ertl
John Ertl, a professor working in Canada in the 1970s, invented a neural efficiency analyzer to more effectively measure intelligence. He believed traditional intelligence tests were limited to understanding an abstract degree of intelligence. Ertl's system measured the speed and efficiency of electrical activity in the brain using an electroencephalogram (EEG).

Francis Galton
Sir Francis Galton (1822–1911), an English anthropologist and explorer, was one of the first individuals to study intelligence in the late 1800s. A cousin of Charles Darwin, Galton coined the term *eugenics* and believed that intelligence was genetically determined and could be promoted through selective parenting.

J.P. Guilford
American psychologist J.P. Guilford (1897–1987) conducted psychometric studies of human intelligence and creativity in the early 1900s. He believed intelligence tests were limited and overly one-dimensional, and didn't factor in the diversity of human abilities, thinking, and creativity.

Arthur Jensen
Arthur Jensen (1923–2012) supported the g Factor Theory and believed intelligence consisted of two distinct sets of abilities. Level I accounted for simple associative learning and memory, while Level II involved more abstract and conceptual reasoning. Jensen also believed that genetic factors were the most influential indicator of intelligence. In 1998, he published the book *The g Factor: The Science of Mental Ability.*

Charles Spearman
English psychologist Charles Spearman (1863–1945) was responsible for bringing statistical analysis to intelligence testing. In the early 1900s, Spearman proposed the g Factor Theory for general intelligence, which laid the foundation for analyzing intelligence tests. Prior to his work, tests weren't highly correlated with the factors they attempted to measure.

Robert Sternberg
American psychologist and psychometrician Robert Sternberg (1949–) has made numerous contributions to the field of psychology. He has both authored and co-authored various publications that include articles, books, and book chapters. He has served as a past President of the American Psychological Association (APA) and serves on the editorial boards of prominent journal publications, one of which includes *American Psychologist*. The main focus of his research has consisted of intelligence, creativity, and wisdom. Among his most significant contributions to psychology, he devised the triarchic theory of intelligence.

The **triarchic theory of intelligence** takes a more cognitive approach to intelligence by focusing on three types of intelligence, which include **practical** (successfully functioning in one's environment), **creative** (devising new ideas), and **analytical** (engaging in information assessment and problem solving) intelligence. Sternberg focuses on **successful intelligence**. Individuals displaying successful intelligence can express and attain their own version of success with respect to their culture. These individuals are able to adjust to and change their environment in ways best suited to their needs.

Lewis Terman

American psychologist and author Lewis Terman (1877–1956) is considered a pioneer in the field of educational psychology. His most notable contributions to the field of psychology consist of his revisions to the **Stanford-Binet Intelligence Scales**, longitudinal studies of children with high intelligence, and the positive psychology of talent. Terman revised the Stanford-Binet by suggesting that one's IQ be reflective of their mental age/chronological age multiplied by 100. Revisions to this test still remain in use as a means of measuring intelligence in both children and adults alike. Terman studied intelligence in children with the intended aim of classifying them accordingly and setting them on the most appropriate vocational path, because it was his view that IQ was an inherited trait that served as the strongest predictor of one's ability to succeed in the world. In his longitudinal study of gifted children, Terman found that high intelligence in children was correlated with significant achievements in adult life, leading to this psychology of talent.

David Wechsler

In the 1950s, American psychologist David Wechsler (1896–1981) developed intelligence tests for adults and children. His tests were adept at identifying learning disabilities in children. Wechsler began his career developing personality tests for the U.S. military. He disagreed with some aspects of the Stanford-Binet Intelligence Scale, and believed intelligence had both verbal and performance components. He also believed factors other than pure intellect influenced intellectual behavior. Wechsler's tests are still used today for adults, as well as school-age and primary-age children. They include the Wechsler Adult Intelligence Scale (WAIS-IV), the Wechsler Intelligence Scale for Children (WISC-IV), and the Wechsler Preschool and Primary Scale of Intelligence (WPPSI-III).

Psychometric Principles and Intelligence Testing

How Psychologists Design Tests

Types of Tests

Achievement tests measure knowledge of a specific subject and are primarily used in education. Examples include exit exams for high school diplomas and tests used in the Common Core for educational standards. The General Education Development (GED) and the California Achievement Test are both achievement tests that measure learning.

Aptitude tests measure the capacity for learning and can be used as part of a job application. These tests can measure abstract/conceptual reasoning, verbal reasoning, and/or numerical reasoning. Examples include the Wonderlic Cognitive Ability Test, the Differential Aptitude Test (DAT), the Minnesota Clerical Test, and the Career Ability Placement Survey (CAPS).

Intelligence tests measure mental capability and potential. One example is the Wechsler Adult Intelligence Scale (WAIS-IV), currently in its fourth edition. The Wechsler Intelligence Scale for Children (WISC-IV), also in its fourth edition, is used for children six years of age to sixteen years eleven months of age, and can be completed without reading or writing. There's a separate version of the test for children aged two years six months to seven years seven months, known as the Wechsler Preschool and Primary Scale of Intelligence (WPPSI-III). Examples of other intelligence tests are the Stanford-Binet Intelligence Scale, the Woodcock-Johnson Tests of Cognitive Abilities, and the Kaufman Assessment Battery for Children.

Occupational tests can assess skills, values, or interests as they relate to vocational and occupational choices. Examples include the Strong Interest Inventory, the Self-Directed Search, the O*Net Interest Profiler, the Career Assessment Inventory, and the Kuder Career Interests Assessment.

Personality tests can be objective (rating-scale based) or projective (self-reporting based), and help the counselor and client understand personality traits and underlying beliefs and behaviors. The Myers-Briggs Type Inventory (MBTI) provides a specific psychological type, reflecting the work of Carl Jung. It's often used as part of the career development process. Other rating scale personality tests include the Minnesota Multiphasic Personality Inventory (MMPI-2), the Beck Depression Inventory, and the Tennessee Self-Concept Scale. The Rorschach (inkblot) and the Thematic Apperception Test are both projective tests, designed to reveal unconscious thoughts, motives, and views.

Types of Reliability

Reliability in testing is the degree to which the assessment tool produces consistent and stable results. There are four types of reliability:

Test-Retest Reliability involves administering the same test twice to a group of individuals, then correlating the scores to evaluate stability.

Parallel-Forms Reliability (also referred to as **equivalence**) involves administering two different versions of an assessment that measure the same set of skills, knowledge, etc. and then correlating the results. A test can be written and split into two parts, thus creating parallel versions.

Inter-Rater Reliability (also referred to as **inter-observer**) checks to see that raters (those administering, grading, or judging a measure) do so in agreement. Each rater should value the same measures and at the same degree to ensure consistency. Inter-rater reliability prevents overly subjective ratings, since each rater is measuring on the same terms.

Internal Consistency refers to how well a test or assessment measures what it's intended to measure, while producing similar results each time. Questions on an assessment should be similar and in agreement, but not repetitive. High internal consistency indicates that a measure is reliable.

- **Average Inter-Item Correlation** is used to determine if scores on one item relate to the scores on all of the other items in that scale. Ensuring that each correlation between items is a form of redundancy to ensure the same content is assessed with each question.

- **Split-Half Reliability** is the random division of questions into two sets. Results of both halves are compared to ensure correlation.

Validity

Validity refers to how well a test or assessment measures what it's intended to measure. For example, an assessment on depression should only measure the degree to which an individual meets the diagnostic criteria for depression. Though validity does indicate reliability, a test can be reliable but not be valid. There are four major types of validity, with subtypes:

Content Validity ensures that the test questions align with the content or study area. This can be measured by two subtypes of validation:

- o **Face Validity** refers to a commonsense view that a test measures what it should and looks accurate from a non-professional viewpoint.

- o **Curricular Validity** is evaluated by experts, and measures that a test aligns with the curriculum being tested. For example, a high school exit exam should measure the information taught in the high school curriculum.

Criterion Validity measures success and the relationship between a test score and an outcome, such as scores on the SAT and success in college. It's two subtypes are:

- o **Predictive Validity** refers to how useful test scores are at predicting future performance.

- o **Concurrent Validity** is used to determine if measures can be substituted, such as taking an exam in place of a class. Measures must take place concurrently to accurately test for validity.

Construct Validity refers to a test that measures abstract traits or theories, and isn't inadvertently testing another variable. For example, a math test with complex word problems may be assessing reading skills. Two subtypes of validation are needed to assess construct validity:

- o **Convergent Validity** tests whether attributes or measures in different tests that are supposed to be assessing the same things are indeed correlated. For example, two separate vocabulary tests can measure students' word knowledge similarly.

- o **Discriminant Validity** tests whether measure or concepts that are supposed to be different and not related are indeed unrelated.

Consequential Validity refers to the social consequences of testing. Though not all researchers feel it's a true measure of validity, some believe a test must benefit society in order to be considered valid.

Interpreting the Meaning of Scores in Terms of the Normal Curve

To begin, any test or assessment should be given under controlled circumstances. The psychologist or counselor should follow any instructions provided in the test manual. Once completed, the counselor and client can discuss the results together.

Some best practices for interpreting results are listed below:

The psychologist or counselor must thoroughly understand the results

The psychologist or counselor should explain results in easily understood terms, and should be able to provide supporting details and norms as needed

The psychologist or counselor should explain and understand average scores and the meanings of results

The psychologist or counselor should allow the client to ask questions and review aspects of the test to ensure understanding

The psychologist or counselor must explain the ramifications and limitations of any data obtained through testing

A **normal distribution** of data follows the shape of a bell curve and the data set's median, mean, and mode are equal. Therefore, 50 percent of its values are less than the mean and 50 percent are greater than the mean. Data sets that follow this shape can be generalized using normal distributions. Normal distributions are described as **frequency distributions** in which the data set is plotted as percentages rather than true data points. A **relative frequency distribution** is one where the y-axis is between zero and 1, which is the same as 0% to 100%. Within a standard deviation, 68 percent of the values are within 1 standard deviation of the mean, 95 percent of the values are within 2 standard deviations of the mean, and 99.7 percent of the values are within 3 standard deviations of the mean. The number of standard deviations that a data point falls from the mean is called the **z-score.** The formula for the z-score is $Z = \frac{x-\mu}{\sigma}$, where μ is the mean, σ is the standard deviation, and x is the data point. This formula is used to fit any data set that resembles a normal distribution to a standard normal distribution, in a process known as **standardizing.**

Here is a normal distribution with labeled z-scores:

Normal Distribution with Labelled Z-Scores

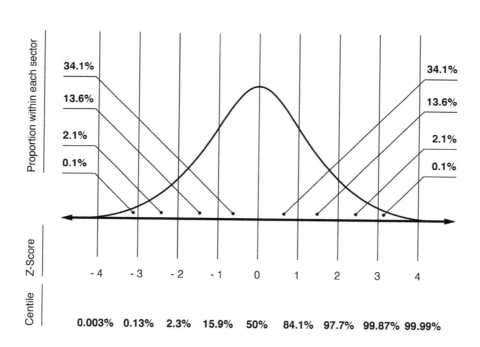

Population percentages can be estimated using normal distributions. For example, the probability that a data point will be less than the mean, or that the z-score will be less than 0, is 50%. Similarly, the probability that a data point will be within 1 standard deviation of the mean, or that the z-score will be

between -1 and 1, is about 68.2%. When using a table, the left column states how many standard deviations (to one decimal place) away from the mean the point is, and the row heading states the second decimal place. The entries in the table corresponding to each column and row give the probability, which is equal to the area.

Relevant Labels Related to Intelligence Testing

Gifted

Giftedness describes an intellectual ability that extends substantially higher than average. While there is no exact definition of giftedness, most longitudinal studies and placement decisions apply this term to those people with IQs in the top two percent of the population, which is basically anything above 130. However, definitions of intellectual giftedness tend to vary across different cultures, especially because cultures have their own distinct views of what constitutes intelligence. Definitions of giftedness range in certain abilities. For example, gifted individuals can have a significant penchant for math, some for art or music, some for science, and others for superior language skills.

Giftedness is categorized into different degrees, or ranges. For instance, **mild giftedness** consists of IQ scores between 115 to 129, **moderate giftedness** between 130 to 144, **high giftedness** between 145 to 159, **exceptional giftedness** between 160 to 179, and **profound giftedness** being IQ scores of 180 or more. The concept of intellectual giftedness translating from childhood traits to adult performances still remains controversial and extensively researched.

Intellectual Disability

Once referred to as mental retardation, an **intellectual disability** describes someone with below-average intelligence or mental aptitude and who has greater difficulty learning the basic skills necessary to function on their own in daily life. The average intelligence is an IQ score of 100. Most people's IQ scores fall somewhere between 85 to 115. However, a person scoring anywhere below 70 or 75 is considered intellectually disabled. While it is possible for people with intellectual disabilities to learn a new set of basic skills, they usually do so at a much slower pace than others, and their ability to function is contingent on the severity of their disability. The lower the IQ, the less likely they are able to function well on their own.

Intellectual disability affects one percent of the population and tends to ranges in the degree of severity. **Mild intellectual disability** consists of IQ scores between 50 to 70, **moderate intellectual disability** is between 35 to 49, **severe intellectual disability** is between 20 to 34, and a **profound intellectual disability** is anything below a score of 20.

Components of Language and Language Acquisition

How Biological, Cognitive, and Cultural Factors Converge to Facilitate Acquisition, Development, and Use of Language

Language is a set of sounds and symbols that have distinct meaning and that are used for communication. There are approximately 5,000 to 7,000 different languages used by humans across the world. Infants are born with the ability to distinguish between sounds found in all languages. However, by about seven months of age, they begin to concentrate on the language or languages that are spoken to them the most. New languages are easiest to learn before the age of seven and become harder to learn through adolescence and then even more so during adulthood.

Theories of Language Development

There are several theories that exist about language development. The **learning theory** proposes that both adults and children learn best when they make a discovery for themselves. In the case of language, infants and adults have conversations even when the infant does not have the ability to speak. Despite this, these interaction build the structure of language in the infant for the time when they are ready to speak.

The **Nativist theory** states that children are born already knowing the laws of language, such as sentence structure and grammar principles. Being around people who are speaking and using these laws allows children to utilize their innate ability as they begin to speak themselves. This theory also supports the idea of **Universal Grammar**, which is the idea that all languages have the same basic underlying structure and that specific languages just utilize this structure with different patterns.

The **Interactionist Theory of Language** relies on the idea that social interaction is important for language development. A child first observes language interaction between other people and then develops the same behavior within themselves. When a child is first learning to speak, the adult leads the conversation but as the interactions continue and the child's skills grow, the child can speak more independently.

Influence of Language on Cognition

Language affects the cognitive process in a person. **Linguistic relativity** is a theory that the language that a person speaks shapes how they view and think about the world around them. Thoughts are often unable to be directly translated between different languages, so the meaning of those thoughts becomes different in the different cultures. Linguistic determinism is the idea that the structure of a language is limited, and therefore limits the knowledge and thought processes that shape that language and the people who speak it.

Brain Areas that Control Language and Speech

Different areas of the brain are responsible for different parts of language processing. Four levels of language comprehension and their associated brain activation are described below:

1. Passive exposure to written words activates the posterior area of the left hemisphere of the brain.

2. Passive exposure to spoken words activates the temporal lobes.

3. Oral repetition of words activates the motor cortex on both sides of the brain, the supplementary motor cortex, and a portion of the cerebellum and insular cortex.

4. Generation of a verb that is associated with a presented noun activates language-related regions in the left hemisphere, including Broca's area.

Appropriate Testing Practices

A variety of ethical issues must be considered before, during, and after any test or assessment is administered. To begin, the counselor must be adequately trained and earn any certifications and supervision necessary to administer and interpret the test. Tests must be appropriate for the needs of the specific client. Next, the client must provide informed consent, and they must understand the purpose and scope of any test. Test results must remain confidential, which includes access to any virtual information. Finally, tests must be validated for the specific client and be unbiased toward the race, ethnicity, and gender of the client.

Unit 6: Developmental Psychology

The Lifespan and Physical Development in Childhood

The Process of Conception and Gestation

Conception describes the process whereby a sperm cell from a fertile man travels into a woman's uterus and merges with her egg cell while it goes down a fallopian tube from the ovary to the uterus. The order of the three stages of prenatal development include germinal, embryonic, and fetal. The **germinal stage** takes place between conception and the first two weeks, which is when the **zygote** (a single cell formed from the fusion of a man's sperm and a woman's egg) begins to undergo rapid division. The **embryonic stage** occurs between the second and eighth week of pregnancy, which is when organs start to develop (**organogenesis**), and it's during this process that the fetus is most prone to birth defects caused by various types of external factors, including drugs, toxins, and extreme environments. The **fetal stage** transpires between week nine up to the fetus's birth. The brain continues to grow and develop during this stage.

Nutrition

Both before and during pregnancy, nutrition and weight management each have a significant impact on infant development. **Prenatal nutrition** relates to nutrient contents that affect a fetus's growth and development. Sustaining a healthy weight while carrying an embryo (**gestation**) decreases the prospect of negative risks associated with congenital birth defects. Prenatal development is a crucial time for healthy infant development, and nutrients are a prime component in ensuring the infants' optimal health and general wellness. Some examples of nutritious foods for infants during prenatal development include lean meats, fruits, low-fat dairy products, vegetables, and whole grains.

Illness

In the vast majority of cases, prenatal development happens normally and very seldomly experiences any deviations from the established patterns of development. If prospective parents take all the necessary precautions that pertain to ensuring their unborn child will undergo healthy growth and development, there should be few if any problems. However, sometimes problems can arise that can negatively affect the health of the fetus. It's important to be aware of the different conditions that can affect the fetus. Some examples of illnesses that can affect the healthy growth and development of a fetus include gestational diabetes, preeclampsia, iron deficiency anemia, and infections.

Gestational diabetes occurs when exceedingly high blood sugar levels are detected during pregnancy, which increases the infant's risk of being born too large. Treatment for this issue consists of ensuring the mother controls her blood sugar levels via a healthy diet and regular exercise, or medication if these levels remain high. **Preeclampsia** describes a rapid or abrupt development of high blood pressure around the twentieth week of pregnancy. The only treatment for this issue is to deliver the baby preterm. **Iron deficiency anemia** involves a low red blood cell count. Iron and folic acid supplements are the treatment of choice for this problem. **Infections** that can affect pregnancy normally involve sexually transmitted diseases, which can impact not just the pregnant woman but also the fetus, as well as the delivery of the fetus. Receiving regular prenatal care from a healthcare provider can not only help in obtaining necessary treatment as early as possible, but also potentially prevent any health problems from occurring.

103

Substance Abuse

Research has demonstrated that pregnant women using drugs such as alcohol, tobacco, marijuana, opioids, and other illicit substances, as well as misusing prescription drugs, can significantly affect the health of a fetus, and even increase the risk of a stillbirth. Many of these substances can easily pass through the woman's placenta, so when a pregnant woman engages in substance abuse, these substances can also reach the fetus. Another potential result of drug use during pregnancy is **neonatal abstinence syndrome**, which involves the fetus experiencing withdrawal symptoms soon after being born. Drugs that increase this risk during pregnancy include opioids, alcohol, benzodiazepines, barbiturates, and even caffeine. The full extent of a fetus's withdrawal symptoms is contingent on which drugs were used, how frequently the pregnant mother used these drugs, the manner in which her body metabolized the drugs, and whether the infant was born prematurely or underwent a full term before birth.

If a mother drinks alcohol during pregnancy, the fetus could develop **fetal alcohol syndrome**, which can result in a combination of behavioral, learning, and physical problems throughout their growth and development. Tobacco use while pregnant can result in birth defects or an increased risk of **sudden infant death syndrome**, which is the unexplained death of an infant before they reach their first year of life. Using illegal drugs such as cocaine and methamphetamine, or misusing prescription drugs such as opioids, can also possibly result in birth defects, withdrawal symptoms, underweight babies, or even the loss of the baby.

Teratogens

A **teratogen** describes an environmental agent that can cause potential birth defects. One of the most sensitive times for a developing fetus is ten to fourteen days after conception, because this is when the prenatal fetus starts becoming more susceptible to these different teratogenic agents. During organogenesis, there are certain organs developing during certain periods of time. A teratogen can interfere with this development, resulting in structural and functional problems of the organs. The central nervous system is especially prone to the detrimental effects of teratogens because the central nervous system is the baby's brain and spinal cord.

Genetic predispositions carried by both the mother and infant can influence the type or degree of abnormalities caused by a teratogenic agent. For example, how the mother metabolizes a particular drug will determine the metabolites to which the baby is exposed, as well as the total interval of that exposure. The developmental stage a baby is in during exposure can also be a factor. Generally speaking, the fetus's genetic predisposition to a certain teratogenic agent tends to have an effect on how everything will turn out.

Some specific examples of teratogens include mercury, nuclear fallout radiation, potassium iodide, lead, alcohol, illegal drugs, prescription drugs, saunas, a disease affecting the mother, and even maternal psychological stress. While some of these agents are avoidable, there are others that are unavoidable, which could include anything required to treat a medical condition. Specialists can assess a baby's risk of being affected by teratogens after their exposure to certain environments.

The Interaction of Nature and Nurture in the Determination of Behavior

The **nature versus nurture debate** describes how particular behavioral features are a product of either genetic or environmental influences. While this debate persists, most psychological researchers are now aware of how both genes and environment play a vital role in an individual's growth and development. In psychology, **epigenetics** outlines how gene expression is influenced by environmental factors to help

shape a person's behavior and general development. In other words, environmental factors can impact the expression of genes. Genes and one's environment communicate back and forth and work in tandem to create traits, and also influence our physical development. **Physical development** involves a process that begins in infancy and persists up into late adolescence. It focuses on the development of gross and fine motor skills, and also puberty. Physical development is related to numerous environmental factors. In fact, one of the most important factors that contribute to an individual's growth and development is their culture.

People raised in different cultures receive specific environmental inputs, ranging from language, parenting style, and social interactions. Every culture has their own rich tapestry of traditions, beliefs, values, laws, norms, and practices that set them apart from other cultures and contribute to a person's uniqueness. Culture also shapes an individual's perspective of the world around them, which, in turn, influences their behavior and perception of events. What is considered normal in one culture might be considered abnormal or taboo in another, and vice versa. Cultural identity can also affect one's physical development, such as how a child learns and develops both fine and gross motor skills, because parenting styles vary across cultures and are passed down from one generation to another.

For example, various Western societies encourage parents to make sure infants are sleeping on their backs in order to prevent the prospect of sudden infant death syndrome, which, in turn, causes them to spend less time on their stomachs and be slower to crawl or sit up. However, in Jamaican culture, parents tend to promote accelerated development as it relates to sitting by placing their infants waist-deep in holes and supporting their posture with blankets.

Maturation of Motor Skills

American psychologist and educator Arnold Gesell developed what is currently dubbed as the **maturational theory of child development**, which emphasizes the role that nature plays throughout the course of human development. When babies are first born, they enter the world with various innate abilities. For instance, babies come equipped with motor reflexes that help them learn to navigate and explore their surroundings. Newborns also have sensory abilities such as sight, smell, touch, taste, and hearing, which tend to develop relatively fast. Along with sensory development, motor development also tends to progress at a rapid rate. **Motor development** is defined as the ability to coordinate muscles that enable one's physical movements, with specific behaviors and abilities developing at certain ages. For instance, a motor milestone typical of a three-month old is the ability to raise their head while sitting.

A four-month old should be able to roll from their back to their side. A five-month old can roll from back to front. A six-month old can raise their chest and the upper portion of their stomach. A seven-month old can bear weight on one hand and sit alone. An infant eight to ten months old can crawl. An infant eleven to twelve months old can reach for a toy while seated and pull into a standing position. An infant between fifteen and eighteen months can squat, walk alone, and learn to run. A two-year old can run, jump, kick, and climb. A three-year old can balance on one foot. A four-year old can skip, hop, and even do somersaults and ride a tricycle. And by age five, a child can begin learning how to skate and swim. Hence, we see that, as time progresses, maturation of these motor skills occurs.

Maturation describes a hardwired approach to growth and development as it relates to the milestones of a baby's motor skills. However, maturation isn't a passive process but rather points to babies developing these skills by moving around and exploring the world around them. It seems that the role of maturation is more prevalent in the development of early motor skills, such as crawling and walking, than in later motor skills, such as learning to play a sport. While there are cultural variations in how rapidly a baby's motor skills develop, both the timing and sequence of early motor development aren't actually culture bound but rather tend to be quite similar across various cultures worldwide. During maturation and development of movement, an infant typically goes through a certain sequence of reflexes and movements, but that doesn't mean that it's impossible for a child to progress either faster or slower than this sequence compared to other children of a similar age range.

Gesell contended that individual variations in a child's rate of growth were the result of an internal genetic mechanism. According to Gesell, the growth of a child's nervous system—consisting of their brain, spinal cord, and an intricate web of nerve fibers—influences the pace at which children develop over time. Consequently, as their nervous system grows, their minds develop further and their behaviors typically change. While Gesell's maturational theory has influenced both child-rearing methods and primary education approaches, some critics assert that his theory has placed too much emphasis on the role of maturation and not enough on the contributions of learning processes.

Social Development in Childhood

The Influence of Temperament and Other Social Factors on Attachment

In psychology, **temperament** describes consistent individual behavioral variations that are biological in nature and can exist relatively independent of learning and one's value system. A person's temperament involves the general attitude that person has when facing different situations. Psychiatrists Alexander Thomas and Stella Chess identified three types of temperaments in children, which include "easy," "slow-to-warm up," and "difficult" children. **Easy** children are friendly, positive, generally adaptable, and get along well with others. **Slow-to-warm-up** children are more withdrawn and tend to adjust to change at a more gradual pace. **Difficult** children are more negative, intense, and tend to have lower levels of adaptability to new people and environments. Examples of different temperaments can include a child who is quiet and shy and needs time to adjust to a new setting, whereas another child who is more outgoing and sociable and adjusts to new environments with ease. Each child exhibits their own respective temperament.

While temperament is largely biologically based, environment can have some impact on the development of an individual's temperament. For instance, if parents tend to take a proactive approach by serving as positive role models in their child's life, then their child will be more likely to form a temperament vastly different from a child who experiences some kind of abuse growing up. A child's daily interactions outside of the home, such as with friends or romantic interests or teachers, can also impact their temperament. For example, if a child is quick to aggression, there are a variety of factors that can contribute to the development of this type of temperament, which include their parents' sensitivity, their family's educational and socioeconomic status, and their interactions with people in school. The same rule also applies to those children who tend to be more mild-mannered in their general approach.

The Contributions of Major Researchers in the Area of Social Development in Childhood

Albert Bandura
The **social cognitive theory**, popularized by Albert Bandura (1925–), looks at the interaction between the person, environment, and behaviors. The 'person' refers to individual characteristics and traits,

especially cognition or thinking processes. Although they are not constantly equal in influence, each of the three are all continually present and have an impact on each other, which Bandura referred to as **reciprocal determinism**. This theory plays out in an aspect of observational learning that proposes that people not only learn through their own behaviors but from watching other people's actions and observing the consequences they face.

Diana Baumrind

While American developmental psychologist Diana Baumrind (1927–) is known for her critique of the use of deception in psychological research, her major contribution to the field of psychology, specifically as it pertains to our understanding of social development, is her research on different parenting styles. Baumrind outlined three different types of parenting styles, which include authoritarian, permissive, and authoritative. **Authoritarian** parenting is more likely to employ the use of strict disciplinary actions when reprimanding the children. The authoritarian parent tends to be harsh, demanding, low in their level of responsiveness, and abusive, though not all authoritarian parents engage in abuse. For example, an authoritarian parent can approach their children with threats or use physical punishment and intimidation.

Permissive parenting involves being too accommodating to a child's demands and rarely, if ever, reinforcing any rules on a consistent basis. The permissive parent makes no demands but is highly responsive to the demands of their children. For example, a permissive parent doesn't keep a consistent bedtime for their children, negotiates with them in order get their respect, and buys them whatever they want. **Authoritative** parenting uses a "tough but tender" approach. In other words, the authoritative parent isn't indulgent and remains firm yet flexible when setting rules and guidelines for their children to follow. They will only make an exception when the situation might warrant one. Demandingness and responsiveness are on an equal playing field. For example, an authoritative parent will consistently enforce boundaries but also encourage autonomy and independence in their child.

Konrad Lorenz

Austrian zoologist, ornithologist, and ethologist Konrad Lorenz (1903–1989) hatched ducklings and goslings in an incubator to show how the newly hatched birds would imprint on any entity they saw in the hours after hatching. This entity could have been their mother, Lorenz, or a number of inanimate objects. The ducklings or goslings would begin to follow the entity and take on its characteristics. Lorenz defined this period as the critical period for imprinting. This discovery supported the idea that some learned behaviors must take place at pre-determined stages of development.

John Bowlby

British psychologist, psychoanalyst, and psychiatrist John Bowlby (1907–1990) first used the term **attachment.** His work with the attachment theory resulted in the belief that for a child to develop healthily, he or she must be able to have a strong attachment—a loving, nurturing relationship—with at least one main caretaker, typically one of the parents.

The ability to form a strong attachment at this age provided security, stability, and self-esteem for the individual later in life. It also promoted independence and the desire to seek out new learning opportunities, which, in turn, provided better opportunities for individual development. Those with weaker attachments in infancy and young childhood might be more anxious and tentative, as well as less willing to engage in new experiences.

Harry Harlow

Bowlby was a doctoral student of American psychologist Harry Harlow (1905–1981), who worked with monkeys to understand and explain human behavior and development related to mother-baby interaction and social isolation. Through his experiments, he suggested that infants have an innate need to be held close, kept warm, shown affection, and nourished—not only with food, water, and shelter, but also through love and physical closeness. Harlow observed that infant monkeys who did not receive these things showed signs of social impairment, aloofness, aggression, and other atypical behaviors. These monkeys also failed to show nurturing behaviors to any offspring produced. He believed these findings held true in humans.

Mary Ainsworth

Mary Ainsworth (1931–1999) was an American-Canadian psychologist known for her work regarding emotional attachment in infants and the Strange Situation experiment, which looked at the attachment relationships between adults and babies between the ages of nine and eighteen months.

Sigmund Freud

Austrian doctor Sigmund Freud (1856–1839) is known as the founder of **psychoanalysis**, which is essentially aimed at using dialogue and dream interpretation and analysis to help make the unconscious conscious. He devised techniques such as **free association** (uncensored expressions of consciousness), outlined the role the unconscious plays in influencing behavior and the underlying mechanisms of repression, created a personality theory composed of the **id** (instinct), **ego** (reality), and **superego** (morality), postulated the notions of the **libido** (sex drive) and **death drive**, and discovered **transference** (client projection) and **countertransference** (therapist projection). However, along with those contributions, another significant contribution Freud made to the field of psychology was his theory of psychosexual development. Freud's **psychosexual development theory** posited that people move through five stages of sexual development as their lives progress, which includes the oral, anal, phallic, latency, and genital stage.

The **oral** stage is the first stage, starting at eighteen months, where the mouth serves as the infant's primary erogenous zone. The **anal** stage is the second stage, which occurs between eighteen months to three years of age, and where the anus serves as the infant's primary erogenous zone. The **phallic** stage is the third stage, which occurs between ages three to six, and involves the genitals serving as the child's primary erogenous zone. The **latency** stage is the fourth stage, which begins at age five and persists until puberty, and involves the child repressing sexual urges and **sublimating**, or channeling, these unacceptable impulses into constructive actions such as hobbies, schoolwork, and friendships. The **genital stage** is the fifth and final stage, which occurs after puberty, and involves the development of a strong sexual interest.

Daniel Levinson

American psychologist Daniel Levinson (1920–1994) focused his studies on adult subjects to create his **Stage-Crisis View**, in which there are stable periods and transitional periods in life, and suggested stages of development throughout the lifespan:

- Early adult transition: age seventeen to twenty-two
- Entering the adult world: age twenty-two to twenty-eight
- Age thirty transition: age twenty-eight to thirty-three
- Settling down: age thirty-three to forty
- Mid-life transition: age forty to forty-five
- Entering middle adulthood: age forty-five to fifty
- Late adulthood transition: age sixty to sixty-five
- Late adulthood: age sixty-five to eighty

These stages present social conflicts that must be resolved. Levinson also proposed that a midlife crisis is part of a normal, healthy development. The Stage-Crisis View theory was the premise of his renowned text, *The Seasons of a Man's Life*, which examines the feelings, dreams, and behaviors of men throughout their lifespans and how these influence the way a man structures his life.

The Interaction of Nature and Nurture and Social Development in the Determination of Behavior

As people progress through the years, their behavior can be affected by a combination of their genetic makeup and the environment in which they were raised. The nature side of this debate has stated that one's genes will impact their response to a situation regardless of their surrounding environment, which, in turn, affects their behavior, personality, and general perception of the world around them. But on the nurture side of this debate, how and where a person is raised, along with any cultural expectations, are said to influence how one behaves and the personality type they develop.

However, most research shows that genes and environment often interact with each other to influence an organism's growth and development. Most researchers have realized that it is the interaction of one's innate biological factors with their external environmental factors that influences and facilitates human growth and development. Cognitive, behavioral, and emotional advancements that typically occur at certain points in one's life warrant genetically-based changes and experiences in one's social environment. Culture is a prime example of how environment can affect a person's behavior and result in a certain personality type. Along with physical development, social development can also be influenced by one's cultural setting.

In psychology, **social development** describes how people form necessary social and emotional skills throughout the course of their lifespan. Childhood and adolescence tend to be particular areas of focus in one's development. A healthy social development enables people to develop positive relationships with family, friends, and numerous other people they encounter in their lives. As people grow and mature, they learn to become better emotional regulators by managing their feelings and their needs, and by becoming more attune to the feelings and needs of others and responding accordingly. A child's personality, opportunities for socialization, observed learning experiences, and developmental disorders can each affect their social development throughout their lives. For instance, a child who is already quick to anger and bears witness to violent and aggressive behaviors could later end up having a particularly difficult time learning how to appropriately interact with others. Because people living in different

cultures vary in how they perceive themselves and relate to others, they also tend to view things differently.

For example, when explaining a personal experience that stands out to them, European-American children will tend to focus more on details, remember specific events, and emphasize their views on them. However, Asian children will tend to pay more attention to describing everyone they met and how they seemed to relate to them.

How Parenting styles influence Development

There are four primary types of parenting styles. Each of these styles involve parenting in a particular way, which can have different effects on children.

Authoritarian: This type of parenting is all about control. Parents who use this style are mostly concerned with setting rules and ensuring their children abide by the rules. Typically, there is a strict and set punishment procedure as well. Children who are raised under this type of parenting style often have issues with social development and communication. These children often go on to use this type of interactions in their relationships outside of their family.

Uninvolved/Neglectful: This type of parenting style is essentially the opposite of the authoritarian style. These parents hardly parent their children and delegate control and care to secondary caregivers or to the children themselves. Children raised in these type environments often have issues with impulse control, authority, and rule following outside of their homes.

Indulgent/Permissive: This type of parenting style is very loving and involved with the child. However, this approach to parenting does not typically use rules appropriately or set healthy boundaries. Parents using this style are often more concerned with being a friend figure to their children rather than a traditional parent. Children raised in this manner are often very creative; however, they also tend to be entitled with little self-control and act selfishly in their relationships.

Authoritative: This type of parenting style is generally regarded as the most desirable type. Parents using this style of parenting will allow their children increasing levels of independence appropriate for their age. Parents will also have clear cut rules and linked consequences. Children who grow up in these type of households are usually seen with increased self-sufficiency and better social skills and self-control.

Cognitive Development in Childhood

The Maturation of Cognitive Abilities

Piaget's Theory of Cognitive Development

Piaget was the first to systematically study cognitive development. He believed children have a basic cognitive structure and continually restructure cognitive frameworks over time through maturation and experiences.

Some of the key terms in this theory are as follows:

Schema: Introduced by Piaget, a concept or a mental framework that allows a person to understand and organize new information

Assimilation: The way in which an individual understands and incorporates new information into his or her pre-existing cognitive framework (schema)

Accommodation: In contrast to assimilation, involves altering one's pre-existing cognitive framework in order to adjust to new information

Equilibrium: Occurs when a child can successfully assimilate new information

Disequilibrium: Occurs when a child cannot successfully assimilate new information

Equilibration: The mechanism that ensures equilibrium takes place

Piaget also recognized and defined the following **four stages of cognitive development:**

Stage 1: Sensorimotor Stage (birth to age 2)

The infant becomes aware of being an entity separate from the environment.

Object permanence occurs as the baby realizes that people or objects still exist, even if they are out of sight. Object permanence builds a sense of security as the baby learns that though "mommy" has left the room, she will still return. This reduces the fear of abandonment and increases the baby's confidence about the environment.

Stage 2: Pre-operational Stage (age 2 to age 7)

The child moves from being barely verbal to using language to describe people, places, and things.

The child remains egocentric and unable to clearly understand the viewpoint of others.

The process of quantifying and qualifying emerges, and the child can sort, categorize, and analyze in a rough, unpolished form.

Stage 3: Concrete Operational Stage (age 7 to age 11)

The ability to problem solve and reach logical conclusions evolves.

By age 10 or 11, children begin to doubt magical stories, such as the Tooth Fairy or the Easter Bunny.

Previously-held beliefs are questioned.

Stage 4: Formal Operational Stage (age 12 through remaining lifetime)
A. More complex processes can now be assimilated.
B. Egocentrism diminishes.
C. One assimilates and accommodates beliefs that others have needs and feelings too.
D. New schemas are created.
E. The individual seeks his or her niche in life in terms of talents, goals, and preferences.

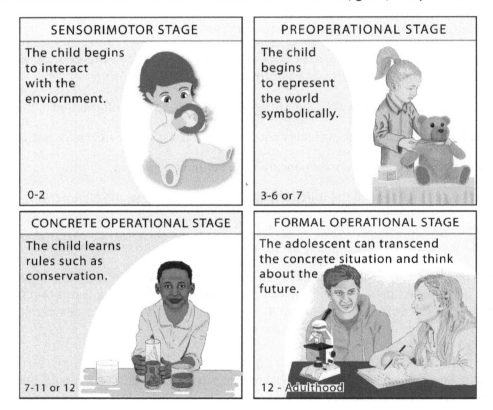

The Contributions of Major Researchers in the Area of Cognitive Development in Childhood

Lev Vygotsky

Soviet developmental psychologist Lev Vygotsky (1896–1934) was the founder of the **sociocultural theory of development**, which posits that mental abilities are shaped by culture and how people in a society interact with one another. Along with this contribution, Vygotsky is also known for devising the concepts of intrapersonal communication and the zone of proximal development.

Intrapersonal communication refers to a communicator's internal use of both language and thought, which encompasses different types of inner speech. Examples of these types include reading aloud and repeating something heard. The **zone of proximal development** describes the difference between what a learner is capable of doing without help and what they are unable to do alone but become able to achieve over time with the proper guidance. This guidance can come from a peer or an adult knowledgeable in certain areas, and through a combination of social interaction and sense-making, develops the ability to work independently. An example of this is a student who initially becomes frustrated when working on multiplication problems alone but becomes better able to perform this task after working with a parent or educator.

Jean Piaget

As mentioned previously, Jean Piaget (1896–1980) was the first to systematically study cognitive development. He believed children have a basic cognitive structure and continually restructure cognitive frameworks over time through maturation and experiences. Piaget's work, which outlined developmental stages, was the first to argue that children's method of thinking varies considerably from that of adults. Piaget's stages demonstrate how he believed children's cognitive abilities change and develop over time, acquiring new skills at every stage. He also argued that intelligence was not set, but develops as a result of both biological and environmental factors. Piaget's theory included the concept of schemas, which can be explained as frameworks or pattern of behaviors in response to a specific stimulus or information.

Gesell

American pediatrician and psychologist Arnold Gesell (1880–1961) conducted longitudinal observational studies over fifty years to produce several theories regarding human development. His **maturationist theory** states that beginning at the fetal stage, individuals will follow set, linear steps of physical and cognitive development. Gesell argued that human development is primarily governed by an individual's genetic makeup. External influences, such as society, parents, siblings, and teachers, are most effective when their actions support the physiological progress that will take place.

Adolescent Development

Maturational Challenges in Adolescence

Adolescence is a period of development in which significant biological, psychological, and social changes take place.

In both sexes, biological changes stem from a shift in hormone production that results in physical growth spurts as well as the further development of sexual and reproductive characteristics. Males experience increased levels of testosterone, resulting in a visible Adam's apple, a voice that is deeper in pitch, an increase in lean muscle mass, the onset of facial hair, and the ability to ejaculate seminal fluid from the penis. Females experience increased levels of estrogen, which encourages fat deposits (e.g., breasts) and a wider hip structure. The increased amount of body fat is necessary for females to begin menstruation, which is a monthly release of an unfertilized egg from one of the two ovaries.

Both sexes also experience in an increase in body hair (although males typically grow more body hair than females), an increase in functioning sweat glands (and therefore body odor), and changes to the cardiovascular system. Due to these biological changes that encourage reproduction, both sexes may feel more desire for the opposite sex and the urge to engage in sexual behaviors. Females tend to experience puberty and maturation first, while males appear to lag some years behind.

A number of cognitive, psychological, and emotional changes also occur. These are also hormone-driven changes. The adolescent brain changes in physical composition and in its use of neural pathways, especially in areas that regulate mood and behavior. Adolescents also experience different interactions in their environment and with their primary peers that affect how their cognition is shaped. Compared to children's brains, adolescent brains are primed to think more critically, hold attention and focus for longer, and have better personal self-control; however, these abilities are not fully developed until the mid- to late-twenties in most people.

Some researchers believe that although increased cognitive abilities related to critical thinking and personal control are present, the social and emotional areas that also influence the outward presentation of these skills develop at a different rate. This imbalance may contribute to the stereotype of adolescent behavior (e.g., emotional, impulsive, moody). It is also believed that the adolescent brain favors high-risk situations and is more motivated by social and cultural reward. This may have an evolutionary basis; seemingly risky situations, such as leaving the family home, interacting with strangers, and seeking new experiences, often lead to a less familial mate who provides more gene variation for higher reproductive fitness. However, these behaviors often come at a high cost in modern society, such as unsafe sex practices that result in disease transmission or teenage pregnancies.

Coupled with the biological changes of adolescence, as well as with cultural norms within specific environments, adolescents may appear to undergo tremendous changes in personality. This can be a rough adjustment for the adolescent's family of origin. Newly-formed cognitive skills, such as critical thinking and the awareness of other perspectives in the world, may contribute to the adolescent questioning or rebelling against family norms and values as the adolescent tries to form their unique identity. It may be difficult for parents to view emotional outbursts or unstable moods, as well as risky behaviors. Adolescents tend to favor the opinions of peers rather than that of family members or elder relatives; trying to balance peer pressure with family values can increase conflicts between parents and adolescents. Through these changes, the adolescent is ultimately preparing for independence and moving away from the family group.

Adulthood and Aging

The Development of Decisions Related to Intimacy as People Mature

Intimacy refers to the closeness between two people. The types of intimacy that people seek out, and even the types of intimacy experienced between the same two people over a long period of time, often shift over the lifespan. As children, humans have deeply personal bonds with their regular caregivers; these relationships influence how people interact in relationships as they age. Beyond caregivers, children may develop close bonds with friends or peer groups in school and experience the intimacy of friendship. The intimacy of friendship is likely to remain as a part of people's lives throughout their lifespan and is an important component of overall well-being. Having intimate friendships allows people to learn how to relate to one another, have shared experiences over common interests, and find community in others. Friendship contributes to a sense of having social support, belonging, and people with whom to experience daily life.

Adolescents often start to seek out **romantic and sexual intimacy**, which allows them to experience physical and loving closeness with another person. Healthy romantic intimacy allows one to be open

with personal desires and fears with another person while knowing the relationship will endure this vulnerability. In young and middle adulthood, people typically strongly desire romantic and sexual intimacy in their lives. They may seek out partners who primarily fulfill only a physical desire or sexual attraction.

As people age further, however, romantic and sexual intimacy tends to become less important than deep and companionate intimacy. **Companionate intimacy** refers to a type of closeness that can last years without being broken down and allows people to share in multiple aspects of life together. In Western cultures, people often seek marriage with the hopes of achieving sexual, romantic, and companionate intimacy in a primary and constant relationship. The ability to build intimacy that lasts through the course of a lifetime is a skill that requires effort from both parties in the relationship. It often requires open and honest communication, physical (although not always sexual) intimacy, and supporting one another through various obstacles and problems. Working on spirituality, participating in a shared hobby, parenting children, and carving out alone time for personal goals can also help strengthen companionate intimacy.

The Physical and Cognitive Changes that Emerge Through the Lifespan

From development within the mother's womb to the latest stages of adulthood, humans experience a number of physical and cognitive changes. The **fetal stage** is the first period of rapid growth and neurological development. A **zygote** begins as the size of a poppy seed, yet quickly undergoes mitosis to become an **embryo** in the second week of pregnancy. By the eighth week of pregnancy, the embryo has grown into a **fetus** with a neural plate. From the preliminary structure of the neural plate until birth, the brain undergoes a remarkable amount of growth in size and function; some studies show that over one hundred billion neurons are formed by the second trimester of pregnancy. **Neural pathways** between these cells begin to develop immediately and are affected by the mother's nutrition, exercise, stress levels, and other environmental factors.

In the two years after birth, babies continue to rapidly grow in size and develop physical strength and coordination. They typically follow established physical and motor milestones, such as holding their heads up, rolling over from back to front and vice-versa, sitting unassisted, crawling, pulling up to a standing position, and walking clumsily. **Cognitive abilities** during this period are supported through both verbal and nonverbal communication from caregivers, such as talking, cooing, reading, singing, eye contact, and facial expressions. Babies may respond positively or negatively based on the type of interaction that occurs.

While temperament does have a large genetic component, many of these early interactions with caregivers can also heavily influence a child's disposition and attachment patterns to others. Babies also learn through sensory and tactile experiences during this age period. Playing with different textures and materials, hearing different types of music, and experiencing different environments teaches infants and toddlers different patterns in the world, cause and effect relationships, and supports neural pathways linked to creativity.

In childhood, cognitive functioning remains influenced by personal experience. Children are able to understand the world immediately around them through their own experience, but often cannot understand that their unique environment is part of a larger system until they reach the pre-teen years. However, cognitive functioning in the areas of memory, information processing, and attention advance throughout the grade school years. **Gross and fine motor skills** are developed through repetitive practice, which continues to be important to maintaining functional mobility through the lifespan.

Compared to these periods of rapid advancements in cognition and physical abilities, it may appear that people begin to slow down in both areas as they reach middle age and late adulthood. However, studies show that many individuals remain alert, focused, and mentally and physically active through middle age and late adulthood. A number of influential factors can support or hinder cognitive and physical health throughout the lifespan. Genetic predispositions to certain neurological disorders, such as dementia or Alzheimer's disease, can result in visible cognitive impairment in adulthood. Lifestyle factors play an incredible role in maintaining cognitive and physical abilities. Recent research links nutrition as a critical factor in brain health.

Medical professionals have often recommended that cognitive function in infants and young children is supported by fatty acid consumption and other dietary fat sources (e.g., omega-3 fatty acids, whole milk), but new research indicates that unsaturated fat consumption also supports brain health in older individuals. On the other hand, highly processed foods containing high levels of fats and sugar are associated with cognitive decline. **Type 3 diabetes** refers to a new category of metabolic disorder linked with Alzheimer's disease and may be exacerbated by these types of foods. Active lifestyles also support brain and physical health, with physical exercise supporting the production of mood and cognition neurotransmitters like **brain-derived neurotrophic factor (BDNF)**, and mental activities such as crosswords and logic puzzles supporting the maintenance of neural pathways. Regularly engaging in novel experiences or learning new information also supports cognitive functioning, while periods of intense stress can cause both acute and long-term cognitive decline.

The Contributions of Key Researchers in the Area of Adulthood and Aging

Erik Erikson

Erik Erikson (1902–1994) proposed a lifespan theory of psychosocial development as an alternative to Freud's psychosexual stages. According to Erikson's epigenetic principle of maturation, human beings pass through eight developmental stages, each of which builds upon the preceding stages and sets the groundwork for the stages that follow.

Erikson's Psychosocial Stages of Development

Stage	Age	Psychosocial Crisis	Basic Virtue
1	Infancy (0 to 1½)	Trust vs. mistrust	Hope
2	Early Childhood (1½ to 3)	Autonomy vs. shame	Will
3	Play Age (3 to 5)	Initiative vs. guilt	Purpose
4	School Age (5 to 12)	Industry vs. inferiority	Competency
5	Adolescence (12 to 18)	Ego identity vs. role confusion	Fidelity
6	Young Adult (18 to 40)	Intimacy vs. isolation	Love
7	Adult hood (40 to 65)	Generativity vs. stagnation	Care
8	Maturity (65+)	Ego integrity vs. despair	Wisdom

All eight stages are present at birth, but remain latent until both an innate schedule and an individual's cultural upbringing cause a stage to begin to unfold.

An individual does not have to "master" a stage to proceed to the next stage, and the outcome of a particular stage may later be changed by an individual's life experiences. As with Freud's theory, Erikson proposed that each stage of development is characterized by a crisis; however, for Erikson, the crisis involves a conflict between the needs of the developing individual and the needs of society. Successfully mastering a stage and its psychosocial crisis leads to the development of a healthy personality and possession of basic virtues.

Erikson's theory centers around the development of ego identity, or a sense of self that is acquired by interacting with the social environment.

Psychosocial Stages

The first stage is **Trust vs. Mistrust**. This stage is centered in infancy (birth to eighteen months). An infant with consistent and stable care will develop a sense of trust that extends beyond the primary caregiver and is necessary for feeling secure in the world and in future relationships. An infant who does not develop trust becomes fearful and sees the world as an unsafe, unpredictable place. Mastery of this stage results in the virtue of **hope.**

The second stage is **Autonomy vs. Shame and Doubt**. This stage occurs during early childhood (eighteen months to three years). The focus of this stage is development of personal control, as the stage typically occurs when young children are beginning to gain motor control, explore the physical environment, and satisfy some of their own basic needs (e.g., by starting to dress themselves, eat independently, and use the toilet). Mastery results in a sense of autonomy; however, if a child's caregiver has expectations that are too high, restricts a toddler's independence, or belittles the child, shame and doubt may develop instead. The virtue acquired during this stage is **will**.

The third stage is **Initiative vs. Guilt.** This stage occurs in the preschool/play age (three to five years). Through play, being active, and planning activities, children in this stage begin taking risks and initiating tasks for specific reasons. Initiative is developed when adults support children's exploration and assist them in making good choices for themselves. Lack of support during this phase may instead cause the child to experience guilt related to his or her wants and needs. The virtue resulting from this stage is **purpose**.

The fourth stage is **Industry vs. Inferiority.** This stage occurs during childhood/school age (five to twelve years). During this stage, teachers and peers play a much larger role in a child's life and social interactions. As cognitive ability increases, children are able to understand more complex concepts, acquire skills such as reading and writing, and begin to form their own opinions and values. Per Erikson's theory, the early school years are essential to a child's sense of self-confidence. If children are encouraged and praised, they learn to take pride in accomplishments and to display industrious, goal-oriented behavior. If they experience discouragement, ridicule, or lack of opportunities for success, they may doubt their own abilities and develop feelings of inferiority. The virtue associated with this stage is **competence.**

The fifth stage is **Identity vs. Role Confusion** (or **Diffusion**). This stage occurs in adolescence (twelve to eighteen years). During the adolescent phase, as their bodies are rapidly maturing, children exert greater independence, often exhibit rebellious behavior, and begin to develop a sense of who they are as human beings. Establishment of ego identity is the crucial task of this developmental stage. If adolescents successfully navigate this stage, they emerge with a sense of self, an understanding of who they want to be, and comfort within their sex role. On the other hand, adolescents who are unable to find a solid sense of self and their place in the society around them may instead experience role confusion. The virtue associated with this stage is **fidelity** (being able to show one's true self to others and to relate to them in a genuine and sincere manner).

The sixth stage is **Intimacy vs. Isolation.** This stage occurs during young adulthood (eighteen to forty years). During this stage, young adults explore relationships and learn to commit to others beyond their immediate family. Erikson proposed that successful ego identity development during adolescence was crucial in order for adults to develop intimate relationships with others successfully during this subsequent stage. The virtue resulting from this stage is **love.**

The seventh stage is **Generativity vs. Stagnation.** This stage occurs in adulthood (forty to sixty-five years). During this stage, individuals turn their focus to family, careers, contributing to the world around them, and guiding the next generation. The virtue resulting from mastery of this stage is **care.**

The eighth stage is **Integrity vs. Despair.** This stage occurs during maturity (sixty-five years or older). Older adulthood is a time of existential reflection. Erikson proposed that looking back upon accomplishments and finding meaning in one's life results in satisfaction and ego integrity. Alternatively, those who are dissatisfied with their past may experience despair and regret. The virtue associated with this stage is **wisdom.**

Moral Development

The Contributions of Major Researchers in the Area of Moral Development

Lawrence Kohlberg

Lawrence Kohlberg (1927–1987), an American psychologist, is known for his work examining how people develop morals. His theory of moral development stated that individuals progress sequentially through three levels, each with two stages. Moral development tends to begin in the preschool to young childhood age range.

Preconventional Morality

The first level, preconventional morality, is when individuals are influenced by reward and punishment.

> Stage 1: Orientation to obedience and punishment: Children act as prescribed by a figure of authority.

> Stage 2: Individualism and exchange: Children begin to understand that there are gray areas to "right" and "wrong."

Conventional Morality

The second level, conventional morality, occurs when individuals behave morally to win external approval by peers or society and to cultivate positive relationships.

> Stage 3: Good relationships: Individuals seek to gain approval from others.

> Stage 4: Maintaining social order: Moral behavior is determined by social and cultural law, legal obligations, and one's sense of duty.

Postconventional Morality

The third level, postconventional morality, occurs when individuals engage in abstract thinking and development of personal moral principles.

> Stage 5: Social contract and individual rights: Individuals act in a way that considers society and its welfare, rather than maintaining a singular motivation of self-interest as the basis for moral behavior.

> Stage 6: Universal principles: Moral thinking is influenced by respecting universal justice for all people.

Kohlberg believed that one could not progress to a stage without mastering the one before it and that many never reach stages five or six.

Carol Gilligan

Carol Gilligan (1936–) was a student and researcher of Lawrence Kohlberg. Gilligan argued that women underwent completely different personal and social experiences from men to shape their moral standings, and that Kohlberg only considered men's experiences when he developed his theories.

Comparing and Contrasting Models of Moral Development

Psychologists Erik Eriksson, Jean Piaget, and Lawrence Kohlberg provided the most well-known models relating to moral development. Eriksson's and Piaget's models focused more on social and emotional development, but also emphasized how intricately these phases influence a person's concept of morality. Eriksson and Piaget proposed their models in the 1930s. In the late 1950s, Kohlberg built off these ideas (especially Piaget's theories) to develop his widely accepted six stages of moral development.

As previously described, Eriksson proposed an eight-stage theory of emotional development that focused on how people develop emotions based on interactions that occur in their environment. He especially highlighted interactions with parents and caregivers as formative in the development of such as trust and distrust, autonomy and shame, initiative and guilt, industry and inferiority, and secure identity and identity confusion. Based on personal experience and upbringing, people likely develop one or the other of each pairing throughout their childhoods. More complex emotional pairings, such as intimacy and isolation, generativity and stagnation, and purpose and despair, come through in later years as people find mates, have children, take on careers, and have other experiences that contribute to their sense of self. Through these learned behaviors, people determine subjective moral and ethical ways to behave based on their personal narrative and the situation at hand.

Piaget focused on cognitive development as a determinant of behavior and decision making. His stages of development center on what the brain is capable of logically understanding through different periods of the lifespan, thus driving choice and behavior. Piaget believed that these capabilities are roughly the same across cultures during the same periods of the lifespan (e.g., a two-year-old living in a remote East Asian village will have roughly the same cognitive abilities as a two-year-old living in a Western metropolis) and that people advance through the same stages in order: a **sensorimotor stage**, where the person learns through sensory interactions; a **preoperational stage**, where the person begins to think through symbols and use language to better understand the world; a **concrete operational stage**, where the person becomes more logical and rational but is limited to concrete experiences; and finally, a **formal operational stage** where the person is able to theorize, hypothesize, and come to conclusions without a concrete experience.

Through each of these stages, people make moral and ethical decisions based on what their brain is capable of perceiving, understanding, and rationalizing. For example, a young child in the sensorimotor stage may throw a block at a caregiver simply to see what happens to the block. They do not realize this might cause pain to the caregiver. An adult in the formal operational stage would preemptively realize that throwing an object at another person could cause pain, and their choice to throw the object may provide information about their personal moral beliefs.

Kohlberg theorized that morality varied across age ranges; consequently, the **age ranges** associated with each of his stages of development are not absolute. In the first two stages, obedience and self-interest, people learn to obey commands in order to avoid negative experiences in their own self-interest. The next two stages, conformity and order, are stages in which people learn how to act within their society. These conventions and norms give rise to what a person may believe to be moral and ethical traditions. In the final stages of social contract orientation and universal human ethics, people understand and abide their own beliefs of what is moral and ethical rather than abiding by society or authority rules. Kohlberg believes not all people reach these stages, often as a result of the parameters of the society in which they live. Ultimately, Kohlberg utilized both environmental experiences and personal cognition as influential factors that work in tandem to shape a person's moral development.

Gender and Sexual Orientation

How Sex and Gender Influence Socialization and Other Aspects of Development

Sex refers to the biological characteristics of an individual, whereas **gender** refers to the personal identity or social role given to the individual. Two primary sexes exist: the **male sex**, characterized by an *xy* chromosome that gives rise to reproductive organs such as the testes, penis, and urethra, and the **female sex,** characterized by an *xx* chromosome that gives rise to reproductive organs such as the ovaries, uterus, and vagina. Genders may be male, female, or a number of other identifiers that vary by culture and society. Societies in which male and female genders are the two primary norms are known as **gender binary systems**, and socialization based on gender norms often factors into individual development. Gender socialization can be quite engrained in culture as a result of history, rituals, practices, portrayals in mainstream media, and other social behaviors.

Gender socialization may present as early as during the prenatal period. For example, friends and relatives may give expecting parents certain types of gifts based solely on the sex of the child (e.g., pink clothes for girls, blue clothes for boys). These types of norms can continue into childhood, adolescence, and adulthood, even though evidence-based research indicates that there is minimal biological (apart from reproductive processes) and cognitive difference between the two sexes. These types of norms may condition each sex to behave in a way that they believe to be socially acceptable. Yet, some of these norms can be restrictive and even harmful, contributing to centuries of inequalities in schooling, work opportunities, and social liberties.

For example, women could not vote in the United States until the early 1900s and were rarely seen in high-ranking professional positions until recent decades. Additionally, research shows that women are often overlooked in professions that pay higher and sometimes even discouraged from pursuing coursework that leads to such professions. Men, on the other hand, have long accepted cultural norms

of appearing tough and without softer emotions, which can be detrimental to their mental health and interpersonal relationships that are critical for overall well-being.

Unit 7: Motivation, Emotion, and Personality

Theories of Motivation

Basic Motivational Concepts

Motivation, a psychological construct, is the direction and intensity of an individual's effort. There are several forms of motivation including intrinsic and extrinsic motivation, achievement motivation, and motivation associated with skill development. It should be noted that individuals generally experience more than one type of motivation, and these can vary depending on the activity being performed, perceptions of competency, the level of importance the individual places on the activity, in addition to other factors.

The behavior of all living organisms is driven by **motivation**, which refers to the reasons why an organism acts the way that it does. Most types of motivation stem from the need to uphold the organism's own survival or that of their offspring, although some theories (such as **Maslow's Hierarchy of Needs**) suggest that more complex organisms, such as humans, may act in ways to fulfill a larger purpose or personal meaning.

Instincts

The **instinct theory of motivation** states that organisms are motivated primarily by survival, and all organisms are born with innate abilities and urges that drive behavior. These behaviors are not learned; the organism simply knows what to do in order to survive. For example, all infants will display "rooting" behavior, in which they seek out a bottle or breast nipple in order to feed. Nearly all babies, if they feel sensation near their cheek or mouth, will turn their mouth toward the sensation and instinctively begin to suck. This supports the feeding relationship with a caregiver and ensures the infant's survival. Various animals are also born with natural survival instincts. Psychologist Konrad Lorenz is well known for discovering the concept of **imprinting**, which describes how many animals attach to a parent or location immediately upon birth. Many behaviors associated with mating, such as courting rituals, are also believed to be instinctive across animals. Protecting the younger members of a group is also considered an instinctive behavior across animal species.

Incentives

Incentives are rewards or things (tangible or intangible) that are attractive to someone. For example, trophies or medals for winning a race, or the personal satisfaction of running one's fastest marathon time can be attractive incentives. **Incentive theory** posits that people are motivated to behave the way they do based on rewards. This can be applied for both getting a behavior to occur or extinguishing it. In order for this premise to work, the reward has to be attractive to the individual and realistic/possible. If there is no way that the person can realistically get the reward, then they will not be motivated to engage in the behavior. A weakness of this theory is that it often is not applied successfully to groups, as a reward for one person may not hold universal attraction to others.

Intrinsic Versus Extrinsic Motivation

Intrinsic motivation is an individual's internal desire for his or her behavior to be competent and self-determined. It originates from the person's love and interest in the activity and personal satisfaction (i.e., inherent reward) in performing it. Intrinsic motivation is generally considered the best form of

motivation. Intrinsic motivation can help one maintain focus on achieving short-term goals that require consistent effort.

Extrinsic motivation, used extensively in sports and careers, comes from external sources (e.g., coaches, teammates, managers) in the form of individualized rewards such as praise from coaches and supervisors, bonuses or raises, social acceptance, avoidance of punishment, and the desire for positive reinforcement.

Over-Justification Effect

Many behaviors are motivated by the possibility of receiving an external incentive or reward. For example, a new college graduate who finds thrill in solving complex problems may seek out a challenging job that inherently comes with high compensation. The **over-justification effect** occurs when initial intrinsic motivation declines upon receipt of the external incentive or reward. In the example of the ambitious college graduate, the graduate may lose the internal motivation to work at the same challenging pace after receiving a few large paychecks. This phenomenon may occur as a result of shifting one's focus to the reward (e.g., the paycheck) rather than embracing and enjoying what the initial motivation was (e.g., the thrill of solving a problem). One way to possibly diminish the over-justification effect is to provide external rewards only when the behavior is performed well or at an established standard. In the case of the ambitious college graduate, the graduate is more likely to remain intrinsically motivated on the job if the compensation package is tied to high performance and productivity.

Self-Efficacy

Self-efficacy is a concept that was first theorized by psychologist Albert Bandura. The term refers to one's confidence in one's own abilities to complete specific tasks, especially those that impact one's own life and experiences. Feelings of high self-efficacy in relation to a particular task is associated with higher levels of motivation to complete the task. As a result, shaping self-efficacy is often a component of behavior change interventions, as someone who believes they are capable of changing a behavior is more likely to be motivated to go through the steps of behavior change.

Studies indicate that even small increases in feelings of self-efficacy increase one's motivation in completing a task. For example, a person who is trying to increase their vegetable intake may be more motivated to stick with a nutrition plan if they successfully learn how to prepare three easy meals that are plant-based. Self-efficacy is also highly correlated with resiliency in the face of stressors as well as with self-confidence. Stronger senses of self-efficacy can be developed through setting feasible but challenging goals and incrementally mastering the steps needed to achieve each goal, seeking role models that one relates to who have achieved a desired goal, and developing a personal introspection and mindfulness practice to support bouncing back from failures.

Achievement Motivation

Achievement motivation reflects an individual's effort to master a specific task, attain excellence, perform better than others, and overcome obstacles. There are two types of achievement motivation. The **motive to achieve success** (MAS) is characterized by a desire to challenge and evaluate one's ability and be proud of accomplishments. People with greater MAS like challenging situations, where the likelihood of success or failure is approximately the same. The **motive to avoid failure** (MAF) is characterized by the desire to avoid being perceived as a failure, preserve one's ego and self-confidence, and minimize shame. People with greater MAF prefer either easy situations where they will likely succeed and avoid shame or difficult situations where success is unlikely and feelings of shame are minimized. In the athletic arena, athletes with high levels of achievement motivation are more competitive and generally perform better than athletes with lower levels of achievement motivation.

Comparing and Contrasting Motivational Theories

Drive Reduction Theory
Drive reduction theory was developed by Clark Hull. Essentially, the theory is that the drive or motivation behind any behavior is an attempt to create homeostasis. When an internal system is imbalanced in some way, the person is driven to behave in such a way that would restore equilibrium to the imbalanced system. For example, if someone is hungry, they will be driven to eat. Drive reduction theory set the path for many research experiments. The strength of the theory is that it explains the motivation to meet basic physiological needs. The weakness is the fact that the theory cannot be generalized to motivations that are not biologically based or arousal reducing (for example, eating when not hungry or pursuing a hobby simply for leisure).

Arousal Theory
According to arousal theory, everyone has a different optimal level of arousal, under which they perform best. This theory attempts to explain why some people engage in higher-risk behaviors than others (ex. sky diving, race car driving). Operating at someone's ideal arousal state involves striking a balance between being under-aroused (too calm or blasé), and being too anxious and amped up. This concept speaks to **Yerkes-Dodson law**, which is an empirical relationship between one's state of arousal and his or her performance. Performance suffers at states of hypo- or hyperarousal. If someone is too aroused, then they may seek out activities to lower their arousal state. These will typically be things that are considered to be relaxing. Alternately, if someone is very under aroused, then they will seek out activities that will lead them to a higher arousal state. A weakness of this theory is that it fails to explain more complex social activities.

Evolutionary Theory of Motivation
The premise behind the evolutionary theory of motivation, or **instinct theory**, is that humans have a biological predisposition to behave in certain ways that will aid in their survival. An example of this would be the way an infant instinctively roots for a breast when hungry. This theory is broken down into three areas: behavior, perception, and emotion. The strength of instinct theory is that it can explain certain behaviors that are common amongst animals and humans. The weaknesses are that this theory cannot explain every behavior and it is very difficult to observe or assess scientifically.

Maslow's Theory
Maslow's Hierarchy of Needs states that there are certain basic needs that must be met in order before one can get to the higher more abstract needs. These needs are presented in a pyramid with the needs going from most basic at the wide base to the least essential at the peak with the categories of physiological, safety, love/belonging, esteem, and self-actualization. The idea is that until someone's lowest, basic needs are being met, they are not going to be motivated to reach higher levels of need. The issues with this theory are that it cannot be easily tested and does not take into account the differences of individuals. The theory, however, is intuitive.

Cognitive Dissonance Theory
Cognitive dissonance refers to mental discomfort that occurs when two competing sets of values or behaviors exist in the same context. The **cognitive dissonance theory of motivation** refers to instances in which a discrepancy exists between a person's beliefs and behaviors. For example, a relatively

wealthy person who volunteers to support people who live in poverty may feel discomfort at enjoying and possessing luxurious material items in their personal life. Cognitive dissonance is commonly seen in people who want to change personal health behaviors. For example, a woman who has heart disease may know that she should reduce her consumption of processed foods, yet she does not.

There are often environmental or social factors at play that lead to feelings of cognitive dissonance. In general, mental discomfort can be relieved by taking steps that minimize the dissonance. In the case of the wealthy volunteer, for example, the volunteer may minimize personal spending and instead donate those funds to a reputable poverty charity. Other methods may reduce the cognitive dissonance for the person, yet still remain detrimental to the person's overall well-being. This often comes in the form of justification or rationalizing that relieves the dissonance. In the example of the woman with heart disease who consumes too much processed food, she may rationalize the behavior by saying there is no time to cook healthy meals after work. This may temporarily relieve the dissonance, yet it does not address the root cause of the health issue.

Classic Research Findings in Specific Motivations

Eating

Eating is a behavior that is necessary in order to receive nutrients to keep the body and its systems functioning. The motivation to eat is driven through feelings of hunger, which are regulated by various hormones, as well as through learned cues. From a physiological perspective, the hormones ghrelin and leptin control feelings of hunger and satiety in the body. **Ghrelin** is released into the blood stream in order to stimulate appetite, whereas **leptin** is released to signal feelings of fullness. In healthy individuals, these work in tandem to maintain an optimal level of energy stores in the body. Some studies indicate that these hormones may not work effectively or the system does not respond appropriately to them in individuals with hormonal imbalances and metabolic disorders. Additionally, some foods such as refined sugars and highly processed additives affect the reward centers of the brain and induce cravings for more of the same or similar foods. Comparatively, some neuroimaging studies of patients with eating disorders show that their brains ignore hunger and satiety cues found in healthy individuals.

Across most cultures, eating is also tied to emotions and learned behaviors. Food is used in celebration, such as the ritual of cutting and eating cake to mark birthdays. It is also used in times of comfort. Consider illness and funerals, two events in which a common social practice is to take prepared meals to the family in support. Research also shows that people are who are depressed or chronically sleep-deprived may seek foods high in carbohydrates and sugars to stimulate the reward centers of the brain or to address energy shortages. Additionally, eating can occur out of habit or conditioning. For example, a person whose office has a lunch break at noon each day may feel hunger around noon over the weekends, even at home. People who snack while watching television may feel hungry every time they sit down to watch a show, even if they have just eaten a full meal.

Sex

Sex is a behavior that is necessary for reproduction to occur but is also pursued for intimacy and pleasure. People are motivated to have sex through feelings of desire, which have hormonal and learned bases. During puberty, the phase when reproductive systems in the human body become further developed, people may experience an increase in sexual motivation and the physical desire to have sex. As both sexes are capable of reproduction at this stage, these urges likely have an evolutionary basis that supports survival of the species. Hormone therapy, medications, nutrition, hormone disorders, and

congenital disorders can impact the hormonal cycles that trigger the onset of puberty, as well as sexual drive and the ability to reproduce.

Sexual motivation is also largely driven by cognitive and psychological impulses. Some neuroimaging studies show that damage to areas of the limbic system of the brain can reduce sexual motivation; however, people that have damage to reproductive organs and cannot physically have sex can still feel strong sexual urges. Finally, learned behaviors and personal experience with sexual interactions in childhood and young adulthood often strongly influence one's personal sexual motivations.

Social
Socializing behavior supports survival through community connection and support. **Social motivation** refers to people's desire to connect and engage with others, and for neurotypical individuals, this type of connection is critical for overall well-being. From an evolutionary standpoint, surviving successfully without social support is rare; people rely on one another for different strengths, intellectual stimulation, emotional connection, as partners for reproduction, to barter assets, and to have a sense of belonging and purpose. Specific social motivators are subjective, largely dependent on an individual's personality and needs in life.

For example, an introverted person may generally prefer to spend time alone but will socialize with work colleagues or mentors in order to keep a job that provides their primary income for living. A single person who wants to enter a romantic relationship may be socially motivated to interact with others who could be a good partner for multiple reasons (e.g., similar values, opinions on child-raising, shared cultural beliefs); whereas a happily married individual may socialize with others over a single shared hobby. New research findings, although preliminary, indicate that neurologically atypical individuals may have vastly different social motivation systems. For example, autism spectrum disorders have largely been studied from a cognitive basis, but preliminary research shows that differences in social motivation may significantly contribute to behaviors associated with the spectrum.

Contributions of Key Researchers in the Psychological Field of Motivation and Emotion

William James
William James (1842–1910) is considered the father of American Psychology. James was the founder of functionalism and co-wrote the *James-Lange Theory of Emotion*, which states that emotions come about as answers to events. People have a response to an event that is physiological in nature. Then they interpret that event, which spurs the emotional response.

Alfred Kinsey
Alfred Kinsey (1894–1956) is well known for his extensive research in the field of sexual behavior. He is known for founding the Institute for Research in Sex, Gender, and Reproduction. Kinsey also wrote two books about sexual behavior in both males and females. These books became known collectively as the "Kinsey Reports." Kinsey also came up with the Kinsey Scale, which is a heterosexual-homosexual rating scale.

Abraham Maslow

Abraham Maslow (1908–1970) developed Maslow's Hierarchy of Needs. This states that a person will not be motivated to work toward higher level needs until his or her basic needs are met. Maslow also co-founded the *Journal of Humanistic Psychology*. In his later years, Maslow pondered why some people do not go on to seek fulfillment of higher-level needs once their basic needs are met.

Stanley Schachter

Stanley Schachter (1922–1997) was a co-founder of the **Two Factor Theory of Emotion**. This theory states there are two parts to emotion: physiological arousal and cognitive label. Schachter also conducted studies on obesity.

Hans Selye

Hans Selye (1907–1982) developed the **General Adaptation Syndrome (GAS)**, which considers how our bodies respond to and handle stress.

Specific Topics in Motivation

The Biological Underpinnings of Motivation

Abraham Maslow is the most notable researcher in the area of basic human needs. As mentioned, **Maslow's Hierarchy of Needs** from his 1943 work *A Theory of Human Motivation*, is a theory typically depicted as a pyramid, with the most fundamental needs forming the base. Maslow proposed that people are motivated to meet their most basic needs before turning their attention to the fulfillment of more advanced needs.

Maslow theorized that human needs could be described in the form of a pyramid, with the base of the pyramid representing the most basic needs and the higher layers representing loftier goals and needs. Unless the basic needs are met, a person cannot move on to higher needs. For example, a homeless woman living under a bridge will need food, shelter, and safety before she can consider dealing with her alcoholism. The foundational layer in Maslow's hierarchy is physiological needs, and the final layer at the pinnacle of the pyramid is self-transcendence.

Maslow's Hierarchy of Needs

Maslow's Hierarchy of Needs

Physiological Needs: These needs must be met first and pertain to what humans need to survive. These include basics, such as food, water, clothing, and housing.

Safety Needs: Once primary needs are met, the person may now focus on safety issues, including safety from abuse and neglect, natural disaster, or war.

Love and Belonging: Once the first levels of needs have been satisfied, people are next driven to find a sense of acceptance and belonging within social groups, such as family, community, or religious organizations. Maslow suggests that humans have a basic need for love, affection, and sexual intimacy. Failure to achieve this level can lead to difficulty in forming and maintaining close relationships with others.

Esteem: The need for esteem is driven by a desire for recognition, respect, and acceptance within a social context.

Self-Actualization: The U.S. Army slogan, "Be All You Can Be," expresses this layer of need. Reaching one's highest potential is the focus. According to Maslow, this cannot be achieved until all the other needs are mastered.

Self-Transcendence: This level was devised by Maslow in his later years because he felt that self-actualization did not completely satisfy his image of a person reaching his or her highest potential. To achieve self-transcendence, one must commit to a goal that is outside of oneself, such as practicing altruism or finding a deeper level of spirituality.

Some human motivators are more biologically based and others are more strongly influenced by sociocultural factors, although biology and environment play a role in both. Biological factors involved in hunger motivation include the lateral and ventromedial areas of the hypothalamus, metabolic rate, and glucose levels. However, hunger is also influenced by social factors such as body perception and cultural customs around food. Sex drive, though powerfully influenced by the biology of hormones such as testosterone and progesterone, is also motivated by social constructs and social norms for sexual behavior. Substance addiction includes both biological and sociocultural motivation, as it impacts a person physically, psychologically, and socially.

Theories of Emotion

Comparing and Contrasting Major Theories of Emotion

Emotion is a state of mind or instinctive feeling that is derived from the situation or mood that a person is in.

James–Lange Theory
The **James-Lange theory of emotion** proposes that emotions are felt in response to bodily changes that are already occurring. It is the body's response to a stimulus that triggers the emotional response. For example, the hair on the back of a person's neck stands up before the feeling of fear is processed in the brain and then physically experienced with awareness.

Cannon–Bard Theory
The **Cannon-Bard theory** proposes that the role of emotion is to help a person deal with changes in the environment. It focuses on the connection between emotion and the autonomic nervous system, which comprises the sympathetic nervous system and the parasympathetic nervous system. The sympathetic nervous system makes changes such as increasing heart rate, increasing breathing rate, and causing reflex actions, and the parasympathetic nervous system works at a slower rate to dampen or inhibit physiological responses. The Cannon-Bard theory proposes that the brain is oversees which emotion is an appropriate response to the stimulus that is being processed. The cerebral cortex simultaneously decides on the emotion and activates the sympathetic nervous system so that the body is ready for an immediate response once the decision is made.

Schachter Two-Factor Theory
There are two parts to the **Schachter-Singer theory of emotion:** the physiological arousal and the cognitive label. The theory proposes that when an emotion is experienced, a physiological change is felt first. Then, the person searches the environment for clues to help identify the cause of the physiological change and label the emotion. Identification of emotion in this manner can lead to misinterpretation of the feelings a person is experiencing, which is a realistic scenario.

Evolutionary Theories
Primary emotions occur directly as a result of a specific event. They typically occur as an immediate response, rather than secondary emotions that result after a period of thought and analysis. Primary emotions often motivate behaviors that ensure survival. These emotions may be considered instinctual or intuitive. From an evolutionary perspective, it is believed that primary emotions are derived from the brain's limbic system. Physician Paul Maclean is best known for identifying the limbic system and explaining its evolution over time. The **limbic system** appears to be the oldest structure in the brain; it produces emotion as a physiological response to external stimuli. In turn, this motivates the human

being to act in a specific way that fulfills a basic survival need such as food, water, shelter, or reproduction.

For example, a nomadic tribe member would need to remain highly alert to threats such as predators; fear would motivate this tribe member's sympathetic nervous system to enter a "fight or flight" mode quickly in the event of danger. The limbic system is also associated with learning and memory; therefore, it teaches the body to respond in habitual patterns to external stimuli. In contemporary times, it is believed the limbic system produces emotions to different stressors that are not necessarily "fight or flight" situations (e.g., traffic, work deadlines) and may create unhealthy stress conditions in the body. People who have experienced trauma likely have altered states of appropriate primary emotional response. Evolutionary psychologists view human behavior as a direct result of biological influences resulting from evolution and natural selection. Based on the initial work of Charles Darwin, this field of psychology asserts that behavior is internally driven by mechanisms meant to protect survival and reproduction.

Charles Darwin's work on evolution and natural selection set the foundation for biopsychology. Traits, like sexual drive and emotions, have developed as a result of evolution and natural selection in order to facilitate the survival of the human species. Darwin's work supported his theory that animals and humans descended from a single ancestor and that both shared a significant number of genes. The discovery of this genetic commonality not only led to comparative psychology or utilizing animal studies to learn more about humans, but it also set the stage to study how genetics and biology affect and drive behavior.

Richard Lazarus's Appraisal Theory

Richard Lazarus's appraisal theory states that people take inventory of a situation or environment in which they are in, and this appraisal then causes emotions. Lazarus's theory states that because every person's perspective about a situation is going to be different based on personality, personal experience, and other factors that influence judgment, events will cause different emotions subjective to the people who are appraising them. For example, a combat veteran might appraise an amusement park and find it to be crowded and noisy. This appraisal may create a heightened sense of fear or alertness based on their personal experience of war. Meanwhile, a young child who has no history of trauma may arrive to the amusement park and feel a sense of anticipation and joy at the various sights and sounds. Lazarus based his theory on the earlier research of Magda Arnold. The appraisal theory is met with some controversy, as a number of other researchers believe physiological arousal precedes an emotional response.

Joseph LeDoux's Theory

Joseph LeDoux's theory focuses on the link between emotions as a response to fear or danger. LeDoux's research shows that the brain has specific learning pathways that activate in response to fear, and that stored "threat memories" play a role in producing emotions relating to fear. This type of "threat conditioning," in which the amygdala plays a large role, may influence certain types of emotional and mood disorders, such as anxiety, paranoia, or phobia. LeDoux's research indicates that therapies that disrupt a person's conditional fear response can be especially useful in patients who have experienced trauma and therefore have dysfunctional threat conditioning. Additionally, LeDoux's theory focuses on how a person who is experiencing the fear response transitions from simply experiencing fear to the response. People experience intense fear in response to triggers that retrieve the initial threat memory, and this can cause a sense of decision or action paralysis during their fear experience. This can keep them in a constant mental loop of feeling fear when a true danger is not present. Working with the

conditioning of this response circuit can aid patients with anxiety and other fear-related disorders move into using healthier, action-oriented coping tools.

Paul Ekman's Research on Cross-Cultural Displays of Emotion

Paul Ekman is a renowned psychologist and pioneer in research relating to emotion. Much of his work focuses on nonverbal signals of emotion, including body cues and facial expressions. Ekman studied the facial muscle movements that result in outward expression, identifying thousands of facial muscle movements that are linked to emotion. **Micro-expressions**, or facial movements that last for a fraction of a second, can be the most revealing part of emotional expression.

Ekman is most famously known for identifying emotions that appear to exist universally across cultures, even in isolated tribal cultures that did not have access to rituals or media outside of their immediate community. His six universal emotions are fear, anger, disgust, joy, loneliness, and surprise. Ekman also determined that although universal emotions were expressed through the same neural circuitry and facial musculature across cultures, subjective cultural and social norms impacted how emotions were expressed. For example, in cultures where positivity and group harmony were idealized, people who felt anger would employ additional facial expressions to shield the emotion when other members from their community were present. Finally, Ekman worked intensively in the field of deception. His research contributed to a better understanding of the social influences that lead people to deceive others, as well as the expressions and body language that indicate someone is lying.

Facial Feedback Hypothesis

The basis for the **facial feedback hypothesis** was originally proposed by Charles Darwin. It states that physiological cues by the body serve as causal factors to emotion. Further, Darwin hypothesized that even thinking about certain emotional situations would elicit an emotional response; on the other hand, softening one's facial cues would also soften the emotional response. Psychologist William James expanded on this hypothesis to suggest that becoming aware of physical and physiological changes in the body are what ultimately cause a person's emotional response.

Modern researchers developed these ideas further by testing facial feedback responses with participants. For example, participants would view images or experience events that were intended to cause a specific emotion but were asked to consciously soften or intensify facial muscle movements. While these trials did show some evidence to support the facial feedback hypothesis, it remains difficult to prove. Subjects always begin trials with some degree of understanding about the process, often due to ethics requirements and due to participants generally understanding what the study was focusing on during the trials. Subjects' facial emotions are also strongly influenced when they know they are being observed; this is simply a part of human conditioning. These obstacles create bias in the findings.

How Cultural Influences Shape Emotional Expression

Three Components of Emotion

There are three components of emotion. The **cognitive** part of emotion is how a person experiences the emotion and verbally describes how they are feeling. The **physiological** part is the part of emotion that is expressed through bodily responses, such as tears that come when a person feels sad. The **behavioral** component is how a person's actions change in response to an emotion. For example, a person may become defensive in response to a threat.

Universal Emotions

There are six emotions that are universally recognized in all cultures: fear, anger, happiness or joy, surprise, disgust, and sadness. Each has a distinct facial expression and physiological response associated with it as well.

Fear: A feeling induced by perceived danger or threat

Anger: A strong emotional response to a perception of threat, hurt, or provocation

Happiness or **Joy:** A feeling of great pleasure and positive emotions

Surprise: A feeling of astonishment from something unexpected

Disgust: A feeling of repulsion in response to something unpleasant or offensive

Sadness: An emotional pain associated with a feeling of loss, helplessness, or disappointment

Adaptive Role of Emotion

Emotions cause humans to be adaptive and respond to how they are feeling. They provide motivation for action and change. For example, if a person does not study and ends up doing poorly on a test, he or she feels sad. This sadness motivates the person to study more for the next test in order to avoid feeling sad again. The same motivation exists for feelings of happiness—activities that elicit feelings of pleasure are likely to be pursued and repeated. Charles Darwin believed that the adaptive nature of emotions allowed humans to survive and reproduce in line with his theory of natural selection.

The Role of Biological Processes in Perceiving Emotion

Brain Regions Involved in the Generation and Experience of Emotions

Different regions of the brain are activated by the generation and experience of different emotions. The **amygdala** is responsible for intense affective emotions, such as love and fear. They **hypothalamus** is involved with the feelings of both pleasure and rage. The **cingulate gyrus** is a part of the brain that coordinates present sights and smells with previous emotions. It also regulates feelings of aggression.

The Role of the Limbic System in Emotion

The **limbic system** is a complex set of structures in the brain, including the hypothalamus, hippocampus, and amygdala, among others. It is involved in the recognition of emotion and the formation of emotional memories. Although each structure of the complex system is responsible for a different part of the emotion-eliciting process, the whole system works together as one to connect the cognitive, physiological, and behavioral components of emotions.

Emotion and the Autonomic Nervous System

The generation, recognition, expression, and experience of emotion are largely mediated by the autonomic nervous system. There are two types of patterned activity that are exhibited by the autonomic nervous system in response to emotions: coherence and specificity. **Coherence** is the organization and coordination of activity within the autonomic nervous system as well as between the autonomic nervous system and other response systems, such as facial expressions and cognitive emotional experience. **Specificity** is the idea that each emotion activates a different response and activity from the autonomic nervous system.

Physiological Markers of Emotion

Changes in the autonomic nervous system are the most obvious physiological signs of emotion. This system controls the smooth muscle, cardiac muscle, and glands in the body and mediates increases and decreases in heart rate, increased and decreased blood flow to the face, which results in blushing or turning pale, and sweating, among many other things.

Stress and Coping

Theories of Stress and the Effects of Stress on Psychological and Physical Well-Being

Stress is the emotional strain that a person feels from circumstances that are demanding or that do not provide assurance of a positive outcome.

The Nature of Stress
Appraisal

An **appraisal** is an evaluation of what is happening between a person and the environment around them. Appraisals establish a person's feelings towards a situation and help determine the amount of stress involved. The **primary appraisal** is the first assessment of whether or not the situation is harmful to a person's well-being. The **secondary appraisal** follows the primary appraisal and is an evaluation of the options and resources available for coping with the situation. A person experiences stress when the available resources are not enough to completely manage or cope with the situation.

Different Types of Stressors

A **stressor** is an event that causes a person to experience feelings of stress. The three main types of stressors are cataclysmic events, personal stressors, and chronic stressors. **Cataclysmic events** occur suddenly and involve many people, such as earthquakes or mass transit accidents. **Personal stressors** are events that cause personal life changes, such as the loss of a job or death of a family member. These events usually cause an immediate, emotional reaction that tapers off over time. In some cases, however, a personal stressor may cause a person to experience post-traumatic stress disorder (PTSD), which has long-term effects, such as nightmares and flashbacks. **Chronic stressors** are events that occur often, sometimes daily, such as getting stuck in traffic or working long hours. These stressors are often small but can summate over time and negatively affect a person's well-being.

Effects of Stress on Psychological Functions

The ability to cope with stress is an important part of maintaining a person's state of good health. Stress can affect a person's immune system and increase one's susceptibility to illness. Chronic stress, coupled with a lack of effective coping mechanisms, can also affect a person's psychological state and lead to depression and anxiety. Chronic stressors persist over a long time and require a person's body to cope on a daily basis. The body's energy stores get depleted faster as well. These physiological effects impair a person's psychological state over time and do not allow them to function normally.

Stress Outcomes
Physiological

The physiological response of the body to stress is often referred to as a **fight-or-flight response**. The stress stimuli cause a chain of chemical and hormonal reactions in the body that will either prepare a person to fight the stressor or flee from the stressor to avoid any harm. The body increases production of both adrenaline and cortisol. **Adrenaline** keeps the body in a state of readiness; it increases a person's heart rate and causes some muscles to tighten. **Cortisol** helps the body get ready to deal with stressor as well, as helps it return to a normal state after the situation is over. It first helps to increase production of blood sugar to provide the body with extra energy and then helps the blood sugar level return to normal. Cortisol also regulates the acidic/alkaline balance of the body.

Emotional

When a person has appropriate coping resources, small amounts of stress can help motivate them to take action or make a change. The emotional response can be positive and stimulating. Prolonged stress, on the other hand, can take a toll on a person's emotional well-being. The body's hormonal and chemical response to stressors is very fast. When the response lasts too long or becomes too intense, the byproducts of the hormones and chemicals can become sedative-like and cause a person to feel fatigued. The feelings of low self-confidence can often become part of a pattern when the same stressors are encountered repeatedly, which can eventually lead to depression.

Behavioral

Stress affects a person's behavior in two stages: the short-term and the long-term. Following the idea that stressful stimuli cause the body to prepare itself for either fight or flight, in the short-term, the brain starts to automate some habitual behaviors. For example, while under stress, a person may take the milk out of the refrigerator several times after they have already poured themselves a glass. The brain focuses in on preparing the body for the stressful situation. In the long-term, the body may feel the effects of the overproduced stress hormones by being over-stimulated or under-stimulated. Over-stimulation may cause a person to be ill-tempered. It can cause people to grind their teeth or bite their nails and may affect appetite. Under-stimulation may cause a person to feel a loss of energy that inhibits motivation and daily functioning and may lead to a feeling of being burnt out.

Managing Stress

There are many things that people can do to manage the stress that they feel. First, it is important to identify the stressors. Acute stressors are often easier to identify than chronic stressors. Stress is a part of daily life and having appropriate coping mechanisms can help people maintain their healthy physical and emotional well-being. Exercising is a positive way to manage stress. Physical activity releases endorphins that make a person feel good and elevate their mood. It helps to distract a person from the stress in their life and reduces tension and frustration. The maximum benefit comes from exercising for at least thirty minutes in order to feel the effects of the endorphins, elevate the heart rate, and relieve stress.

Stress also causes a person's muscles to tighten as part of the fight-or-flight response. Relaxation can help loosen the muscles and relieve stress. Stretching, massages, and getting a good night's sleep can all help to ease the tension in muscles. Deep breathing is also a quick way of relaxing the muscles and getting some relief from stress.

Spirituality is a broader form of stress relief. It includes the development of a personal value system, connecting with oneself, and searching for more meaning in life. While in many cases spirituality is connected to a religion, it can also be found with a connection to nature, music, or art, among many other things. It helps a person feel a sense of purpose in their community and in the world, which can help relieve mental anxiety about smaller stressors in life.

General Adaptation Theory

General Adaptation Syndrome (GAS) establishes that there are three stages that prepare the body to handle danger when encountering a stressful situation. The first stage is alarm. This stage occurs after the dangerous situation is introduced. During this stage, cortisol and epinephrine are released by the body. This is when the body prepares for fight or flight. The second stage of GAS is resistance. In this stage, the body tries to restore homeostasis and fight the physiological changes that have occurred since the dangerous situation was introduced. Exhaustion is the final stage. During this stage, the resources have decreased and if the stress continues, then the body will continue to debilitate.

Stress-Related Illnesses

Short periods of stress (e.g., exercise, problem solving) can be beneficial for the mind and body, but prolonged periods of stress are linked to chronic health illnesses. When the body experiences stress, it activates the **sympathetic nervous system (SNS)**. The SNS is part of the nervous system and responsible for creating response behaviors relating to fighting or fleeing the stressor. These response behaviors include increased stress hormone production, extended periods of muscle contraction, and heightened inflammatory response. During prolonged periods of stress, the SNS remains activated.

The **parasympathetic nervous system (PNS)**, the part of the nervous system that is responsible for rest, recovery, digestion, immunity, and other normal body processes, becomes suppressed. Over time, this can lead to immune system disorders, gastrointestinal disorders, cardiovascular disorders, mood disorders, musculoskeletal disorders, and sleep disorders. Illnesses directly linked with chronic stress include autoimmune diseases, depression, anxiety, heart disease, dementia, and ulcers. People who frequently experience stress or are under chronic stress also experience higher incidences of back, neck, and shoulder pain, as well as a higher incidence of acute illnesses like the common cold. They are also less likely to benefit from preventative measures such as vaccinations, simply due to the immune system remaining in a constantly weakened state.

Lewin's Motivational Conflicts Theory

Kurt Lewin's motivational conflicts theory focuses on how people manage approaching or avoiding certain situations, and the conflicts these can cause. It is typically used in the context of how people are motivated to interact with situations in which there are both positive aspects (that would motivate them to approach the situation) and negative aspects (that would motivate them to avoid the situation). For example, consider a new father who has been offered a major promotion at work. However, the new role requires extensive weekly travel. This father is likely to feel motivational conflict at taking a new job that would provide more income for his family but would require him to be away from the family often.

Lewin also stated that people might feel conflict when faced with two different, albeit positive, pathways. For example, a woman who receives two job offers that she loves may experience motivational conflict about which job to accept in the end. Both situations will ultimately benefit her, but she will have to eventually choose to avoid one in order to approach the other. Finally, people may have to pick between two negative experiences. They may want to avoid both but are required to eventually approach one. For example, a teenager who hates doing chores may have to choose between doing the family dishes each week or folding the family laundry each week. They may not want to do either but will have to pick one in order to avoid conflict in the family system.

Unhealthy Behaviors

In response to stress, people often turn to coping behaviors to soothe their central nervous system. Some of these often cause short-term periods of stress relief but ultimately cause additional health issues or prolong the stress cycle. Common unhealthy behaviors related to stress coping include smoking cigarettes and drinking alcohol. Often, people begin these behaviors as a way to escape the stressor. Smoking provides a physical activity to engage in away from the situation, while alcohol serves as a physiological depressant. Over time, withdrawal from these substances (even in people who only socially smoke or drink) can cause a physiological stress response that causes cravings for the substance in order to relieve the stress response. In the long term, chronic smoking or drinking alcohol can cause a host of health issues, including addiction, cancer, cardiovascular disease, liver disease, lung disease, and depression. People may also turn to recreational drugs to cope with stress, which causes the same cycle of addiction and may have a higher fatality rate.

Unhealthy eating behaviors are also linked to stress coping. Foods that are high in fat and sugar reward areas of the brain that regulate dopamine production and mood; people often crave these kinds of food in response to stress and fatigue. Food also holds a psychological comfort for many people; they may associate certain foods with comfort and relaxation and use these foods to cope. Foods that are high in fat and sugar cause system inflammation in the body, cravings and withdrawal behaviors akin to addiction, metabolic disorders, and obesity. People may also control intake of food during times of high stress if they feel they are unable to control the stressful aspects of their lives. Controlling and limiting food intake can result in extreme weight loss, malnutrition, obsessive compulsive disorders, and eating disorders.

Introduction to Personality

Describing and Comparing Research Methods that Psychologists Use to Investigate Personality

Case Studies
Case studies may be used to examine the personality traits, behaviors, and interactions of people who have been categorized in some way. For example, they are often used to observe and document behaviors in people who are from the same demographic (e.g., children) or who have a specific type of personality disorder. Theories regarding temperament and attachment primarily emerged as the result of numerous case studies that observed interactions between infants and young children and their caregivers.

Case studies can also help researchers investigate the influence that a particular environment or context has on the way someone's personality emerges. For example, a researcher may observe the behaviors of an introverted person in a quiet, empty setting such as a library in the evening, and then compare this person's behaviors in a loud, crowded setting such as a night club. The ability to compare in-depth observation notes with various contextual factors allows researchers to better understand subjective, multi-causal topics like personality. Because personality often emerges as a result of genetic components, environmental components, and personal history, case studies allow researchers to examine these components in individuals and then compare themes across various observations.

Surveys
Surveys are an important quantitative self-reporting mechanism that can be utilized to investigate personality and traits related to personality. They can be used to collect and analyze traits about the individual, as well as collect personal opinions and values, which allows researchers to collect a broad range of personality data from a single subject. Surveys are an easy measurement tool to distribute to participants and to collect results, especially in today's digital era.

A number of online survey software programs will email participants, analyze responses, and track trends, which can save time for the researcher. Researchers should note that personality traits are a sensitive topic, and survey respondents may worry about judgment when answering surveys that contain questions about their personal traits. Therefore, personality surveys may be subject to bias, as respondents may answer in ways that do not truly reflect facts about them and opinions they hold. Bias may be stronger during interview surveys, rather than paper surveys; paper surveys may provide a stronger appearance of confidentiality. Therefore, paper survey methods may provide more accurate results when trying to collect information relating to personality.

Personalities Inventories

Personality inventories are often taken by participants in order to better understand different aspects of oneself. They are often contextualized for specific scenarios, and therefore should match the end goal of a participant. For example, a participant who is struggling with mental health concerns may take a variety of personality inventories to collect trends relating to potential pathologies. Common inventories that indicate pathologies include the **Minnesota Multiphasic Personality Inventory (MMPI)** and the **Personality Assessment Inventory**.

Personality inventories are used more often in clinical settings to make diagnoses, as compared to **personality surveys**, which are more likely to collect broad swaths of data for information purposes. Personality inventories are also commonly used when making a decision that is likely to have a long-term impact. For example, an employer may administer a comprehensive personality inventory, such as the **Myers-Briggs Type Indicator**, when interviewing a job candidate to make sure the candidate is a good cultural fit for the organization and for the roles and responsibilities of the job. These types of personality inventories provide an overview of someone's traits, likes, dislikes, and preferences, rather than point to pathological diagnoses, to provide information about how someone may act in a specific environment.

The Contributions of Major Researchers in Personality Theory

Alfred Adler

Alfred Adler (1870–1937), an Austrian medical doctor and psychotherapist, is known for establishing the school of individual psychology and for work on the inferiority complex and how it shapes personality. Alfred Adler believed that birth order, as well as other sibling contexts, played a major role in how an individual's personality was shaped. He attributed traits to each child relative to when they were born in comparison to their other living siblings, and he attributed traits to only children, twins, adopted children, and children born after the death of an older sibling. Additionally, he felt that if all siblings were of the same sex, this context would hold a specific influence toward each sibling. Children who were the only one of a given sex among a group of siblings of the opposite sex (e.g., the only sister in a group of brothers) would be influenced by their sibling context as well.

Albert Bandura

Albert Bandura (1925–) was an American psychologist who theorized that learning takes place socially through observation and imitation of others and that not all behaviors are conditioned.

Paul Costa and Robert McCrae

Psychologists Paul Costa (1942–) and Robert McCrae (1949–) are known for their intensive research on personality traits, personality changes across aging, and the development of the Five Factor model. The **Five Factor model** accounts for five initial traits (later revised to six traits) that make up the personality.

These are neuroticism, extraversion, openness to experience, agreeableness, and conscientiousness. These traits appear to be influenced by genetics, culture, and stage of life. For example, adolescents typically score high in extraversion, but most adults move closer toward the introversion side of the spectrum (even if they are still an extraverted individual). Almost all people move toward agreeableness and conscientiousness as they age. Regardless, most people's score along each trait stabilizes, with slight fluctuations, by adulthood. Scoring high or low in certain traits does not indicate a pathology; the scoring spectrum of each trait is simply used to provide information about someone's personality. This model has upheld vigorous testing across cultures and retroactively across various time periods. Costa and Mcrae also developed a widely used personality assessment, known as the **NEO personality inventory**, based on the five factors. The latest revision took place in 2010.

Sigmund Freud

Sigmund Freud (1856–1839) is best known for pioneering the field of psychoanalysis. He utilized the technique of **free association** in his patients, during which he encouraged patients to talk freely about concerns, memories, and especially dreams that they could remember. Freud believed dreams held insights from the subconscious and unconscious minds that were repressed fears, desires, or events that were causing pathologies. Much of Freud's work focused on a person's relationship with and memories of sex; he believed that neuroses and other mental disorders did not present unless the patient had a repressed sexual memory or sexual trauma. Freud also posited psychoanalytic ideas that focused on psychosexual development in both sexes, and introduced the concepts of the id, the ego, and the superego as the three primary components of the human psyche.

The **id** represents base desires, the **superego** represents extreme morality, and the **ego** tries to manage the polar opposite desires of both. While many of Freud's psychoanalytic theories have declined in popularity in modern times, he was a pivotal thought leader in the early 1900s. Some of his other concepts, such as repression, the influence of early childhood memories on personality, and the insights available from the subconscious, remain important parts of modern therapeutic interventions.

Carl Jung

Carl Jung (1875–1961) pioneered **analytical psychology**. Jung is well known for developing the concepts of **archetypes** and **archetypical images**, which represent collective, universal, and recurring themes across societies through a variety of images and ideas in cultural mediums. Jung is also known for first introducing the personality concepts of **introversion**, referring to people who prefer quiet environments, limited stimuli, and find energy in solo activities, and **extraversion**, referring to people who prefer more sensory input and find energy when among groups. Other key concepts that Jung proposed include **synchronization**, or the presence of related yet unexpected coincidences, and **individuation**, or the way each individual must find, determine, and pursue their path to personal fulfillment.

Many of Jung's theories can be seen in ancient texts, as he studied a number of stories and religious texts to derive themes that led to his ideas of individuation. He believed that spiritual practices could strongly support, and even eliminate, psychological ailments such as depression or addiction. Jung's theories continue to drive a number of business management and organizational development practices, and New Age spirituality. His ideas are seen in popular art and literary media, and his archetypes serve as the foundation of the popular Myers-Brigg Personality Indicator.

Abraham Maslow

Abraham Maslow (1908–1970) is best known for pioneering **humanistic psychology**, a field focused on how people develop, pursue, and achieve their highest talents and potential. Humanistic psychology was unique at the time of its inception; most fields of psychology focused on pathologies, while the humanistic field focused on personal development and success.

Maslow is also renowned for establishing **Maslow's Hierarchy of Needs**, a theory which ranks personal human needs over the course of a lifetime. The Hierarchy is depicted in a pyramid shape; a person must achieve a stage before moving on to the next step in the hierarchy. The stages, in order, include basic needs, such as food, water, and shelter; safety and security needs, such as income and employment; love and belonging needs, such as friendship, family, and romantic love; self-esteem needs, such as confidence, accomplishments, and sense of self; and finally, self-actualization. **Self-actualization** encompasses all activities that contribute to personal meaning and personal purpose on the Earth. According to Maslow, reaching this stage is the ultimate goal for human beings; without achieving self-actualization, people may always struggle with internal existential conflicts. However, he also believed that many people never achieve the true stages of self-esteem and self-actualization.

Carl Rogers

Carl Rogers (1902–1987) expanded the ideas of humanistic psychology to include the influence of a person's environment on their path to self-actualization. While he also believed all people ultimately want to achieve self-actualization, he felt that the presence of environments and systems that supported people's development and well-being (e.g., nurturing school environments, meaningful relationships) were critical for success. Rogers believed that the key factors that supported personal growth included genuineness, acceptance, and empathy from the social systems around the individual.

He also stated the idea that everyone's journey to self-actualization will look different because everyone's definition of self-actualization will be different. Rogers posited that self-actualization takes place when one becomes clear about what they believe to be their ideal self; when this ideal aligns with the person's self-concept, then self-actualization has occurred. Rogers also felt that early childhood experiences were key to this process. Negative experiences, especially those that contributed to negative self-esteem or self-concept, would muddle one's path to self-actualization. He also established an idea of the **fully functioning person**, with traits such as open-mindedness, creativity, sense of trust in self, creativity, and general fulfillment in life. This concept has been met with some criticism by other researchers, saying it often does not translate across cultures.

Psychoanalytic Theories of Personality

Comparing and Contrasting the Psychoanalytic Theories of Personality with Other Theories of Personality

There are several noted theories as to how personality is formed. In 400 B.C.E., Hippocrates attempted to identify personalities based on four temperaments. He called these **humors**, and these were associated with body fluid presence, such as phlegm or bile.

In the 1940s, William Sheldon came up with his body type theories that included the **endomorph**—an overweight or short and stocky individual, with an easy-going personality; the **mesomorph**—a muscular person, with an aggressive personality; and the **ectomorph**—a thin and lanky individual, with an artistic or intellectual personality.

Freud's Theory

Freud believed the personality was composed of the id, the ego and superego. The **id** refers to a person's unconscious, with its suppressed desires and unresolved conflicts, whereas the **ego** and **superego** are more influenced by the conscious mind. He believed that these three components were often in conflict with one another and that how one resolved these conflicts determined personality. He also stressed the importance of childhood experience in personality development.

Freud also focused on human development, especially relating to sexuality. Freud theorized that each stage of human development is characterized by a sexual focus on a different bodily area (**erogenous zone**), which can serve as a source of either pleasure or frustration. He believed that **libido** (psychosexual energy) is the determinant of behavior during each of five fixed stages, and that if a developing child experiences frustration during one of these stages, a resulting **fixation** (or lingering focus) on that stage will occur.

To understand Freud's developmental stages fully, one must also understand his conceptualization of the human personality.

Freud describes three levels of the mind as follows:

> **Consciousness:** the part of the mind that holds accessible and current thoughts

> **Pre-consciousness:** the area that holds thoughts that can be accessed by memory

> **Unconscious:** where the mind motivates behaviors, and contains thoughts, feelings, and impulses that are not easily accessible

Freud believed that the personality, or **psyche**, consists of three parts called the **Psychic Apparatus**, each of which develops at a different time.

Id

The **id** is the most basic and primitive part of the human psyche, based on instincts and all of the biological aspects of a person's being. An infant's personality consists only of the id, as the other aspects have not yet developed. The id is entirely unconscious and operates on the pleasure principle, seeking immediate gratification of every urge. It has two instincts: a death instinct called **thanatos** and a survival instinct called **eros**. The energy from eros is called the **libido.**

Ego

The **ego** is the second personality component that begins to develop over the first few years of life. The ego is responsible for meeting the needs of id in a socially-acceptable, realistic manner. Unlike the id, the ego operates on the reality principle, which allows it to consider pros and cons, to have awareness that other people have feelings, and to delay gratification when necessary.

Super Ego

The **super ego** is the final personality component, developed by about age five. The super ego is essentially a person's internal moral system or sense of right and wrong. The super ego suppresses the instincts and urges of the id, but also attempts to convince the ego to act idealistically, rather than realistically.

In a healthy personality, there is balance between the three personality components. The individual has **ego strength**—the ability to function well in the world despite the conflicting pressures that the id and super ego place upon the ego.

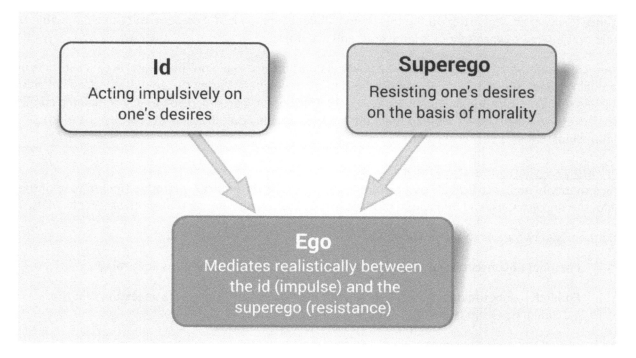

Five Stages of Psychosexual Development

Oral Stage (Birth to Eighteen Months): The infant satisfies its libido by feeding and by exploring the environment, primarily by putting objects in its mouth. The id dominates the oral stage of development, and every action an infant undertakes is guided by the pleasure principle. The key task of this phase is weaning from the breast, which also results in the infant's first experience of loss. Too much or too little focus on oral gratification at this stage was theorized to lead to an oral fixation and an immature personality. Examples of an oral fixation were believed to be excessive eating, drinking, or smoking.

Anal Stage (Eighteen Months to Three Years): The key task of this stage is toilet training, which causes a conflict between the id (which wants immediate gratification of the urge to eliminate waste) and the ego (which requires delay of gratification necessary to use the toilet). A positive experience with toilet training was believed to lead to a sense of competence that continues into adulthood. Anal-retentive personality results from overly-strict toilet training, characterized by rigid and obsessive thinking. Likewise, anal-expulsive personality results from a lax approach to toilet training, characterized by disorganization and messiness.

Phallic Stage (Three to Six Years): The libidinal focus during this stage is on the genital area, and it is during this stage that children learn to differentiate between males and females. The Oedipus and Electra complexes are a component of the phallic stage of psychosexual stages of development, occurring between three and five years of age. Freud believed that, in this stage, individuals become aware of differences in anatomy and social characteristics between the two genders. The **Oedipus Complex** develops during this stage; Freud believed that a young boy views his father as a rival for his mother's attention and the boy may want to eliminate his father in order to take his place. Similar to the Oedipus Complex, the **Electra Complex** says that a young girl may view her mother as her rival. Freud

also believed that girls experience penis envy. The key task of this stage is identification with the same-sex parent, and Freud believed these complexes resolved themselves when the young child took on the characteristics of the same-sex parent and therefore further developed aspects of their identity.

Latency (Six years to Puberty): During this period, libidinal energy is still present, but the child is able to direct that energy toward school, friendships, and activities.

Genital Stage (Puberty to Adulthood): The libidinal focus is once again on the genital area (as it is during the phallic stage), but at this point, the psyche is more developed. During the genital stage, an individual achieves sexual maturation, becomes independent of his or her parents, resolves any remaining conflict from the earlier stages, and is able to function as a responsible adult in terms of both work and relationships.

Carl Jung's Psychoanalytic Theory

Jung's theory is similar to Freud's psychoanalytic theory, with differences related to the purpose of the libido, the unconscious, and behavioral motives. Libido is a psychic energy that motivates individuals.

Jung theorized two parts to the unconscious:

Personal unconscious: contains information not accessible to the conscious mind

Collective unconscious (transpersonal): the memories from a person's ancestors that the individual has from birth

Jung identified this collective unconscious into four main archetypes.

Persona: the artificial self that individuals show to the world to hide who they really are

Anima/Animas: the masculine qualities that women express to society and the feminine qualities that men express to society

Shadow: similar to Freud's id, signifies raw needs and desires

Self: the unconscious and conscious mind come together to form a unified whole; occurs as a consequence of individuation

Object Relations Theory was developed as an offshoot of Freud's theory. Melanie Klein is the person most closely associated with Object Relations Theory. In this theory, **object** typically refers to a person; thus, the theory is concerned with relationships between people, and it particularly emphasizes the relationship between the mother and child. A basic idea is that all people are driven to develop relationships with others, and failure in early interpersonal relationships causes later dysfunction.

- **External object:** a person, thing, or place
- **Internal object:** one's idea or mental representation of an actual object

Behaviorism and Social Cognitive Theories of Personality

Comparing and Contrasting the Behaviorist and Social Cognitive Theories of Personality with Other Theories of Personality

Behaviorist theories of personality focus primarily on how a person learns to behave, and that behaviors are heavily influenced by the environment with which a person interacts. Psychologists who employ behaviorist methods focus on actions of an individual that can be directly observed rather than what is self-reported by the individual. Well-known behaviorists include John Watson, Albert Bandura, and B. F. Skinner. Watson is considered the pioneer of **behaviorism**. He focused on the way people react to situations and environments but did not place importance on cognitive and mental responses. In general, he believed cognitive, mental, and some emotional responses could not be observed and documented; therefore, they could not be accurately studied as a part of personality.

He also believed that fear, anger, and love were emotions that people were born with, but their outward manifestation only occurred as a result of learned, conditioned behavior. Skinner is best known for the concept of operant conditioning. **Operant conditioning** refers to a process in which behavior is learned through positive or negative reinforcements, as well as positive or negative punishments. **Positive reinforcements** provide a reward for a behavior, while **negative reinforcements** remove an unpleasant stimulus in response to a behavior; both mechanisms create more of the initial behavior. **Positive punishments** add a disciplinary action that reduces a behavior, while **negative punishments** remove a desired stimulus to reduce a behavior. Bandura agreed with the conditioning mechanisms utilized by other behaviorists but believed that behavior was also learned based on interactions with others. He expanded traditional behaviorist theories to include a social cognitive component, stating that behavior is often learned through imitating and modeling influences in a person's environment.

Other fields of personality psychology rely heavily on **self-report**, whether that information is verbally provided during a counseling session or provided through a written assessment. For example, psychotherapists ask clients to report on early childhood memories or situational feelings. This information is then used to assess different aspects of behavior and influence behavior change. **Psychodynamic theories** rely heavily on an individual's subconscious and unconscious mind, including components such as repressed early childhood memories or dream states. Most behaviorists, however, did not believe that early childhood experiences played a major role in personality development. Instead, they believed that personality was fluid over the lifespan; it shifted based on the different environments that someone experienced. Behaviorism also does not focus on the role of consciousness, or other introspective components, in personality development in the way utilized by other fields of psychology.

Humanistic Theories of Personality

Comparing and Contrasting Humanistic Theories of Personality With Other Theories of Personality

Carl Rogers was a proponent of the **humanistic theory** of personality development. This approach emphasized self-perception and a desire for striving to become the best person one can become. His theory was based on the basic goodness and potential of each person.

The humanistic school of thought focuses on individuals reaching their full potential and viewing a person as a whole, not as solely governed by internal drives or external forces. The humanist perspective views human behavior in terms of choices that are influenced by a combination of factors including the environment, biology and physical and emotional factors. Humanistic theories focus on people's subjective views and experiences, not on objective and measurable experimentation. Due to this subjectivity, the humanistic theory and its interventions are not as reliably tested by the scientific method as some other perspectives, like behaviorism. Abraham Maslow, with his Hierarchy of Human Needs, is one of the major contributors to humanism.

Carl Rogers was also considered a leader in the development of humanism. Rogers introduced the person-centered approach. This approach was influenced by Maslow's concept of self-actualization, but expanded on it by adding that having a supportive and encouraging environment is crucial for a person to achieve growth and self-actualization.

How Cultural Context Can Facilitate or Constrain Personality Development

Research from psychological studies and anthropological studies indicate that culture plays an influential role on personality development and self-concept. Although individuals grow up with unique experiences with a culture, the shared norms and rituals experienced throughout the lifespan can provide similarities in personality across a group of people who grew up in the same society. Personality differences between members from two different cultural societies may be quite outwardly visible.

Additionally, culture influences the personal values, goals, and consequently behaviors, of individuals in the society; this plays a role in the way a person's self-concept develops. For example, gender roles often arise from cultural norms, yet some of these behaviors inadvertently end up being attributed to personality rather than an external influence. Recent research indicates that while some personality traits are genetic, cultural and social influences play a strong role in the way someone develops self-concept, self-esteem, contextual behaviors, and how they outwardly reflect aspects of personality.

Collectivistic Versus Individualistic Cultures

Collectivistic cultures, most commonly seen in Eastern countries, Latin countries, Caribbean countries, and African countries, focus on the goals of a group (e.g., a social community, a family, a work team). These group goals take priority over individual needs and desires. Collectivistic cultures value community, families, social relationships, and bettering the society as a whole. Individualistic cultures, most commonly seen in Western countries, prioritize personal needs over group needs. These cultures value traits such as power, assertiveness, and independence.

People who come from a collectivistic society are more likely to develop self-concepts that are integrated with that of others, such as their role in the family or in the communities to which they belong. They are more likely to attribute successes to the group rather than take credit personally, even in initiatives they personally lead. People who grow up in **individualistic societies**, however, may describe themselves in terms that relate to their individual interests, goals, or profession. They may seem more competitive or emphasize personal accomplishments in conversation.

Trait Theories of Personality

Comparing and Contrasting Trait Theories of Personality with Other Theories of Personality

Gordon Allport developed the trait theory of personality development. He believed that certain personalities were comprised of clusters of traits and that these traits could be categorized into cardinal, central, and secondary traits.

Holland's Theory and Hexagon

Holland developed a theory in which personality was the basic factor in career choice. He created the **Vocational Preference Inventory** and **Self-Directed Search (SDS)** to assess traits and match them with specific occupations. He believed that individuals want careers with like-minded others of similar personalities. Most individuals fall into at least one of six personality types, depicted by a hexagon, which shows the correlation between jobs and personality traits.

Holland's Six Personality Types

Realistic types enjoy working with their hands: building, fixing, assembling, and operating tools and equipment. People with these personalities can enjoy working outdoors. Occupations of interest include engineer, mechanic, pilot, electrician, computer technologist, sportsperson, and park ranger.

Investigative types enjoy problem-solving, research, and discovery. People with these personalities like to observe, investigate, and experiment. Investigative individuals have excellent analytical, communication, and calculation skills. They can be best suited for careers in science, which include medical, health, and research occupations.

Artistic types express themselves through art, music, drama, and creative design. They enjoy performing, singing, dancing, planning, and presenting. Occupations of interest include artist, illustrator, fashion designer, photographer, and musician.

Social types like working with people. These personalities enjoy meeting new people, teaching, training, and coaching. They are skilled at treating others (as in a health setting) as well as providing care and support. Careers of interest can include athletic trainer, nurse, counselor, social worker, and dental hygienist.

Enterprising types like to meet people and enjoy working in business. They like talking, leading people, influencing, and encouraging others. People with these personalities are skilled at organizing, planning, developing, selling, promoting, and persuading. Careers of interest include lawyer, accountant, promoter, entrepreneur, manager, and business owner.

Conventional types like working with data and numbers. They enjoy accuracy, organization, and clear procedures. Conventional types are skilled at tasks that require orientation to detail. They excel at recordkeeping, handling money, working independently, and organization. Occupations of interest include librarian, office worker, bank clerk, and computer operator.

Measuring Personality

Personality Assessment Strategies and Their Reliability and Validity

While **personality** seems like a highly subjective, multifactorial concept, psychologists have developed ways to quantitatively and qualitatively assess various aspects of personality. Personality assessment instruments are most commonly used to identify pathologies or disorders, provide knowledge or understanding in order to support a client's personal or professional goals, or collect anthropological information about a sample population. Evidence-based instruments are valid and reliable, meaning that they measure what they are supposed to measure and produce consistent findings across multiple instances of testing.

Personality Inventories

Personality inventories are most commonly used by career counselors and other career professionals (e.g., human resource managers) to determine information about an individual's preferences, values, attitudes, beliefs, strengths, weaknesses, and social interactions. However, some personality inventories are also used in clinical settings to determine pathologies. Personality inventories are designed as objective measurement instruments, meaning that they are largely free from researcher bias. Inventories typically collect a broad range of information and aim to quantify the data collected. However, the results may still be biased if the participant taking the inventory does not answer honestly. Because aspects of personality can be a sensitive subject, participants may feel hesitant answering all items with complete candor, especially if they feel like the results may not be completely anonymous or confidential. Commonly used personality inventories include the **Myers-Briggs Type Indicator**, the **Minnesota Multiphasic Personality Inventory,** and the **16PF**.

Projective tests

Projective tests are those that collect data that are interpreted by the administering practitioner. Consequently, these types of tests are more prone to researcher bias than more objective personality inventories. Often, the practitioner who administers these tests has an established relationship with the patient or client; they can use the additional knowledge that they have (e.g., childhood experiences, medical history) as part of the final analysis. Projective tests typically aim to study people's subconscious and unconscious psyches. They are commonly used by practitioners in psychodynamic fields. The **Rorschach inkblot test** is a well-known projective measure. In this test, the client views various inkblots and provides an interpretation of what they see. The **Thematic Apperception Test** is another widely used projective measure that asks the client to view vague pictures and provide a background story. It is believed that the answers that clients give to seemingly featureless images provides valuable insight into various aspects of their personalities, subconscious beliefs, or unconscious memories.

Unit 8: Clinical Psychology

Introduction to Psychological Disorders

Psychological disorders can be difficult to define because they are based on determining what qualifies as normal or abnormal behavior. Psychological disorders are characterized by behaviors that are not only abnormal, but are maladaptive, distressing to the individual and disruptive to daily functioning.

The *Diagnostic and Statistical Manual of Mental Disorders (DSM)*

Psychological disorders are classified using the *Diagnostic and Statistical Manual of Mental Disorders, 5th Edition (DSM-V)*, which is published by the American Psychiatric Association. It is the primary reference used to make diagnoses pertaining to psychological disorders and conditions. Within this manual, the various disorders are listed and the diagnostic criteria are provided. The DSM is periodically updated to integrate new research findings, and the newest edition was released in May, 2013. The DSM-5 includes several broad categories of psychological disorders, including mood disorders, dissociative disorders, anxiety disorders, and personality disorders.

Contemporary and Historical Conceptions of What Constitutes Psychological Disorders

The perception of what constitutes psychological disorders has varied widely over time. As the human understanding of different mental conditions has advanced, clinical diagnostic assessments also changed. Ancient texts and documentation indicate that mental disorders have always existed; however, the physiological factors were not well understood. As a result, ancient civilizations branded psychological disorders as supernatural experiences or a manifestation of religious evil. The idea that psychological disorders may have some basis in physiology was popularized by Greek and Roman philosophers, included Plato and Aristotle, although the physician Hippocrates first began treating patients with psychological disorders in the same way he treated patients with physical symptoms.

Behaviors that are not part of a society's norm have often been deemed as a psychological disorder. For example, sexual orientation and preferences that fell outside heteronormative behaviors were classified as psychological disorders. Homosexuality was classified as a disorder in the DSM until the late 1980s, and patients were often subjected to debasing methods of treatment. Even as the evidence base around psychological disorders grows, patients remain stigmatized as they have throughout history. In the eighteenth and nineteenth centuries in the United States, patients with mental disorders were often isolated, against their will, in unsanitary institutions and subjected to inhumane treatments and care. Women, especially, were poorly treated when showing symptoms of mood disorders that were often related to hormonal changes or imbalances.

While various federal policies advocating for mental health research, education, and services have been passed in the United States since the 1940s, the associated social stigmas have been slow to change. In developing countries, mental health disorders such as depression or schizophrenia often still lead to isolation within the community, as people fear the patient is contagious, cursed, or has been possessed by a supernatural force of evil.

The Intersection Between Psychology and the Legal System

Confidentiality

The field of psychology and the legal system have a clear overlap. Not only can practitioners support the legal system in cases, but the legal system also has laws in place for practitioners to follow. Psychological disorders may lead to deviant, and even illegal, behavior. A number of notorious criminals have been eventually diagnosed with some form of psychological disorder. Mental health assessments have become an integral part of the United States legal system when evaluating criminal cases and passing sentencing judgments. Forensic psychology is a field in which a practitioner evaluates crime scenes and develops a psychological profile of the criminal in order to create a reliable list of potential suspects. Additionally, individuals with mental illnesses have some legal protections in place so that lesser crimes are judged and sentenced appropriately.

Confidentiality

Confidentiality is an important part of the practitioner-client relationship. The **Health Insurance Portability and Accountability Act of 1996 (HIPAA)** protects an adult individual's health information, including mental health visits and treatments. With the client's verbal permission, the practitioner may share information about the client's diagnosis and treatment plan (e.g., with family members or employers). If the practitioner deems that the client is not sound of mind to make appropriate decisions, the practitioner may share necessary information without the client's consent. Typically, this may occur if the client makes statements that indicate they may commit harm to themselves or to others.

Additionally, if a client who has been receiving mental health treatments commits a crime and is undergoing due process in court, the judge may require that the practitioner shares information about the patient. In these cases, the practitioner should only share limited information that is directly relevant to the case. In general, direct, and comprehensive notes from client therapy sessions should never be shared with family or court systems; rather, a relevant overview or expert testimony provided by the practitioner is sufficient. Wrongful or excessive disclosure may result in legal claims against the practitioner.

Insanity Defense

In the court, the **insanity defense** is in support of a defendant who has been accused of a crime. The insanity defense provides a statement that the alleged crime was committed directly as a result of a psychiatric illness or other reason that results in impaired mental judgment. Insanity defenses generally only apply to the defendant's mental health state at the time of the alleged crime; the defendant often has to undergo additional assessment to determine if they are competent to stand a trial. If a defendant is found not guilty as a result of an insanity defense, they are often mandated to undergo extensive psychiatric rehabilitation. Often, this rehabilitation period lasts longer than a prison sentence for the crime would. Pleading an insanity defense often requires expert testimony from clinicians and practitioners in the mental health field. This defense is considered controversial, with some states refusing to allow it in their courts. As a defense, it is used in less than one percent of trials in the United States.

Psychological Perspectives and Etiology of Disorders

In the United States, approximately 20-25% of the adult population struggles with some type of mental disorder in a given year. The rate of serious psychological disorders is less, at roughly 4-8%. The United

States has a high rate of mental disorders compared to other countries. Anxiety disorders are the most common type of psychological disorder, followed by mood disorders.

The Strengths and Limitations of Various Approaches to Explaining Psychological Disorders

As mentioned, clinicians in the United States currently utilizes the fifth edition of the **Diagnostic and Statistical Manual (DSM-V)** in categorizing and diagnosing psychological disorders. Patients are assessed for a variety of symptoms, and clinicians review the DSM to determine how those symptoms can be categorized. Additionally, clinicians try to understand what resulting behaviors or outcomes are linked to such symptoms. If a patient is showing abnormal behaviors that are not causing any detriment to themselves or others, they will likely not be diagnosed with a psychological disorder. As new research comes out, the DSM is updated to reflect accurate diagnoses and humane treatment interventions. The latest edition also includes notes on behaviors that are different than social norms, stating that these are not necessarily disorders unless a physiological dysfunction, harm to self, or harm to others is involved. This is an important distinction between newer editions and early editions.

Diagnostic tools such as the **DSM-V** or the tenth edition of the **International Classification of Diseases (ICD-10)**, an international compendium that classifies various diseases including psychological ones, help clinicians apply a standardized, unbiased approach to diagnoses. However, mental health assessment outcomes can vary by patient and by the cultures and norms that are prevalent in a particular society. As all humans are uniquely different and there are over seven billion variations on the planet, some argue that mental health classification systems cannot truly capture or define abnormal behavior. The human brain and concepts relating to that of the human psyche still leave much to be understood, including the level of variation that can normally occur between different minds. Additionally, due to the cultural and social influences on brain and cognitive development, a standardized diagnostic tool may result in incorrect diagnoses or ones that can cause severe social stigma in some cultures.

The Positive and Negative Consequences of Diagnostic Labels

For clients who do not feel their best and do not know why, having a **diagnostic label** that explains their symptoms can provide clarity around their personal health problems. If the diagnostic label also provides opportunities for successful therapeutic interventions, it can provide incredible hope and positive health outcomes for clients. However, diagnostic labeling also appears to come at some costs. Research shows that utilizing a label may change how clients view themselves, as well as how they are viewed by their loved ones. These confirmatory views of the label may influence how clients behave, as well as influence the interactions that occur between clients and their loved ones.

For example, consider a man who receives a diagnosis of social anxiety. He shares this diagnosis with his wife, who loves going on social outings that sometimes make her husband uncomfortable. She begins to make plans alone, knowing that her husband does not enjoy most of the outings as much as she does. However, they both ignore the few times where has truly enjoyed himself and made friends who provide a sense of community that is important for his overall well-being. Over time, he becomes more isolated and lonelier, which is detrimental to his well-being and strains his relationship with his spouse. Additionally, many labels still carry stigma, which can also affect one's sense of overall well-being.

The Rosenhan Study

The **Rosenhan Study** examined psychological diagnoses and labels, and how disorders are difficult to reliably diagnose and validate. In this study, psychologist David Rosenhan and members from his research team purposefully acted in a way to receive a particular diagnosis and gain admittance to a mental health hospital. Upon acting out hallucinatory symptoms, the team was, in fact, diagnosed with a mental health disorder and institutionalized. Upon admission, each team member began acting normally and no longer displayed any symptoms associated with the initial diagnosis. Yet, they were forced to label themselves with the diagnosis, take medication for it, and remain hospitalized. Rosenhan, himself, was institutionalized for over two months.

During this period, the team reported inhumane treatment, with basic behaviors being labelled as pathologies. In a follow-up to this study after disclosing the experimental nature, Rosenhan asked hospital staff to identify other false patients that had been admitted. Although Rosenhan had not brought any other people into the facility apart from his initial team, the hospital staff selected over forty patients and identified them as not having any disorders. As a result of this experiment, Rosenhan concluded that diagnostic labels can be harmful, unreliable, and invalid. He proposed treating specific behaviors in mental health facilities rather than using umbrella labels which could be misleading.

Neurodevelopmental and Schizophrenic Spectrum Disorders

The Major Diagnostic Categories of Neurodevelopmental and Schizophrenic Spectrum Disorders

Schizophrenia
Schizophrenia is one of the more genetically-determined psychological disorders and usually involves psychotic symptoms such as hallucinations and delusions, in which a person loses touch with reality. Auditory or visual **hallucinations** are when a person perceives something that is not there. **Delusions** are false beliefs, such as a delusion of grandeur in which a person believes they are the president of the United States. Odd or disorganized speech and catatonia are other symptoms of schizophrenia.

Schizophrenia has a strong genetic component, with a correlation between high levels of dopamine and schizophrenia. Anti-psychotic medications used in the treatment of schizophrenia serve to decrease the levels of dopamine, but also have the risk of causing tardive dyskinesia or Parkinson's disease, which are both associated with low levels of dopamine. Schizophrenia has also been shown to have a high genetic predisposition, with biological family members of those with schizophrenia being more likely to develop the disorder.

Dissociative Disorders
Dissociative disorders are a controversial category of disorders, characterized by dissociation or detachment within a person's consciousness. The most well-known and debated dissociative disorder is **dissociative identity disorder** (formerly **multiple personality disorder**). A person with dissociative identity disorder (DID) can develop two or more distinct personalities. These personalities may have different names, genders, ages, and behaviors. Dissociative disorders also include a fugue state and depersonalization disorder.

Personality Disorders
Personality disorders are characterized by maladaptive and enduring patterns of social functioning and interactions, including manipulative or lying behaviors, social avoidance, or anti-social behavior. Some common personality disorders are narcissistic personality disorder, anti-social personality disorder, borderline personality disorder, and histrionic personality disorder.

Bipolar, Depressive, Anxiety, and Obsessive-Compulsive and Related Disorders

The Major Diagnostic Categories of Anxiety, Bipolar, Depressive, and Obsessive-Compulsive Disorders

Anxiety Disorders

Anxiety disorders are characterized by persistent worry, anxiety, or fear. They may also include maladaptive patterns of behavior that are intended to reduce the fear or anxiety. This category of disorders includes generalized anxiety disorder, post-traumatic stress disorder (PTSD), specific phobias, panic disorder, and obsessive-compulsive disorder.

Bipolar and Related Disorders

Bipolar disorder (formerly **manic-depressive disorder**) is considered a mood disorder and involves a mood that fluctuates between depression and mania or hypomania. The length and severity of the cycles of elevated mood and depressed mood vary from person to person. **Cyclothymia** is a related disorder in which a person experiences a fluctuation between minor depression (**dysthymia**) and mild mania (**hypomania**). Children who experience this fluctuating mood are diagnosed with **disruptive mood dysregulation disorder** rather than bipolar disorder.

Depressive Disorders

Major depressive disorder (MDD) is characterized by a depressed, sad, or hopeless mood. Some other symptoms are changes in sleep and appetite patterns, lethargy, decreased interest in previously-enjoyed activities, and suicidal ideation. These symptoms must persist for at least two weeks to receive a diagnosis of MDD. **Persistent depressive disorder, or dysthymia,** is another depressive disorder. It is a milder form of depression than MDD and persists for at least two years.

Mood disorders, including depression, are connected to levels of neurotransmitters in the brain. Specifically, serotonin, norepinephrine, and dopamine levels can affect a person's mood. Although not as strong as in schizophrenia, research indicates that there is a genetic predisposition to depression.

Obsessive–Compulsive Disorder

Obsessive-compulsive disorder is a specific type of anxiety disorder that consists of obsessive and recurring thoughts, and compulsive behaviors that are meant to reduce the stress related to the obsessive thoughts. For example, a person who has persistent thoughts related to cleanliness may engage in compulsive behaviors that would reduce the risk of germs, such as repetitive washing of hands.

Trauma- and Stressor- Related, Dissociative, and Somatic Symptom and Related Disorders

The Major Diagnostic Categories of Trauma- and Stressor-Related Disorders

Trauma- and Stressor-Related Disorders

Trauma related disorders, most notably PTSD, develop in reaction to stressful and traumatic experiences that a person has endured. For example, experiencing a rape or a natural disaster can lead a person to a trauma-related disorder. These disorders involve fear responses to triggers, anxiety, depression, insomnia, hyper-arousal, etc.

Somatic Symptom and Related Disorders

Somatic symptom disorders are psychological disorders that manifest with physical symptoms even though there is no identifiable physical cause for the symptom. Conversion disorder and illness anxiety disorder (formerly **hypochondriasis**) are two examples of somatic symptom disorders.

Feeding and Eating, Substance and Addictive, and Personality Disorders

The Major Diagnostic Categories of Eating, Addictive, and Personality Disorders

Feeding and eating disorders both relate to the intake of food, although in different ways. Feeding disorders refer to the rejection of certain foods for a minimum of one month, often due to a sensory issue, that results in malnutrition or growth deficiencies.

Feeding Disorders
Avoidant/Restrictive Food Intake Disorder

The DSM-V names one major feeding disorder, known as **avoidant/restrictive food intake disorder (ARFID)**. It is primarily used as a classification for children but may be used to diagnose adults who restrict food but do not fit the criteria for restrictive eating disorders. Children diagnosed with AFRID are often also diagnosed with sensory processing disorders, autism spectrum disorders, and/or obsessive-compulsive disorders; AFRID is often not a stand-alone diagnosis in children.

Eating Disorders

Eating disorders refer to a disorder of behavioral eating habits and may be diagnosed in children and adults.

Anorexia Nervosa

Anorexia nervosa is an eating disorder in which food intake is severely restricted and extreme weight loss often occurs. The effects of this self-imposed starvation can vary from mild nutritional deficits to cardiac failure and death. It may also occur with a paranoia of becoming fat; more commonly, it may result as a coping mechanism for someone who is experiencing loss of control or chaos in their personal life.

Bulimia Nervosa

Bulimia nervosa is characterized by periods of overeating followed by a restrictive or purge period (e.g., vomiting, excessive exercise, etc.). People with bulimia can sustain significant damage to the mouth and teeth as a result of the effects of gastric acids associated with the vomiting.

Binge Eating Disorder

Binge eating disorder refers to cyclic periods of extreme, often compulsory overeating without the purging component seen in bulimia.

Eating Disorders Not Otherwise Specified

In addition to these three disorders, the DSM-V also includes a category for eating disorders not otherwise specified, which refers to any type of abnormal eating habit that does not fall under listed eating or feeding disorders.

Substance and Addictive Disorders

Substance and addictive disorders include abuse, overuse, dependence upon, or addiction to particular substances. Common substance issues include alcoholism and recreational and illegal drug use. Addictive disorders may relate to substances or to behaviors relating to rewards and pleasure, such as gambling, sex, and even social media feedback. Across these types of disorders, the brain rewires its ability to derive pleasure, causing a need for more of the initial substance or behavior. Symptoms include using the substance or engaging in the behavior on a regular basis, lying about use or frequency, engaging in risky behavior, legal and occupational trouble, and isolation from friends and family.

Personality Disorders

Personality disorders cover a wide range of unhealthy behaviors that ultimately impact an individual and/or their loved ones in a negative way. Personality disorders are grouped into three primary clusters: A, B, and C. **Cluster A personality disorders** include behaviors that are extremely paranoid, delusional, or hallucinatory. They include disorders such paranoid personality disorder and schizotypal personality disorder. These types of disorders are characterized by extreme distrust of others, heightened emotional responses to normal stimuli and interactions, limited general affect, and low interpersonal skills.

Cluster B personality disorders include disorders relating to extreme moods or unpredictable behaviors, such as narcissistic personality disorder, histrionic personality disorder, or borderline personality disorder. These types of disorders are often characterized by extreme and unpredictable emotional outbursts, an inflated sense of ego, impulsive and risky behaviors, disregard for other people and their feelings, and dramatic interactions.

Cluster C personality disorders include those related to anxious behaviors and thought patterns. They include disorders such as avoidant personality disorder and obsessive-compulsive disorder. These types of disorders are characterized by extreme sensitivity, isolation, taking neutral comments personally, strict and rigid patterns of behavior in order to promote a sense of predictability and security, and awkward interpersonal communication.

Introduction to Treatment of Psychological Disorders

The Central Characteristics of Psychotherapeutic Intervention

Building Counselor and Client Relationships

Creating rapport with clients requires mental health providers (such as therapists, counselors, and psychologists) to engage in specific approaches using appropriate therapeutic techniques. (For readability, the term "counselor" will be used in this section to represent mental health providers in general, with the understanding that the same responsibilities apply to any of the diverse mental health practitioner roles.) In addition to the use of theory, counselors must convey a genuine attitude of empathy and respect for their clients. Using positive regard, as well as a nonjudgmental style, is essential to creating a sense of comfort and willingness for clients to open up to their counselor. Counselors should carefully evaluate each client and develop a plan for services that will best meet his or her needs. The plan should be communicated and agreed upon with the clients, ensuring that they feel the provider is trustworthy and competent.

Initial Phase of Relationship Building

At the onset of the process, the counselor and client will progress through the initial relationship building phase, which has four specific phases. These phases may be completed at varying paces, depending on both parties. Some phases can be completed quickly, while others may take several sessions.

Phase 1. Initiation, or entry phase: This is the introduction to the counseling process, which sets the stage for the development of the client/counselor relationship.

Phase 2. Clarification phase: This phase defines the problem and need for the therapeutic relationship.

Phase 3. Structure phase: The counselor defines the specifics of the relationship, its intended outcomes, and responsibilities of both parties.

Phase 4. Relationship phase: The client and provider have developed a relationship and will work toward mutually agreed-upon goals.

Stages of Positive Interaction

Once a working relationship is established, the client and counselor will need to develop and maintain positive interactions to ensure the effectiveness of counseling. Positive interactions ensure the therapeutic relationship advances and supports clients in meeting their goals. The counseling relationship has four stages.

Stage 1. Exploration of feelings and definition of problem: Counselors will use rapport-building skills, define the structure of the counseling process and relationship, and work with their clients on goal setting.

Stage 2. Consolidation: This is the process of the clients integrating the information and guidance from the counselor, allowing them to gain additional coping skills and identify alternate ways to solve problems.

Stage 3. Planning: During this phase, clients can begin employing techniques learned in counseling and prepare to manage on their own.

Stage 4. Termination: This is the ending step of the therapeutic relationship. It should occur when clients feel equipped to manage problems independently and have fully integrated techniques learned in counseling.

Silence

Silence can be an effective skill in therapy but must be used carefully, especially in the early stages of the process. Initially, clients may be silent due to many factors, such as fear, resistance, discomfort with opening up, or uncertainty about the process. Counselors who use silence in initial sessions must ensure clients do not perceive the counselor as bored, hostile, or indifferent. As counseling progresses, clients may gain additional comfort with silence and use it as a way to reflect on content, process information, consider options, and gain self-awareness. Newer counselors may have more difficulty with silence, as they may believe they are not being helpful if they are not talking. Silence is also viewed differently by culture, so cultural awareness is important in understanding and using it as a therapeutic tool.

Attending

Attending is the act of the counselor giving clients his or her full attention. Attending to the client shows respect for their needs, can encourage openness, and can create a sense of comfort and support in the counseling process. There are several ways for counselors to attend actively to clients, including maintaining appropriate eye contact, using reassuring body language and gestures, and monitoring their tone and expressions. Counselors can communicate support and a nonjudgmental attitude through an open posture and eye gaze that shows interest but not intimidation. They should use a caring verbal tone and facial expressions, which indicate attention to what their clients are saying, and can be used in addition to silence to create a positive environment for counseling.

Questioning

As part of any counseling session, counselors will ask both open and closed questions. Open questions are more likely to provide helpful information, as they require the client to express feelings, beliefs, and ideas. Open questions often begin with "why," "how," or "when" or "tell me …". Closed questions may be less helpful, as they may elicit brief responses of one or few words.

Counselors do need to be aware of the limitations of asking questions. Any questions asked should have purpose and provide information that will be meaningful to the counselor and the relationship. Curiosity questions should be avoided, as well as asking too many questions, which may feel interrogating to the client. A counselor can ask follow-up questions for clarification as needed. The counselor should provide the client adequate time to answer questions and elaborate but also allow time for the client to talk freely.

Reflecting

Reflecting is a basic counseling skill designed to build rapport and help clients become aware of underlying emotions. Counselors "reflect back" what a client says, both to indicate they are attending and also to analyze and interpret meanings. Reflecting is more than simply paraphrasing a client's words, as it involves more in-depth understanding and an attempt to elicit further information. An example would be a client stating, "I'm not sure what to do about my current relationship. I can't decide if I should stay or leave." The counselor would reflect by stating, "It sounds like you are conflicted about what to do; this is a difficult decision to make," and follow up with a probing question or time for the client to process and react.

Giving Advice

There are two main types of advice: substantive and process. **Substantive advice** can be considered directive and may involve the counselor imposing his or her opinions onto clients. **Process advice** is more empowering and helps clients navigate options for solving their own issues. An example would be a client who is struggling with anxiety. Substantive advice would be the counselor telling the client he or she should practice deep breathing. Process advice, in the same example, would be teaching the client how relaxation techniques can lessen anxiety and providing examples.

Counselors can offer process advice to help clients better understand their problems and possible solutions. Clients may ask for advice, and in some situations, it may be appropriate for the counselor to offer process advice; it is less likely that substantive advice should be given. Providing counseling is more complex than simply giving advice; thus, counselors should explore when, why, and how to give advice, if needed. As the goal of counseling is to help individuals gain a better self-awareness and competence, giving advice may undermine the process by not allowing clients an opportunity to learn ways to solve their own issues both within and after counseling.

Summarizing

Summarizing is another active listening and rapport-building technique. The counselor listens to the content provided by the clients and summarizes the essential points of the conversation. This process can help isolate and clarify the essential aspects of issues and ensure that both the client and the counselor can focus on the most critical tasks. Additionally, summarization can be helpful in goal setting or at the end of a session.

Reassurance

Reassurance is an affirming therapeutic technique used to encourage and support clients. Reassurance can help alleviate doubts and increase confidence. Counselors use reassurance when a client experiences setbacks or an inability to recognize progress. Clients can be reminded of past successes to help bolster their ability to solve current problems. It is important that reassurance is genuine and not overused by counselors to pacify clients, but rather as a tool to validate and inspire continued growth.

Promoting Relaxation

As part of the counseling process, clients may need to learn basic relaxation techniques, which can be simple to learn and practice. Stress can cause increased anxiety and tension; thus, relaxation techniques help reduce both mental and physical stress. Clients may present with racing thoughts, fatigue, or headaches; techniques such as awareness, breath work, and progressive relaxation can be of great benefit. Clients who have a reduction in their stress level may be more engaged in the counseling process and better able to manage difficulties outside of sessions. Meditation is a powerful relaxation tool to help build awareness and the ability to calm oneself. Relaxation can help diminish the activity of stress hormones in the body, reduce feelings of anger and frustration, lower heart rate, and improve confidence.

Setting Goals

Setting goals is an important aspect of the therapeutic process. Talk therapy may seem unstructured or capable of lasting for long periods of time; however, both the client and the counselor are responsible for setting and working toward measurable change. Goals of counseling can include the desire for physical change, such as getting into shape or losing weight, and career aspirations and/or social goals, such as gaining increased support or modifying relationships. Other types of goals can include emotional, spiritual, and intellectual.

Goals can be immediate, short term, or long term, and clients may want to achieve several goals at different paces. Goals can take the form of **SMART goals**, which are specific, measurable, achievable, relevant, and time-bound. **Specific** means detailing why you want to accomplish the goal, what specifically there is to accomplish, who is involved, the setting for the goal, and what kind of resources are involved. **Measurable** means designating a system of tracking your goals in order to stay motivated. **Achievable** is making sure that the goal is realistic, like looking at financial factors or other limitations. **Relevant** means making sure it's the right time for the goal, if it matches your needs, or if the goal seems worthwhile to pursue. Finally, **time-bound** is developing a target date so that there is a clear deadline to focus on.

Goal setting must be specific to each client and should be mutually agreed upon. Setting clear time frames, supported by the counselor, is essential to success. Goal setting may cause issues if goals are too ambitious or vague or have no identifiable benefit. It is also important to explore what motivation exists for a client to work toward a goal. If adequate motivation is present, the counselor also needs to consider what will happen if the goal is not met. In some cases, failure to meet goals can cause a client to become highly discouraged and unwilling to stick with the process of reformulating goals. During the process of working toward goals, a client may realize another goal is better suited. It's important to reevaluate goals during the process to help the client grow and embrace personal change.

Imagery

Guided imagery can be a powerful tool in the counseling process. Guided imagery, which draws upon the mind-body connection, can be used to help the client alleviate anxiety, relax, and control or change negative thoughts or feelings. A counselor, who helps the client envision a place of relaxation and calm, guides the process. The counselor encourages the client to visualize and relax into the details of the image. Clients can also envision the successful outcome of a situation or imagine themselves handling a stressful situation. Once learned, clients can practice imagery on their own to help reduce stress and anxiety.

Coping Skills

Teaching coping skills is an important role of the counselor in the therapeutic relationship. Coping skills enable individuals to manage stressful situations, solve problems, handle uncertainty, and develop resilience. Coping skills can include solution-focused problem solving, removing negative self-talk, learning mindfulness or other stress management techniques, and gaining support through friends, family, and community. Individuals may learn how to identify specific patterns to their feelings and behaviors, and thus, learn new and healthier responses. As there are many ways for individuals to develop and practice coping skills, counselors can provide options and unique plans for clients to best meet their needs.

Additional Counseling Skills

The following are additional counseling skills:

Restating: Clarifying through repeating back the client's words, as understood by the counselor

Reflecting: Restating what the counselor heard from the client, emphasizing any underlying emotional content (can be termed **reflection of feeling**)

Paraphrasing: Repeating back a client's story while providing an empathic response

Summarizing: Reiterating the major points of the counseling discussion

Silence: Moments during which neither the client nor the counselor speak; can be used for reflection but may indicate resistance from the client

Confronting: Technique in which the counselor identifies discrepancies from the client in a supportive manner (counselor may also ask for clarification to determine if content was misheard prior to exposing possible inconsistencies)

Structuring: Used to set goals and agree upon plan for counseling; also used within sessions to make effective use of time and respect boundaries

The Contributions of Major Figures in Psychological Treatment

Aaron Beck

Aaron Beck pioneered the field of **cognitive behavioral therapy**. He also developed a number of widely utilized assessments, including the **Beck Depression Inventory**. He has been influential in developing effective intervention techniques for depressed patients. His primary cognitive therapy technique encourages clients to examine their thought patterns in the present moment, as he believed that patients with depression tend to have more frequent and spontaneous negative thoughts than the average person. In turn, this leads to certain unhealthy behaviors and feelings, which continue the cycle of negative experiences and negative thoughts.

Through becoming aware of the frequency, intensity, and nature of these thoughts, clients with depression could begin to stop the pattern and replace it with a more positive one. This would then lead to positive feelings and behaviors, and then start a positive feedback cycle instead. It would allow the client to interact with their world from a place of positive affect, thus creating more positive experiences and positive thought patterns. This form of therapy expanded beyond clients with depression to interventions in substance abuse, eating disorder, anxiety, and anger cases.

Albert Ellis

Albert Ellis (1913–2007) is known for developing **Rational Emotive Behavior Therapy (REBT)**, a psychotherapeutic method that helps people change or overcome irrational thoughts. It is considered to be one of the first active processes of psychotherapy, moving beyond simply making clients aware of their thoughts and beliefs; rather, it then encourages clients to change their thoughts and beliefs in the way they believe would be most productive for their personal goals. Ellis believed people tend to blame external circumstances for their emotions rather than take the opportunity to review and change their personal beliefs about a particular event (and therefore change their emotions). Through this examination of one's personal emotional response to an event, Ellis would challenge the client to justify whether the emotional response was rational or not.

Ellis argued that most emotional responses result from irrational beliefs; by changing the belief, one could control and retrain their emotional response to seemingly negative situations. This method is commonly used in helping people with people pleasing or subservient behaviors, anxiety disorders, phobias and paranoias, and shyness. Ellis defined the main goals of REBT counseling as gaining acceptance of self and others and dropping inflexible and maladaptive thoughts and behaviors.

Sigmund Freud

Freud's primary contributions to psychology including pioneering the field of **psychoanalysis**, which analyzes an individual's subconscious and unconscious thoughts in their relation to the individual's behaviors and motivations. Freud brought attention to the role of unconscious thoughts, such as those in dreams and from repressed memories, through treatment methods including free association and dream analysis.

As a part of free association, Freud asked patients to speak openly and without stopping. He would analyze this dialogue for patterns and "slips" that gave insight to the patient's subconscious thoughts. He especially placed importance on repressed memories from early childhood and believed these experiences shaped how people behaved into adulthood. Freud believed memories become involuntarily repressed when the initial experience caused pain, fear, or shame in in some way; while he tried to create a standard model for the process of repression, he ultimately concluded it was a subjective experience that varied by individual. Freud is also well known for developing the concepts of the id, the ego, and the superego.

The id represented thoughts and motivations focused on basic, primitive desires, while the superego represented thoughts and motivations based on social norms and morals. The ego attempted to manage the relationship between the two and governed how people outwardly presented themselves in society. Overall, Freud believed all actions were motivated by sexual desires and the fear of dying, which manifested themselves unconsciously. He believed these types of thoughts often came up in dreams, and he utilized his method of dream analysis to examine and label meaningful symbols and imagery in his patients' dreams. He also believed in the concept of **transference**, where patients would project their unconscious beliefs about an important personal figure (e.g., mother or father) onto the therapist. Therefore, analyzing the patient's interactions with the practitioner for instances of transference was also a part of Freud's treatment methodology.

Mary Cover Jones

Mary Cover Jones (1897–1987), a behavior therapist, became renowned in her field at a time when women were rarely seen in science, research, or professor roles at a university. Her work focused on fear reduction through conditioning responses; her most famous study in this area is known as the **"Little Peter" experiment**. In this experiment, Jones worked with a three-year-old with a fear of rabbits. She gradually increased exposure to the rabbit alongside a positive incentive, ultimately desensitizing the fear by creating a classical conditioning response through the use of the incentive. Through this experiment, she discovered that presenting a stimulus that is desirable to the client alongside a stimulus that the client fears can reduce the client's phobia.

This desensitization process, also known as **counterconditioning**, continues to be used in modern therapeutic interventions to reduce or eliminate phobias and anxious behaviors. This approach was different from other behavior therapists, who regularly used flooding techniques to reduce fears. **Flooding**, or intensely experiencing a stimulus that causes fear, can be a more difficult method for clients (especially children). Additionally, Jones is well known for her research into adolescent behaviors, including protective and risk factors for unhealthy behaviors such as drinking. She also examined how adolescent maturity interacts with factors in the environment, discovering that females who mature earlier in adolescence experience more negative interpersonal treatment and socioeconomic outcomes, while boys who mature earlier in adolescence experience more positive interpersonal treatment and socioeconomic outcomes.

Carl Rogers

Carl Rogers (1902–1987) is a renowned figure in the humanistic field of psychology, an area that focuses on the development of human potential. He was one of the leaders in developing **client-centered therapy**, a medium in which the practitioner empowers the client to direct their own therapeutic processes. In fact, Rogers was one of the first practitioners to refer to patients as clients, implying that practitioners and clients were in a collaborative relationship rather than one where the practitioner tried to "fix" the patient. Instead, the practitioner utilizes techniques that encourages clients to develop self-awareness, self-efficacy, and personal goals toward which they direct their own behaviors. Rogers believed that all individuals hoped to self-actualize, and that in order to do so, they must be able to know what comprises their concept of the ideal self. With this understanding, individuals can examine their current concept of self and determine what actions need to be taken to align the two separate concepts.

B. F. Skinner

As mentioned numerous times, B. F. Skinner was a behaviorist psychologist, largely focusing on visible, outward expressions of behavior that could be documented. He emphasized the roles of the environment and external stimuli in behavior conditioning, stating that negative responses to a behavior would eliminate the behavior, while positive responses would result in more of the same behavior. Skinner used this premise to develop his concept of operant conditioning, a framework for learning behaviors. In **operant conditioning**, reinforcements are used to increase behaviors, while punishments are used to decrease behaviors. He developed the Skinner Box as a tool to study these ideas.

The **Skinner Box** focused on the behaviors of a rat placed in the box. Certain behaviors within the box resulted in food being produced for the rat, a positive reinforcement. After a few trials, the rat would regularly exhibit the behavior needed for the food to arrive in the box. Additionally, Skinner conducted a **negative reinforcement trial** (where an unpleasant stimulus is removed upon the expression of a certain behavior) with rats in the box. He placed an electric grid in the box that unpleasantly buzzed the rat, but if the rat pressed a button it would cause the buzzing to stop. After a few trials, rats would learn to immediately press the button that eliminated the buzz after being placed in the Skinner Box.

Joseph Wolpe

Joseph Wolpe (1915–1997) was a notable behaviorist and an influential mentor to Mary Cover Jones. His work focused on desensitization and anxiety reduction. Wolpe believed that dysfunctional behaviors are learned, and therefore could be unlearned. His studies often introduced a phobia or anxiety, provided a technique for relaxation, then introduced the fear and the relaxation technique at the same time in order to encourage the unlearning response. Wolpe also believed that fears and phobias may result from indirect negative associations in the client's psyche, and part of his process focused on discovering the root cause of the phobia before introducing the unlearning technique. These processes continue to be used today not only in client counseling sessions but also as organizational management tools in which participants learn to manage conflicts and healthily assert personal beliefs and boundaries.

Psychological Perspectives and Treatment of Disorders

Major Treatment Orientations Used in Therapy

Pioneers in the field of psychology developed a number of different ways in which to better understand psychological disorders and create successful intervention therapies. Some therapies are no longer widely practiced, even if they experienced popularity at some point in history. Additionally, different types of therapies may be better suited for specific contexts or demographics. As more scientific evidence becomes available to explain psychological disorders and what types of interventions are truly necessary or helpful, practitioners may shift their treatment orientations.

Behavioral

Behavioral therapy, which comes from behaviorist theories in psychology, intends to reinforce positive behaviors and decrease or eliminate undesirable behaviors. This type of therapy relies heavily on methods derived from theories of conditioning. **Classical conditioning**, first introduced by physiologist Ivan Pavlov, utilizes certain stimuli to elicit specific responses. The process first determines an already existing relationship between a stimulus and a response. Pavlov, for example, determined that dogs automatically salivate in response to smelling food. In this scenario, both the food and the dog's reaction to the food are unconditioned. Upon determining this relationship, Pavlov introduced the sound of a bell. The sound of the bell is considered a neutral stimulus, because the dog has no association affiliated with it.

In his famous experiment, Pavlov chimed the bell every time the dog was presented with food. After multiple repetitions of this experiment, Pavlov chimed the bell without presenting any food to the dog; the dog salivated upon hearing the bell. This response to a stimulus that was originally neutral is called a **conditioned response**. Pavlov also noticed that if he continued to sound the bell without presenting any food, the dog eventually stopped salivating in response to the bell. Eliminating a conditioned response is known as **extinction**. In this same way, a neutral stimulus can be introduced alongside a triggering stimulus to change a person's behavior over time. This practice is commonly used to reduce or eliminate phobias.

Common classical conditioning techniques in therapy include **flooding**, where an individual may be exposed to a stimulus that provokes an undesired response without the ability to leave the environment or stimulus, **systematic desensitization**, where an individual learns to condition a relaxation response toward a stimulus that initially caused fear, and **aversion**, where an unwanted conditioned response to a stimulus becomes an unpleasant experience for the individual.

Operant conditioning, introduced by psychologist B. F. Skinner, refers to the process of creating an association between a behavior and a consequent reward or punishment. Behaviors strengthen or weaken depending on what occurs immediately after the behavior, and how an individual perceives the experience. In response to displaying a behavior, individuals may experience positive or negative reinforcement that encourages continuation of that behavior. **Positive reinforcement** occurs when a behavior produces a desirable outcome, whereas **negative reinforcement** occurs when a behavior takes away an undesirable outcome. Positive and negative punishments can also condition behavior. **Positive punishment** refers to an instance where an undesirable outcome occurs immediately after a behavior.

Negative punishment occurs when behavior results in the loss of a desirable outcome. In therapeutic settings, clinicians typically hope to reward and emphasize desirable behaviors to condition these behaviors. Punishment is often ineffective, especially with younger individuals. Reinforcing positive behaviors through operant conditioning is often a systematic and gradual process, as small, consecutive goals are often more feasible for a client who is trying to make a large change. However, different types of reward schedules exist that can ultimately lead to a conditioned behavior.

Continuous reinforcement, fixed-ratio schedules, variable-ratio schedules, fixed-interval schedules, and **variable-interval schedules** are the most common types of behavior reinforcement schedules. Incidentally, many of these reward schedules exist in our society and can cause psychological issues. For example, many casino games use a variable-ratio reward schedule, where variable, unpredictable instances of a behavior (playing the game) result in a reward (a payout). These types of reward systems can cause gambling addictions. Other behavior reward systems used in early childhood education, such as sticker incentives for reading a book, are a type of fixed-ratio reward schedule. These systems may encourage the behavior of reading, but may not encourage a sustainable, intrinsic motivation to read.

Cognitive

Cognitive treatments focus on interventions that target mental processes such as reasoning, judgment, memory, decision making, attention, and perception. This field became exceedingly popular in the 1970s, and theorists in this area often drew comparisons between the human brain and the central processing unit of a computer. Cognitive approaches resulted from psychologists believing that behaviorist theories were too limited in scope, as they largely ignored the complex mental processes and introspection that drive behavior. Cognitive psychologists refer to these mental processes—the ones that take place between the perception of a stimulus and the associated behavior—as mediational processes.

Cognitive treatments often aim to treat disorders that affect mental processing, such as Alzheimer's disease, dementia, or attention deficit disorder. They also may be used to help individuals who have experienced a traumatic brain injury that affects cognitive functioning. Practitioners in this field employ techniques that can help their clients improve long- or short-term memory recall, focus, or increase the amount of information they are able to store and retrieve. Practitioners often specialize in an area of cognition (e.g., decision making, and cognitive processes related to this function).

Beyond injuries and disease, cognitive treatments may help individuals who are simply trying to improve their mental performance. For example, a chief executive officer of an international corporation may seek therapeutic solutions from a cognitive psychologist in order to make the complex leadership and management decisions that drive the company.

Additionally, cognitive therapies encourage individuals to introspect through methods such as journaling, meditation, and guided imagery techniques. Practitioners may also encourage their clients to validate negative thought patterns or rehearse scenarios that historically have caused distress. For example, consider a female patient with social anxiety who feels that her mind goes blank when she has to talk to someone she does not know well. A psychologist who utilizes a cognitive approach may ask this individual to role-play multiple scenarios of talking to a stranger, encouraging quicker retrieval of information for conversation when the "real-time" conversation takes place.

Psychodynamic

Psychodynamic therapy focuses on individuals' unconscious and subconscious beliefs and memories, and how these aspects drive current behavior and self-concept. This form of treatment encourages individuals to examine their own thoughts, beliefs, attitudes, values, and emotions in order to apply this knowledge to better understanding their current (especially problematic) behaviors. Often, treatment begins with examining the client's childhood and formative years, including relationships with

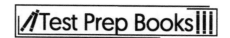

caregivers, interests, desires, traumatic events, and repressed memories. Psychodynamic therapies are a form of "talk therapy," in which the practitioner encourages clients to discuss their introspective findings freely. The practitioner and the client may collaboratively find patterns in the client's behavior, or the practitioner may take the lead in pointing out behavioral patterns to the client.

Often, individuals who are receiving psychodynamic therapy are exploring the full range of their emotions for the first time. They may also be able to acknowledge feelings of which they previously were unaware. During these sessions, coping or defense mechanisms may become apparent. For example, clients may begin discussing a sensitive memory and may stop talking or switch the topic in the middle of the discussion. This can be a cue to the practitioner to gently guide the client back to the topic, as it may be a primary, yet unresolved, source of mental or behavioral distress for the client.

Humanistic
Carl Rogers developed the person-centered, or humanistic, approach to counseling, which stressed the importance of the counseling relationship, as well as the need to evaluate therapy for effectiveness. Rogers believed that three core conditions must exist for therapy to facilitate change: empathy, positive regard, and congruence. Rogers's work was continued by Robert Carkhuff, who created a five-point scale to measure the core conditions and effectiveness of a counselor. This scale attempts to measure the degree to which the counselor is providing effective levels of empathy, genuineness, concreteness, and respect.

Level 1: Therapist is contradictory in statements and nonverbal cues and exhibits defensiveness.

Level 2: Therapist is superficially professional but lacks genuineness.

Level 3: Therapist does not express defensiveness; there is implied but not overt professionalism.

Level 4: Therapist is genuine and non-defensive.

Level 5: Therapist is open and honest and accurately and genuinely reflects ideas and reactions to client.

In his 1967 book, *Toward Effective Counseling and Psychotherapy*, Carkhuff found that therapeutic interventions did not always have a long-term positive impact, and in some cases, clients worsened after counseling. Carkhuff's findings were summarized in a famous quote that "therapy may be for better or for worse." This led him to conduct further research on specific attributes of the counselor that contributed to successful outcomes.

Psychodynamic
Psychodynamic therapies also often focus on a client's interpersonal relationships and communication skills. This type of therapy can be especially useful for clients who are experiencing personal conflicts due to interpersonal obstacles, such as an inability to set personal boundaries or to clearly communicate personal needs to others. Additionally, this type of therapy can help clients identify sources of both internal and external distress; with time, clients can learn how to develop healthy coping mechanisms and resiliency toward these sources of distress.

The cognitive school of thought focuses on mental functions like memory, problem solving, and language. Jean Piaget proposed the theory of cognitive development that provides an explanation for how a child's mind develops and perceives the world. Piaget argued that cognitive development progresses through the following four different stages:

> Sensorimotor – (0-2 years): The major development during this stage, which takes place from birth to two years of age, is **object permanence**, which is the ability of a child to know an object exists even when it cannot be seen.

> Preoperational – (2 -7 years): The significant developmental milestone that takes place in this stage is the ability for the child to use symbolism. Children are able to use a thing or a word to represent something else (e.g., using a doll to represent a friend).

> Concrete Operational - (7-11 years): During the concreate operational stage, children begin to think more logically or operationally. At this stage, a child would be able to determine how puzzle pieces fit together without physically interlocking the pieces.

> Formal Operational – (12 years – adulthood): This is the last stage in Piaget's model. During this stage, children and adults use complex logic, reasoning, and creative problem solving. An example of this is the ability to make a linear connection between items. At this stage, a person using logic could conclude that if John is shorter than Ted, and Ted is shorter than Bill, then John is shorter than Bill.

Piaget's work, which outlined developmental stages, was the first to argue that children's method of thinking varies considerably from that of adults. Piaget's stages demonstrate how he believed children's cognitive abilities change and develop over time, acquiring new skills at every stage. He also argued that intelligence was not set, but develops as a result of both biological and environmental factors. Piaget's theory included the concept of schemas, which can be explained as frameworks or pattern of behaviors in response to a specific stimulus or information.

Cognitive-Behavioral

Cognitive-behavioral therapy (CBT) approaches are widely used in today's therapeutic settings. CBT brings together the cognitive approach, theories from psychodynamic therapies, and the behavioral approach. CBT focuses on an individual's thoughts and other cognitive processes as well as reviews personal history and memories; the approach examines how all of these affect the person's behavior. Practitioners will typically work with the client to establish a goal to work toward, and various techniques may be used to aid the client in achieving the goal. Techniques may be subjective, based on the client. By combining these different approaches and tailoring the method to the client, CBT clients may experience positive results in a shorter period of time. Additionally, clients are also given techniques to implement and practice outside of sessions, which can further aid the process. The practitioner-client relationship is seen as more collaborative or coaching than what is common in other therapeutic fields.

In general, clients in this type of therapeutic setting are asked to notice and identify their internal dialogue and automatic thought responses. Most people constantly have a stream of thoughts in their mind during their conscious hours; some studies indicate that the majority of these thoughts are reactive and habitual in nature. Most people tend to respond to their thoughts and actions based on what is taking place around them, rather than consciously and intentionally producing a specific response. Additionally, these reactions are programmed patterns; people tend to primarily react negatively or positively. The way a person instinctively reacts to an event is often a result of their personal lived experience, although there are also genetic and evolutionary components involved.

Aaron Beck, the pioneer of CBT, believed these responses were shaped in early childhood and become automatic without intervention. Beck believed unproductive or maladaptive thoughts, and their consequent behaviors, could be retrained to produce more productive and positive feelings. This process begins with learning to become aware of one's personal thought, feeling, and behavior patterns. CBT practitioners believe that clients give meaning to certain events that cause negative feelings; by shifting the meaning that clients associate with events, their perceptions and thought patterns can literally create new, positive associations. This opens up the avenue to new, positive behaviors.

CBT is a treatment with a great deal of evidence-based support. Rigorous trials utilizing this approach have been completed successfully and have gone through peer-review and publication in scholarly journals. This technique is commonly used to help with depression, anxiety, substance abuse, disrupting bad habits and creating new habits, and for achieving very specific goals.

Sociocultural

Sociocultural treatments highlight the influence of one's social environment, including the impact that family members, friendships, community, and cultural factors play on an individual's thoughts, feelings, and behaviors. The language, rituals, social norms, gender roles, and values within a society have been shown to greatly influence cognitive processes.

This approach was pioneered by psychologist Lev Vygotsky, who lived in the former Soviet Union under the Communist Party. He emphasized the role of community in creating values and meaning in early childhood. While other popular developmental psychologists at the time believed cognition preceded learning abilities, Vygotsky believed that social learning sets the foundation for cognition. Vygotsky did not finish detailing his theories due to an early death, but he did establish principles that led to the sociocultural approach in treatments.

This approach focuses heavily on childhood development. It emphasizes the role of a teacher or tutor with whom a child can have meaningful dialogue, and from whom a child learns to model behavior and interpersonal relationships. This approach believes that much of what a child learns is passed down from language, rituals, and beliefs in the immediate and extended family. Language and dialogue exposure at an early age shapes specific neural pathways associated with language comprehension (including memory and recall) and refines the necessary motor skills for speaking.

Additionally, Vygotsky believed that interests around the child shaped the child's personal interests; for example, a child who grew up in an environment where play, exploration, and building were encouraged would likely continue to be drawn to these types of activities as they grew up. Children with involved mentors, whether those are caregivers, teachers, or extended family members, are likely to experience the full potential of their cognitive abilities as a result of the nurturing social input. Vygotsky referred to this experience as **scaffolding**.

Therapies that incorporate the sociocultural approach may often be those that focus on early childhood development, such as in the case of a child who is not meeting emotional or social developmental milestones. Additionally, clinicians may inquire about a client's sociocultural upbringing if they are working with someone who is from a different background (e.g., an immigrant or refugee) as this can influence the success of treatment options.

The Effectiveness of Specific Treatments for Specific Problems

The effectiveness of specific treatments determines largely on the type of disorder, the experience and approach of the practitioner, and the client. Effective treatments rely on a good fit between these different aspects—the therapist has treated the disorder successfully before, the disorder has been successfully treated in a clinical setting, the client and practitioner have a good working relationship, and so on. Some psychological disorders simply do not have any known treatments that can effectively "cure" the disorder or allow for a typical quality of life; interventions that manage these disorders and prevent afflicted clients from doing harm to themselves or others may exist. Clients who voluntarily seek treatment often have particular behaviors or outcomes in their lives that they are trying to address.

Practitioners, their clients, and sometimes additional stakeholders (such as family members or legal counsel) may work together to establish goals; reaching these goals is often an indicator that treatment has occurred successfully. Assessing effectiveness this way can be subjective, relying on the client's or practitioner's perception that a dysfunction has been addressed. Additionally, clients who go into treatment at the request of a third party (e.g., a court order that requires substance abuse counseling in the case of a drunk driving accident) may simply attend treatment to meet external requirements, rather than addressing and treating an existing disorder.

Some methods of treatment have been rigorously and scientifically tested as approaches to specific disorders, and they have been shown to show a high positive correlation with successful outcomes. Additionally, patient and therapist characteristics have also been tested to determine what personal and professional characteristics lead to successful outcomes. Peer-reviewed research indicates that obsessive-compulsive disorders and psychotic disorders often require medication in order for the client to lead a normal life, although many clients with psychotic disorders may need constant clinical supervision. Mood disorders, such as depression and anxiety, can often be successfully treated with cognitive therapies that focus on disrupting certain thought patterns.

Phobias and behavioral problems, such as substance abuse, are often best treated through methods rooted in cognitive-behavior or behavioral approaches, such as the process of systematic desensitization or through behavior conditioning. Clients who achieve the most success are those who voluntarily seek out counseling services for a specific behavior or outcome that they have self-identified as problematic, those who have an intrinsic desire to change a personal behavior or outcome, and those with a strong social support system. Successful practitioners often have history working with the disorder at hand, are able to establish clear, professional boundaries between themselves and the client, and utilize empirical methods that have been associated with successful counseling outcomes.

How Cultural and Ethnic Context Influence Choice and Success of Treatment

Cultural and ethnic contexts often drive if and how people choose to seek psychological treatments. These contexts may also determine the manner in which treatments are carried out. Research indicates that beliefs about what causes psychological disorders varies across cultures and ethnicities. For example, studies show that African-American groups regard social support systems as an important component of mental well-being, and attribute psychological disorders to a disruption in one's personal support system. This demographic also views financial concerns as a primary cause of stress and mental health concerns, and they report higher levels of distrust in medical providers. Therefore, they may be less likely to seek out conventional treatments or continue them upon starting. Studies also show that African-American groups are more likely to turn to spiritual communities in times of mental distress.

Asian Americans, comparatively, have reported that they believe mental health disorders are caused by physiological conditions and problems in one's immediate or extended family. Mental health disorders in this demographic often present as physical health issues (e.g., migraines or back pain), and the physical health issues are what prompts the patient to seek health care. Asian-American groups also are less willing to openly discuss mental health, with a long cultural history of associated stigma in many Eastern countries. A number of Eastern cultures believe discussing mental health issues disrupts or burdens one's social support system. As many Eastern cultures are collectivist societies, a mental health burden may also impact a family's public or social image. Asian-American groups also report feeling more comfortable with providers that are of the same ethnicity.

Latin-American groups report mental health issues around family concerns and stress associated with migration. Latin cultures also experience stigmatization of mental health diagnoses and report feeling less comfortable speaking about their mental health. This demographic also values privacy, and it holds fears about deportation that often prevents them from seeking any type of medical care. The majority of people without health insurance in the United States are Latin-American groups.

Across all ethnic minorities, there are common reports of feeling misunderstood, experiencing discrimination, an inability to pay for psychological services, and struggling with language barriers. These may all serve as obstacles for receiving effective treatment, and public health studies indicate that minorities have higher rates of chronic illnesses (which are linked to higher rates of mental health disorders) as well as higher rates of untreated psychological disorders.

Prevention Strategies that Build Resilience and Promote Competence

Resilience refers to one's ability to successfully navigate stressful situations and return to a balanced mental, physical, and emotional state of health. Stress is a normal part of life. Short periods of stress can actually provide benefits. For example, lifting weights places stress on certain muscles, but ultimately increases physical strength and supports a healthy metabolism. Chronic periods of stress, however, can result in a host of health issues. While people have different thresholds for stress based on their personality, personal history, and other subjective experiences, there are personal development methods that help people become more resilient, bounce back from stressful situations more quickly, and improve their overall ability to cope with general stressors.

These methods are a mix of cognitive and behavioral techniques that include reframing stressful events as temporary challenges from which one can learn and improve, committing to specific goals and the discipline necessary to achieve those goals, and directing energy only toward situations within one's control. Additionally, people with high levels of resiliency tend to focus on objectives, processes, and specific events, rather than viewing setbacks as an indicator of their personal shortcomings. For example, a resilient student who receives a poor grade on an essay would acknowledge they did poorly on one assignment, and they would then examine ways to improve for the next assignment. A student who is lacking resiliency may feel utterly defeated, berate themselves for never doing anything right, and toss the paper in the trash without giving it another look.

Resiliency and competence come with personal intention for growth, and from active experience with failure. Often, one must examine personal belief systems and thought patterns to determine if these are hindering or supporting resiliency. People who are trying to build a stronger sense of resiliency and competence can try questioning their limiting and negative beliefs, and practice more confident and empowering thoughts. They can also practice compartmentalizing their experiences so that if they

experience failure, they can examine the event on its own rather than linking it to their personal characteristics or other unrelated experiences.

Treatment of Disorders from the Biological Perspective

The Effectiveness of Specific Treatments Used to Address Specific Problems From a Biological Perspective

The **biological perspective** in psychology examines how someone's personal biology, such as genetics, hormones, structural features in the brain, and other physiological factors influence their psyche and psychopathologies. **Biological interventions** often utilize medication or treatments that directly influence the brain or neurotransmitters in order to produce desired behaviors or outcomes. A number of psychological disorders may only achieve positive outcomes through pharmacotherapy. Only **psychiatrists**—medical doctors who are trained in psychotherapy methods—are able to also prescribe medications to address psychological disorders.

Psychotic disorders, such as schizophrenia, do not effectively respond to psychotherapy methods. Prescription medications that are known to effectively manage difficult symptoms of schizophrenia, such as hallucinations and delusions, include risperidone and clozapine. Personality disorders are also commonly treated with medications that reduce symptoms of depression and anxiety, such as selective serotonin reuptake inhibitors, tricyclic antidepressants, dopamine reuptake blockers, and benzodiazepines. Additionally, clients with anxiety and depression disorders who do not respond to psychotherapy and lifestyle changes may also benefit from these medications.

Some psychological disorders may result from **structural abnormalities** in the brain, such as congenital defects, traumatic brain injuries, or the presence of brain tumors. These can result in mood disorders or involuntary emotional reactions that may be managed through pharmacotherapy. Additionally, physical brain abnormalities can result in cognitive issues such as dementia, short- and long-term memory loss, acute aggressive behaviors, or loss of motor skills; people who experience these issues often also experience depression from the sudden loss in quality of life. Effective treatment in these situations generally involves cognitive rehabilitation, a type of intervention in which cognitive exercises are performed to support and rearticulate neural pathways responsible for specific functions. Cognitive behavior therapies and mindfulness meditation techniques may also support positive outcomes. In cases of structural abnormalities or tumors that contribute to psychological disorders, surgery or radiation may be required.

Evaluating Strengths, Weaknesses, and Empirical Support for Treatments of Disorders

Comparing and Contrasting Different Treatment Methods

Individual

Individual therapy refers to any form of one-on-one treatment method between a practitioner and a client. These sessions maintain privacy for the client and allow practitioners to focus their undivided attention on a single person. Practitioners may work in a guiding role, where they lead the complete framework and delivery of the intervention and establish a baseline and goals for the patient. Decades ago, practitioners typically took on authoritarian roles where they prescribed judgment of situations and

ordered treatments; modern day therapy sessions are often more collaborative in nature. Practitioners may also take on a coaching role, where they create general parameters within which to work (such as the therapeutic approach used) but encourage and empower their clients to direct treatment, decide which areas to focus on, and determine if they feel like progress is being made. Due to the private nature of individual therapy, practitioners are not allowed to disclose confidential information unless it is court ordered, there is a threat of harm to the client or others, the client is a minor, or the client is medically or legally declared to be mentally incapacitated.

Individual therapy is often most beneficial when a client is trying to learn more about themselves or wants to address a highly specific, personal problem. These aspects are in contrast to **group therapy**, a type of intervention which may work with a group of unrelated people who want to address the same issue (e.g., substance abuse) or a family who wants to work toward a goal together (e.g., address intergenerational coping mechanisms).

Individual therapy may be more costly than other types of therapy, but it can produce better outcomes due to its tailored approach. People who pursue individual therapy may also benefit from some aspects of group therapy, such as the social encouragement and empathy that comes from participating in a complementary support group.

Group

Individuals seeking counseling may benefit from group work in addition to, or in place of, individual counseling. Groups focus on nonpathological issues, such as personal, physical/medical, social, or vocational, and act to support and encourage growth. Groups are popular for addictions, eating disorders or weight loss, grief, anxiety, and parenting. They can be homogenous and share demographic information and goals or can be heterogeneous and diverse with multifaceted goals. Group members benefit from the process through sharing and the ability to learn new ways to react and cope with difficulties. It is essential that groups have a trained leader to help create structure, boundaries, and rules and keep the group on track.

Gerald Caplan, known for his crisis intervention theories, defined three levels of groups. **Primary groups** focus on healthy living and coping strategies. These groups, also referred to as **support, guidance**, or **psychoeducational groups**, may help prevent unwanted consequences by teaching healthier alternatives. **Secondary groups** deal more with existing problems and work to reduce or prevent their severity. Also referred to as **counseling groups**, they focus on short-term concerns. **Tertiary groups** are designed for individuals with more serious pathology and include members who are likely receiving individual psychotherapy in addition to the group.

Types of Groups and Primary Goals

Guidance/psychoeducational: This type of group is designed to teach or guide individuals to develop or maintain specific skills. This group is used to help prevent problems (such as substance abuse or teen pregnancy) and teach alternative options, problem solving, and coping skills. They are considered structured groups, as there are defined tasks and goals.

Counseling: This type of group provides additional support to members experiencing stress but not major psychological issues.

Psychotherapy: This type of group provides a therapeutic intervention for members experiencing more acute issues and must be led by a trained counselor or psychotherapist.

Self-help: This is a more informal group that does not have a designated leader. Alcoholics Anonymous is a self-help group.

T-group: This is an experiential or training group designed to help individuals facilitate change.

Task: This group is formed to complete a specific task or goal. These can include committees, focus groups, or work groups.

Psychoanalytic: These groups are based on Freudian theories and used to gain conscious awareness of unconscious conflicts. These groups can be intense and long term but are designed to facilitate major insights and change.

Cognitive behavioral: This is a task-focused group to help individuals understand how thoughts impact behaviors and develop more functional patterns.

Stages of a Group

Several theories outline the developmental stages of a group. One of the most well-known is Bruce Tuckman's four-stage model: forming, storming, norming, and performing. **Forming** is the stage where the group members are just beginning to get acquainted and may be anxious and less vocal. **Storming** involves conflict, discord, and struggles to agree upon a leader. **Norming** is the agreement stage, during which a leader is chosen and conflicts begin to resolve. **Performing** is the point at which the group becomes effective at achieving defined tasks. A fifth stage, **Adjourning**, was added, which defines the point at which the group terminates.

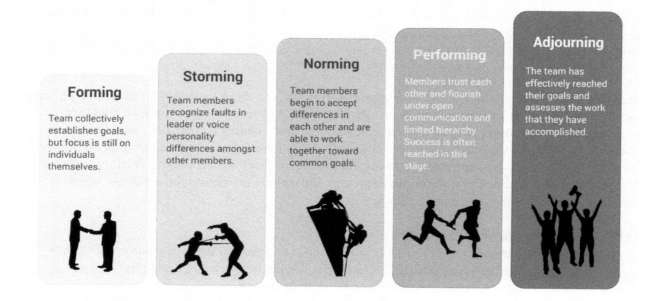

Forming

Team collectively establishes goals, but focus is still on individuals themselves.

Storming

Team members recognize faults in leader or voice personality differences amongst other members.

Norming

Team members begin to accept differences in each other and are able to work together toward common goals.

Performing

Members trust each other and flourish under open communication and limited hierarchy. Success is often reached in this stage.

Adjourning

The team has effectively reached their goals and assesses the work that they have accomplished.

Other group development theories include that of Irvin D. Yalom, whose three-stage model included orientation, conflict/dominance, and development of cohesiveness. Gerald Corey's stages included initial, transition, working, and termination. All three theories share similar progressions of the group process.

Purpose of Family Counseling

Just as individuals need help and support, family units need guidance in dealing with problems, coping with stressors, and learning ways to function more effectively. The goals of family counseling are to identify and change dysfunctional patterns, increase communication, and use the power of relationships to heal and stabilize the family unit. Family counseling can include nuclear families, extended families, and anyone who has an impact on the familial relationship. Family counseling helps to build love and support, thus creating stronger and healthier families.

Psychoanalytic Theory and Group Work

Based on Freudian theories, psychoanalytic groups are intensive and long-term forms of group therapy. These groups focus on early childhood relationships, unconscious processes, and the resolution of past relationship conflicts. Group members may use each other and the group leader to re-experience past relationships and work to develop insight and self-awareness. Transference and countertransference are essential processes in psychoanalytic groups, and the leader's role is to facilitate analysis, interpretation, and resolution of individual and group dynamics.

Gestalt Theory and Group Work

Based on the work of Fritz Perls, Gestalt group work began as an alternative to the more intense psychoanalytic group process. **Gestalt**, from the German word for *shape* or *form*, encourages increased emotional awareness, freedom, and self-direction. It is a holistic model that helps clients focus on the present and work toward personal growth and balance. Specific techniques used are experimental exercises, such as the empty chair technique, where a client uses an empty chair to resolve feelings toward a specific person or sits in the chair to act as that person.

Person-Centered Theory and Group Work

Applying the Rogerian principles of genuineness, positive regard, and empathy, person-centered group work is designed to help individuals increase self-awareness, self-acceptance, and openness and decrease defensiveness. The group leader is nondirective and may act as more of a member than an expert. Person-centered groups may progress more organically, as there is less structure and more focus on listening and reflection.

Behavioral Counseling Groups

Behavioral groups are more structured and designed to help extinguish unwanted behaviors or increase more functional thoughts and actions. Behavior modification techniques such as reinforcement, modeling, extinction, and desensitization are used. The leader of a behavioral group is an expert and directive and sets a clear agenda. These groups focus less on emotional content and processing and more on increasing levels of functioning through behavior modification.

Transactional Analysis Theory and Group Work

Through the study of psychoanalysis and human interaction, Eric Berne developed transactional analysis, which is easily applied to group settings. The focus of the work is on human interactions and helping individuals develop autonomy by learning awareness, spontaneity, and the capacity for intimacy. Group members support each other through positive interactions that help empower them to make better decisions. Group leaders have three main functions: protection, permission, and potency. These involve keeping members safe, providing directives, and using appropriate counseling interventions. Examples of these functions would be protecting by communication the message that the group and counselor will be there when the client is scared or worried, and the group and therapist give the client permission to do whatever he or she was previously told wasn't allowed (such as communicating feelings or asking for what he or she needs). Finally, the degree to which the client is protecting or giving permission to him or herself will affect the therapeutic potency (or how much the mind, internal self-talk, and emotions are affected).

Reality Theory and Group Work

Reality theory focuses on the present; the goal is for members to understand consequences of decisions and learn to get their basic needs met. Basic needs include survival, love, belonging, power, freedom, and fun. Once their needs are met, members can focus on controlling their behavior. The leader's role is to instill trust in the members, help them provide each other feedback, and teach them to apply what is learned in therapy to their life.

Structured vs. Unstructured Group Sessions

Structured exercises are important, especially at the start of a new group, to help members open up and gain trust with one another. Research has shown that too much structure can be detrimental for a group and causes overreliance on the leader. Yalom found that excessive structure could also cause the group to skip over necessary stages of development. It was also found that leaders of highly structured groups were more popular with the members; however, the group overall was less effective.

Adlerian Theory and Group Work

Alfred Adler was one of the first psychologists to use group counseling, as he believed that individuals needed social structure to facilitate change. He found issues resulted from a lack of social connections, which could be addressed through a therapy group. Adlerian group therapy has four main goals: first, establishing and maintaining relationships with group members; second, understanding each individual's functioning based on his or her social and family experiences; third, gaining awareness and insight from interactions with, and feedback from, group members; and fourth, bringing change into action through reorientation to society with improved self-esteem. Adlerian group leaders act as guides and role models and are actively involved with the group.

Rational-Emotive Method

Rational-emotive behavioral theories state that one's feelings and beliefs arise from one's thoughts. The rational-emotive method is typically used as an intervention for clients experiencing negative emotions, feelings, and thought patterns. It is commonly used to treat conditions such as depression or aggression, and it is also used to address unhealthy habits and self-sabotaging behaviors. Often, clients may be not aware that they hold negative or limiting beliefs that drive their behaviors and contribute to the events that take place in their lives. The rational-emotive method helps clients become aware of their habitual thoughts and behavior patterns. Then, they are able to identify how negativity or irrational beliefs contribute to their present conditions, personal challenges, and inability to meet desired goals.

This method works well with clients who are hoping to simply feel happier in their daily lives, overcome unhelpful habits, or achieve a personal or professional goal. It also works well to support people in better understanding their self-concept, self-esteem, and personal needs; this method can help clients eliminate narratives they have heard during their life (e.g., expectations from society or caregivers) and embrace authentic personal values and belief systems. Practitioners who utilize this method can sometimes be quite direct in their interactions with clients, pointing out when a belief may be negative or irrational. This is different than some of the more collaborative approaches seen in modern day therapeutic interventions. Some researchers and practitioners criticize this method as an approach for clients who have experienced extreme trauma such as early childhood sexual abuse, believing the

method minimizes or invalidates the emotional burden unique to survivors of assault, war, and other highly volatile experiences.

Psychoanalytic/Psychodynamic Method

The **psychodynamic perspective** explores the psychology of personality and asserts that personality is developed as a result of unconscious drives, or an individual's inner motivations and childhood experiences. This perspective was developed as a result of the work of Sigmund Freud. Freud introduced psychoanalytic theory, which proposed three components of the mind including the conscious, preconscious and unconscious minds. The **conscious mind** contains thoughts that a person is aware of. The **pre-conscious mind** contains information that a person can retrieve if needed. The **unconscious mind** stores thoughts and experiences a person is not aware of, however, still affects the individual's personality, feelings and actions. Freud also proposed three distinct personality components including the id, ego and the superego. The **id** is seeks pleasure and is impulsive in doing so. The **superego** develops as a result of societal influence and provides a framework for morality. The **ego** manages the conflict between the id and the superego.

Freud also proposed several stages of human development, psychosexual in nature, that occur before the age of 5. A disruption at any of the stages would affect an individual's personality development. Freud's psychosexual development stages include oral, anal, phallic, latency and genital. Another major contribution by Freud is the concept of defense mechanisms. These protective mechanisms occur at unconscious levels and reduce anxiety and stress in an individual. Some of the more well-known defense mechanisms are repression or preventing uncomfortable thoughts and feelings from reaching consciousness and projection, which is when an individual projects or assigns his or her own feelings on to another person to avoid stress about those feelings.

Client-Centered Method

The **client-centered method** is a highly collaborative method of therapy that encourages clients to take an active, leading role in their own treatment. It works under the principle that all people, when supported appropriately, will move in ways that serve their individual growth and healing. This method was pioneered to be as nondirective as possible, and practitioners often let clients guide the topics of the session while they work to provide a nonjudgmental and supportive environment that allows the client to talk openly. Practitioners who use this method are most effective if they can avoid talking about their personal experiences, empathize with the client, serve as an active listener, and provide relevant information when asked. In the client-centered method, practitioners take on a facilitation role and try to support clients in discovering the answers to their personal questions on their own.

Proponents of this approach believe it builds self-confidence and self-efficacy in clients. By leading their own recovery, clients become empowered to gradually learn self-reliance in navigating their personal problems and obstacles in life. Clients build trust in themselves and in their ability to develop and implement resolutions. This method can be beneficial when working with people who suffer from depression, anxiety, low self-esteem, and low self-confidence. It can also support people who suffer from substance abuse, addiction, and other self-sabotaging coping mechanisms. This method may be difficult to utilize with clients who have psychotic disorders, have been medically or legally deemed as not sound of mind, or are in treatment involuntarily. The client-centered approach usually requires that participants are intrinsically motivated to introspect, analyze personal beliefs and behaviors, and actively work toward established goals in order to achieve positive outcomes.

Cognitive Method

The **cognitive method** addresses the way people think, hold beliefs, make decisions, and carry out other cognitive processes. Generally, a practitioner will work with a client to identify habitual and automatic thought patterns, internal dialogue, and factors that shape the client's perception of the world. This method focuses intensely on internal factors that may not initially appear to be clearly linked to personal behaviors. The cognitive approach was popularized with the advent of computer systems, which operated on clear flowchart mechanisms—if a certain input is entered into a system, a certain output will result, and an internal analysis within the operating system takes place in between the input and the output. The cognitive approach addresses human behavior in a similar way. It accounts for the stimuli (or inputs) that people sense and perceive around them, which ultimately results in a behavior (or outputs); between the initial perception of the stimuli and the corresponding behavior, a host of cognitive processes take place in a person's brain and consciousness.

This approach added a helpful layer to behavioral methods, which typically did not account for the influence of cognition on behavior. Cognitive methods are especially helpful in interventions for mood disorders, such as depression, due to their ability to help clients quickly become aware of internal mental patterns that can result in mood disorders (e.g., negative self-schemas, automatic negative dialogue). These methods can also be effective in treating clients who are addressing a specific cognitive task, such as wanting to increase their memory recall or reduce indecisiveness. Aging clients who want to maintain their brain health may also benefit from services provided by a practitioner trained in the cognitive field. Finally, the cognitive approach can help clients who have faced trauma to the structure of the brain that impacts cognitive processes. Practitioners may utilize games and both mental and physical exercises that help clients rehabilitate neural functions after events like a stroke or head injury.

Cognitive approaches on their own may not necessarily result in any type of behavior change, and some practitioners find this method more theoretical in nature rather than one that can be pragmatically used with clients who are hoping to change a behavior. Additionally, some researchers critique this approach because of the parallels to computer systems. Critics state that humans are more complex than computers and human actions cannot be reduced to simplistic input and output explanations.

Behavioral Method

The **behavioral perspective** differs from previous schools of thought, like the psychodynamic and functionalist perspectives that emerged during the 1800's. Behaviorism focuses solely on observable behaviors as compared to internal feelings, responses or thoughts. Behaviorists study how behaviors are reinforced or decreased in response to external stimuli.

John Watson, influenced by Pavlov's concept of conditioning, believed that all behavior could be explained by reactions to external stimulus, which resulted in the development of the behaviorism school of thought. Watson disagreed with previous theories that attributed human behavior to internal drives. Watson expanded on Pavlov's conditioning experiment with animals and demonstrated that human behavior could be impacted by conditioning. B.F. Skinner continued work on behaviorism and introduced the concept of operant conditioning.

Sociocultural Method

The **sociocultural method** considers how a person's social influences and culture upbringing impact belief systems and behavior. Clients' self-perception is greatly influenced by their social and cultural environments, and their belief systems, attitudes, norms, goals, and motivations are often shaped through these influences, as well. Practitioners who utilize this approach may not typically work in

individual therapy sessions; rather, they are likely to be found in research settings where they examine factors of society and culture and how human behavior, collectively, is affected. However, practitioners who work in individual therapy often utilize sociocultural research to better understand their clients and to be more sensitive to clients who come from different walks of life.

Sociocultural methods examine variables such as race, social class, income level, cultural practices for each gender, and family dynamics. These methods can be especially helpful when working with immigrants who are trying to assimilate to a new environment and native-born children of immigrants who experience one culture at home and another culture in school or at work. Sociocultural methods are also helpful when working with any minority group, as most minorities in the United States report feeling vulnerable, untrusting, and susceptible to prejudice and discrimination when compared to majority groups.

Sociocultural influences can also be used to work with clients who need clarity around self-identity, who struggle with self-esteem, and who generally want to develop their sense of self-concept. Often, these are tied to narratives provided by the society and household in which one grew up. Clients may embody gender norms, gender roles, and other stereotypes with which they do not genuinely identify; a better understanding of how these beliefs were absorbed can help clients move toward developing a stronger self-concept. It is important that practitioners who utilize sociocultural methods also consider cognitive and behavioral approaches, as taking a purely sociocultural approach is likely to not provide an effective intervention that results in a sustained behavior change.

Biopsychosocial Method

The **biological** or **biopsychological** school of thought looks at how human physiology and biology including hormones, genes and the brain affect human psychology. This perspective asserts that cognitive processes are genetic, and behavior is driven by biology. For instance, a biological psychologist would look for biological influences for the causes of depression. Examples may be brain chemistry or injury as well as a person's genetic predisposition. The biopsychosocial model first developed by George Engel in 1977 utilizes multiple schools of thought including biology, social, environmental and psychological. This perspective is used frequently in modern psychology.

Cognitive-Behavioral Method

Cognitive-behavioral methods are frequently used in both individual and group therapy settings. Such methods begin by asking clients to become aware of automatic and embedded thought patterns, beliefs, attitudes, and reactions. Then, clients are asked to link these to behaviors. Finally, they are provided tools to reinforce or unlearn relevant behaviors that move them toward an established outcome or goal. By integrating the benefits of both cognitive approaches and behavioral approaches, practitioners increase the chances of client success. Cognitive-behavioral methods allow clients to better understand what drives their behaviors while also providing the necessary tools for change. As a result, these methods can be used to treat a wide range of disorders, including addiction and mood disorders.

They can also be used to simply address and resolve bad habits while replacing them with beneficial habits. Cognitive-behavioral methods are often used to build resiliency and incorporate ways to healthily cope with stress. Practitioners will often provide practices and work for clients to do on their own time, outside of sessions. As a result, clients work toward their goals continuously and may experience positive outcomes and breakthroughs more quickly than through other approaches. Peer-reviewed meta-analyses of this method indicate that over eighty percent of adults who participate in cognitive-behavioral therapy sessions experience or report positive outcomes as a result. The limitations

175

for this approach are minimal and mostly pertain to the lack of knowledge that still exists around cognitive processing.

Unit 9: Social Psychology

Attribution Theory and Person Perception

Applying Attribution Theory to Explain Motives

Attribution theory states that people attribute the behavior they observe in others either to their situation or their disposition, or unchanging qualities.

Fundamental Attribution Error
The **fundamental attribution error** happens when someone mistakenly attributes observed behavior to someone's disposition rather than their situation. There are also cultural variations when it comes to attribution styles. Western cultures that are more individualistic tend to attribute behaviors to a person's disposition. On the other hand, some collectivist Asian cultures are more likely to consider situational factors in behavior attribution.

The attitudes people have toward other people, situations, or things will strongly influence their behaviors. Attribution theory asserts that people attribute someone's behavior either to their disposition or their situation. This will then influence actions toward that person. Icek Ajzen's **theory of planned behavior** (TPB) states that a combination of perceived behavioral control, attitudes, and normative beliefs work together to influence behavior.

Self-Serving Bias
The **self-serving bias** refers to a personal tendency to believe that positive events in one's life are due to their personal efforts, traits, or character, while negative events in one's life are due to circumstances outside of personal control. This bias appears to be common across the population, although somewhat less skewed in people who have been diagnosed with depression. Culturally, individualistic societies are more likely to experience a stronger self-serving bias. People with depression appear to have a smaller self-serving bias; they may even experience a phenomenon known as a flipped self-serving bias.

In a **flipped self-serving bias**, people attribute negative events in their lives to personal flaws, and do not take any ownership or credit for the positive events that occur. It is believed that self-serving biases occur to maintain one's sense of self-concept and self-esteem. They are most commonly seen in workplace settings. Biases appear more extreme in interpersonal relationships where the people involved do not know each other well; the closer two people's relationship, the less intense either person's self-serving bias becomes. In personality pathologies, such as narcissism, self-serving biases are often higher than average.

False Consensus Effect
The **false consensus effect** refers to the phenomenon of people believing their personal values, beliefs, systems, and attitudes are the norm. People have the natural tendency to overestimate the number of other people who share the same viewpoint as them, creating false assumption of group consensus on one or more ideas. The false consensus effect is highlighted in groups where people have similar interests and opinions; an individual in this group is more likely to believe the similarities extend to the population at large.

In recent culture, this type of phenomenon has been seen in relation to political viewpoints that are shared on social media. As people tend to interact virtually more with people and media that are similar to their personal viewpoints, software algorithms often eliminate perspectives that are different from the users' perspectives. For the end user, this creates a virtual bubble of opinions and perspectives that are largely similar. From a psychological standpoint, when people are presented with evidence that goes against their primary consensus, they believe the information is flawed in some way.

Confirmation Bias

Confirmation bias occurs when a person is seeking out evidence that supports a desired result. Often, that person will ignore or avoid seeking out evidence against the desired result. Generally, people tend to lean toward having a confirmation bias; this often drives personal behavior and decision making. Confirmation biases appear to become stronger around emotional or vulnerable topics. For example, childhood vaccines have become hotly debated in recent years, with both pro-vaccine and anti-vaccine groups citing various sources of evidence that support their viewpoint. Yet, confirmation bias is strong in this context due to the parental emotion involved—parents want to make the safest choice for their children. In topics or debates that do not necessarily impact an individual directly, they may be more open to listening to various and differing sources of evidence before taking a stance. Additionally, confirmation bias may be influenced by people's need to seek positive over negative information, to justify a cost decision, or to avoid creating cognitive dissonance.

Just-World Hypothesis

The **just-world hypothesis**, a social psychology concept, predicts that people inherently try to view events as part of a fair and morally-balanced world. It states that people typically judge those who are in unfortunate situations and believe they somehow deserve or caused the situation to occur. Psychologists believe the just-world concept allows people to make sense of negative events that would otherwise cause emotional or psychological distress; however, this viewpoint can also result in people invalidating or negating perspectives of those that might have been victimized in a situation.

In the study that first illustrated this concept, psychologist **Melvin Lerner** showed footage of a woman receiving electric shocks. No other context was provided to participants. Yet, viewers shared negative perceptions of the woman and made arguments that she likely deserved the treatment. This was a controversial study in the 1960s that led to further examination of how people justify negative events, especially those in which people are suffering, in order to mentally maintain a semblance of the world as a fair and ethical place. Later research showed that the more people view the world as a fair place, they more they also believe that those in unfortunate circumstances (e.g., poverty, domestic violence situations) ultimately brought the situation upon themselves.

Halo Effect

The **halo effect** is a form of bias in which a person takes an initial positive impression of another person and extrapolates that into assuming other positive qualities about that person's character. Most commonly, this is seen with attractiveness; research shows that people often assume attractive people have a host of other positive qualities (e.g., smarter, funnier, wealthier) even without evidence that supports those assumptions.

The halo effect is also commonly seen in student-teacher interactions. Students tend to judge teachers based off initial impressions of age, warmth, and socialness. Younger teachers who are friendly and warm in the initial interaction are more likely to be rated as more knowledgeable and skilled instructors, even without evidence that clearly indicates this. Studies also show that teachers tend to view quieter

students as better behaved and more intelligent, even before reviewing work or assessments. This concept is heavily relied upon in marketing, advertising, and political campaigns. People report that it is often difficult to challenge the halo effect, even if they are aware of its presence, due to its inherently subliminal nature.

The Impact of Social and Cultural Categories on Self-Concept and Relations with Others

Self-esteem is the feeling of personal value or worth, and **self-efficacy** is an individual's feeling of competence in accomplishing a task. Someone who has strong self-esteem and self-efficacy will be proactive and confident, both socially and vocationally. Having an internal locus of control vs. external locus of control also plays a role in one's identity. An **internal locus of control** is when someone has the perception that he or she have control over his or her environment. An **external locus of control** is when someone believes that his or her future and life are controlled by factors outside of himself or herself. Those with an internal locus of control have a stronger self-concept and self-identity, leading to superior achievement, greater emotional stability, and more individual responsibility for behaviors.

Identity is best understood as a person's view of self, which may include the many different aspects of race, gender, age, sexual orientation, and class. Chronological and felt age, as well as economic class, can contribute significantly to one's identity. All aspects of identity are influenced by social factors and issues of discrimination and prejudice based on specific identity characteristics.

Gender
Gender refers to a person's subjective experience of being male or female. **Sexual orientation** has to do with sexual attraction, and includes those who identify as homosexual, heterosexual, asexual, or bisexual.

Gender identity is a person's understanding of his or her own gender, especially as it relates to being male or female (or something else). **Gender expression** is one's outward presentation (e.g., clothing, hair style, physical appearance) and behaviors that communicate or show their gender identity. **Sexual orientation** is a more complex concept as it refers to the sexual attraction one feels toward others.

Types of Gender Identity
Bi-gender: An individual who fluctuates between the self-image of traditionally male and female stereotypes and identifies with both genders.

Gender Nonconforming: An individual who has a gender identity or expression that is different that the norms associated with the gender they were assigned at birth.

Genderqueer: A term for an individual who may think of themselves as both male and female, a third or other gender, or moving between the two binary genders.

Transgender: A generalized term referring to a variety of sexual identities that do not fit under more traditional categories, a person who feels to be of a different gender than was assigned at birth.

Transsexual: A person who identifies emotionally and psychologically, and sometimes physically, with the gender other than that assigned at birth; lives as a person of the opposite gender.

Those who are transgender or transsexual may be homosexual, heterosexual, or asexual. Sexual identity and sexual attraction are independent.

Being transgender can be defined as identifying as a gender other than they the gender one was assigned at birth. Publicly sharing that one is transgender can be difficult for some individuals. Transgender individuals may live in a community where their identity is not positively accepted or is misunderstood, and they may feel shamed or ridiculed. It may be a difficult experience for close family members to understand the perspective of a transgender individual, which can affect the cohesiveness of family relationships and the family unit. Transgender individuals may also feel a lack of acknowledgement when others fail to use the correct pronouns or respect other identity wishes.

Some transgender individuals choose to medically transition to the gender they identify as. This is a procedure that requires physical, emotional, and psychological support. Individuals not receiving support during their transition can experience extreme feelings of sadness, isolation, and lack of belonging. Medically transitioning individuals also undergo hormonal changes in addition to surgical procedures, and these can cause unexpected feelings and reactions in the individual. There are also medical risks that go along with both the surgical and hormonal procedures of transitioning that the individual has to be aware of and manage. Finally, after the transition is complete, individuals may struggle with living as someone who is relatively unfamiliar to their friends, family members, and colleagues. The transgender person may or may not experience support and acceptance in these groups and relationships, and some group members may even act aggressively toward the transgender person.

If this is the case, it may be helpful to find support groups where transgender individuals can find not only friendship and community, but also guidance on how to navigate their new life, society, friends and relationships, and medical recovery.

Race

Race typically denotes distinctive physical characteristics, such as skin color, while **ethnicity** encompasses all of a person's cultural traditions and background.

The following lists Sue & Sue's Stages of Racial/Cultural Identity Development:

Conformity
The individual displays a distinct preference for the dominant culture and holds negative views of his or her own racial and/or cultural groups. He or she may also experience shame or embarrassment.

Dissonance
The individual undergoes a period of re-thinking or challenging his or her beliefs. For the first time, the individual examines and appreciates positive aspects of his or her own racial/cultural group.

Resistance and Immersion
The individual shows preference for minority views and actively rejects the views of the dominant culture, experiencing pride about and connection to his or her racial or cultural group.

Introspection
The individual becomes aware of the negative impact of the resistance and immersion stage and may realize that he or she does not actually disagree with all majority views or endorse all minority views.

Integrative Awareness

The individual is able to appreciate both his or her own culture and differing cultures.

The following lists William Cross's Stages of Identity Development for people of color:

Pre-Encounter

Unless prompted to do so, children do not critically evaluate the race-related messages that they receive from the world around them.

Encounter

Often experienced in early adolescence, the individual has one or more experiences that are related to race. Although it is possible for the experiences to be positive, this is often when an individual first experiences racism or discrimination and begins to understand the personal impact of his or her race.

Immersion-Emersion

After experiencing a race-related incident, the individual strongly identifies with his or her racial group and may seek out information about history and culture.

Internalization

Racial identity is solidified, and the individual experiences a sense of security in identifying with his or her race.

Internalization-Commitment

Racial identity is taken one step further into activism pertaining to issues related to the experiences of the individual's racial group.

Ethnicity

Race refers to biologically-distinct populations within the human species. **Ethnicity** is a cultural term referring to the common customs, language, and heritage of a category of people. **Ethnic identity** is the identification with a particular group of people who share one's culture and heritage.

Culture, race, and ethnicity can greatly impact one's self-image, whether one is part of a privileged population or of a minority or disenfranchised population. One's ethnic and racial background provides a sense of belonging and identity. Depending on a country's treatment of a particular group, self-image can be negatively impacted through racism and discrimination. Non-whites are more likely to be arrested than whites and often receive harsher sentences for similar offenses. Racial jokes and racial slurs are common. Stereotypes abound, and some people judge entire racial groups based on the behavior of a few. Such treatment consistently impacts the self-esteem of those in minority groups.

As children become aware of the environment and the culture in which they live, they inevitably notice a lack of prominent non-white politicians, entertainers, CEOs, and multi-millionaires. Non-white Americans—who grew up in the fifties or earlier—were denied access to restaurants, theaters, high schools, professions, universities, and recreational activities. Even within the last fifty to sixty years, African Americans who had achieved great status in the fields of music, sports, and entertainment were still denied access to certain clubs, hotels, or restaurants.

Every person must explore and come to terms with his or her own culture, ethnicity, and race. Sometimes, this even means rejecting cultural aspects with which he or she disagrees and embracing new and evolving cultural norms. This is a significant part of self-identity development for teenagers and young adults, as they are part of a new generation that may be culturally different from their parents. Those that have more exposure to other cultures and backgrounds likely will have a more open perspective and will be better able to evaluate their own culture and ethnicity objectively.

The Impact of Self-Fulfilling Prophecy on Behavior

Self-fulfilling prophecies are beliefs or expectations someone has about a person, which cause them to act in a certain way toward that person, thus eliciting the very behavior they expect of them. This has been clearly observed in experiments conducted with school teachers and children, where the teachers were given faulty expectations about students, either that they were more or less intelligent than they actually were. The students' performances reflected the expectations of their teachers, because the teachers treated the students according to the expectations they had of them.

Attitude Formation and Attitude Change

Important Figures and Research in the Areas of Attitude Formation and Change

Leon Festinger

Leon Festinger (1919–1989) played a critical role in the field of social psychology by contributing the social comparison and cognitive dissonance theories. The **social comparison theory**, which he posed first, states that people inherently judge themselves based on how they compare to others around them. This evaluation serves as a component of how people develop their self-concept. Later, his **cognitive dissonance theory** stated that people generally hope to keep their personal beliefs and attitudes uncompromised. When a threat occurs to a person's belief system, they feel compelled to rectify the dissonance. People will attempt to address dissonance through changing a behavior, seeking out more information to justify the original beliefs, or shifting personal beliefs and attitudes to reduce the discrepancy. However, eliminating cognitive dissonance is not always successful.

Festinger also conducted an experiment to depict his concept of forced compliance. In this experiment, he asked people to perform a task they did not choose or necessarily want to do. He found that this forced compliance created a cognitive dissonance that generally resulted in tension in the participant. Festinger is also credited with the concept of the **proximity effect**, which states that people are more likely to develop social relationships with those who are physically close to them (e.g., an adjacent neighbor, a coworker at an adjacent desk).

Attitude Formation and Change

Just as attitude can influence behavior, behavioral change can influence attitude change. For instance, the action of smiling can encourage the feeling of happiness. The action of role playing can create attitudes in line with the role being played. Secondly, when those presenting a particular message are considered more attractive, knowledgeable in their field, or trustworthy, it is more likely that the listener will accept the speaker's message and change his or her attitude. Finally, social factors can affect attitude change. Attitudes are formed and altered by observing others and people tend to conform to the beliefs of their peers and society.

The **foot-in-door phenomenon** refers to when someone influences another person to do a greater behavior or action, by first getting them to agree to a small step. If someone has loaned a friend $5, the loaner may later be willing to increase the loan to $20. The first action, though small, leads to an attitude that allows for a greater action. Role-playing is another behavior that can powerfully influence

attitudes. Philip Zimbardo's prison experiment, in which students were asked to role play guards and prisoners, is a classic example of the power of role playing. The participants' attitudes were so influenced by their roles that they began to act in dangerous and extreme ways.

The attitudes people have toward other people, situations, or things will strongly influence their behaviors. **Attribution theory** asserts that people attribute someone's behavior either to their disposition or their situation. This will then influence actions toward that person. Icek Ajzen's **theory of planned behavior** (TPB) states that a combination of perceived behavioral control, attitudes, and normative beliefs work together to influence behavior.

Central Route to Persuasion

The **central route to persuasion** is a cognitive function that explains how people may shift personal beliefs, values, and attitudes based on an external influence. The central route is a deeper, systematic, and analytical method of persuasion in which the person who is listening to or viewing a message actively absorbs the information, thinks about the message, and considers their own perspective and beliefs. From here, they acknowledge that the content is meaningful or valuable to them in some way; they are persuaded directly by the message itself. This tactic is commonly seen in political campaigns, infomercial advertising, and health marketing. For example, consider pre-primary presidential debates that take place between hopeful candidates. In these events, each candidate provides information and content with the sole intention of persuading potential voters to cast a vote for the candidate's platform. Candidates utilize the central route to persuade potential voters by providing direct messaging for the viewer to analyze. It must also be assumed that for the central route to persuasion to work successfully, the person who is receiving the message is open to actively listening and taking the time to consider the content.

Peripheral Route to Persuasion

The **peripheral route to persuasion** occurs when a person shifts their beliefs, attitudes, or values based on less obvious reasons. Often, these reasons are not even directly related to the content being presented. People are most likely to be persuaded by the peripheral route if they perceive the messenger to be credible or an expert, if they do not know enough about a topic to confidently argue against the presented message, or if they ultimately hold a type of bias. A common example of persuasion through the peripheral route is the voter who always votes down a certain party's line, even if they are unsure of the actual stances that candidates in the party hold. From the perspective of the messenger, the peripheral route of persuasion should always be considered when delivering content. As people, in general, are only deeply engaged and willing to devote time to a few topics at any given time, they are often persuaded (or not) through peripheral means. Therefore, messengers should consider aspects beyond just content delivery; they may also want to consider the demographic data associated with the intended audience, what value the topic holds with the intended audience, and whether or not the delivered content appears to come from an expert source.

Cognitive Dissonance

Cognitive dissonance theory states that when a person holds two conflicting beliefs, or acts in a way that is inconsistent with his or her beliefs, the person will experience tension or dissonance. In an effort to reduce this tension, the person will act to reduce this tension by changing their attitudes or actions.

Elaboration Likelihood Model

The **elaboration likelihood model** seeks to explain attitude changes that lead to behavioral changes and decision making. These changes happen primarily through persuasion. A person engaged in the **central**

route to persuasion will assess the true characteristics of a thing or the actual issues being debated. The **peripheral route to persuasion**, on the other hand, relies on secondary and superficial means rather than the actual issues. For example, someone may be persuaded to purchase a particular item because it was advertised by a famous or attractive person, rather than because on the quality of the item itself. When there is high cognitive engagement, or elaboration, there is a higher chance that the central route to persuasion will be utilized, which typically leads to more long-term and enduring changes in attitude.

Conformity, Compliance, and Obedience

The Contributions of Key Researchers in the Areas of Conformity, Compliance, and Obedience

Solomon Asch

Solomon Asch (1907–1996) pioneered concepts of conformity in the social psychology domain. He stated that a person's interactions with others and their behaviors in public were influenced heavily by the environment, and that people generally will try to fit in with their environment. His ideas first came to fruition during the World War II years, as he tried to understand the role and influence of Nazi propaganda. Asch's pivotal studies on conformity experimented with how much people would shift personal values and beliefs in order to fit in with a larger group or environment. His conformity studies showed that people would concede to the opinions and actions of the group that surrounded them even if those opinions and actions went largely against their personal beliefs. While these studies provided information relating to social pressures, it also showed how horrific events in humanity could easily start and maintain themselves. Asch was also a primary mentor to Stanley Milgram.

Stanley Milgram

Stanley Milgram (1933–1984) is best known for his studies on obedience behaviors, including his eponymous experiment. Like Asch, Milgram's work resulted from an interest in better understanding social psychology factors of the Nazi regime and events relating to the Holocaust. Milgram's experiment tested different factors that contribute to one's obedience to authority and occurred alongside the trial of SS office Adolf Eichmann. During these periods of trials that decided upon charges and sentencing for Nazi officials, social and political commentary centered on whether lower-ranking officers simply had to obey orders.

In the experiment, the participant was asked by a designated authority figure to deliver certain voltages of shocks to another participant. The participant receiving shocks was actually an actor who was not actually hurt, but acted as though they were seizing, unable to talk, and in extreme pain. Milgram and a panel of other scientific experts hypothesized that no participant would voluntarily deliver a high level of shock upon seeing these outcomes. Yet, the majority of participants delivered shocks at the highest setting upon instruction from the authority figure. Most of them appeared to be highly uncomfortable and upset at doing so, yet still obeyed the command. From this experiment, Milgram illustrated how people would obey authority even if they deeply disagreed with or were bothered by the action they were performing. This experiment was received with a great deal of ethical criticism.

Philip Zimbardo

Philip Zimbardo (1933–) was a contemporary of Stanley Milgram and is best known for the **Stanford prison experiment**. This experiment examined the impact of role and authority upon an individual's psyche. A second goal was to better understand the role of personality versus the influences of a specific environment. Zimbardo assigned random male undergraduate students the role of guard in the trial,

while others were assigned role of prisoners. Zimbardo told the acting guards that they could punish the acting prisoners with any means apart from physical violence. The acting guards began implementing punishments such removing bedding, enforcing sleep deprivation, and other dehumanizing acts. With no intervention, they continued to increase the frequency and intensity of punishments, even after acting prisoners began showing visible signs of mental abuse.

Both sets of participants took on the personas they were assigned, showing how roles, labeling, social expectations, environment, and lack of peer intervention can give rise to dehumanizing and humiliating behaviors. Many of these participants were normal, well-functioning citizens who showed healthy mental and physical faculties. Like the Milgram experiment, this study was received with significant criticism in regard to potential ethical violations.

How Individuals Respond to Expectations of Others

There are many ways in which a social context can influence individual behavior, either positively or negatively. **Social psychology** looks at the person-environment interaction and explores the many ways the social setting influences a person's attitudes and actions.

Attitudes toward, and influenced by, those around play a major role in a person's behaviors. **Attribution theory** has to do with how one views the behavior of others, whether attributing their behaviors to disposition or situation. If one wrongly attributes someone's negative action to his/her disposition—the **fundamental attribution error**—then one may think more negatively about others than is deserved.

The concept of **conformity**—the tendency for a person to conform personal behaviors to the behaviors of those around him or her—helps explain everything from style trends to mass genocide. Solomon Asch performed a study which showed that people tend to conform to the people around them, even if it means giving an answer that they know is false. The phenomenon of conformity stems from the idea that people act in a way to get approval from others and to avoid disapproval, called **normative social influence**. Another impact of the social sphere that people live in is **deindividuation**, in which a person loses a sense of personal responsibility or individualism. This may happen in crowds at a concert or sports event, or a riot, leading people to behave in ways they would not normally behave if they did not feel anonymous and emotionally-charged by the social setting.

People tend to automatically form groups, often developing the in-group and out-group. The **in-group** consists of those who are part of the group, who share its identity and unifying characteristics. The **out-group** consists of those outside the group, particularly those who may be in opposition or share opposite beliefs to those in the in-group. This in-group and out-group concept may lead to patriotism or working together towards a common goal, but it may also lead to prejudice and discrimination. Groups also tend to engage in **group think**, where no one is willing to share an opinion contrary to the group, or **group polarization**, in which people in the group become stronger and stronger in their opinions as they spend time with others who hold similar beliefs.

Some other key concepts related to the effects of social context on behavior are social loafing and social facilitation. **Social loafing** happens in a context of shared responsibility for a task. In this case, there is a tendency for some people to abdicate responsibility, assuming that others will fulfill the obligations of the work. **Social facilitation**, on the other hand, is when having an audience inspires people to perform tasks they do well even better. Alternatively, it can also cause them to do worse in tasks they find more difficult or challenging.

Environment and social context shape perceptions of how someone acts, speaks, or dresses. Something that would be perceived as normal and appropriate in a particular environment may not be perceived in the same way in a different environment, such as wearing a bathing suit to the grocery store. Additionally, a positive or comfortable environment may cause others to be viewed more positively, whereas a negative environment may have the opposite effect.

Groupthink

Groupthink occurs when people in a group are unwilling to express ideas in opposition to everyone else, due to a desire to maintain harmony. This results in the group making a unanimous decision even though some people may secretly disagree. Negatively, groupthink can prevent all the options from being fully and reasonably explored which may lead to poor decision-making.

Collective Behavior

Collective behavior occurs when groups of people share in the same activity under special circumstances. One obvious example of collective behavior is **fads**, which are short-lived popular trends in behavior, speech, or clothing. **Mass hysteria** results when something happens that causes a widespread and irrational fear among people. The universal panic can result in mass responses that can be as dangerous as the threat that caused the hysteria. **Riots** are when a group of people engage in a spontaneous emotional reaction, often involving violence. Riots are very often in protest of something perceived as negative, but they can also occur spontaneously in joyful reaction to a positive outcome or event.

Group Influences on Behavior and Mental Processes

The Structure and Function of Different Kinds of Group Behavior

Humans end up in groups due to both voluntary and involuntary reasons. Evolutionarily, humans have grouped together to cooperatively collect and utilize resources, provide protection to one another, indulge in entertainment, provide a sense of belonging, and create familial units. In contemporary times, these reasons still exist. Additionally, people group together involuntarily in workplaces, areas of interest and recreation, (e.g., shopping malls and sports arenas), and by geographical proximity. Today, groups can be defined as **formal groups**, which are placed together for a clearly defined purpose, and **informal groups**, in which people organically come together (often for social well-being purposes). Formal groups typically have defined norms, rituals, and governing structures. Informal groups are typically defined by a shared interest or a shared likeness. To be defined as a **group**, all members must exist relatively interdependently and contribute something to the overall value and dynamic of the group.

Additionally, people can exist as a part of primary or secondary groups. **Primary groups** are typically small in size, and members likely have closer and more intimate bonds. **Secondary groups** are larger with less intimate bonds; they often comprise different primary groups. Research indicates that all groups move through certain stages when shaping their dynamic and interactions. As mentioned before, these stages are known as **forming**, **storming**, **norming**, **performing**, and **adjourning**. In the first stage, group members may awkwardly come together and try to better understand other members of the group. As they move into storming, they may take on individual and hierarchical group roles. Norming groups have functioning processes and an interdependent dynamic; strengthening these aspects allows the group to move into performing, where the group becomes functional and operates well together.

Not all groups move into the adjourning phase, unless the groups were formed for a specific task (e.g., a project with a deadline within a company).

The Impact of the Presence of Others on Individual Behavior

The **bystander effect** is a phenomenon in which the greater the number of people around someone in an emergency situation (e.g., heart attack, assault), the less likely anyone is to help. A common assumption within a large group of bystanders is that someone else in the group will step forward to help the person in need; ultimately, this results in nobody helping. Additionally, people tend to modulate their own behaviors based on the behaviors displayed by the rest of the group. This effect was first recognized during the relatively public murder of a woman, Kitty Genovese, in New York City. Genovese was stabbed repeatedly by an assailant in full view of a group, and nobody attempted to intervene.

The bystander effect was repeatedly tested through the 1960s and 1970s in experimental emergency situations. These tests reliably showed that people were more likely to aid the "victim" if there were no, or very few, other people around. In the last five years, the bystander effect seems to have changed. In some studies, people appear to be more likely to help someone in distress regardless of bystanders; in fact, some trials even show that aid increases with more bystanders around. This shift could be a result of increased knowledge about the bystander effect or the advent of social media, where many situations are now recorded and placed online by bystanders. This often results in public criticism against those who do not help, and therefore, could have shifted the psychological landscape of the bystander effect.

Social Facilitation
Social facilitation refers to the concept that people tend to perform better, when engaging in familiar tasks, in the presence of an audience. Social facilitation can also occur when others are simply around and there is the possibility that there may be attention drawn to one's actions, even if that external attention is never actually given. For example, a college student working in a classroom with peers and an instructor is more likely to engage in their workload, versus working alone in a room. Comparatively, it should be noted that the social facilitation effect does not extend to tasks that are relatively unfamiliar. When someone has an audience when practicing an unfamiliar task, that person is more likely to flounder and make mistakes rather than improve personal performance.

Social inhibition
Social inhibition refers to avoidance behaviors that pertain specifically to social situations and interactions. It typically takes place when someone hopes to avoid disapproval, judgment, or general criticisms from others. Social inhibition is commonly seen in people who are prone to periods of anxiety and depression, have low self-esteem, or have a personal history of trauma, abuse, and/or neglect. It is also correlated with traits like neuroticism and perfectionism. Social inhibition can be seen in daily life for people who experience it; it can also serve as a precursor to an array of anxiety disorders. It can begin in early childhood. For example, infants who are predisposed to social inhibition may show withdrawal behaviors or a lack of resiliency in foreign or stressful situations. Caregivers may contribute to the development of social inhibition by withholding affection and nurturing behaviors. In adolescence, social inhibition is largely driven by peer reactions to one's personal appearance. People with early inclinations toward social inhibition are likely, without therapy or intervention, to carry these behaviors into adulthood. Social inhibition should not be confused with introversion, a personality trait.

Group Polarization

Group polarization refers to the phenomenon that when a people gather with others who hold similar beliefs, they will become stronger in their shared beliefs. When the majority of the group either opposes or supports a particular idea, they are more likely to make a more extreme decision than they would do as an individual.

Deindividuation

In psychology, **deindividuation** refers to a group behavior in which individual members lose their personal beliefs or values. The single members of the group may have previously expressed certain beliefs and values but take on the uniformity of the group when members are together. This concept is normally referenced in temporary situations of group behavior, such as in riots, but can also be used to define behaviors that last for longer durations, such as in the semblance and group mentality seen in cults. Additionally, deindividuation can also be seen in groups that promote positive messages or behaviors. Philip Zimbardo, of the Stanford prison experiment, examined this concept as part of the prison study. Deindividuation is also commonly seen in groups where uniformity is highly valued, such as in the military.

Diffusion of Responsibility

Diffusion of responsibility is an important concept that is part of the bystander effect. It explains how people are less likely to act when other people are around, assuming that someone else will take a necessary action. This is most commonly used in the context of emergency or social situations. In general, the larger a group of people, the less likely any one person is to assume responsibility for a specific action. For example, consider a group of twenty employees tasked with completing a project deliverable in thirty days. Without clear guidance, direction, or assigned tasks, the group is more likely than not to simply not complete anything related to the project during the thirty-day timeframe. People are also more likely to diffuse responsibility out to the group if a required action is to be done anonymously, if they are not singled out specifically to complete the task, or if they have not been explicitly designated as a leader within the group.

In-group/Out-Group Bias

When discussing people and the communities to which they belong, a person's **in-group** refers to a group that they self-identify as belonging to. Common in-groups that a person identifies with may include family, recreational interest, profession, political affiliation, geography, and so on. Some people may also choose to identify in-groups based on race, religion, sex, or other discriminatory factors. All other groups are considered **out-groups**. **In-group bias** refers to the favoritism that one shows to their in-group; this can extend to belittling or looking unfavorably upon an out-group. **Out-group bias** occurs less commonly but can take place if a member of a group is striving to achieve or obtain something not found within their in-group. A number of studies on in-group and out-group stereotyping have taken place. People are more likely to stereotype against people they perceive as being in an out-group. If people themselves experience out-group stereotyping, they are less likely to have in-group biases and more likely to treat out-group members with kindness and respect.

Reciprocity Norms

People have the tendency to reciprocate generosity that is shown to them. This is explained by the **reciprocity norm**, which states that when one receives a favor or experiences kindness from someone, they feel obligated to return the favor or experience. The reciprocity norm is commonly utilized in marketing and other persuasive contexts. For example, vendors who are competing to provide a particular service may bring gift bags to initial meetings with a potential client. From an evolutionary

perspective, reciprocity norms support cooperative, communal efforts within the human species that ultimately contribute to survival of the group. Modern day reciprocity norms, especially in industrialized countries, may have more capitalistic intents. Consumers may want to take pause when receiving a favor to evaluate possible reasons behind the action.

Social Norms

Social norms are the unspoken expectations of behavior in a culture or society. Norms may be established through formal laws and regulations but are often unofficially assumed. Social norms are the underlying structure of every society and are necessary to the smooth and cohesive functioning of a group of people.

Sanctions

Sanctions are a form of behavioral reinforcement used to encourage conformity to social norms. They can be mild or severe, depending on how norms have been violated. Many sanctions are informal, whether verbal praise of a particular behavior or shaming when someone does not conform. but formal legal sanctions may also be used in extreme cases where there is a deviation from social norms. Formal and informal sanctions may be implemented by peers, parents, police, teachers, or others.

Folkways, Mores, and Taboos

Folkways are simply everyday customs that are common to a particular population or society. They are the daily habits and behaviors of a culture, such as shaking someone's hand upon being introduced to them. **Mores,** by nature, have a moral emphasis behind them; these behaviors are considered either right or wrong and are often established through religion. Lying or cheating, for example, are considered morally unacceptable in many cultures. Those who engage in mores will usually receive informal sanctions from others, being shamed or ostracized in some way. **Taboos** are actions that are so strongly forbidden by the culture that a person is universally rejected or ostracized from the group because of the behavior. An example of this may be incest or pedophilia.

Anomie

Emile Durkheim developed the term **anomie**, which refers to a mismatch between individual needs, norms or morals, and the expectations of the society. When there is a breakdown of values or norms, there is a de-integration of individuals and the social structure. This can result when social norms fail to evolve and grow with the changing population and the needs of the individual people. Social norms then serve to frustrate or hinder people from reaching their goals. People, instead of being led by appropriate and moral norms of society are left to create and pursue their own norms, which can result in individualism and isolation.

Deviance Perspectives

Deviance is a behavior that violates or dramatically departs from social norms. Some behavior is considered deviant in a particular context while being perfectly normal in another setting or group. The **differential association** perspective of deviance states that deviant behavior is learned and that people who engage in deviance have adopted it through observing others. **Labeling theory** looks at the power of labels and how those with social power or influence can assign the label of deviant to certain behaviors. Those who are labeled in a certain way may either change their behaviors in order to conform to social norms or they may embrace those behaviors more fully as their identity. Finally, the **strain theory** puts the blame on the social system or structure. One major way this plays out is when society has certain expected goals of individuals but does not provide the means by which people can achieve those goals. As a result of this strain, people may resort to deviant behavior, such as criminal activity.

Social Traps

Social traps refer to short-term social decisions that, in the long run, ultimately result in harm for an individual, a small group, a large society, or the human population as a whole. Often, these short-term decisions are made as a resolution to a problem but often do not address the root cause of the problem or result in additional issues later down the road. Deforestation, especially in rainforests, is commonly cited as an example for a social trap. While it can provide lumber for trade and space for agricultural practices in the short-term, the long-term impacts of carbon emissions and climate shifts cause health and survival concerns for the entire global population. Social traps can be categorized into the following groups: **ignorance social traps**, where someone makes a decision without proper education or knowledge; **reinforcement social traps**, where a small initial decision results in a snowball effect of poor decisions; **tragedy of the commons**, in which people think their individual decisions will not result in a collective poor outcome, but they do; and **nesting traps**, in which people make short-term decisions due to the community in which they are nested.

Prisoner's Dilemma

The **prisoner's dilemma** is a concept derived from game theory. It serves as a means for examining cooperation and strategy within a partnership or group. It resulted from an experiment conducted by a mathematician named Albert Tucker, although the original concepts of the dilemma were formulated by mathematicians Merrill Flood and Melvin Dresher. In general versions of the experiment, two people are charged with a crime and placed in separate rooms so that they are unable to talk to one another. Each party is told that if they both confess, they will both receive extensive jail time. If only one party confesses and the other does not, the one who confesses will be punished. If neither party confesses, both will receive some jail time.

Ultimately, the decision tree of the prisoner's dilemma shows that when participants act in their own self-interest when deciding, the resulting outcome for all participants is worse, statistically, than if they work cooperatively. This logic can be extrapolated to a number of other contexts, such as choosing to work independently in a company setting versus collaborating with a group. Typically, collaborative efforts will result in higher overall rewards than independent, self-serving efforts.

Conflict Resolution

Conflict resolution refers to any modality in which parties work together to reach a mutually agreeable fix for a problem. Some strategies are more effective than others. Conflict resolutions styles can be avoidant, yielding, competitive, or cooperative. In **avoidant styles**, one party passively withdraws from engaging in the conflict, therefore allowing the conflict to resolve in a way that does not truly involve them. While this may result in an end to the conflict, it can cause personal resentments or feeling like one has lost control or power in a situation. This style is commonly seen in intercultural communications when the parties come from different backgrounds. For example, some management studies indicate that employees from collectivist cultures tend to communicate in a softer, less direct way than employees who were born and raised in the United States.

This mismatch in communication styles sometimes leads to nonnative employees feeling overlooked and undervalued when their input is not understood or received as they intended. **Yielding styles** tend to take place when one person places a higher regard on the other person's values or feelings than on their own. This can result from an imbalance of power or low self-esteem. It may resolve a conflict but

can eventually cause personal issues for the person who is yielding. **Competitive styles** can result in high levels of aggression from both parties. Both parties are often seeking power or control of the situation, and there is often little regard for the other's views or feelings. **Cooperative styles** tend to address the root cause of the conflict and work from a place from compromise, where each party feels heard and valued and the resolution is mutually agreed upon as satisfactory. It requires direct, empathetic, and respectful communication.

Superordinate Goals

Superordinate goals are those that bring parties with two opposing perspectives together. Often, a superordinate goal is one that is imperative on a larger scale or benefits both parties, therefore encouraging the opposing parties to work together. Working on a superordinate goal sometimes results out of necessity (e.g., to ensure survival). Additionally, it may be employed as a management or interpersonal relationship tool to foster collaboration between individuals who otherwise do not get along. For example, a marriage and family therapist may work with a couple who is considering divorce by guiding them toward a superordinate goal that highlights their relationship strengths. In general, creating superordinate goals can break down communication and relationship obstacles, encourage cooperation, and remove factors that may have been creating stagnation within an entity.

Bias, Prejudice, and Discrimination

Processes that contribute to differential treatment of group members

In-Group/Out-Group Dynamics

Those considered to be part of the **in-group** are the ones who share a common identity that joins them. Anyone without the same shared characteristics (such as race or religion) as those in the in-group is considered different and part of the **out-group**.

Ethnocentrism

Ethnocentrism is the tendency to view one's own ethnicity more positively than other ethnicities, and to view everything about one's own culture as better than other cultures. On the other hand, **cultural relativism** views each culture as being equally valid and good, although different from each other.

Prejudice

Prejudice—the perceived opinions and beliefs that cause someone to feel or act in a negative manner toward a particular group—can present itself in several forms. The following are some examples:

- **Anti-Semitism:** prejudice against the Jewish religion and culture
- **Racism:** prejudice against a particular race
- **Sexism:** prejudice against one or the other sex
- **Ageism:** prejudice against someone based on age, either young or old
- **Classism:** prejudice against someone based on his or her socio-economic class
- **Ableism:** prejudice against someone with disabilities or handicaps
- **Homophobia:** prejudice against the gay and lesbian community
- **Transphobia:** prejudice against the transgender community
- **Nationalism:** prejudice against non-natives in a specific country

Prejudice may also present itself as discrimination against someone due to immigration status, national origin, religion, or weight.

Prejudice is most often a negative belief about others that is based on pre-judging with limited information and faulty assumptions. Unfortunately, prejudice can, and is, shown toward people due to their race, gender, sexual orientation, religion, and many other factors.

Power, Prestige, and Class

Some common contributors to prejudice have to do with a person's position, reputation, or economic status. Those with more political or personal **power** may be prejudiced against those who are perceived as weaker. **Prestige** has to do with a person's position or job, which can contribute to prejudice against those in less prestigious positions. Finally, a person's **class** or socioeconomic status can serve as a trigger for prejudice against those in lower socioeconomic positions.

Status is the position that someone has within a group or society and how they fit into the social structure. **Achieved status**, good or bad, covers everything that a person earns or acquires in their life through their own efforts and choices, whether financial, vocational, or educational positions. **Ascribed status** is what a person obtains by no individual choice or effort, including race or socioeconomic status inherited at birth.

The Role of Emotion in Prejudice

People tend to show prejudice toward those whom they feel certain emotions, such as disgust, pity, or envy. These emotions are felt toward those who are part of various outgroups, whereas positive emotions are felt toward those who are in the same group or category as oneself.

The Role of Cognition in Prejudice

The human brain, in processing and retrieving memories, tends to categorize information about others. These mental groupings can lead to oversimplified categorizations and reduce complex human beings to specific labels or characteristics. **Belief perseverance**—the tendency to persist in one's beliefs no matter what the contrary evidence may be—can lead people to hold onto the faulty ideas they have developed about certain groups or types of people.

Stereotypes

Stereotypes are the labeling or categorizing of people based on fixed ideas about the group to which they belong, thus leading to assumptions about others based solely on their group membership. These generalizations can lead to prejudice and discrimination.

Bias

Biases are any factors that contribute to preferential beliefs, values, or behaviors. They generally result in negative outcomes, such as racial, gender-based, age-based, or other forms of discrimination. Unfair biases most commonly result from pervasive stereotypes. Based on personal history and sociocultural influences, people may develop subconscious biases to which they remain unaware unless they actively engage in introspective practices. Researchers who conduct scientific trials typically have to incorporate procedures that eliminate personal biases and confirmation biases when they design experiments.

For example, conducting double-blind studies limits bias from both the people conducting the experiment as well as participants who are involved in the experiment. Healthcare practitioners, and other members of the community who work in social or educational services, also must be especially mindful of personal biases. Workers in these fields often interact with vulnerable populations, and personal biases can impact the quality and humanity of their work. For example, a psychologist who has personally experienced infidelity from a previous romantic partner may have difficulty remaining

objective when working with a couple who is trying to overcome an instance of infidelity in their own relationship.

Discrimination

Discrimination is the unfair or unequal treatment of a person or group, based upon a characteristic, such as race, ethnicity, religion, age, sex, or sexual orientation. There are several forms of discrimination that minorities experience:

Direct Discrimination: The unfair treatment based on someone's characteristics. An example would be refusing to hire someone because of their ethnicity.

Indirect Discrimination: Situations in which a policy applies the same to everyone, but a person or group of people are negatively impacted due to certain characteristics. For example, a company might require that everyone help unload shipments that come to the office. The policy is the same for everyone, but it's discriminatory towards any disabled employees. In a workplace environment, indirect discrimination can sometimes be allowed if there's a compelling reason for the requirement. For example, firefighters have to meet certain physical criteria due to the nature of their work.

Harassment: Unwanted bullying or humiliation intentionally directed to a person of minority status.

Victimization: The unfair treatment received when a person reports discrimination and is not supported by authorities.

Effects of discrimination on the individual may include depression, anxiety, and other mental health issues; and medical/health-related problems caused by lack of access to health resources. Effects of discrimination on society include diminished resources (e.g. employment, educational opportunities, healthcare) and a culture characterized by fear, anger, or apathy.

Scapegoat Theory

The **scapegoat theory** states that people tend to blame external sources for their personal problems, creating divisions, out-groups, and often unfounded blame toward the source that is allegedly causing a problem. This theory is only used in contexts where people do not take personal accountability for failures, and it should not be applied to situations where an external force truly is present. One of the most commonly cited social examples for the scapegoat theory is that of Adolf Hitler's perspective of the Jewish population during Nazi Germany. Hitler stated that Jews were more successful than German nationals, and he persuaded German nationals to discriminate and kill Jewish people.

In general, social scapegoating tends to occur toward people who are relatively powerless in a society or do not have the means to fight back. During Nazi Germany, Jewish populations did not have the resources or power to rise against the country's military and federal laws. From a more psychoanalytical perspective, psychologists believe individual people tend to scapegoat when they are unable to objectively examine their own shortcomings and work at improving their own skills. For example, a person who is relatively lazy at work and is overlooked for a promotion may scapegoat the person who receives the promotion by saying it is due to reasons other than competency and merit.

Stereotype

A **stereotype** refers to a generalized, often negative, belief about an entire group of people. Certainly, some people within a group may embody characteristics of the stereotype, but it is unlikely that all members of a group would. Stereotypes are often inaccurate and often cause harm to members of the group, as others assume negative characteristics about people within the group that may be unfounded or unjust. Some stereotypes are intended to be positive but can still have ill-effects. This can place an onus on other members of the group to live up to impossible standards, or to live in a way with which they do not identify. For example, consider a family with three children in high school. Two of the children love the topics of, and excel at, science subjects, so teachers incorrectly assume the third child also loves and excels in science. This may result in unfair treatment or pressure to perform in class, and the third child may feel shame or guilt when underperforming. The third child may feel uncomfortable asking for additional tutoring, or they may feel unable to pursue topics that they truly are passionate about.

Out-Group Homogeneity Bias

The **out-group homogeneity bias** explains how people see more diversity within their perceived in-group yet see people in perceived out-groups as homogenous. For example, an undergraduate college student may view all instructors in their classes as salaried professors of the university, when in fact, many instructors are graduate students or adjunct Masters'-level lecturers. Out-group homogeneity bias is most commonly seen in race and cultures. People tend to be able to easily identify different characteristics in members of their own race and culture demographics, yet they are often unable to discern these same differences in people of a different race and culture. From social and evolutionary perspectives, this may be due to the fact that people more closely study and more frequently interact with people in their in-group as a way to develop intimacy and build trust. However, the out-group homogeneity bias can result in excessive divisions and stereotyping.

Mere-Exposure Effect

The **mere-exposure effect**, also commonly known as the **familiarity effect** or **familiarity principle**, states that people are more likely to prefer things that are familiar. This is seen across inanimate objects, animals, events, facilities, and other people. In experimental trials, people who are exposed to a new item repeatedly are more likely to choose that item even if a second, more desirable item is later introduced. Marketing agencies often subliminally utilize this tactic when advertising messages, companies, and products. Additionally, this effect can explain poor decision making in some people. For example, people who had dysfunctional relationships with a primary caregiver are more likely to end up with romantic partners who have the same dysfunctional traits due to the perceived familiarity.

Altruism and Aggression

The Variables that Contribute to Altruism and Aggression

Altruism is defined as behaviors that are performed with the intention of physically, emotionally, mentally, financially, or otherwise helping others. **Aggression** is defined as behaviors that are performed with the intention of harming others across these various aspects. While these are two behaviors that seem to be on opposite sides of the behavior spectrum, the variables that drive them have some commonalities. For example, in order to act on either an altruistic or aggressive impulse, people must have an end goal in mind and must be capable of reading the emotions and responses of others. Both behaviors also appear to have biological and evolutionary underpinnings. Altruism appears to be rooted

in creating community, engaging the support and protection of others, and showcasing oneself in a positive light.

People tend to be more altruistic toward family and people they know versus strangers. Altruism is also linked to helping oneself feel better and have a more positive self-concept. Researchers continue to debate whether any form of altruism is truly selfless, or if every altruistic act still benefits the person doing it even in slight, subconscious ways. Aggression appears to be rooted in threat response and creating a sense of power and control. It appears to be largely innate, although extreme stress and trauma can have an epigenetic effect that may make some people predisposed to displaying higher levels of aggression. Additionally, aggression can result from traumatic brain injuries, and it can be learned if someone is placed in an environment where aggression is openly and often displayed. Historically, men are more likely to show aggression than women, and they are more likely to show physical aggression. Women are more likely than men to show passive, relational, verbal, and emotional aggression.

Interpersonal Attraction

The Variables that Contribute to Attraction

Interpersonal attraction, from an evolutionary standpoint, resulted from variables that would translate into in the highest possibility of reproductive fitness and species survival. In modern times, this theory holds some basis but has been criticized, as not all romantic partners can or want to have children. However, some of the biological variables still hold true. **Pheromones** are hormones that have scent giving biological cues to a potential partner, including sensory information about sexual orientation and individual genetics. These hormones can be found in sweat, tears, and other biological fluids. While most people are not aware that they are receiving this information, they are most likely to be attracted to others with a high level of genetic variation from their own, as this ensures the highest chance of reproductive survival. Furthermore, people are more likely to be repelled by the pheromones of those with close genetic compositions.

In addition to pheromones as a physical variable for attraction, people also tend to be attracted to those who have symmetrical, showy physical features. Studies indicate that women are more attracted to men who are taller with broader shoulders, while men are more attracted to women with a lower waist-to-hip ratio. A lower waist-to-hip ratio is also correlated with better health outcomes, so this ratio may go beyond a factor that is visually pleasing to also indicate a partner who will have better health.

From a sociocultural standpoint, attraction results from exposure, familiarity, lust, and similarities in values, beliefs, and attitudes. People are most likely to be attracted to those that they see and interact with on a regular basis. People tend to look for others who appear confident, have visual markers that indicate success and health, and have resources (whether they are physical, emotional, or financial) to care for a partner and potential offspring. In modern society, people look for emotional factors such as trustworthiness, kindness, loyalty, genuine friendship, and recreational compatibility. People also seek compatibility in areas that are important to modern day life, such as intellectual compatibility, religious beliefs, financial practices, ideas around child-rearing, work-life-home balance, and personal development. Compatibility in these aspects correlates with long-lasting partnerships in modern times.

Practice Questions

1. What term is used to describe a study that is repeated in order to support or refute the results obtained in the original research study?
   - a. Falsifiability
   - b. Face validity
   - c. Replication
   - d. Operational definition
   - e. Construct validity

2. Which of the following describes the third phase of the five stages of the scientific process?
   - a. Communicating the results
   - b. Conducting a test
   - c. Forming a prediction
   - d. Interpreting the data
   - e. Making an observation

3. A study is conducted to understand the similarities and/or differences between identical twins raised together, and those not raised together. Researchers observe these participants from childhood to adulthood to learn how being brought up in different environments influences their habits and traits. What type of research method is being employed here?
   - a. Cross-sectional study
   - b. The Delphi method
   - c. Interview
   - d. Longitudinal study
   - e. Questionnaire

4. Which of the following statements is NOT true of cross-sectional studies?
   - a. This method gathers preliminary information and makes inferences about potential relationships.
   - b. The sample population involves a comparison of different people with similar features.
   - c. This approach evaluates information about variables obtained at a specific point in time.
   - d. These studies are used to outline traits that exist in a certain group.
   - e. This type of research is used to determine cause-and-effect relationships between variables.

5. What is considered a STRENGTH of case studies?
   - a. They offer insights for future research.
   - b. They are easy to replicate.
   - c. They are generalizable to a large population.
   - d. They consist of large sample sizes.
   - e. They are resistant to researcher bias.

6. A man remains convinced that evolution is a hoax. Despite all the evidence presented to him in support of evolution, he dismisses it as biased propaganda pushed by nonbelievers, while at the same time, he favors information on creation science websites arguing against evolution. Which of the following concepts is MOST applicable in this scenario?
- a. Top-down design
- b. Motivated reasoning
- c. Schematic processing
- d. Bottom-up design
- e. Proactive interference

7. A hungry customer enters a diner, orders their meal, eats the food, pays the bill, leaves a tip, and then departs from the diner. What is this scenario describing?
- a. An archetype
- b. A rubric
- c. A script
- d. A social role
- e. An example of operant conditioning

8. Which of the following statements BEST describes the evolutionary theory of sleep?
- a. Sleep rids the brain of toxins and waste products accumulated throughout the previous day.
- b. Non-REM sleep restores physical functions.
- c. Sleep helps process information gathered during the day.
- d. Sleep allows all species to conserve energy.
- e. Sleep acts as nutrition for the brain.

9. Which of the following has been demonstrated by split-brain research?
- a. The cerebellum manages voluntary motions including balance, coordination, posture, and speech.
- b. There is no risk of functional impairments after cutting the corpus callosum.
- c. The right hemisphere is dominant in visual-motor skills.
- d. The left hemisphere is responsible for controlling the left side of the body.
- e. The occipital lobe contains a visual receiving area and a visual association area.

10. You're driving a car, and a nearby road sign that you pass seems to go by very quickly, but other objects that are farther away appear almost stationary. What is this phenomenon called?
- a. Perspective
- b. Aerial perspective
- c. Interposition
- d. Convergence
- e. Motion parallax

11. Which of the following describes an amount by which something needs to be changed for any alterations to be observed?
- a. Bayesian inference
- b. Just noticeable difference
- c. Two-point threshold
- d. Attitude scaling
- e. Retinal disparity

12. Of these figures, which one is best known for devising a theory of consciousness that is backed by neuroscientific research?
    a. Michael Gazzaniga
    b. Wilhelm Wundt
    c. Eugen Bleuler
    d. David Hubel
    e. William James

13. Which theory of visual perception describes how one's perception of reality is developed by understanding the whole object structure as opposed to merely the sum of its parts?
    a. Gibson theory of perception
    b. Gestalt theory of perception
    c. Empirical theory of perception
    d. Self-perception theory
    e. Cognitive dissonance theory

14. A man looks at an image, but because of his eyes' inability to focus light evenly, the image appears blurry and darkened. What sensory impairment is this man most likely experiencing?
    a. Myopia
    b. Hyperopia
    c. Presbyopia
    d. Astigmatism
    e. Visual illusion

15. When the brain is no longer able to receive signal transmissions from the auditory nerve, what type of hearing impairment is MOST likely occurring?
    a. Neural hearing loss
    b. Sensorineural hearing loss
    c. Conductive hearing loss
    d. Mixed hearing loss
    e. Tinnitus

16. A woman is able to taste chocolate whenever she hears the word "factory." Which form of synesthesia is this woman experiencing?
    a. Grapheme-color
    b. Chromesthesia
    c. Auditory-tactile
    d. Misophonia
    e. Lexical-gustatory

17. What is the function of the postcentral gyrus (also known as the primary somatosensory cortex)?
    a. Controlling the voluntary movements of skeletal muscles
    b. Separating the frontal lobe from the parietal lobe
    c. Serving as the main receptive area for one's sense of touch
    d. Contributing to short-term memory processing and other cognitive functions
    e. Separating both the frontal lobe and parietal lobe from the temporal lobe

18. Which brain region is responsible for language processing and speech production?
    a. Broca's area
    b. Wernicke's area
    c. Central sulcus of Rolando
    d. Supramarginal gyrus
    e. Olfactory bulb

19. Which of the following is LEAST accurate concerning the cortical homunculus?
    a. It is a neurological map serving as a distorted depiction of the human body.
    b. It is dedicated to processing sensory or motor functions for different parts of the body.
    c. Nerves transmitted from the hands cover sizable areas of the brain.
    d. It represents the proportional size of each area of the body in schematic form.
    e. Nerves transmitted from one's arms or torso cover only a small amount of cortical brain regions.

20. After spending a few minutes looking at a red object, Harold soon finds himself seeing a green afterglow. Which concept is most applicable in this situation?
    a. Dark adaptation
    b. Opponent process theory of color
    c. Melanin production
    d. Trichromatic theory of color
    e. Rayleigh scattering

21. Which of the following outlines the CORRECT order in which the sensation of pain is processed?
    a. Transduction, modulation, transmission, conduction, perception
    b. Transmission, perception, conduction, modulation, transduction
    c. Transduction, transmission, modulation, perception, conduction
    d. Transmission, conduction, transduction, perception, modulation
    e. Transduction, conduction, transmission, modulation, perception

22. Which of these statements MOST accurately reflects the differences between rods and cones?
    a. Rods process vision at higher levels of light and spatial acuities, and facilitate color vision; cones process vision at lower levels of light and spatial acuities, and don't facilitate color vision.
    b. Rods process vision at lower levels of light and spatial acuities, and don't facilitate color vision; cones process vision at higher levels of light and spatial acuities, and can facilitate color vision.
    c. Rods process vision at lower levels of light and spatial acuities, and facilitate color vision; cones process vision at higher levels of light and spatial acuities, and don't facilitate color vision.
    d. Rods process vision at lower levels of light, higher spatial acuities, and don't facilitate color vision; cones process vision at higher levels of light, lower spatial acuities, and facilitate color.
    e. Rods process vision at lower levels of light, higher spatial acuities, and facilitate color vision; cones process vision at higher levels of light, lower spatial acuities, and don't facilitate color vision.

23. Which of the following statements about visual perception is accurate?
    a. Light enters through the retina, which helps focus that light onto the photoreceptors in the cornea to translate it into an image.
    b. Bottom-up processing is data-based; top-down processing is knowledge-based.
    c. Visual perception is one of the least studied topics in psychology.
    d. The exact function of photoreceptors in the retina still remains a mystery.
    e. Vision is the only one of our five basic senses that doesn't have to pass through the thalamus.

24. A research participant is blindfolded and given a weight to hold. The researcher gradually increases the weight and asks the participant to respond when they first feel the increase. The researcher finds that the participant's response is proportional to the weight's relative increase. Which of the following concepts applies to this experiment?
   a. Monocular cue
   b. Binocular cue
   c. Weber-Fechner law
   d. Chemoaffinity hypothesis
   e. Optimal probabilistic reasoning

25. A young woman goes to an ice cream parlor. Trying to decide what to get, she asks an employee their recommendations. After the employee patiently and politely answers all her questions, she makes a purchase, and says that she appreciates the service so much that she plans on coming back there more often. As a result, the young woman develops a favorable perception and memory of this particular ice cream parlor. What phenomenon in psychology is this describing?
   a. Schema
   b. Perceptual constancy
   c. Retrospective analysis
   d. Parapraxis
   e. Context effect

26. What significant contribution did Sigmund Freud make to the field of psychology?
   a. The discovery of simple cells and complex cells
   b. Revealing that electrically stimulating a part of the vagus nerve slows down heart activity
   c. Developing the field of psychophysics
   d. Conceptualizing the significant role that the unconscious plays in influencing human behavior
   e. Being among one of the first researchers to study the phenomenon of split brains in humans

27. Which of the following is NOT true about sleeping disorders?
   a. Sleep disorders impact one third of the American population.
   b. A sleep disorder is suspected when difficulty sleeping occurs frequently.
   c. Sleeping disorders aren't known to have any significant negative impact on health.
   d. Lifestyle changes can be used to help treat sleep disorders.
   e. There is no one exact factor that causes sleep disorders.

28. When describing neuroplasticity, which of these statements is accurate?
   a. Neuroplasticity generally occurs under extreme circumstances only.
   b. Plasticity occurs to a greater extent in the developing brain compared to the adult brain.
   c. Damaged brain functions have no chance of being recovered.
   d. Environmental cues have been found to have little to no impact on brain plasticity.
   e. Psychology has virtually no understanding of the underlying mechanisms of plasticity.

29. A man suffering from epileptic seizures undergoes a surgery in which the goal involves carefully removing brain areas where these seizures are known to originate, while simultaneously leaving the rest of the brain completely intact. What is the name of this procedure being performed?
   a. Gamma knife
   b. Autopsy
   c. Necropsy
   d. Lesioning
   e. Transorbital lobotomy

30. What neuroimaging technique is used to determine where neurons are firing by measuring levels of sugar glucose in the brain?
   a. Positron emission topography
   b. Electroencephalogram
   c. Functional magnetic resonance imaging
   d. Magnetic resonance imaging
   e. Ablation experiment

31. Which of the following BEST illustrates the process of natural selection?
   a. The careful manipulation of heredity in certain flowers to create the perfect hybrid
   b. A giraffe developing an elongated neck over a lifetime of struggling to reach high tree branches
   c. The wings of penguins becoming smaller due to disuse
   d. Crossbreeding dogs for some of their desired characteristics
   e. Lizards developing longer leg bones to climb up during floods and escape ground predators

32. Experiences and environments influence the expression of genes, which in turn helps to shape behavior. What term is used to describe this process?
   a. Adaptation
   b. Neurogenesis
   c. Epigenetics
   d. Gene editing
   e. Eugenics

33. What theory proposes that the stimulation of brain circuits during REM sleep serves as the reason that we dream?
   a. Information consolidation theory
   b. Activation-synthesis model
   c. Psychoanalytic theory
   d. Neurocognitive theory
   e. Jungian dream theory

34. A couple decides at last minute to have a date night, and they know their favorite restaurant is open until 11:00 p.m., so they decide to go there for dinner. The time that the restaurant closes represents factual information stored away for conscious recall. Which type of memory is being described?
   a. Procedural memory
   b. Declarative memory
   c. Iconic memory
   d. Echoic memory
   e. Haptic memory

35. As one's years of schooling increase, the more likely they are to have a higher income. What concept does this example represent?
    a. A positive correlation
    b. A negative correlation
    c. An initial value
    d. An intercept
    e. A bimodal distribution

36. A student is taught how to perform long division but does not display that knowledge until they have to take an important test. What type of learning does this example demonstrate?
    a. Social learning
    b. Insight learning
    c. Latent learning
    d. Observational learning
    e. Emotional learning

37. Which statement MOST accurately reflects the Rescorla-Wagner model of conditioning?
    a. Researchers perceive conditioning as merely an automatic process.
    b. The pairing of two different stimuli always results in the same type of conditioning.
    c. No information processing takes place in conditioning.
    d. Conditioning is more effective if the signal of a conditioned stimulus reliably predicts the appearance of an unconditioned stimulus.
    e. Not many theoretical developments or experimental findings have been impacted by it as of yet.

38. To raise their child, a parent sets clear limits on behavior, consistently enforces boundaries, and uses positive discipline. Which type of parenting style is being used in this example?
    a. Permissive
    b. Authoritative
    c. Authoritarian
    d. Uninvolved
    e. Helicopter

39. Which of the following depicts the correct order of the four stages of memory processing?
    a. Encoding, storage, consolidation, retrieval
    b. Consolidation, encoding, storage, retrieval
    c. Storage, encoding, retrieval, consolidation
    d. Encoding, consolidation, storage, retrieval
    e. Encoding, consolidation, retrieval, storage

40. After years of practice, Jennifer retained many of her lessons and became an exceptional piano player. What type of memory is Jennifer demonstrating?
    a. Declarative memory
    b. Procedural memory
    c. Sensory memory
    d. Episodic memory
    e. Semantic memory

41. After seeing a box, Derek remembers he needs to bring a package to the post office to mail to a relative living out of state. What type of memory is Derek demonstrating?
    a. Haptic memory
    b. Echoic memory
    c. Iconic memory
    d. Retrospective memory
    e. Prospective memory

42. In order to avoid getting into an argument with his roommate, Eric decides to clean up the mess he made in the kitchen. What technique is being used in this example?
    a. Positive punishment
    b. Positive reinforcement
    c. Negative punishment
    d. Negative reinforcement
    e. Systematic desensitization

43. A research participant is shown photographs of landscapes while experiencing electric shocks, which in turn causes them distress as they start associating the pictures with the shocks. What is occurring in this experiment?
    a. Fear conditioning
    b. Reward training
    c. Autoshaping
    d. Flooding
    e. Exposure therapy

44. Which of the following is NOT an example of a classical conditioning experiment?
    a. Giving rats sweetened water either with or without radiation to assess how they respond to it
    b. Training dogs to respond to a neutral stimulus
    c. Administering shocks to dogs to convince them they cannot escape a negative situation
    d. Introducing a reward in order to get a rat to press a lever
    e. Pairing loud noises with a white rat to condition a research participant to start fearing the rat

45. Which of the following statements is the LEAST accurate?
    a. Contingency hasn't been shown to be successful in helping people modify their behaviors.
    b. Behaviorists have learned that an animal's learning abilities can be constrained by their biology.
    c. The frontal lobe and hippocampus are each known to play important roles in short-term memory.
    d. Correlation does not imply causation.
    e. Intelligence tends to be viewed in different ways across various cultures.

46. Which serves as the BEST example of higher-order conditioning?
    a. A researcher pairs food with the sound of a bell to elicit a response.
    b. The sound of a bell is paired with the presence of light until an association is made between them.
    c. A child doing poorly on tests will start feeling that nothing they do will ever change that outcome.
    d. Children watch adults hit a blow-up doll then start engaging in the same behavior.
    e. A child does not engage in a behavior after observing a sibling being scolded for the same behavior.

47. Upon hearing a loud noise, Harold jumps in panic. What does Harold's jumping demonstrate?
    a. An unconditioned stimulus
    b. A neutral stimulus
    c. A conditioned response
    d. An unconditioned response
    e. A modified behavior

48. Your dog responds to the command "roll over." One day, he just stops listening to you, but then days later, he rolls over again. What behavioral phenomenon is occurring in this scenario?
    a. Extinction
    b. Acquisition
    c. Stimulus discrimination
    d. Stimulus generalization
    e. Spontaneous recovery

49. Which of these major figures is MOST known for devising the triangular theory of love?
    a. Howard Gardner
    b. Arnold Gesell
    c. Robert Sternberg
    d. Ivan Pavlov
    e. Diana Baumrind

50. Which figure is MOST known for pioneering factor analysis?
    a. Raymond Cattell
    b. Martin Seligman
    c. John Bowlby
    d. Charles Spearman
    e. Sabina Spielrein

51. Which of these researchers is BEST known for their studies on taste aversion?
    a. John Garcia
    b. Carl Jung
    c. Lewis Terman
    d. Lev Vygotsky
    e. Aaron Beck

52. Which of the following BEST reflects one of the views of John B. Watson?
    a. Introspection has a major impact on behavior.
    b. A psychologist's goal should be to understand the mind's inner workings.
    c. Assumptions and findings should be based on purely observable data.
    d. Language is not a learned phenomenon.
    e. Behaviorism is only applicable to nonhuman subjects.

53. What is the correct order of the three stages of prenatal development?
    a. Embryonic, germinal, fetal
    b. Germinal, embryonic, fetal
    c. Germinal, fetal, embryonic
    d. Fetal, germinal, embryonic
    e. Embryonic, fetal, germinal

54. Which term BEST describes the process whereby organs first start developing?
    a. Epigenetics
    b. Maturation
    c. Gestation
    d. Organogenesis
    e. Conception

55. Which of the following is NOT considered a teratogenic agent?
    a. Prescription drugs
    b. Saunas
    c. Computers
    d. Potassium iodide
    e. Maternal stress

56. What is the fourth stage of the psychosexual theory of development?
    a. Oral
    b. Genital
    c. Anal
    d. Phallic
    e. Latency

57. A student is initially irritated when trying to perform math problems on their own but becomes more capable of performing this task after working with a teacher. What concept does this example represent?
    a. Social development
    b. Physical development
    c. Free association
    d. Zone of proximal development
    e. Biofeedback

58. A person buys a new complex puzzle set that consists of ten thousand pieces, which requires some creative solutions to solve in a reasonable amount of time. What process is being employed in this particular scenario?
    a. Fluid intelligence
    b. Crystallized intelligence
    c. Processing speed
    d. Successful intelligence
    e. Factor analysis

59. According to the theory of multiple intelligences, which category of intelligence would an actor be most likely to fall under?
    a. Naturalistic intelligence
    b. Intrapersonal intelligence
    c. Interpersonal intelligence
    d. Bodily-kinesthetic intelligence
    e. Visual-spatial intelligence

60. Which of the following statements is MOST accurate about the Flynn effect?
    a. Research conducted worldwide hasn't found any decline in IQ scores across other countries.
    b. Researchers are finding that scores related to abstract problem solving are the ones on the rise.
    c. Performances on the Raven's Progressive Matrices have been decreasing over the past century.
    d. Researchers have narrowed down the cause of this effect to one specific factor.
    e. James Flynn has been reluctant to offer any opinions on what could account for this effect.

61. Which of the following general statements regarding intelligence is LEAST accurate?
    a. The *g* factor investigates cognitive abilities and human intelligence.
    b. There is no exact definition of giftedness.
    c. There are no known cases of savant syndrome developing because of an acquired brain injury.
    d. Those with intellectual disabilities aren't able to function on their own regardless of their severity.
    e. A criticism of intelligence tests is that they don't focus enough on noncognitive abilities.

62. What are researchers Alexander Thomas and Stella Chess known for identifying?
    a. A personality theory consisting of the id, ego, and superego
    b. Authoritative, authoritarian, and permissive parenting styles
    c. The analytical psychology theory of the anima and animus
    d. Insights that involve selective-encoding, selective-comparison, and selection-combination
    e. Three temperaments where children are classified as easy, slow-to-warm-up, or difficult

63. Which statement about prenatal development is MOST accurate?
    a. Nutrition hasn't been shown to play a significant role in ensuring the well-being of a fetus.
    b. Even parents who take all the necessary precautions are unable to prevent illnesses in infants.
    c. Maintaining a healthy weight while carrying an embryo decreases the possibility of negative risks.
    d. Substance use during pregnancy isn't known to result in any long-term problems for infants.
    e. The developmental stage of a baby has no bearing on an infant's susceptibility to teratogens.

64. Which concept is attributed to Sigmund Freud?
    a. Sensorimotor development
    b. Learned helplessness
    c. Countertransference
    d. Collective unconscious
    e. Affective forecasting

65. Which theory proposes that mental abilities are influenced in part by people's interactions in a societal setting?
    a. Psychosocial theory of development
    b. Moral theory of development
    c. Cognitive theory of development
    d. Sociocultural theory of development
    e. Attachment theory of development

66. Which defense mechanism involves channeling negative or unacceptable urges into positive and constructive actions or behaviors?
   a. Repression
   b. Sublimation
   c. Projection
   d. Reaction formation
   e. Displacement

67. When there's a near-perfect relationship between one's glove size and hand length, which of the following would have been used to efficiently assess the relationship between these variables?
   a. Abstract measure
   b. Chunking
   c. Correlation coefficient
   d. Rehearsal
   e. Lines of best fit

68. Which of the following is NOT an example of a coping strategy?
   a. Deep breathing
   b. Journaling
   c. Meditating
   d. Talking with others
   e. Having a visual reminder about daily goals

69. Males experience which of the following physical changes during puberty?
   a. An increase of hair follicles on the scalp
   b. An increase in fat deposits
   c. An increase in hip-to-waist ratio
   d. An increase in lean muscle mass
   e. A development of higher arches in the feet

70. Melissa is a young girl who has always been very close with her two parents. Recently, however, she has acted moodily and stopped spending evenings talking with her parents. Instead, she spends most of the evening on her phone talking to her friends. When Melissa wanted a second opinion on her clothing or a new hairstyle, she usually asked her mom. Now, she almost never asks her mom; instead, she takes pictures of her new options and sends them to her best friend. One day, Melissa notices a few spots of blood in her underwear when she is going to the bathroom. She gets completely frazzled and is unsure of what to do, or who to ask. What is Melissa likely experiencing?
   a. She is developing an Adam's apple.
   b. She is experiencing menopause.
   c. She is going through puberty and the adolescent stage.
   d. She is depressed.
   e. She is having a body image disorder.

71. Which of the following developmental concepts strongly influences people's ability to become intimate?
    a. Rooting reflex
    b. Attachment style
    c. Type of birth experience
    d. Prenatal vitamin consumption by the mother
    e. Imprinting

72. At what age have over one hundred billion neurons been formed in an individual?
    a. By age three
    b. By age twenty in females and age twenty-five in males
    c. By the seventh month of pregnancy, as a fetus
    d. By age eleven
    e. By age seventy-five

73. The incidence and progression of which disease is likely influenced by the consumption of highly processed, high-fat, high sugar foods?
    a. Type 1 diabetes
    b. Congenital adrenal hyperplasia
    c. Spina bifida
    d. Gestational diabetes
    e. Type 3 diabetes

74. Nav is a 70-year-old man who has recently retired from a career as an engineer. Though Nav ended his career at a C-Suite level in which he mostly managed the work of others, he used his lunch periods every day to complete online courses in technology subjects that were new to him. He also completes the newspaper crossword puzzle every morning, and he does a walking meditation each evening for about thirty minutes. Which health outcome is Nav most likely to avoid from engaging in these lifestyle habits?
    a. Knee replacement surgery
    b. Hormonal imbalances
    c. Tooth decay
    d. Cognitive decline
    e. Spinal degeneration

75. A young boy is having a birthday party. He receives a variety of gifts from his friends: a train set and track, a dump truck, some puzzles, a coloring book, and a bubble machine. One of his peers from a school, a young girl, gives him a shiny crown and a pink wand as a present. The boy is excited about this gift when he opens it, and he starts to put the crown on his head. Both of his parents immediately stop him and say, "Oh, that's a perfect gift for a little girl! But we will have to exchange it for something else this weekend." What is this story an example of?
    a. Homophobia
    b. Gender socialization
    c. Gender identity
    d. Anti-feminism
    e. Gender roles

76. Societies that consider male and female as the two primary genders are known as what kind of societies?
   a. Gender nonconforming
   b. Gender fluid
   c. Gender binary
   d. Gender homogenous
   e. Contemporary

77. Most animals species' behavior is largely driven by what urge?
   a. Motivation for species survival
   b. Motivation for species recreational time
   c. Seeking a higher purpose
   d. Supporting immediate family members
   e. The need to hoard resources in order to prepare for hibernation

78. Which of the following is NOT an innate reflex displayed by human newborns?
   a. Rooting reflex
   b. Moro reflex
   c. Coo reflex
   d. Grasp reflex
   e. Suck reflex

79. Which of the following is considered an instinctive behavior across animals?
   a. Imprinting
   b. Attachment styles
   c. Courting
   d. Mating with a single partner for life
   e. Latch reflex

80. A father is in the process of toilet training his two-and-a-half-year-old son, who has shown an interest in using the toilet. For each time his son uses the toilet without prompting, the father places a bright, shiny sticker on a chart. This system works well for two weeks. The son regularly uses the toilet and feels very excited to receive a sticker on his chart. After a few weeks, though, the son begins having at least one accident per day and does not seem too concerned about it. When his dad offers a sticker for using the toilet, the boy seems unaffected. When the father tells his son that he will not get a sticker if he has an accident, the son remains unaffected. What concept is this illustrating?
   a. The over-justification effect
   b. Classical conditioning
   c. Cognitive dissonance
   d. Appraisal
   e. Moro reflex

Use the following vignette to answers Questions 81 and 82.

Talli is a woman who is trying to commit to eating fewer refined sweets as a part of an overall goal to manage her blood sugar levels, which are borderline pre-diabetic. For as long as she can remember, she has eaten dessert every night after dinner.

209

81. Because she has always had dessert after dinner, Talli does not believe she can skip it. She wonders if perhaps she should simply try decreasing her portion size. On the first night, she takes a smaller piece of dessert but ends up getting another piece because she does not feel satisfied. She then decides there is no way she can skip dessert. What does Talli seem to be lacking?
    a. A normal circadian rhythm
    b. Smaller bowls to aid with her visual perspective of the food
    c. A sense of self-efficacy
    d. Confirmation bias
    e. Medications to curb her appetite

82. A few days later, after unsuccessfully eliminating sweets from her diet, Talli thinks hard about her sugar intake. She understands her doctor has told her she is borderline pre-diabetic, but she also feels that she does not engage in other unhealthy health habits, such as smoking, drinking, or sun tanning. As a result, she decides it is probably okay if her only indulgences are sweets. What is Talli trying to do with this line of thought?
    a. Motivate herself
    b. Reduce her personal cognitive dissonance
    c. Minimize her risk for diabetes
    d. Increase her self-efficacy
    e. Eliminate her confirmation bias

83. Which hormones, respectively, stimulate appetite and signal fullness?
    a. Oxytocin and prolactin
    b. Testosterone and estrogen
    c. Insulin and glucagon
    d. Ghrelin and leptin
    e. Cortisol and thyroid-stimulating hormone

84. What types of food do people who are depressed or chronically sleep-deprived tend to crave?
    a. Fats
    b. Carbohydrates
    c. Proteins
    d. Oils
    e. None of the above

85. Paul has an hour-long commute every morning and afternoon during rush hour traffic. To try to make his drive more pleasant, he plans on listening to two interesting podcasts each day. He also buys himself a large vanilla cappuccino each morning and afternoon before starting the drive. Recently, Paul learned he is being transferred to a worksite that is only ten minutes from his house. On his first day at the new site, he is able to sleep in, drink coffee at home, and even go for a short walk with his dog before leaving for work. As soon as he gets in his car, though, he immediately craves a large vanilla cappuccino. What is the craving an example of?
    a. Dopamine reward response
    b. An addiction
    c. Operant conditioning
    d. Classical conditioning
    e. Modeling

86. Neurological differences in social motivation may serve as the primary underlying factor that contributes to which disorder?
   a. Depression
   b. Anxiety
   c. Introversion
   d. Tourette syndrome
   e. Autism

87. Which of the following groups of people are likely to have dysfunctional states of primary emotion response?
   a. Combat veterans
   b. Toddlers
   c. Newborns
   d. Females experiencing menopause
   e. Teenage males

88. Which of the following, from an evolutionary development standpoint, is widely accepted as the oldest structure in the brain?
   a. The pons
   b. The corpus callosum
   c. The frontal neocortex
   d. The limbic system
   e. The metencephalon

89. Kaya and Amie are best friends who are planning a beach vacation together. Kaya is also planning to bring her one-year-old daughter on the trip. Together, she and Amie spend a day looking at vacation rental homes for the trip. Amie finds a high-rise condo that seems perfect. She shows it to Kaya, excitedly pointing out the beach view, the luxurious amenities, and a balcony that they can relax on. Kaya immediately becomes frustrated and vetoes the idea, saying she is worried about her daughter hitting her head on some of the sharp corners and that the balcony is too high. What is this an example of?
   a. Conflict resolution
   b. Imprinting
   c. Piaget's stages of development
   d. Appraisal theory
   e. Cross-cultural conflict

90. Which of the following is NOT considered to be a universal emotion across cultures?
   a. Fear
   b. Anger
   c. Joy
   d. Surprise
   e. Love

91. Chronic stress is positively correlated with which of the following cognitive diseases?
    a. Dementia
    b. Hashimoto's disease
    c. Lupus
    d. Multiple sclerosis
    e. Down syndrome

92. Ophelia is a doctoral student who is examining how daycare settings contribute to attachment styles. Her university has a daycare center on campus that offers childcare to faculty and staff. After obtaining permission from parents who use the facility, she observes three different children interact with their parents and records notes about attachment behaviors that the children display. On a different day, she sits in the daycare center, watches drop-off for these three children, and observes them for a few hours in the center. She continues to make notes about their attachment behaviors, especially as the children interact with teachers and peers. What research method is Ophelia using?
    a. Randomized trial
    b. Anecdotal
    c. Survey
    d. Case study
    e. Personality inventory

93. Andy is a hiring manager who is considering four different candidates for a data analyst position. The best fit for the position is someone who is highly detail oriented, enjoys spending time alone reviewing spreadsheets, and prefers a structured work environment. While all four candidates have verbally stated that they have these qualities, Andy would like to further validate their responses, as turnover in this particular job would deeply impact the company's productivity. What would be a good assessment for Andy to utilize in this situation?
    a. The Myers-Briggs Type Indicator
    b. The Beck Depression Inventory
    c. The Minnesota Multiphasic Personality Inventory
    d. The Thematic Apperception Test
    e. The Rorschach Test

94. Which field of psychology was the FIRST to take the unique approach of focusing on human potential and development, rather than pathologies?
    a. Psychoanalytical
    b. Humanistic
    c. Behaviorist
    d. Cognitive
    e. Forensic

95. Frank is a 30-year-old male who previously experienced some personal crises that left him homeless. With the support of his community's social services, Frank was able to move into subsidized housing and utilize food stamps for meals. Approximately a month later, Frank found a job at a local software company. His job provided him with additional training, to which Frank dedicated himself. Through his hard work and the professional development opportunities, he moved from an entry-level role to a supervisory role at the company. The increased pay allowed Frank to move out of subsidized housing and purchase a two-bedroom home in town. According to Maslow, what type of activity is Frank most likely to pursue next?
    a. Looking for a bigger house
    b. Buying a new car
    c. Going back to school
    d. Becoming involved in his new community and perhaps dating
    e. The peaceful acceptance that his time on earth will eventually end

96. Which of the following figures in psychology is MOST likely to believe that early childhood memories and dream states play an important role in understanding one's present-day problems?
    a. Albert Bandura
    b. B. F. Skinner
    c. Mary Cover Jones
    d. John Watson
    e. Sigmund Freud

97. Which of the following is the BEST example of someone from a collectivist society?
    a. A son whose elderly parents live with him, his wife, and his three kids
    b. A rock climber who treks solo across the world, occasionally seeing her family on Thanksgiving
    c. A manager who takes full credit for his team's work, since he was the one who directed all operations
    d. An American college student who spends a summer abroad
    e. A teacher who has her students engage in academic competition for a prize

98. Which of the following traits was once diagnosed as a psychological disorder in the United States, but no longer is?
    a. Autism spectrum disorder
    b. Occupational burnout
    c. Homosexuality
    d. HIV
    e. Seasonal affective disorder

99. Which of the following defenses is used in less than one percent of criminal trials in the United States?
    a. Group defamation
    b. Insanity defense
    c. Self-defense
    d. Stand your ground
    e. Justifiable homicide

100. Bonnie, a 52-year-old woman, has recently been diagnosed with depression. She likely has had depression since she was a teenager, but only recently received a formal diagnosis. Bonnie often struggles to leave her home, or to even to get out of bed, but does feel better if she sees friends or exercises with her partner. However, since receiving a diagnosis, she constantly tells her partner that she can't go out for a walk or to dinner. She says she feels better if she stays in bed and naps, and that it is now medically explained why she needs to do so. However, most evenings she finds herself teary-eyed and wondering if anyone even misses her. What is Bonnie's case an example of?

    a. The side effects of pharmaceuticals
    b. Disparities in the healthcare system for women
    c. A negative consequence of diagnostic labeling
    d. The Rosenhan effect
    e. Compliance

101. What is the desensitization process commonly used to treat?

    a. Addiction
    b. Phobias and anxiety
    c. Post-partum depression
    d. Binge eating
    e. Sleep apnea

102. Receiving a paycheck every two weeks for performing a job is what kind of reinforcement?

    a. Continuous
    b. Fixed-ratio
    c. Variable-ratio
    d. Fixed-interval
    e. Variable-interval

103. Which of the following cases is most likely to benefit from a cognitive approach intervention?

    a. A woman who is grieving after the loss of her father
    b. A man who has emotional outbursts after having a stroke
    c. A child who will not make eye contact with caregivers
    d. A boy who is having nightmares about dying
    e. A woman who is trying to quit smoking

104. Eoin has started therapy sessions to manage family stress. Although he is an adult with children of his own, Eoin's parents place unfair demands on his time and finances, expecting him to pay for their mortgage and spend all of his free time helping with their household chores. Eoin's therapist asks him questions about how he views his role in his relationship with his parents. Then, she provides him with some examples of script he can use when he next speaks with his parents that will allow him to establish boundaries with them. She encourages him to use the script as often as possible before the next session. What type of therapy is Eoin receiving?

    a. Cognitive-behavioral therapy
    b. Pharmaceutical therapy
    c. Acting therapy
    d. Art therapy
    e. Psychoanalytic therapy

105. Priya is a young wife and mother. She dreams about pursuing doctoral studies, but her husband and in-laws say that it will be a struggle to raise the children without her constantly around. When she was a child, Priya's mom taught her how to cook meals that would provide for a large family. Priya also helped take care of her three younger siblings, including changing their diapers, packing their lunches, and reading bedtime stories. Priya knows she is great mother and homemaker. Although Priya completed her undergraduate studies, she feels that her dream to obtain a doctorate will likely remain a dream. What is Priya's story an example of?
   a. Stockholm syndrome
   b. Low self-esteem
   c. Sociocultural influences
   d. Work-life struggles
   e. Communism

106. Which of the following figures emphasized the importance of mentors and teachers in a young child's life?
   a. Mary Cover Jones
   b. Lev Vygotsky
   c. Sigmund Freud
   d. Abraham Maslow
   e. Aaron Beck

107. Which of the following positively correlates with effective treatment?
   a. Clients who voluntarily attend therapy
   b. Clients who attend therapy due to a third-party requirement
   c. Clients who have been diagnosed with a psychotic disorder
   d. Practitioners who use anecdotal evidence to treat clients
   e. Clients who are ashamed of legal troubles that resulted from behavioral issues

108. Which of the following is NOT an example of the influence of cultural context?
   a. Jane, an Asian-American, is diagnosed with depression but will only see her primary care provider for symptoms of fatigue.
   b. Mark, an African-American, is diagnosed with Type 2 diabetes but thinks his doctor is trying to get him to come in for more visits.
   c. Miranda, an Irish-American, believes everyone should have access to health insurance that covers mental health visits.
   d. Jagjit, an Indian-American, tries to talk to his mother about anxiety but she brushes off his concerns by saying everyone in their family is mentally strong.
   e. Jose, a Latin-American, thinks he might drink too much alcohol but doesn't feel comfortable telling his cousins, who also drink often.

109. Emmie has always been a high achiever who struggles immensely when she fails at something. A friend of hers pointed out that Emmie avoids activities in which she thinks she might fail. Emmie starts noticing her thoughts and realizes she often thinks that if she does not achieve certain standards, people will not like her. Her friend helps her question if this is actually true. Emmie is not sure, but she considers trying rock-climbing. She does not think she is strong enough, and knows she might fail at her first attempt, but she still wants to try it. What is Emmie trying to build?
   a. Competency
   b. Resilience
   c. Lean muscle mass
   d. Friendships
   e. Her hierarchy of needs

110. Risperidone and clozapine are used for what purpose?
   a. As pharmaceutical interventions to manage symptoms of schizophrenia
   b. As pharmaceutical interventions to manage symptoms of mild to moderate depression
   c. As pharmaceutical interventions to manage symptoms of bipolar disorder
   d. As pharmaceutical interventions to manage symptoms of obsessive compulsive disorder
   e. As pharmaceutical interventions to manage symptoms of anxiety

111. Direct and blunt dialogue from the therapist, and the potential to invalidate the feelings of trauma survivors, are criticisms of which treatment method?
   a. Individual therapy
   b. Client-centered therapy
   c. Group therapy
   d. Cognitive method
   e. Rational-emotive method

112. Which psychological approach highlights the similarities between the human mind and a computer?
   a. Psychoanalytical
   b. Machine learning
   c. Behavioral
   d. Cognitive
   e. Artificial intelligence

Use the following vignette to answer Questions 113–115.

> Louie's well-connected uncle introduces him to an executive at a renowned tech company in which he was an early startup investor. He provides Louie with a solid reference, and Louie gets a desirable job managing a team of software developers.

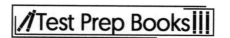

113. Even though Louie just graduated from college, he was selected over an intern who had been working with the company for six months. Louie commends himself for being a great candidate with a 4.0 GPA. Later, when Louie's team produces a horrible application that crashes repeatedly and is ultimately deemed a failure, Louie blames his team for not putting in enough effort. What is Louie exhibiting?
    a. A confirmation bias
    b. A self-serving bias
    c. The just-world hypothesis
    d. Narcissism
    e. Self-esteem

114. A new intern joins Louie's team for the next project. The new intern has heard about the failure of the last project, but since Louie is in a position of power, she assumes he is well experienced, and the failure was an anomaly. She later hears from others that Louie did not manage that project well but considering that Louie always appears so poised and polished, is always at work early, and always on his computer, she thinks there is no way he could be a poor manager. What is the new intern's perception an example of?
    a. Confirmation bias
    b. Halo effect
    c. Bystander effect
    d. Hazing
    e. False consensus

115. After Louie's next three projects launch successfully, he is mysteriously let go by the company. No one is really sure why he was fired. Some of his team members seem upset; they had started to finally all work functionally and effectively as a group. One of his team members, however, says, "I'm sure he had it coming to him after that first failure. That was the biggest project out of the bunch. Anyway, I heard he only got this job because of his uncle. He really wasn't great at his job." What is this team member's commentary an example of?
    a. Just-world hypothesis
    b. False consensus effect
    c. The halo effect
    d. Social loafing
    e. Deindividuation

116. Which of the following groups are MOST likely to exhibit qualities associated with deindividuation?
    a. Green card holders taking a citizenship test at a U.S. Immigration office
    b. High school students at a school with no dress code
    c. A preschool classroom
    d. Military officials
    e. Homeless mothers

117. A pharmaceutical rep is visiting a doctor's office to offer a comparable price on a commonly prescribed drug. He brings the office manager a flier, a pricing sheet, a few samples, and a large basket of gourmet holiday cookies. Based on the concept of the reciprocity norm, how is the office manager likely to respond?

    a. Feel pleased by the gift, and share the cookies with her staff

    b. Ask the rep to stop soliciting the office

    c. Tell the rep that cookies are not very healthy

    d. Ignore other patients in the waiting room, as they don't have gifts for the office

    e. Place an order for a three-month supply of the medication

118. Every Thursday evening, Ken runs with a group in his town. The group is open to anybody in the community, and all interested people meet at 6:00 p.m. at a local running shoe store. It's not a scenic route, but he enjoys the comradery. One day, a new running shoe store opens in the town. It's in a better location, and also holds group runs through a pristine nature trail. Ken hears through the grapevine that they also offer snacks at the end of the run and are even raffling off new running shoes. Yet, Ken prefers to stay at the original store. What is this an example of?

    a. Mere-exposure effect

    b. Scapegoating

    c. Altruism

    d. Prisoner's dilemma

    e. Social inhibition

119. Samantha is a skilled health education presenter who travels to different worksites and presents wellness topics. Before every workshop, she tries to practice her presentation at home. She always struggles with her sentences, feels awkward, and becomes unmotivated to continue. She wonders, before every presentation, if she will fumble through the real thing. Yet her workshops always go exceedingly well, and she leaves feeling energized and fulfilled from her work. What is Samantha experiencing?

    a. Imposter syndrome

    b. Social facilitation

    c. Social loafing

    d. Conformity

    e. Chronic brain fog

Free-Response Questions

1. Daniel is an author who is writing a personal development book. He hopes to talk to people near the end of their lives and extract different themes about how people learn lessons and develop at different stages. Daniel begins interviewing residents in his grandfather's community-living home and hospice center. Most of the residents are over eighty years old, and they are thrilled to share their earliest memories and their recent stories. Daniel asks each interviewee to share how they feel they grew and developed as a person over the course of their lives, and what their most important life lessons are.

Provide a sample interview response for each of Erik Eriksson's developmental stages, listed below, that shows what the experience of each stage might look like in the average American:

Trust versus Mistrust

Autonomy versus Shame and Doubt

Initiative versus Guilt

Industry versus Inferiority

Identity versus Confusion

Intimacy versus Isolation

Generativity versus Stagnation

Integrity versus Despair

2. Researchers are interested in studying whether research participants who were feeling aggressive would be less aggressive after experiencing catharsis (also known as an emotional release). One day, 10 individuals separately met with a researcher named Russell. They were each asked to write an opinion paper about the political climate in the United States, which Russell would later take the time to assess. After each participant wrote their respective paper, Russell took each individual aside into another room and told them that it was the most poorly written paper he ever read and that they should be ashamed of their work. Later that day, another set of 10 individuals each wrote a paper on the same topic, and Russell gave them all the same response. After hearing Russel's appraisal of their work, the first group was asked to repeatedly hit a training dummy, while the second group was asked to sit idly alone in a room for five minutes. After either hitting the dummy or watching cartoons, each research participant was given the chance to blow a whistle as loudly as they could whenever they saw Russell approach them. The researchers operationally defined aggression as how loud each participant blew their whistle. Researchers posited that the participants who hit the training dummy would be less likely to blow their whistle loudly at Russell, if at all. The following table indicates how loud, in decibels, each participant from each group blew their whistle at Russell. The order of listed values is not significant. Assume all differences are significant.

Sat Idly	Hit a Training Dummy
0	105
0	70
7	65
0	50
0	110
3	85
5	45
10	55
15	60
8	35

Part A

Identify each of the following in this study:

- Experimental group:
- Control group:
- Independent variable:
- Dependent variable:

Part B

Explain whether the hypothesis of the researchers was supported or refuted:

Describe how to modify one ethical flaw in this particular research study:

Calculate the loudness of the whistle (in decibels) for the group that repeatedly hit the training dummy:

3. Jason is scheduled for his annual checkup with his pediatric dentist. Jason hates having to go to the dentist because he doesn't like all the tools the dentist has to use with him during his checkup. While Jason's parents are reluctant to bring him in for this reason, they know it is important for his health, so they devise a way to get Jason to go. Jason's father proposes that they go for a ride to the toy store, which is five minutes away from the dentist's office. After Jason agrees to go, Jason's mother says that if he is on his best behavior at the dentist's office, they will buy Jason his favorite action figure. While initially hesitant, Jason agrees to go to the dentist's office, and he is well-mannered during his entire time there. Afterward, his parents buy Jason the action figure.

Please explain how each of the following concepts is related to this particular scenario.

- Positive reinforcement

- Associational learning

- Hippocampus

- Foot-in-the-door phenomenon

- Approach-avoidance conflict

Answer Responses

1. C: Choice *C* is replication, which describes research that is repeated to see if an original study's results are consistent with results obtained in subsequent studies, which in turn would indicate that the original results are valid and reliable. Choice *A* is incorrect because falsifiability actually describes how some proposition or theory has the ability to be proven wrong. Choice *B* is incorrect because face validity entails using a test that measures a concept it purports to measure. Choice *D* is incorrect because operational definition describes procedures that outline a series of necessary tests used to determine the nature of a certain variable. Choice *E* is incorrect because construct validity refers to how accurately a test measures the construct it is supposed to measure.

2. B: Choice *B* entails the third step of the scientific process. Conducting a test is done after a researcher makes an observation and generates a hypothesis. Choice *A* is incorrect because communicating the results is the final step researchers take after testing is completed and the results have been interpreted. Choice *C* is incorrect because forming a prediction actually constitutes the second step to take before the testing phase begins. Choice *D* is incorrect because interpreting data follows conducting the test. Choice *E* is incorrect because the scientific method starts with making an observation before undertaking all the other steps.

3. D: Choice *D,* longitudinal study, is correct because a longitudinal study is the research method where researchers repetitively collect information on the same participants over an extended timeframe, often over many years. In the example given with identical twins, it's not uncommon for researchers to employ the use of a longitudinal study. Choice *A* is incorrect because cross-sectional studies are used to evaluate data about variables obtained at a certain point in time across a sample population, which consists of different people with similar characteristics. Choice *B* is incorrect because the Delphi method ascertains the variety of opinions on a subject of interest, examines issues of clinical relevance, and devises a consensus on more contentious problems. Choice *C* is incorrect because an interview is a method carried out in person, over the telephone, or via telecommunication over the computer. The researcher can be formal or informal and might use a checklist or some form to record the research participant's responses. Choice *E* is incorrect because a questionnaire is used to gather information from a large group of people who may not be able to attend an interview or participate in experiments due to time constraints.

4. E: Choice *E* doesn't apply to cross-sectional studies. Regarded as descriptive research, cross-sectional studies wouldn't be used to determine causality. Researchers would use causal or relational studies to determine a cause-and-effect relationship between variables. The other choices are incorrect because they are indeed true of cross-sectional studies. Choice *A* is incorrect because cross-sectional studies are used as a means of obtaining initial data and drawing inferences about a possible relationship between variables. Choice *B* is incorrect because the population in cross-sectional studies do consist of different people with similar traits being compared to one another. Choice *C* is incorrect because one of the ways in which cross-sectional studies are differentiated from longitudinal studies is that the former involves evaluating variable information obtained over a specific point in time, as opposed to over an extended timeframe. Choice *D* is incorrect because cross-sectional studies do focus on describing the traits of a group.

5. A: Choice *A* states that a case study has the ability to provide insights for future studies, which is indeed considered one of the strengths a case study offers. Some other strengths of case studies include how they offer detailed information and allow researchers to study impractical scenarios. Choices *B* and *C* are incorrect because case studies are actually difficult to replicate because the information provided in the original study won't directly match information in follow-up studies, rendering those original results unreliable and correspondingly ungeneralizable to a larger group. Choices *D* and *E* are incorrect because case studies actually tend to consist of a small sample size, which serves as a reason for a case study's lack of generalizability. This also makes these studies especially prone to bias. Some other reasons that case studies are particularly susceptible to bias include the selection of research participants being non-randomized and also because of the possibility of researchers asking the research participants leading questions during interviews.

6. B: Choice *B*, motivated reasoning, describes how a person's judgments are predisposed to bias by self-serving motivations, causing them to favor any information confirming their predetermined beliefs while simultaneously rejecting other information opposing those beliefs. This best explains why the man listed in the example was resistant to the evidence supporting evolution, yet was in favor of the creation science arguments against it. Choice *A* is incorrect because top-down design describes making use of one's prior knowledge and experiences to increase their understanding of an event, and in turn, help them interpret stimuli. Choice *C* is incorrect because schematic processing involves a heuristic technique used to both encode and retrieve memories in a manner not requiring much effort. Choice *D* is incorrect because bottom-up design consists of processing sensory information that can help analyze stimuli. Choice *E* is incorrect because proactive interference describes the tendency of previously learned information to hinder one's ability to learn new material, whereas retroactive interference describes how learning new information hinders one's recall of previously learned material.

7. C: Choice *C*, a script, is correct because a script outlines a series of behaviors expected in a certain situation. In the given example, the customer at the restaurant follows a script by engaging in a set of behaviors acquired through habit and routine practice. Choice *A* is incorrect because an archetype describes inborn tendencies that serve to help influence human behavior and personality, all of which evolved from experiences over time, such as a compassionate and generous caregiver with a genuine and committed desire to helping others in need. Choice *B* is incorrect because a rubric is more a method of scoring based on certain evaluative criteria, which is something an educator might use to grade student assignments. Choice *D* is incorrect because a social role describes a sequence of connected behaviors and actions carried out in a particular social situation, such as the role of a teacher in a classroom setting. Choice *E* is incorrect because operant conditioning actually pertains to a learning process demonstrating how the strength of a behavior is modified by either reinforcement or punishment. One example is a young student finishing their homework because they know they'll be rewarded and praised for completing it.

8. D: Choice *D* describes the notion that sleep allows all species to conserve energy as they sleep, to avoid being awake during certain times that would otherwise put them in harm's way, which is precisely what the evolutionary theory of sleep proposes. Choice *A* is incorrect because it is actually the clean-up theory of sleep that contends how sleep acts as the brain's means of ridding itself of toxins and waste products accumulated throughout the previous day. Choice *B* is incorrect because the concept that NREM sleep helps restore physical functions and REM sleep restores mental functions is actually posited by the repair and restoration theory of sleep. Choice *C* is incorrect because the idea that sleep helps in processing information gathered during the day is derived from the information consolidation theory of sleep. Choice *E* is incorrect because the idea that sleep is a type of nutrition for the brain is actually based on a separate concept reported by organizations such as the National Sleep Foundation and American Nutrition Association.

9. C: Choice *C* outlines how visual-motor skills are more prominent in the brain's right hemisphere, a fact which was demonstrated in the split-brain research performed by researchers Roger Sperry and Michael Gazzaniga. Generally speaking, split-brain research offered insights into interhemispheric communication and a first-order approximation of each hemisphere's functions. Choice *A* is incorrect because, while it is true that the cerebellum is responsible for voluntary movements, this wasn't discovered during the split-brain study. In fact, the function of the cerebellum was first discovered in 1809 by an Italian anatomist named Luigi Rolando. Another brain region—the central sulcus of Rolando—is actually named after him. Choice *B* is incorrect because functional impairments were actually found to occur after cutting the corpus callosum. This impairment is referred to as split-brain syndrome, which describes how this separation affects the right hemisphere's ability to properly transfer information over to the left hemisphere, and in rare cases, can even result in a sort of split personality occurring in the patient. Choice *D* is incorrect because split-brain research revealed that the left hemisphere is actually responsible for controlling the right side of the body, and the right hemisphere controls the left side of the body. Choice *E* is incorrect because, while the occipital lobe does contain both a visual receiving area and a visual association area, Sperry and Gazzaniga's split-brain study did not discover this fact.

10. E: Choice *E* mentions a phenomenon in depth perception known as motion parallax, which is a monocular depth cue describing how objects viewed in close proximity appear to move at a fast pace, while objects viewed from a distance appear almost stationary. This best explains the phenomenon you, the fictitious driver, were experiencing in the question prompt. Choice *A* is incorrect because perspective entails watching the narrowing of a scene the farther it goes off into the distance. Choice *B* is incorrect because aerial perspective describes the phenomenon of how images increasing in their rate of distance start to appear blurrier to the observer. Choice *C* is incorrect because interposition, also referred to as overlap, occurs when an object is perceived as being closer when it partially obstructs the view of another object. Choice *D* is incorrect because convergence is actually a binocular depth cue that outlines the concurrent inward movement of each eye toward one another when viewing an object, which stretches the eye muscle and aids in depth perception.

11. B: Choice *B* is a concept found in Weber's law called the just noticeable difference, which describes how much something must be changed in order for any difference to be noticed. For instance, if you were given two objects of different weights, the just noticeable difference would be the minimum weight difference between them that you could discern most of the time. Choice *A* is incorrect because the Bayesian inference is a statistical method used to modify the probability of a hypothesis as more information becomes readily available. Making use of sensory data and previous knowledge serves as a feature of this concept. Choice *C* is incorrect because what the two-point threshold describes is the smallest separation in which two points simultaneously applied to a person's skin can be distinguished from one another. Choice *D* is incorrect because attitude scaling is a concept that involves the ability to objectively measure attitude. Weber and Fechner's research has been helpful in this endeavor. Choice *E* is incorrect because retinal disparity is actually a binocular depth cue describing how the brain evaluates a scene's depth by using two images of the same scene obtained from relatively different angles. For example, if you held out an object in front of your nose, closed one of your eyes, and kept switching back and forth between each eye that was closed, you'd find that each eye would offer you a very different view of that object.

12. A: Choice *A* is American psychologist Michael Gazzaniga, who became renowned for his research with split-brain patients. After discovering that the two hemispheres can function independently and autonomously of one another, Gazzaniga formed a theory of consciousness that is currently supported by neuroscientific research. Choice *B* is incorrect because Wilhelm Wundt was a German physician known for opening the first laboratory for experimental psychology at the University of Leipzig in Germany in 1879. Choice *C* is incorrect because Eugen Bleuler was a Swiss doctor most known for his contributions to better understanding mental illness. He coined terms such as ambivalence, autism, depth psychology, schizoid, and schizophrenia. Choice *D* is incorrect because David Hubel was a Canadian-American neurophysiologist who, alongside fellow researcher Torsten Wiesel, is known for his research into the structure and function of the visual cortex. Both researchers received the Nobel Prize in Physiology or Medicine for their work related to how the brain was able to process visual information. Choice *E* is incorrect because William James was an American philosopher and psychologist best known for his theories on pragmatism, functionalism, and stream of consciousness. Pragmatism posits that an idea's abstract truth can never be completely proven, and that philosophy should be geared toward its overall usefulness. Functionalism posits how thought and behavior can help an individual function in the world. Stream of consciousness contends that consciousness isn't experienced as successive ideas but rather as a blended stream.

13. B. Choice *B*, Gestalt theory, contends that the whole is greater than the sum of its parts. As it relates to visual perception, Gestalt principles use closure, the figure-ground relationship, proximity or similarity, and the law of good continuation to help shed light on how people organize incoming sensory information. Choice *A* is incorrect because the Gibson theory of perception argues that the mind can directly perceive stimuli from one's environment without the need of any other cognitive processing. Choice *C* is incorrect because the empirical theory of perception states that, rather than analyzing the various components of sensory information, sensory systems integrate information about properties of the world and attach incoming stimuli to this information. Choice *D* is incorrect because self-perception theory maintains that people form attitudes by observing their own behavior and inferring what attitudes caused those behaviors. Choice *E* is incorrect because the cognitive dissonance theory describes how a person is capable of holding two contradictory thoughts at the same time, which causes them to develop a sense of discomfort and in turn do anything to help decrease that dissonance.

14. D: Choice *D* is astigmatism, which is a visual impairment that entails light being unevenly focused in the eye and causing images to become blurry or shadowed. This impairment best applies to what the man in the given scenario was experiencing. Choice *A* is incorrect because myopia, also known as nearsightedness, occurs when the eye's lens focuses an image in front of the retina rather than on the retina itself, which results in poor distance viewing. Choice *B* is incorrect because hyperopia, also called farsightedness, occurs when distant objects are seen more clearly than nearby ones. Blurriness in hyperopia is likelier to happen in more severe instances. Choice *C* is incorrect because presbyopia is a normal part of aging where the eyes gradually lose the ability to focus on nearby objects. Choice *E* is incorrect because a visual illusion isn't necessarily an impairment, but instead indicates a contradiction between an eye's visual input and the brain's interpretation of that input. When this phenomenon occurs, the observer perceives images in a way that differs from objective reality, which in turn results in the visual illusion.

15. A: Choice *A*, neural hearing loss, happens when the brain is no longer able to receive signals from the auditory nerve. The brain experiences problems processing information in sound. These problems can include issues understanding speech and discerning the source of the sound. Choice *B* is incorrect because sensorineural hearing loss occurs when there is damage to the hair cells of the cochlea of the ear to the point it affects the inner ear. Choice *C* is incorrect because conductive hearing loss is an impairment—such as excessive ear wax, ear infections, fluid build-up, a punctured eardrum, or even abnormal bone growth—that prevents sound from passing through either the outer or middle ear. Choice *D* is incorrect because mixed hearing loss is actually when conductive and sensorineural hearing loss concur. Choice *E* is incorrect because tinnitus isn't necessarily hearing loss. While the ringing or

buzzing sound in one or both ears can obviously interfere with hearing, tinnitus itself isn't known to cause hearing loss.

16. E: Choice, lexical-gustatory synesthesia, is a rare form of synesthesia where the person will experience certain tastes after hearing certain types of words. The given example of the woman being able to taste chocolate whenever she hears the word "factory" points to her having this rare form of synesthesia. Choice A is incorrect because grapheme-color is a common form of synesthesia where the person can see letters and numbers (graphemes) in certain colors, though the color of each grapheme tends to vary from one person to another. Choice B is incorrect because chromesthesia is another common form of synesthesia that entails sounds being associated with colors. Everyday sounds can trigger the perception of color in those with this type of synesthesia. Choice C is incorrect because auditory-tactile involves experiencing bodily sensations after hearing certain sounds, such as a certain word causing the person to feel touched despite not being physically touched. Choice D is incorrect because misophonia is a neurological disorder where emotions such as anger, fear, and disgust are triggered by certain sounds, which can range from dripping water to chewing or repetitive pencil tapping.

17. C: Choice C correctly describes that the postcentral gyrus, or primary somatosensory cortex, is responsible for a person's sense of touch. The somatosensory cortex is located in the parietal lobe and is vital for processing sensations of touch, and after this information is processed, a person can learn to identify objects via this touch sensation. Choice A is incorrect because it is the precentral gyrus, or primary motor area, that controls the voluntary movements of skeletal muscles. Choice B is incorrect because it is the central sulcus of Rolando that helps to keep the frontal lobe separated from the parietal lobe. Choice D is incorrect because it is the superior frontal gyrus that focuses on processing short-term information (or working memory) and contributes to other higher cognitive functions, such as self-awareness. Choice E is incorrect because the lateral Sylvian fissure is the brain feature separating the frontal and parietal lobe from the temporal lobe.

18. A: Choice A is Broca's area, or the inferior frontal gyrus, which is the brain area responsible for speech production and language processing. Damage to this brain region can result in Broca's aphasia, or expressive aphasia, which consists of partial loss of the ability to produce language, whether manual, spoken, or written. Choice B is incorrect because Wernicke's area, or the superior temporal gyrus, is the region responsible for the comprehension of language. Damage to this area can result in Wernicke's aphasia, or receptive aphasia, which consists of having a difficult time understanding spoken or written language. Choice C is incorrect because the function of the central sulcus of Rolando is separating the frontal lobe and the parietal lobe. Choice D is incorrect because the function of the supramarginal gyrus (part of the somatosensory cortex) is to identify gestures and postures and interpret tactile data, as well as space and limb location. Choice E is incorrect because the function of the olfactory bulb, which is in the forebrain and considered one of the oldest structures of the brain, is odor detection. Olfaction (smell) is our only sense that can actually bypass the thalamus and travel directly to our forebrain.

19. D: Choice D states that the activity of the cortical homunculus represents the proportional size of each body area, but this is inaccurate. In fact, it actually indicates the complexity of the performed activity. Choice A is incorrect because the cortical homunculus is considered a neurological map acting as a distorted representation of the human body, in terms of activity. Choice B is incorrect because the function of this region involves processing sensory or motor functions for different bodily locations. Choices C and E are incorrect because nerve signals transmitted from the hands do terminate over considerably large portions of the brain, while those nerves transmitted from the arms or torso tend to cover much smaller amounts of the brain's cortical areas.

225

20. B: Choice *B* is the opponent process theory of color, which states that color perception is controlled by three receptor complexes (red-green, blue-yellow, and black-white). According to this color theory, these color complexes are only able to detect one of the colors at a time because each color opposes one another. In the example of Harold seeing a green afterglow after looking at a red object for an extended timeframe, the opponent process theory would be most applicable. Choice *A* is incorrect because dark adaptation describes how the pupils of our eyes dilate and the sensitivity of our retinal rods increases as we gradually adjust to lower light intensities. Choice *C* is incorrect because melanin is actually an amino acid that is responsible for giving structures such as our hair, skin, and eyes their natural pigment. Tanning is another example of melanin production occurring. Choice *D* is incorrect because the trichromatic theory of color describes our subjective experience of color. The three receptors in the retina of the eye that process the perception of color each have their own peak sensitivity; one to the color green, one to red, and another one to blue. According to this theory, when these colors are combined, it produces all the colors we are able to perceive. Choice *E* is incorrect because Rayleigh scattering occurs when light scatters via particles in a particular conduit, though there's no change in the wavelength. This phenomenon accounts for why we perceive the sky as blue. Blue light is scattered relatively more effectively than red light.

21. E: Choice *E* represents the correct order in which the sensation of pain is processed (nociception). Nociception starts with transduction (or conversion), progresses to conduction, is followed by transmission, transitions to modulation, and finally culminates in perception. Choice *A* is incorrect because conduction occurs before transmission, which is then followed by modulation. Choice *B* is incorrect because the process starts with transduction before undertaking the subsequent order of conduction, transmission, modulation, and perception. Choice *C* is incorrect because transmission follows conduction and modulation precedes perception. Choice *D* is incorrect because transduction precedes conduction, followed by transmission, and then perception follows modulation.

22. B: Choice *B* accurately represents the differences between rods and cones in our eyes. With rods, vision is processed at lower levels of light and spatial acuities, and rods don't facilitate color vision; whereas with cones, vision is processed at higher levels of light and spatial acuities, and they do facilitate color vision. Choice *A* is incorrect because, in this instance, the roles are reversed. Rods don't process higher light levels and spatial acuities, and don't facilitate color; cones don't process lower light levels and spatial acuities, and do facilitate color. Choice *C* is incorrect because rods don't facilitate color vision and cones do facilitate color. Choice *D* is incorrect because rods process lower spatial acuities and cones process higher spatial acuities. Choice *E* is incorrect because rods process lower spatial acuities and don't facilitate color, whereas cones process higher spatial acuities and do facilitate color.

23. B: Choice *B* serves as the most accurate statement about visual perception. Bottom-up processing is data-based. When an object is being viewed, its representation is built up from an image that the eye's retina has processed. Top-down processing is more knowledge-based. The observer uses their pre-existing knowledge to identify an object and further mediate how visual information is processed. Choice *A* is incorrect because light enters through the cornea (not the retina), which helps focus that light onto the photoreceptors in the retina (not the cornea) to translate it into an image,. Choice *C* is incorrect because visual perception is in fact one of the most extensively studied topics in the field of psychology. Choice *D* is incorrect because researchers are already well aware of the function of the photoreceptors in the retina of the eye. Photoreceptors respond to light and transduce light into signals that are transmitted to the brain. Choice *E* is incorrect because it is actually smell, not vision, that doesn't have to pass through the thalamus before being transmitted to its respective region of the brain.

24. C: Choice *C* is the Weber-Fechner law, which is named after researchers Ernst Weber and Gustav Fechner. With regard to human perception, this law describes the relationship between the actual change in a physical stimulus and the perception of that change. The example used to outline this concept was an actual experiment Weber conducted to demonstrate this phenomenon. Choice *A* is incorrect because a monocular depth cue is used to describe how depth information is provided when one eye is used to view a scene. Choice *B* is incorrect because a binocular depth cue entails when both eyes are providing information about depth. Choice *D* is incorrect because the chemoaffinity hypothesis was proposed by Roger Sperry to describe how neurons generate connections with specific targets based on how they interact with distinct molecular markers during development. In this hypothesis, it is the genotype of an organism that determines the initial diagram for wiring. Choice *E* is incorrect because optimal probabilistic reasoning is actually synonymous with the Bayesian inference, which describes a statistical method used to revise the probability of a hypothesis as more information becomes readily available.

25. E: Choice *E* is the context effect, which describes how environmental factors in an event affect how a person ends up perceiving and remembering that event. This concept is most applicable to the given example of the woman in the ice cream parlor experiencing friendly service, making a purchase, and developing a favorable impression of the parlor that will likely result in her returning there again in the future. Choice *A* is incorrect because a schema actually describes a cognitive framework that people use to organize and interpret information acquired from the surrounding world. Examples of schemas include academic rubrics, archetypes, scripts, social schemas, stereotypes, and worldviews. Choice *B* is incorrect because perceptual constancy describes how we perceive an object as constant despite our sensation of the object changing. Choice *C* is incorrect because retrospective analysis is actually another term for a retrospective study, which is a research method used when an event's outcome is already known. Choice *D* is incorrect because a parapraxis is actually synonymous with a Freudian slip, which describes an error in speech or action due to interference from an unconscious wish or thought process.

26. D: Choice *D* describes how Sigmund Freud, who established the field of psychoanalysis, contributed significantly to the field of psychology with his conceptualization of the important role the unconscious plays in influencing human behavior. He posited that awareness exists below the surface and that unconscious thoughts can motivate our behaviors. He used psychoanalysis to help people bring their unconscious thoughts into conscious awareness. Choice *A* is incorrect because the discovery of simple and complex cells was actually made by researchers David Hubel and Torsten Wiesel. Choice *B* is incorrect because the discovery of how the vagus nerve affects heart activity was made by researcher Ernst Weber. Choice *C* is incorrect because it was actually Gustav Fechner who developed psychophysics. Choice *E* is incorrect because it was researchers Roger Sperry and Michael Gazzaniga who studied split brains.

27. C: Choice *C* says that sleep disorders aren't known to have any significant negative implications for one's health, which is actually not true. In fact, a lack of sleep can adversely affect a person's physical health, along with their energy levels, relationships, and task performance. Sleep problems can also cause fatigue, irritability, inattentiveness, difficulty falling or staying asleep, and recurring naps throughout the day. They are also known to impact one's mental health as well by contributing to anxiety and depression. Each of these issues can substantially impair one's ability to function on a daily basis. Choices *A* and *B* are incorrect because sleep disorders do impact a third of the American population, particularly those between the ages of twenty to sixty, and are commonly suspected when difficulty sleeping is chronic and not simply the result of external factors that impact sleep only occasionally. Choices *D* and *E* are incorrect because lifestyle changes, along with medical treatments, can be used to help treat sleep disorders. Treatments for sleep disorders tend to vary because there is no single causal factor for them.

28. B: Choice *B* describes the accurate finding that, while neuroplasticity can last throughout the entirety of an individual's lifespan, developing brains tend to demonstrate plasticity to a greater extent compared to the adult brain. Choice *A* is incorrect because neuroplasticity can actually result from normal experiences as well as be a means of recovering from traumatic brain injuries, the latter of which serve as the scientific basis for treating acquired neurological injuries. Choice *C* is incorrect because research into brain plasticity has shown that damaged brain functions can recover by transferring over to undamaged brain regions, which allows the brain to help compensate for a particular functional deficit. This is known as functional plasticity. Choice *D* is incorrect because environmental cues have been found to be one among numerous factors that can affect neuroplasticity. These other factors include behavior, emotion, experience, learning, the repetition of stimuli, and thought. Choice *E* is incorrect because extensive research on plasticity has helped researchers gain more of an understanding of its underlying mechanisms.

29. D: Choice *D*, lesioning, is a research method that involves certain regions of the brain being either disabled or removed entirely as a means of learning their specific functions. Researchers study brain lesions that are the result of illness, injury, or damage inflicted by the researcher. In the given example, the man suffering from epileptic seizures was undergoing this lesioning procedure to address his seizure activity. Choice *A* is incorrect because gamma knife describes a type of radiation therapy used as a treatment method for tumors and other brain abnormalities. However, gamma knife isn't technically surgery in the traditional sense because there are no incisions being made. Choice *B* is incorrect because an autopsy consists of extensively examining a corpse via dissection to determine the cause, mode, and manner of death, or to evaluate the degree of any present underlying disease or injury. Choice *C* is incorrect because necropsy is similar to an autopsy in that it's performed to determine the cause of death in nonhuman animals. Choice *E* is incorrect because a transorbital lobotomy was a psychosurgical procedure performed between the late 1940s and late 1960s on patients suffering from certain psychiatric problems. Lobotomies have since fallen out of favor; however, in the rare instance they are performed today, they are much more sophisticated now than they were in their heyday.

30. A: Choice *A*, positron emission topography (PET) scan, is the neuroimaging device used to illustrate where neurons are firing by using radioactive tracers. The reason this works is because the tracers bond with brain glucose, which the brain uses as fuel. Choice *B* is incorrect because the function of the electroencephalogram (EEG) is to measure electrical activity in the brain in the form of brainwaves. It is often used to study certain psychological states, such as wakefulness and sleepiness, and is also useful in helping to diagnose seizures and other medical issues resulting in either overactive or underactive brain regions. Choice *C* is incorrect because functional magnetic resonance imaging (fMRI) is used to measure brain functioning through the combination of numerous images on a computer taken a fraction of a second apart. Choice *D* is incorrect because magnetic resonance imaging (MRI) is a neuroimaging device that helps to distinguish grey matter, white matter, and cerebrospinal fluid. Choice *E* is incorrect because an ablation experiment is another term used to describe the surgical procedure of lesioning.

31. E: The best example of natural selection given is Choice *E*, where lizards develop longer leg bones as a means of climbing up tall objects so as to avoid floods or escape ground-based predators. The reason this serves as the best example of natural selection is because natural selection consists of those traits, whether physical or psychological, that allow an organism to adapt to an everchanging world. In turn, this increases the organism's likelihood of survival and reproduction. Choice *A* is incorrect because this example of carefully manipulating heredity in flowers to create a perfect hybrid is actually indicative of

artificial selection, which describes the intentional reproduction of certain organisms in a population primarily for their desirable traits. It is synonymous with selective breeding. Choice *B* is incorrect because this example of a giraffe developing a long neck after struggling to reach high branches represents the now discredited Lamarckian theory of inheritance, which posited that traits were altered over an organism's lifetime and could be passed down to their offspring. Choice *C* is incorrect because this example of a penguin's wings getting smaller due to disuse serves as another example of the Lamarckian version of inheritance. Choice *D* is incorrect because the example of crossbreeding dogs for their desired traits represents artificial selection.

32. C: Choice *C* is epigenetics, which is the term that describes a framework in the field of psychology used to better understand the ways in which gene expressions are influenced by our experiences and environments as a means of shaping our behavior. Scientists have studied identical twins that were separated at birth and subsequently adopted into different homes and environments in order to observe how different upbringings and experiences would affect their behavior. Choice *A* is incorrect because adaptation actually describes a phenomenon in Darwinian evolution that involves an organism modifying their behavior, physiology, and practices in order to better adapt to their environment. Bird calls and migrations are examples of adaptation. Choice *B* is incorrect because neurogenesis describes the brain's ability to create new neurons. While it is important as an embryo develops, neurogenesis actually persists in certain brain areas, such as the hippocampus, even after one's birth and throughout the entirety of their lifespan. Choice *D* is incorrect because gene editing describes the process of inserting, deleting, or replacing DNA in a cell or organism at a specific site in their genome. Choice *E* is incorrect because eugenics described a set of practices that were aimed at improving people via controlled breeding to increase the incidence of desirable inherited traits.

33. B: Choice *B* is the activation synthesis model, which is a theory of dreaming describing how dreams are the products of brain circuitry that become activated during the process of REM sleep. Choice *A* is incorrect because the information consolidation theory posits that sleep serves as a means of processing information acquired during the previous day. Choice *C* is incorrect because the psychoanalytic theory of sleep proposed that dreams represent one's unconscious desires, motivations, and thoughts. Freud once referred to dreams as "the royal road to the unconscious." Choice *D* is incorrect because the neurocognitive theory of dreaming suggests that dreams are akin to mind-wandering in that they're imaginative yet realistic simulations of one's waking life. Choice *E* is incorrect because the Jungian theory of dreams contends that dreams perform the work of integrating our conscious and unconscious lives.

34. B: Choice *B* is declarative memory, also referred to as explicit memory. This type of memory involves the recall of facts and events. Declarative memories can be consciously remembered. The example of the couple recalling the hour that their favorite restaurant closes best describes declarative memory. Choice *A* is incorrect because procedural memory—also called implicit memory—describes the unconscious retention of various skills, which can include tying a shoelace, playing an instrument, or driving a car. Choices *C, D,* and *E* are incorrect because each of these types of memory describe different types of sensory memory. Iconic memory is used for visual stimuli, echoic memory is used for auditory stimuli, and haptic memory is used for touch.

35. A: Choice *A* is positive correlation, which involves two variables headed in the same direction. In other words, if one variable increases, then the other variable also increases. In the given example, as schooling increases, a person's likelihood of generating a higher income also increases, thus indicating a positive correlation because both variables are showing an increase. However, it's also important to note that if both variables were decreasing, the same rule would apply because both variables would be decreasing. Choice *B* is incorrect because a negative correlation indicates variables are moving in opposite directions. In other words, if one variable increases, then the other variable decreases, or vice versa. For example, as a student's absences to class increases, their grades decrease, thus indicating a negative correlation because there's an inverse relationship between these variables. Choice *C* is incorrect because an initial value indicates the output value when the input of a linear function comes out to zero. In other words, *Y* is the initial value when *X* is zero. Choice *D* is incorrect because an intercept indicates where a straight line crosses either the *X*-axis, or the *Y*-axis, on a graph. Choice *E* is incorrect because a bimodal distribution describes when two values are occurring most frequently. For example, a histogram of test scores that is bimodal will have two peaks—one for each of the most frequently-earned test scores.

36. C: Choice *C* is correct because latent learning is a type of learning and information retention that occurs unconsciously and without reinforcement or any kind of motivation, and that isn't displayed until the time comes to apply that learned information. In the given example, a student learns division, but doesn't display that knowledge until presented with an important test where that learning could be applied. Choice *A* is incorrect because social learning posits that a new behavior can be obtained via observing and imitating others performing that behavior, and subsequently the observer becomes motivated to recreate the learned behavior. For example, watching a commercial featuring a product that upon use will make us more appealing to others, and then modeling that behavior by buying and using the advertised product. Choice *B* is incorrect because insight learning focuses on finding a solution to a problem via a sudden realization and without any continuous trials. For example, you come across a tough problem on a test, and right before you decide to move on to the next question, the equation that will yield the answer suddenly comes to mind. Choice *D* is incorrect because observational learning involves learning that happens by watching how others behave. For example, a young child doesn't take a piece of candy out of a tray without permission after observing their older sibling being reprimanded for doing so. Choice *E* is incorrect because emotional learning involves using identifiable skills to regulate one's emotions and identify the emotional state of others by learning to see things from a different perspective.

37. D: Choice *D* states that conditioning is rendered more effective if the signal of a conditioned stimulus reliably predicts the appearance of an unconditioned stimulus, which Rescorla used to demonstrate the role cognitive processes play in classical conditioning. Choice *A* is incorrect because, while researchers once perceived conditioning as simply automatic, Rescorla's research changed that perspective. Choice *B* is incorrect because Rescorla's research actually showed that pairing two different stimuli together doesn't always result in the same conditioning. Choice *C* is incorrect because Rescorla did in fact demonstrate the important role that information processing plays in conditioning. Choice *E* is incorrect because many theoretical developments and experimental findings have indeed been influenced by Rescorla's model over the years.

38. B: Choice *B*, the authoritative parenting style, is correct because this style involves parents who are considered firm yet flexible when setting rules and guidelines for their children. In the given example, a parent who enforces boundaries, uses positive discipline, and generally sets clear restrictions on behavior is an example of authoritative parenting. Choice *A* is incorrect because permissive parenting involves parents who cater too much to their child's demands and hardly ever consistently reinforce any rules. Choice *C* is incorrect because authoritarian parenting features parents who use strict discipline when punishing their children. Choice *D* is incorrect because indulgent parenting is essentially another example of permissive parenting. Choice *E* is incorrect because helicopter parenting refers to those parents who pay too much attention to their children's experiences and problems, particularly as they relate to that child's academic success.

39. D: Choice *D* correctly lists the order of the four processing stages of memory: encoding, consolidation, storage, and retrieval. Encoding consists of breaking information down and converting it into a construct that is stored in the brain. Consolidation involves stabilizing or solidifying information that has already been encoded. Storage is placing new information into memory for later retrieval. And retrieval refers to retrieving information from storage. Choice *A* is incorrect because consolidation occurs before the processing of storing information. Choice *B* is incorrect because the process of encoding precedes the consolidation stage. Choice *C* is incorrect because the brain cannot store information that hasn't been encoded and information needs to be consolidated and stored in the brain in order for a memory to be retrieved. Choice *E* is incorrect because information first needs to be stored in the brain before a memory can be later retrieved.

40. B: Choice *B* is procedural memory, also called implicit memory, which involves retaining motor skills such as talking, walking, or playing an instrument. In the given example, Jennifer becomes a skilled piano player after years of practice and retaining several lessons, thus demonstrating a type of procedural memory. Choice *A* is incorrect because declarative memory, also called explicit memory, describes the conscious and intentional recollection of certain information, unlike procedural memory, which is more unconscious. Choice *C* is incorrect because sensory memory refers to the short-term retention of sensory information even after the original stimulus has passed. Choice *D* is incorrect because episodic memory involves consciously recalling personal, autobiographical events that occurred at a certain point in time. Episodic memory is one example of an explicit memory. Choice *E* is incorrect because semantic memory involves consciously recalling factual information. Semantic memory is also another type of explicit memory.

41. E: Choice *E* is prospective memory, which is a type of memory where one recalls a planned intention or to perform a specific plan of action in the future. In the given example, Derek remembering to send a package after seeing a box describes a scenario that exemplifies prospective memory. Choice *A* is incorrect because haptic memory is actually a type of sensory memory that focuses specifically on touch stimuli. Choice *B* is incorrect because echoic memory is another type of sensory memory that focuses specifically on auditory stimuli. Choice *C* is incorrect because iconic memory is another type of sensory memory; it focuses specifically on visual stimuli. Choice *D* is incorrect because retrospective memory actually involves remembering something from the past.

42. D: Choice *D* is negative reinforcement, which involves removing something unpleasant as a means of reinforcing a desired behavior. In the given example, Eric cleans up a mess to avoid arguing with his roommate. Cleaning up the mess constitutes the behavior, whereas the avoidance of an argument serves as the removal of an unpleasant stimulus. Choice *A* is incorrect because positive punishment refers to introducing an unpleasant stimulus as a means of decreasing an unwanted behavior. The prime difference between reinforcement and punishment is that reinforcement aims to increase a desired behavior, whereas punishment is used to decrease an unwanted behavior. Choice *B* is incorrect because positive reinforcement describes how a pleasant stimulus is added in the form of a reward in order to increase a desired behavior. Choice *C* is incorrect because negative punishment focuses on removing an unpleasant stimulus as a means of decreasing an unwanted behavior. Choice *E* is incorrect because systematic desensitization actually describes exposing someone to anxiety-evoking stimuli in order to help them overcome a phobia. And then after this type of treatment has been successful, the person is taught relaxation methods.

43. A: Choice *A* is fear conditioning, which describes a kind of learning where aversive stimuli are gradually associated with an otherwise neutral stimulus in order to produce a fear response. In the given example, a research participant repeatedly experiences electric shocks while looking at pictures of landscapes, and as a result, begins to associate the shocks with the landscapes, which in turn causes the participant significant distress. Choice *B* is incorrect because reward training is a training technique used to reinforce a desired behavior via the introduction of a reward. Choice *C* is incorrect because autoshaping involves changing an existing response into a more desired behavior via successive trials and reinforcement of precise behavioral segments. Choice *D* is incorrect because flooding is a therapeutic method that involves putting someone in a situation where they would face a phobia at its worst as a means of demonstrating the irrationality of their fear. Choice *E* is incorrect because exposure therapy is similar in purpose to the flooding technique.

44. D: Choice *D* involves having a rat press a lever by introducing a reward, which is more an example of operant conditioning as opposed to classical conditioning. This relates to the work of behaviorist B.F. Skinner, who demonstrated how positive reinforcement worked by placing a hungry rat in a box. Classical conditioning pertains to pairing two stimuli together in order to generate a new learned response, whereas operant conditioning utilizes reinforcement or punishment as a means of modifying behavior. The rat's reward is a type of reinforcer used to increase the likelihood of the rat repeating the desired behavior of pressing a lever. Choice *A* is incorrect because giving rats sweetened water with or without radiation in order to assess their response was actually a classical conditioning experiment conducted by John Garcia to test the phenomenon of taste aversion. Choice *B* is incorrect because training dogs to respond to a neutral stimulus when that neutral stimulus is paired with an unconditioned stimulus is an example of Ivan Pavlov's famous dog experiment, which serves as a well-known example of classical conditioning. Choice *C* is incorrect because shocking dogs to convince them they cannot escape a negative situation is actually an example of research conducted by Martin Seligman to investigate the phenomenon of learned helplessness. Choice *E* is incorrect because this response refers to the "Little Albert" classical conditioning experiment conducted by John B. Watson. In this study, Watson paired loud noises with a white rat until Little Albert eventually came to fear the rat.

45. A: Choice *A* states that contingency hasn't been shown to help people modify their behavior, which is inaccurate. In fact, contingency has helped pave the way for successful behavior modification in the subject of interest. Choice *B* is incorrect because it is true that behaviorists have found that an animal's biological constraints can impact their ability to learn. Choice *C* is incorrect because both the frontal lobe and hippocampus have each been shown to play important roles in short-term memory. Choice *D* is incorrect because correlation isn't synonymous with causation. Correlation simply describes a relationship between two or more variables, whereas causation refers to a cause-effect relationship between variables; thus, correlation does not imply causation. Choice *E* is incorrect because intelligence is indeed defined and viewed differently in various cultures.

46. B: Choice *B* describes a prime example of higher-order conditioning, wherein the sound of a bell being paired with light until an association is formed. Also referred to as second-order conditioning, higher-order conditioning involves a previously neutral stimulus being paired with an already conditioned stimulus to elicit the same conditioned response as the conditioned stimulus. In this example, the bell would serve as the already conditioned stimulus, whereas the light would serve as another previously neutral stimulus, and when paired together, the subject would eventually form an association between them and produce a response. Choice *A* is incorrect because pairing the sound of a bell (conditioned stimulus) with food (unconditioned stimulus) is a prime example of first-order conditioning, which involves pairing a conditioned stimulus and an unconditioned stimulus. Choice *C* is incorrect because a child doing poorly on exams and subsequently feeling unable to ever change that outcome is a prime example of learned helplessness, which happens when someone feels powerless after experiencing a particularly negative and traumatic event. Choice *D* is incorrect because a child imitating the aggressive actions of adults against a blow-up doll actually relates to an experiment

conducted by Albert Bandura to demonstrate social learning. Choice *E* is incorrect because a child not engaging in a bad behavior after seeing someone else scolded for it is an example of observational learning.

47. D: An unconditioned response, Choice *D*, is any reaction that is elicited naturally and automatically from an unconditioned stimulus without any prior learning. In the given example, Harold jumping at the sound of a loud noise would be considered a natural response to such an unconditioned stimulus, hence making it an unconditioned response. Choice *A* is incorrect because it is actually the loud noise that would be considered the unconditioned stimulus, whereas Harold's jumping would serve as the unconditioned response. Choice *B* is incorrect because a neutral stimulus is a stimulus that initially generates no specific response. Plus, in this instance, Harold's jumping would serve as a response, not a stimulus. Choice *C* is incorrect because a conditioned response describes a previously learned response, which is one of the ways it is differentiated from an unconditioned response. Harold's jumping in response to the loud noise was generated naturally and automatically and without any prior learning. Choice *E* is incorrect because behavior modification can involve using positive reinforcement, negative reinforcement, positive punishment, or negative punishment to modify some behavior in human or nonhuman subjects. In the case of Harold, no form of behavior modification is occurring.

48. E: Choice *E* is spontaneous recovery, which describes a conditioned response that can potentially reemerge after a rest period, or a reduced response. In the given example, the dog suddenly rolling over to the "roll over" command after stopping for a brief time is a prime example of spontaneous recovery. Choice *A* is incorrect because extinction involves an unconditioned stimulus and a conditioned stimulus no longer being paired together, which results in a decrease or extinction of a conditioned response. Choice *B* is incorrect because acquisition describes the initial learning phase after a response was already established and gradually strengthened. Choice *C* is incorrect because stimulus discrimination relates to the ability to differentiate between a conditioned stimulus and other stimuli not previously paired with an unconditioned stimulus. Choice *D* is incorrect because stimulus generalization involves a conditioned stimulus generating similar responses once another response was previously conditioned.

49. C: Robert Sternberg, a psychologist and psychometrician, is known for his various contributions to the field of psychology, one of which includes his triangular theory of love. Therefore, Choice *C* is correct. Choice *A* is incorrect because Howard Gardner is an intelligence theorist best known for his theory of multiple intelligences. Choice *B* is incorrect because psychologist and educator Arnold Gesell is most known for his maturational theory of child development. Choice *D* is incorrect because Ivan Pavlov was a physician who is most known for his classical conditioning experiment that involved training dogs by pairing the sound of a bell (conditioned stimulus) with the presence of food (unconditioned stimulus) in order to generate a response from them in the form of salivation. Choice *E* is incorrect because Diana Baumrind is a developmental psychologist who is most known for her research into different parenting styles.

50. D: Psychologist Charles Spearman is known for his numerous contributions to the field of psychology, one of which has involved pioneering factor analysis. Therefore, Choice *D* is correct. Choice *A* is incorrect because psychologist Raymond Cattell is most known for coining the terms fluid intelligence and crystallized intelligence. Choice *B* is incorrect because psychologist Martin Seligman is most known for his research into learned helplessness. Choice *C* is incorrect because psychologist John Bowlby is best known for his attachment theory of development. Choice *E* is incorrect because psychoanalyst Sabina Spielrein is best known as being the first to propose a thesis about instinctual life, based on the life instinct and death instinct, which Sigmund Freud later adapted.

51. A: Psychologist John Garcia is known for his research into conditioned taste aversion; therefore, Choice *A* is correct. Choice *B* is incorrect because psychologist Carl Jung is best known as the founder of analytical psychology and devising his theories on the collective unconscious. He also collaborated with Sigmund Freud and Sabina Spielrein. Choice *C* is incorrect because psychologist Lewis Terman is most known for his revisions to the Stanford-Binet intelligence test and his longitudinal study of gifted children, which led to his psychology of talent. Choice *D* is incorrect because developmental psychologist Lev Vygotsky is most known for developing the sociocultural theory of development. Choice *E* is incorrect because psychologist Aaron Beck is most known for developing cognitive-behavioral therapy.

52. C: Choice *C* outlines how purely observable data should serve as the basis of all theoretical assumptions and experimental findings, which is indeed a view behaviorist John B. Watson held. Choice *A* is incorrect because Watson actually didn't place much of an emphasis on how any type of internal consciousness, including introspection, might impact behavior. He believed it was conditioning that best explained behavior. Choice *B* is incorrect because Watson believed it foolish to interpret the mind's inner workings and believed a psychologist should only concern themselves with observable behaviors. Choice *D* is incorrect because Watson did believe that language was conditioned via imitation and learned by manipulating sounds made with the larynx. Choice *E* is incorrect because Watson actually believed that conditioning explained behavior in both human and nonhuman subjects.

53. B: Prenatal development occurs in three stages in order: germinal stage, embryonic stage, and the fetal stage. Therefore, Choice *B* is correct. Choice *A* is incorrect because it's the germinal stage that precedes the embryonic stage. Choice *C* is incorrect because it's the embryonic stage that precedes the fetal stage of development. Choice *D* is incorrect because the fetal stage doesn't precede the germinal stage and the embryonic stage precedes the fetal stage. Choice *E* is incorrect because the germinal stage precedes both the embryonic and fetal stages.

54. D: Organogenesis is the initial formation of organs during the embryonic stage of development. It typically between the second and eighth week of pregnancy. Thus, Choice *D* is correct. Choice A is incorrect because epigenetics describes how environmental factors impact genetic expression. Choice *B* is incorrect because maturation refers to a hardwired approach to growth and development pertaining to the milestones of motor skills in an infant. Choice *C* is incorrect because gestation is the term of carrying an embryo in the womb after conception and before birth. Choice *E* is incorrect because conception describes the process of sperm from a fertile man traveling to a woman's uterus and merging with her egg as it moves down a fallopian tube from the ovary to the uterus.

55. C: Research conducted over several years has found no evidence of any harmful effects occurring in a fetus as a result of being around computers during pregnancy, thus computers aren't considered a teratogenic agent. Therefore, Choice *C* is correct. Choice A is incorrect because prescriptions drugs are indeed a well-known teratogenic agent. In fact, certain prescription drugs, such as opioids, taken during pregnancy can potentially result in birth defects, withdrawal symptoms, underweight babies, or even the loss of the baby. Choice *B* is incorrect because saunas are another well-known teratogenic agent. Babies are unable to regulate their body temperature while in utero, which means they can't tolerate the severe heat of a sauna. Choice *D* is incorrect because potassium iodide readily crosses the placenta and can result in hypothyroidism if it enters a mother's system during pregnancy. Choice *E* is incorrect because maternal stress is actually another type of teratogenic agent. Maternal stress during pregnancy has been known to cause poor outcomes such as low birthweight, preterm births, and even infant mortality.

56. E: Choice *E* is the latency stage, which begins at age five and continues until puberty, and consists of a child repressing their sexual urges and channeling those unacceptable impulses into constructive outlets. This is considered the fourth stage of psychosexual development. Choice *A* is incorrect because the oral stage starts at eighteen months of age, has the mouth serving as the infant's primary erogenous zone, and is considered the first stage of psychosexual development. Choice *B* is incorrect because the genital stage is the fifth and final stage of psychosexual development. It occurs after puberty and involves the development of strong sexual interests. Choice *C* is incorrect because the anal stage happens between eighteen months to three years of age, with the anus serving as the infant's primary erogenous zone and is considered the second stage. Choice *D* is incorrect because the phallic stage takes place between ages three to six, has the genitals serving as the infant's primary erogenous zone, and is considered the third stage.

57. D: The zone of proximal development (ZPD), Choice *D*, refers to the difference between what a learner is able to do without any help and what they cannot do alone but become capable of doing with some guidance. This was part of Lev Vygotsky's sociocultural theory of development. In the given example, the student being unable to perform math problems on their own, but then flourishing upon receiving help from a teacher, is a prime example of ZPD. Choice *A* is incorrect because social development involves how people develop necessary social and emotional skills during the course of their lives. Choice *B* is incorrect because physical development refers to a process that focuses on the development of gross and fine motor skills, as well as puberty. Choice *C* is incorrect because free association describes a psychoanalytic technique developed by Sigmund Freud that involves uncovering the uncensored expressions of one's inner consciousness. Choice *E* is incorrect because biofeedback describes a technique using audiovisual feedback to help address behavioral responses to stress and increase one's performance and general wellbeing. It can often be used in conjunction with psychotherapy.

58. A: Choice *A* is fluid intelligence, which describes one's ability to use abstract thinking, logic, reasoning, and pattern recognition skills when faced with novel challenges. In the given example, this person would be making use of fluid intelligence in order to devise creative solutions aimed at completing the puzzle in a reasonable timeframe. Choice *B* is incorrect because crystallized intelligence relies more on one's pre-existing knowledge of facts and skills in a certain domain, thus consisting of acquired knowledge gained from previous learning and experience. Reading comprehension serves as one example of this type of intelligence. Choice *C* is incorrect because processing speed describes the length of time it takes for someone to finish a mental task, and while processing speed can help make intelligence operate effectively, intelligence and processing speed are actually mutually exclusive. In other words, one doesn't necessarily predict the other. Choice *D* is incorrect because successful intelligence refers to one's ability to adjust and make alterations to their environment in a manner that best suits their specific needs. Choice *E* is incorrect because factor analysis describes a technique used to discern any variability among observable and correlated data and decrease numerous variables into a lesser number of factors.

59. D: Bodily-kinesthetic intelligence, Choice *D,* refers to one's ability to control the movements of their body and their expert handling of objects. According to the theory of multiple intelligences, people like dancers, soldiers, athletes, and actors tend to have a high degree of this type of intelligence. Choice *A* is incorrect because naturalistic intelligence describes how one cultivates and expresses details about their natural environment and would be more likely to include hunters, gatherers, farmers, and scientists. Choice *B* is incorrect because intrapersonal intelligence refers to one's ability to engage in introspection and self-reflection and would be more likely to be seen as a forte in theologians, entrepreneurs, or counselors. Choice *C* is incorrect because interpersonal intelligence refers to the ability to cooperate and be sensitive to how other people think and would be more likely to include managers, teachers, administrators, and social workers. Choice *E* is incorrect because visual-spatial intelligence consists of such traits as spatial navigation skills, facial and scene recognition, and observation of fine details. Some examples of those likely to fall under this category would include architects, photographers, and physicists.

60. B: The Flynn effect refers to a population's general IQ scores change over time. Choice *B* is correct because researchers are finding more of an increase in abstract problem skills than they originally expected. Most experts have assumed that test scores in specific domains of knowledge (crystallized intelligence) would be increasing, but researchers are discovering that scores related to abstract problem solving (fluid intelligence) are the ones rising. This serves as an example of one of the more surprising elements of the Flynn effect. Choice *A* is incorrect because research has found a decline in IQ scores in countries such as Australia, Britain, Denmark, Finland, France, Norway, Sweden, the Netherlands, and some German-speaking countries. Choice *C* is incorrect because performances on the Raven's Progressive Matrices have demonstrated an increase over the past century. Choice *D* is incorrect because researchers have identified several factors—not just one—that contribute to this effect. These factors include stimulating environments, progresses in early education, an increase in test complexity, an improvement with regard to attitudes about test taking, sufficient nutrition, and new technology. Choice *E* is incorrect because intelligence researcher James Flynn has actually posited that this increase could denote an increase in abstract problem solving rather than intelligence itself.

61. D: Choice *D* is inaccurate and thus, the correct answer. It states that people with intellectual disabilities are not able to function on their own regardless of the level of severity, which is inaccurate. Their ability to function alone depends on the severity of their disability. The lower the IQ, the less likely they will function well alone, although there are no hard and fast rules on this. There are certainly exceptions in both directions. The other choices are true regarding intelligence, so they are incorrect. Choice *A* is incorrect because the *g* factor was devised by intelligence theorist Charles Spearman for the purposes of investigating cognitive abilities and human intelligence. Choice *B* is incorrect because there is indeed no exact definition of giftedness; however, most research does apply this term to those with an IQ in the top two percent of the population. Choice *C* is incorrect because savant syndrome describes a rare condition that some people are either born with or can develop as a result of an acquired brain injury. Choice *E* is incorrect because of the criticisms of intelligence tests is that they focus more on cognitive skills and not enough on the contributions of other noncognitive factors such as emotion, level of motivation, morality, and social skills.

62. E: Researchers Alexander Thomas and Stella Chess are known for identifying three temperaments found in children: easy, slow-to-warm-up, and difficult. Therefore, Choice *E* is correct. Choice *A* is incorrect because Sigmund Freud is known for devising a personality theory consisting of the id, ego, and superego, not Alexander Thomas and Stella Chess. Choice *B* is incorrect because Diana Baumrind is known for her research on authoritative, authoritarian, and permissive parenting styles. Choice *C* is incorrect because the founder of analytical psychology and creator of the notions of the anima (unconscious feminine component of man) and animus (unconscious masculine component of women) was Carl Jung. Robert Sternberg outlined selective-encoding, selective-comparison, and selective-combination in his three-process view of insights, so Choice *D* is incorrect.

63. C: Choice *C* is correct because it states that maintaining a healthy birth weight while carrying an embryo reduces the prospect of negative risks, which is accurate. This process of carrying an embryo is called gestation and sustaining a healthy birth weight during pregnancy can decrease the possibility of associated negative risks. Choice *A* is incorrect because research has shown that prenatal nutrition is

one of the most important factors in ensuring a fetus's well-being. Some examples of nutritious foods for infants during prenatal development consist of lean meats, fruits, low-fat dairy products, vegetables, and whole grains. Choice *B* is incorrect because taking necessary precautions can in fact help prevent the development of illnesses in infants. Receiving regular prenatal care from a healthcare provider can help in obtaining treatment as early as possible and also potentially prevent any health issues from occurring. Choice *D* is incorrect because research shows that abusing substances while pregnant can result in long-term problems for infants. A few examples of some of these problems include neonatal abstinence syndrome, fetal alcohol syndrome, and sudden infant death syndrome. Choice *E* is incorrect because the developmental stage of an infant can indeed affect their susceptibility to teratogens. For instance, an infant in their first trimester is most prone to damage from different teratogenic agents.

64. C: Sigmund Freud is known for identifying countertransference, which describes a therapist's emotional reaction to their client's contribution; therefore, Choice *C* is correct. Choice *A* is incorrect because sensorimotor development is the first of four stages in developmental psychologist Jean Piaget's cognitive theory of development. Choice *B* is incorrect because the concept of learned helplessness is attributed to Martin Seligman, who conducted research on the subject. Choice *D* is incorrect because the collective unconscious is attributed to the theories of Carl Jung, who actually collaborated with Freud. Choice *E* is incorrect because affective forecasting describes one's attempt to predict their emotional state about something in the future. Psychologist Daniel Kahneman and his team first researched this concept in the 1990s, but the term itself was later coined by researchers Daniel Gilbert and Timothy Wilson.

65. D: Lev Vygotsky's sociocultural theory of development, Choice *D,* is correct because it proposes that mental abilities are shaped by cultural settings and the ways in which people in a society interact with each other. Choice *A* is incorrect because psychologist Erik Erikson's psychosocial theory of development was devised to identify eight psychosocial stages that a healthy developing person should move through during their entire lifespan. Choice *B* is incorrect because psychologist Lawrence Kohlberg's moral theory of development, adapted from Jean Piaget, describes six stages of morality outlined within three different levels. He contended that moral development is a continuous process throughout the course of one's life. Choice *C* is incorrect because Jean Piaget's cognitive theory of development posits that children progress through four different stages of mental development. Choice *E* is incorrect because John Bowlby's attachment theory of development focuses on the notion that both a substantial physical and emotional attachment to at least one caregiver serves as a crucial element in one's personal development.

66. B: Sublimation is a defense mechanism that involves channeling negative and potentially destructive impulses into a positive and constructive behaviors or actions. Therefore, Choice *B* is correct. Choice *A* is incorrect because repression involves the unconscious exclusion of painful thoughts, feelings, or memories from one's conscious awareness. Choice *C* is incorrect because projection describes how a person projects undesirable feelings or traits about themselves onto others as a means of protecting their ego. Choice *D* is incorrect because reaction formation refers to how unacceptable feelings are surmounted by exaggerating the exact opposite tendency. For instance, instead of being hostile toward someone you dislike, you go out of your way to be kind to them. Choice *E* is incorrect because displacement involves transferring negative feelings from the original source of the emotion to a person or object perceived as being less threatening.

67. C: Choice *C,* the correlation coefficient, is used to assess the relationship or association between two variables for a given function. In the given example, a correlation coefficient would be used to assess the near perfection correlation between one's glove size and hand length. Choice *A* is incorrect because an abstract measure is actually a type of intelligence test used to test a person's aptitude for logical reasoning and nonverbal skills. Choices *B* and *D* are incorrect because chunking and rehearsal both describe a process one uses to increase their short-term memory capacity. Choice *E* is incorrect because lines of best fit, or trendlines, display the general directions in which points on a graph are localized.

68. E: Keeping a visual reminder of one's daily goals is a self-control method used in an effort to maintain motivation and fulfill personal goals. Therefore, Choice *E* is correct. Choices *A*, *B*, *C*, and *D*, which consist of deep breathing, journaling, meditating, and talking with others, are all examples of coping strategies used to help people adjust to any changes in their daily lives.

69. D: Males increase in lean muscle mass during puberty, compared to females who experience an increase in fat deposits and changes in their hip-to-waist ratio during puberty. Neither sex experiences an increase in hair follicles on the scalp, although they do experience a visible increase of body hair. Neither sex experiences changes to the feet in puberty.

70. C: Withdrawing from one's parents, preferring the company of peers, and experiencing menstruation (vaginal bleeding) are all a result of hormonal shifts that occur in females during puberty and the adolescent stage of the lifespan. These factors were mentioned in the description of Melissa. Therefore, Choice *C* is correct. Adam's apples appear in puberty for males, so Choice *A* is incorrect. Menopause refers to the end of menstruation in a female and typically occurs after child-bearing years; therefore, Choice *B* is incorrect. Choices *D* and *E* are incorrect because there are no concrete indicators that Melissa is depressed or has body image issues in the description.

71. B: People's attachment styles are largely shaped by the temperaments with which they are born and their relationships with their primary caregivers in early childhood. These two aspects deeply impact how people make close friendships, romantic partnerships, and companionate relationships throughout the rest of the lifespans. Thus, Choice *B* is incorrect. Choice *A* is incorrect because the rooting reflex is a physiological instinct in newborns that is related to feeding. Choices *C* and *D* are incorrect because an infant's birth experience and prenatal vitamin exposure do not correlate strongly with intimacy later in life. Imprinting is a concept generally used in the context of certain baby animals, such as ducklings, so Choice *E* is incorrect.

72. C: By the end of the second trimester of pregnancy, a fetus has over one hundred billion neurons. From then till death, neurons and neural pathways are typically pruned down in number based on whether they are being used or not.

73. E: Type 3 diabetes, Choice *E,* is a term used to describe metabolic issues that may contribute to the Alzheimer's disease, and is believed to be exacerbated by highly processed, high-fat, and high-sugar diets. Type 1 diabetes is believed to be largely autoimmune, while gestational diabetes is a temporary condition during pregnancy that likely results from hormonal changes; thus, Choices *A* and *D* are incorrect. Spina bifida and congenital adrenal hyperplasia are issues present at birth, so Choices *B* and *C* are incorrect.

74. D: Nav is engaging in activities that use his cognitive faculties in different ways, such as formally learning new subjects and casually engaging in puzzles. He also is engaging in a combination of gentle exercise and meditation, both known for strengthening cognitive functioning and neurotransmitter activity. Therefore, Choice *D* is correct. None of his lifestyle activities are protective against the other health conditions, although it is not guaranteed that he will experience these issues.

75. B: Gender socialization, Choice *B*, refers to deeply engrained social and cultural expectations that a society can place on each gender. This is often seen with toys, where boys and girls are given different types of toys or colors of toys based on their gender. Through gender socialization, people may grow up with subconscious beliefs about their gender roles (Choice *E*). Exchanging the crown and wand gift for the boy does not clearly appear to have homophobic or anti-feminist intentions; thus, Choices *A* and *D* are incorrect. Gender identity refers to the gender with which one self-identifies; therefore Choice *C* is wrong.

76. C: Societies that imply male and female are the two primary genders, through actions such as only listing those two options on legal paperwork, are known as gender binary societies. The other options are not common descriptors for societies. Some societies are nongender binary, meaning that they accept various gender identities beyond male and female. For example, some tribal communities in Mexico and Indonesia recognize between three to five genders. Some Eastern groups, such as in Thailand and India, recognize a third gender that encompasses both male and female aspects. However, these groups of people are also often ostracized.

77. A: Choice *A* is correct because it is largely accepted that all animals, with the exception of human beings, operate from the motivation for survival of the species (including their own survival and passing on their genetic material). Some psychologists theorize that humans, ultimately, are driven by a need to fulfill a higher purpose and achieve self-actualization.

78. C: The coo reflex is not a real reflex, so Choice *C* is correct. Newborns have a number of innate reflexes that support their ability to feed, attach to caregivers, and prepare for mobility in their early months. The root and suck reflexes (Choices *A* and *E*) encourage the baby to open their mouth and latch on to items that stroke near their cheek, which allows them to accept a breast or bottle for feeding. The grasp reflex (Choice *D*) is believed to encourage motor skills. The Moro reflex (Choice *B*) refers to the way a baby startles when an unexpected stimulus is present.

79. C: Almost all species show courting rituals that lead to finding a mate and reproduction. Therefore, Choice *C* is correct. Imprinting is not a courting ritual; rather, it is primarily seen in some bird species where the young latch on to the first entity they see. Thus, Choice *C* is incorrect. Attachment styles are mostly used to describe humans' relationship patterns, so Choice *B* is wrong. Almost no species select a single partner to mate with for life. Therefore, Choice *D* is incorrect. The latch reflex may sometimes be used to describe the sucking reflex, in which human infants instinctively suck to aid feeding. Because this isn't an instinctive behavior across all animal species, Choice *E* is incorrect.

80. A: The over-justification effect occurs when an initial, intrinsic motivation to perform a behavior diminishes after receiving an external award. In this case, the young boy was no longer motivated by the shiny stickers, even though he initially showed his own interest in using the toilet. The boy was not conditioned in any way to use or avoid the toilet; thus Choice *B* is incorrect. Choice *C* is incorrect because the boy does not appear to experience any cognitive dissonance, a context in which he would experience two thoughts that go against each other. Cognitive dissonance in this situation might look like the boy both wanting stickers but also wanting to continue to wear a diaper. The appraisal theory, in which someone views their environment and makes an emotional judgment, and the Moro reflex, a reflex seen in infants where they throw their arms overhead when startled, do not apply to this type of situation. The boy's environment is not impacting his motivation, nor is he an infant. Therefore, Choices *D* and *E* are incorrect.

81. C: Talli does not seem to believe she can do the task she wants to do, which shows a lack of self-efficacy. This also influences her choice to give up on the task of avoiding dessert on the first day of trying, as low self-efficacy often results in low self-motivation. The vignette and question do not indicate that Talli's circadian rhythm is abnormal, that she is lacking confirmation bias, that she needs different dishes, or that she requires medications. Regardless, there is not enough information to tell whether changes in these areas would have an impact on Talli's situation.

82. B: Cognitive dissonance refers to the discomfort that occurs when a person experiences competing thoughts in the same context. Talli knows she should reduce her sugar intake, but also knows she is not taking the actions to do so. To reduce the dissonance in this context, she tells herself her sugar indulgence is okay because she does not engage in other bad health habits. Choice *A* is incorrect because her self-talk is not motivating her to do anything differently. Choices *B* and *D* are incorrect because she is not minimizing her risk for diabetes through her other healthy habits, nor is she increasing her self-efficacy. Confirmation bias, where Talli would have tried to find evidence for a belief she holds while ignoring contrary evidence, does not apply to this story. Therefore, Choice *E* is incorrect.

83. D: Ghrelin is responsible for stimulating appetite, while leptin is responsible for creating feelings of satiety. Often, people with eating disorders have hormonal issues relating to these two hormones. The other hormones listed apply to reproductive processes, stress response, and metabolism.

84. B: Depressed and chronically sleep-deprived people tend to crave refined carbohydrates and sugar, most likely to activate the reward centers of their brain or to get a quick fix of glucose, which provides energy to the body.

85. D: Paul has learned to associate a neutral stimulus (his car) with a conditioned response (the cappuccino). He is craving the specific cappuccino that he has every morning when he drives to work. This is an example of classical conditioning, so Choice *D* is correct. Paul is not necessarily trying to reward himself or reinforce the behavior of driving, since he no longer has a long commute to deal with. He also is not likely fighting an addictive craving, as he already had coffee shortly before getting into the car. He is also isn't around other people whose behavior he could be modeling.

86. E: Preliminary research strongly indicates that autism spectrum disorders may not be due to cognitive disorders; they may result from differences in social motivation. While neurotypical individuals may be motivated to seek social interaction for a variety of reasons, people with autism spectrum disorders may be lacking biological and environmental mechanisms that motivate them to interact in typical, social ways with others.

87. A: In general, people who have gone through traumatic events such as war or assault, have altered and dysfunctional states of primary emotion response. They may perceive threats that are not truly there, or they might seek out situations that provide a heightened emotional response. While the other groups listed may vary in the ways they show emotions, this is likely due to the stage of development and influence of hormones, which are all normal and natural factors.

88. D: The limbic system, Choice *D*, is believed to be the oldest structure of the brain, and is composed of the thalamus, hypothalamus, amygdala, and other areas that aid in survival and reproductive responses. From an evolutionary standpoint, this allowed the human species to avoid fatal threats, remain alive, and continue reproducing. The other structures are relatively newer components that allowed humans to have more complex cognitive functions, increase information processing, and walk upright.

89. D: The appraisal theory states that people take in a situation and environment, and then have emotions as a result. In this situation, Kaya, a mother, and Amie, who is child-free, have fairly different appraisals of the same environment. Kaya sees the dangers to her child, while Amie sees what might be nice to have on a vacation. Choice *A* is incorrect because while a conflict may arise from this situation, there is no information that indicates conflict resolution will occur. This situation does not describe imprinting, which is a response that different baby bird species have to specific maternal figures. Therefore, Choice *B* is incorrect. Choice *C* is incorrect because this situation is not discussing Piaget's stages of development, which show how people develop over the lifespan. Because Kaya and Amie are best friends, they are unlikely to experience cross-cultural conflict, which normally occurs when two people from different backgrounds do not yet understand one another well. Therefore, Choice *E* is incorrect.

90. E: Love is not one of the universal six emotions as stated by renowned emotion researcher Paul Ekman. The six universal emotions are fear, anger, disgust, joy, loneliness, and surprise.

91. A: Dementia and related diseases, such as Alzheimer's, have been linked to chronic stress. The other diseases listed are actually not true cognitive disorders; they are autoimmune disorders or genetic disorders.

92. D: Case studies are commonly used to observe influences from particular environments and variables, which Ophelia considered as she studied children with their parents and then in a daycare environment. Ophelia hand-selected volunteer parents and children to observe, in depth, in different environments; therefore, she conducted a case study. All data collected are somewhat subjective from Ophelia's observation only; she did not take any anecdotal information from the parents or teachers. Thus, Choice *B* is incorrect. This was certainly not a randomized experiment in which testing took place, nor did Ophelia administer a survey or personality assessment to any of the children. Therefore, Choices *A, C,* and *E* are incorrect.

93. A: The Myers-Brigg Personality Indicator, Choice *A,* is commonly used in workplace settings to see how employees align with job roles. It indicates the environments and personal interaction that people prefer, as well as how they like to operate. While people can indicate certain preferences during an interview, the Myers-Brigg can show how they might operate in the long term. The Beck Depression Inventory (Choice *B*) measures symptoms of depression. The Minnesota Multiphasic Personality Inventory (Choice *C*) is really only used in clinical settings; it is typically too complex for nonclinical personnel to utilize effectively. The Thematic Apperception and Rorschach tests (Choices *D* and *E*) provide insight into someone's social beliefs, and do not necessarily explain working style and preferences.

94. B: Humanistic psychologists, Choice *B,* believe all people are working toward developing their potential and unlocking their purpose in life. With the right tools, this can be achieved. From this approach, almost any person can benefit from receiving psychological therapy. The other fields listed all try to address pathologies or dysfunction through their methods so that the client experiences improved outcomes. The psychoanalytic field (Choice *A*) tries to address pathologies as they might stem from unconscious and subconscious beliefs. The behavioral field (Choice *C*) tries to address pathologies as they manifest into behaviors. The cognitive field (Choice *D*) tries to address pathologies that impact cognitive or neurological functioning. The forensic psychology field (Choice *E*) tries to better understand pathologies that drive criminal intentions and behavior.

95. D: Frank has secured the first two stages of Maslow's Hierarchy of Needs: basic needs, including food and shelter, safety and security, and steady employment. The next stage includes love and belonging needs, such as belonging to a community and pursuing romantic love. Therefore, Choice *D* is correct. Additional schooling and a peaceful acceptance of eventual death fall higher on the pyramid, under self-esteem and self-actualization. Therefore, Choices *C* and *E* are incorrect. Material goods, such as new cars, are not necessarily requirements of moving through the hierarchy. Therefore, Choices *A* and *B* are incorrect.

96. E: Freud comes from a psychoanalytic background, in which childhood memory and dream state analyses are a key part of the therapeutic intervention. The other figures listed are behaviorists, who did not focus on the role of consciousness. Rather, they focused on outward, visible behavior and the physical environment.

97. A: Collectivist cultures value the goals of a group and living with extended family is a common practice. In this dynamic, all members can work together to support each other with physical help and with pooling resources. This is commonly seen in Eastern societies. The other options listed include competitive endeavors and solo achievements, which are commonly seen in individualistic (typically Western) societies.

98. C: Until the 1980s, homosexuality was classified as a psychological disorder in the DSM. Autism spectrum disorder is listed in the DSM-5, as is seasonal affective disorder (although listed as a subset of depression). Thus, Choices *A* and *E* are incorrect. Choices *B* and *D* are incorrect because HIV and occupational burnout have never been listened as discrete diagnoses in any edition of the DSM.

99. B: The insanity defense, in which a defendant claims their mental health was compromised at the time of the crime, is rarely used in court due to the extensive psychiatric rehabilitation that is then legally required. Often, these legal rehabilitations last longer than a prison sentence would. The other options listed are commonly used legal defenses.

100. C: Since receiving a diagnosis, Bonnie uses the diagnosis to avoid events that were often hard for her to undertake but made her feel better afterward. Now, she is actively avoiding things that would likely help her condition and well-being, such as spending time with people who care about her or exercising. Therefore, Bonnie is experiencing a negative consequence of a diagnostic label. Choices *A* and *B* are incorrect because there is no evidence of Bonnie using medications right now or that she is receiving inadequate health care. There is no Rosenhan effect, although Rosenhan is known for bringing light to the negative side of diagnostics; thus, Choice *D* is incorrect. Compliance is not relevant in this context, so Choice *E* is incorrect.

101. B: During the desensitization process, a therapist gradually introduces a stimulus that normally causes fear in a client alongside a stimulus that normally causes joy. It is considered to be a gentle technique for helping people face their fears with the support of items that normally cause relaxation or happiness. Eventually, it allows the client to become less sensitive to the stimulus that once caused fear.

102. D: Receiving a paycheck every two weeks is a fixed reward at the same interval. Receiving pay immediately while working would be a continuous reinforcement, so Choice *A* doesn't apply here. Receiving pay based only on number of completed commission sales would be a fixed-ratio reinforcement; thus, Choice *B* does not apply. Choice *C* is also incorrect because receiving pay unpredictably for random sales would be a variable-ratio reinforcement. Receiving a random amount of pay at unpredictable times throughout the work month would be a variable-interval reinforcement. Thus, Choice *E* is incorrect.

103. B: The cognitive approach works best in clients who are trying to recover from a brain injury or other context in which a structure of the brain has become compromised (e.g., such as a stroke victim). Therefore, the man described in Choice *B* would be a good candidate for this approach. Treating grief and trying to quit smoking likely will need a psychodynamic and/or social support component; therefore, Choices *A* and *E* are incorrect. The child who will not make eye contact (Choice *C*) may need social support, while the boy with nightmares (Choice *D*) may benefit from a psychoanalytic approach.

104. A: In cognitive-behavioral therapy, the client often examines their personal beliefs and narrative and is then given a behavior to implement. Often, this comes in the form of "homework" between sessions. The therapist did not give Eoin any medication, nor did she tell him to try acting or art as a healing modality. Therefore, Choices *B*, *C*, and *D* are incorrect. For a true psychoanalytic approach, she may have asked him about his childhood experiences, which she did not. Thus, Choice *E* is incorrect.

105. C: Priya was raised in a home where she was primarily taught to take care of her family and nurture children, and this is further encouraged by her husband and in-laws. This is the social and cultural context in which she has lived her whole life, which is why pursuing something different seems like it will only remain a dream to her. Choices *A* and *B* are incorrect because she does not appear to be held captive by her family, nor does she seem to have low self-esteem, as she knows she is good at her current role. Choices *D* and *E* are incorrect because there are no clear indicators of work-life imbalances in her home, and there are no indicators that she lives in a Communist society. Rather, she simply seems to live in an older, traditional type of family in which she is unsure of how to pursue something different.

106. B: Lev Vygotsky pioneered the sociocultural approach, which emphasized the important of teachers in a young child's life. Unlike most other developmental psychologists at the time, he believed the learning environment set the foundation for cognitive abilities. Therefore, a good teacher and supportive learning environment was critical for a young child. His theories were likely influenced by the Communist society in which he lived. Mary Cover Jones, Choice *A*, was a behaviorist who primarily worked with the process of counter-conditioning, and in longitudinal studies that focused on the behavior of adolescents. Sigmund Freud, Choice *C*, was a psychoanalyst who tried to analyze the human psyche through the client's subconscious and unconscious thoughts, dreams, and early childhood experiences. Abraham Maslow, Choice *D*, worked in the field of humanistic psychology and focused on ways that people could and would want to pursue self-actualization. Aaron Beck, Choice *E*, was worked in the cognitive field and extensively focusing on depression and negative thoughts.

107. A: Out of all the options listed, only clients who voluntarily seek out therapeutic services are positively correlated with effective treatment services. Clients who seek out services are often goal-oriented with a specific issue they want to address, and so have a more intrinsic desire to improve their situation. Thus, Choice *A* is the best answer. Choices *B* and *E* are incorrect because clients who have been ordered into therapy, such as from legal problems, are not likely to maintain changed behaviors in the long run. Clients with psychotic disorders more likely than not remain unable to resolve their diagnosis. Therefore, Choice *C* is incorrect. Practitioners who utilize peer-reviewed, evidence-based methods are more likely to have effective treatments than those who go off anecdotes, so Choice *E* is incorrect.

108. C: Miranda's advocacy for mental health insurance coverage does not necessarily come from her cultural background; it could be derived from a host of other social, political, health, or economic concerns. The other options are documented beliefs from various cultures that highlight their attitudes and values toward mental health practices, stigmas, and seeking care.

109. B: By noticing her limiting self-beliefs and negative narratives, and by trying an activity in which she might fail, Emmie is building herself up to be more resilient. If she is able to fail at rock-climbing without belittling her self-worth or worrying if people will think less of her, she is one step closer to resilience. Choices A and C are incorrect because Emmie might build competency and lean muscle mass through this type of physical activity, but that is not her primary driver for trying. The question does not state that Emmie is trying this for new friends, and it does not provide enough clues to indicate where Emmie might fall on the hierarchy of needs. Thus, Choices D and E are incorrect.

110. A: Risperidone and clozapine are commonly used to manage hallucinations and delusions that are symptoms of schizophrenia. In patients with moderate to severe symptoms of schizophrenia, this is often the only intervention that can effectively manage symptoms, as most symptoms of schizophrenia cannot be alleviated through nonpharmaceutical therapies.

111. E: Therapists who solely practice the rational-emotive method are quick and direct to point out negative and irrational beliefs held by the client. Whereas group therapy often inherently comes with a built-in support system, client-centered approaches are more collaborative, and cognitive approaches encourage the client to introspect, the rational-emotive method can seem authoritative and brusque in comparison. For survivors of trauma, this approach can minimize their emotional wounds and prevent them from truly processing and releasing painful events. While the rational-emotive method can be a type of individual therapy, the majority of individual therapies are collaborative and tailored to the needs of the client.

112. D: The cognitive approach came to mainstream culture in direct parallel with the advent of computers and personal computing. Similar to how computers require inputs to produce outputs, psychological researchers believed that many behaviors resulted from the perception of specific stimuli. Choice A is incorrect because the psychoanalytic approach focused more internally, without looking so much at the link between sensory inputs and behavioral outputs. Choice C is incorrect because behaviorists primarily studied only the behavior outputs. Choices B and E are incorrect because machine learning is a subset of artificial intelligence, and it is a part of software engineering. These are not terms used in psychology.

113. B: Louie is primarily crediting himself and his GPA for getting the job (ignoring his uncle's powerful reference), and he is blaming his team for the failed product rather than acknowledging any personal control in the matter. This is an example of a self-serving bias, which is Choice B. He is not displaying a confirmation bias, in which a person confirms something they wanted to be true. Therefore, Choice A is incorrect. Choice C is incorrect because this situation also does not contribute to a just-world effect, as there is no indication that anyone feels the event is fair or unfair. This doesn't appear to have anything to do with Louie's self-esteem, and he is not exhibiting traits of narcissism. Therefore, Choices D and E are incorrect.

114. B: This situation is a good example of the halo effect. Recall that the halo effect is a form of bias in which a person takes an initial positive impression of another person and extrapolates that into assuming other positive qualities about that person's character. The new intern is assuming a positive quality (good management) from unrelated traits of Louie's (polished appearance, poise, supervisory role, and time spent on the computer). This is even when evidence to the contrary exists, including opinions from those that have worked with him and a documented failed project. Choice A is incorrect because confirmation bias would occur if the intern had an established belief about Louie that she sought to prove. The bystander effect refers to a lack of personal responsibility or desire to help when others are present, which is not applicable in this question, so Choice C is incorrect. The new intern was

not hazed in any way, so Choice *D* is incorrect. The false consensus effect would have occurred if she assumed everyone held her beliefs about Louie, but there is no indication of this assumption. Therefore, Choice *E* is incorrect.

115. A: This team member is aiming to rationalize an event as fair, even though there is very minimal evidence, at this point, that Louie deserved to be fired based on merit. Yet, this team member is nitpicking at Louie's one failure and the connections of his uncle to justify why Louie was let go. This could be to cover up his own personal fear of losing his job for no understandable reason. Therefore, this scenario exemplifies the just-world hypothesis, which occurs when people judge those who are in unfortunate situations and believe they somehow deserve or caused the situation to occur. Choice *B* is incorrect because the team member is not assuming a false consensus, as he is actually voicing against the majority of the team. He is not extrapolating any positive qualities of Louie's to create a halo effect; instead, he's completely undermining them. Thus, Choice *C* is incorrect. There are no indications of social loafing or deindividuation in the question, so Choices *D* and *E* are incorrect.

116. D: Deindividuation is most commonly seen in groups where uniformity is valued. In the military, servicemembers and officials often have to dress similarly, have similar haircuts and other cosmetic requirements, and work as seamless units in order to function effectively. Therefore, Choice *D* is correct. Green card holders applying for U.S. citizenship are likely to have diverse backgrounds; thus, Choice *A* is incorrect. Choice *B* is incorrect because high school students are at a developmental age where they are experimenting with a variety of behaviors, dressing differently, and finding their personal voice. Choice *C* is incorrect because preschoolers are often not concerned with what their peers think, and they are likely to act uniquely. Homeless mothers are also not likely to conform with one another and are often homeless due to varying, unique circumstances, so Choice *E* is incorrect.

117. E: The reciprocity norm is a concept that is commonly utilized in marketing. From a psychological perspective, people are more likely to feel obligated to respond in kind when someone gives something to them. In this case, the office manager is likely to respond positively to the holiday gift.

118. A: This scenario is an example of the mere-exposure effect, which states that people are more likely to prefer things that are familiar. Ken clearly prefers the store that he is familiar with and has been exposed to longer, even though the new store seems to come with a host of other perks. Ken isn't necessarily buying anything from the store and his runs seem to primarily be for his own benefit, so his actions are not a good example of altruism. Ken enjoys the social experience of running, so he is not showing social inhibition. There is no scapegoat in this story. The prisoner's dilemma does not apply to this situation, as this term focuses on situations where people choose to not cooperate on a task even if it could provide a better outcome for both parties in the end.

119. B: Social facilitation refers to someone's ability to perform tasks they are familiar with better when an audience is present. In Samantha's case, she does better work when she is presenting to someone than when she is trying to practice alone at home. This likely would not be the case if she was new to the material, but as she is familiar with the material, she becomes energized by the audience. Choice *B* doesn't apply because Samantha does not appear think she is not competent at her job, so she is likely not suffering from imposter syndrome. She does not appear to be underperforming, and she is not working as part of a group, which eliminates social loafing (Choice *C*) as the answer. Samantha is also not conforming and there is no evidence to support that she is experiencing chronic brain fog, which would result in prolonged underperformance and cognitive issues. Therefore, Choices *D* and *E* are not correct.

Free-Response Sample Answer

Trust versus Mistrust

"I was adopted when I was fifteen months old. My adoptive parents told me that I lived with a foster family from birth until that time, but that they had three biological children and one other foster child at the time. From my understanding, the foster family provided me with basic needs, like a home, formula, and food, but they told my adoptive parents that they felt they could not provide me with the love and affection they wanted to. Sometimes, I was left to cry because they were just stretched so thin. My adoptive mom told me it took almost a year before I snuggled her back when she tried to hug or console me when I was crying. It would take a long time for me to settle down when crying. I still feel uncomfortable with my own emotions, or even asking for help, at times."

Autonomy versus Shame and Doubt

"As I entered toddlerhood, my adoptive parents tried hard to let me know that I was secure in my home and that they would be there for me. I actually vividly remember starting a preschool program where I cried upon arriving. I just did not want to be away from them, or to be with strangers. My adoptive mom told me once that when I found out I was going to be starting preschool, I asked if I would ever see them again. I remember a few days when both of my adoptive parents came and sat in the room with me as I went about my day. They would begin leaving for short periods of time, and slowly started increasing the length of time. My adoptive mom kept a baby book where she detailed my first month of preschool, and by the third day, I was exploring on my own and happily waving bye to them and going to select a toy to play with by myself. In the baby book, my adoptive mom wrote about how she cried tears of joy in knowing that I was comfortable enough to be independent after all the fears I had initially shown."

Initiative versus Guilt

"This preschool that I went to seemed great, from what I understand. It really helped me overcome some of the obstacles I faced from my foster and adoption situation. My adoptive parents didn't end up having or adopting any other kids, so I learned how to play well with others in this setting. While I used to be shy and skittish when I started at the school, my adoptive dad says that as I got ready for kindergarten, I was one of the most social kids in the class. I would always go up to random kids on the playground and ask if they wanted to play, and then even invite them to my house! My adoptive parents said they had a hard time trying to keep up with my little social life!"

Industry versus Inferiority

"I remember really enjoying school. I loved learning new things, and I think that's how I ultimately became a scientist. As a scientist, I always got to learn something new. But there was one year in elementary school where I almost gave up on science entirely. I think it was third grade. I always had so many questions, and one time, my teacher got so angry because I kept interrupting and asking questions about the lesson. She told me nobody else could learn because of me, and all the other kids stared at me. Now, in hindsight, I can see she was probably just trying to get through the class. But as a young child, I felt so embarrassed. I thought I was annoying, or maybe even dumb if I had so many questions that none of the other kids had. Did they already know the answers? So, for the rest of the year, I didn't really participate or do well in the class. But later on, I had a few amazing teachers who enjoyed my questions and even spent time with me after school helping me work on personal science projects. Now I know there is no such thing as a dumb question, but not everyone will want to help you with the answers."

Identity versus Confusion

"I mentioned that I loved my career as a scientist, but as I started testing during school, taking pre-college courses, and deciding what to major in, I remember having a period of just feeling so lost. Now, I know this probably sounds like a cliché adolescent experience. It felt weird to think I had to commit to a major in college so early on, when there are so many neat things to explore in this lifetime. Every time I took an elective, that topic became my flavor of the month. I learned everything I could about it and wondered if I could have a career in it. Plus, I started becoming interested in boys, and not all of them seemed to want to date a girl who had all these other things going on. It was a hard struggle to know when to pursue the things I was interested in while also wanting attention from my crushes! I remember just not wanting my parents' advice at all, and just wanting to fit in and have a big group of friends that I belonged to. There was also a brief period where I really wanted to know more about my biological parents, but it was a closed adoption, so I never found out much. My adoptive parents helped me find a therapist to talk to about this, and inadvertently I talked to him about all of the other stuff I was dealing with too. It was a blessing in disguise, as I really felt like I got to know myself better by the end."

Intimacy versus Isolation

"Luckily, I realized all those boys and friends I wanted attention from probably wouldn't be around for the long run, but my interests, ideas, and curiosity would be. By the time I started college, I had so many AP credits that I had the opportunity to take three semesters-worth of elective topics that simply just interested me. And wouldn't you know it, in one of those random classes, I met my husband! It was an African drumming class, and he was also taking the class just out of curiosity. I think we both loved each other's curious nature, and until he died a few years ago, we would always try to find new things to do together. We learned that novelty creates intimacy."

Generativity versus Stagnation

"But even during our happy marriage, we had one big mid-life struggle. I was a successful scientist and I also had two beautiful children of my own. It was hard to balance sometimes, but I really felt like I was leaving my mark in the world. I was contributing new knowledge regularly to the public, and I just loved being a mother and teaching all of this new stuff to my kids, too. To see them go pursue their own interests and be successful, happy human beings just brought me such joy. My husband, on the other hand, sometimes felt like he didn't quite have the same close relationship with the kids as I did. He travelled a lot for work, and the time away really dragged on him, but he was in such a niche field and didn't know how to make a career change. He got to the point where he felt like he didn't have a purpose in work or a purpose with the family. He figured it out eventually, and he had a great relationship with our kids later on. I like to think he felt like he left the same legacy and felt fulfilled by his life at the end. But boy, was it hard to know how to support him at the time. I think he really had to figure it out on his own."

Integrity versus Despair

"Now, I'm about to turn 85. I enjoy living in this community, although it can be sad to say goodbye to friends as they come and go. The recreation and friendships are nice, and I live close by to my kids and grandkids. My daughter wanted me to come live with her, but this community is such a slower pace than living with toddlers—whew, no offense! As I look back on my life, I feel at peace that even though it seemed like I had such a rough start, I was able to make something of myself. I am so thankful for my parents. I am a happy, positive person and I try to contribute to others' sense of well-being, too. Some of my friends around here, I don't know that they have that. They start to worry about all the things they might have missed out on. They wonder if they should have spent more time with their kids, or if they should have left a bad marriage. I try to help them find the flowers amidst just what is. That's always possible, too. So, I guess my advice to you, for your book, is that you have to know yourself early on. You have to know what makes you happy and what brings you joy, and pursue those things. If you find out new information about what makes you happy and what values you have, course correct immediately! And always find something to be grateful for, no matter what is going on. I think those are the ways to true fulfillment by the end of your time here."

2. **Part A**

Experimental group: also known as the treatment group, is the group in a research study that actually receives a treatment. In this particular study, the first group of 10 people hitting the training dummy would be considered the experimental group, since the goal of this research is to figure out whether research participants who were feeling aggressive would be less aggressive after experiencing a cathartic emotional release by taking out their anger on a training dummy.

Control group: describes a group in an experiment that does not receive the treatment under investigation, but instead serves as a baseline comparison, or a benchmark, to measure how the other test subjects end up doing comparatively. In this study, the control group would be the second group of 10 people sitting idly for 5 minutes, since this act does not involve any kind of cathartic release and only exists to serve as a baseline comparison to the experimental group.

Independent variable: describes the variable in an experimental study that is changed or manipulated to test the effects on the dependent variable. In this particular study, the independent variable involves the action taken by the participants after hearing the review—that participants vented their aggression by either hitting a training dummy or sitting idly.

Dependent variable: describes the variable in a study that is being tested and measured, and which is dependent on the independent variable. In this study, the dependent variable would be how loud each group participant blew their whistle at the researcher giving them the bad review on their opinion paper. In other words, the dependent variable is their rate of aggression.

Part B

In this study, the original hypothesis of the researchers was that a person's level of aggression would decrease after experiencing a cathartic release in the form of hitting an inanimate object. The louder a research participant blew their whistle, the more aggression they were expressing. If you look back at the table comparing the loudness of the whistle (measured in decibels), between the first group of 10 people who hit a training dummy (experimental group) versus the second group of 10 people who sat doing nothing (control group), you will see that the experimental group blew their whistles at the researcher at a much louder rate than the control group. These results revealed that the experimental group demonstrated more aggressive behavior toward the researcher after hitting the training dummy than did the control group who did nothing. In conclusion, the original hypothesis that catharsis decreases rates of aggression was, in fact, refuted.

An ethical flaw in a research study is something that researchers did wrong and need to correct when conducting their experiment. In this particular experiment, deception was used, so

ethically speaking, researchers should have debriefed the group members as to the true nature of the study.

The volume of the whistle blows was measured in decibels. When you calculate the total loudness of the whistles blown by the experimental group who hit a training dummy, it totaled 680 decibels. As for the control group who sat idly, their total amount of loudness with whistle blowing totaled 48 decibels. Since the volume of the whistle blowing was used to indicate the rate of aggression, this calculation clearly helps demonstrate that catharsis did not reduce the total rate of aggression.

3.

Positive reinforcement: describes a form of behavior modification whereby a subject is rewarded whenever they perform a desired behavior, so that they eventually come to associate the action with a reward. In turn, this reinforces the desired behavior and increases its likelihood of being repeated again in the future. In this instance, positive reinforcement relates to Jason gradually coming to associate going to the dentist with receiving a reward (a toy), thus reinforcing his likelihood of not only going to the dentist again, but also being well-behaved when he is there.

Associational learning: occurs when conditioning is used in order to associate a new response with a certain stimulus. Association is the key to learning, so when ideas or experiences are used to reinforce one another, they become connected to each other, thus making it a powerful learning strategy. In this instance, by pairing a dental visit with the prospect of receiving a reward, Jason will eventually come to associate one with the other, which in turn will increase the likelihood of returning to the dentist and being well-behaved in order to get a reward.

Hippocampus: a complex brain structure located in the temporal lobe and plays a vital role in learning and memory, specifically associative memory, which describes the ability to learn and recall the relationship between unrelated stimuli. In this case, Jason is using his hippocampus to remember the association that has been made between going to the dentist and getting a toy reward.

Foot-in-the-door phenomenon: describes the tendency for people to be more compliant with large requests after initially agreeing to a smaller request. In Jason's case, this phenomenon comes into play when he first agreed to go for a car ride to the toy store (a small request) before ultimately complying with the promise to behave when visiting with the dentist (a large request).

Approach-avoidance conflict: describes when there is a particular goal or scenario that has both positive and negative outcomes or features, which essentially makes it both appealing and unappealing at the same time. In this scenario, Jason is going for a car ride, but to two different destinations—one that is appealing to him and one that is not. For Jason, the toy store serves as the more appealing option, and the dentist visit is the more unappealing one.

Dear AP Psychology Test Taker,

We would like to start by thanking you for purchasing this study guide for your AP Psychology exam. We hope that we exceeded your expectations.

Our goal in creating this study guide was to cover all of the topics that you will see on the test. We also strove to make our practice questions as similar as possible to what you will encounter on test day. With that being said, if you found something that you feel was not up to your standards, please send us an email and let us know.

We would also like to let you know about other books in our catalog that may interest you.

AP Biology

This can be found on Amazon: amazon.com/dp/1628456221

SAT Math 1

amazon.com/dp/1628454717

SAT

amazon.com/dp/1628456396

ACT

amazon.com/dp/162845606X

ACCUPLACER

amazon.com/dp/1628456515

We have study guides in a wide variety of fields. If the one you are looking for isn't listed above, then try searching for it on Amazon or send us an email.

Thanks Again and Happy Testing!
Product Development Team
info@studyguideteam.com

Interested in buying more than 10 copies of our product? Contact us about bulk discounts:

bulkorders@studyguideteam.com

FREE Test Taking Tips DVD Offer

To help us better serve you, we have developed a Test Taking Tips DVD that we would like to give you for FREE. **This DVD covers world-class test taking tips that you can use to be even more successful when you are taking your test.**

All that we ask is that you email us your feedback about your study guide. Please let us know what you thought about it – whether that is good, bad or indifferent.

To get your **FREE Test Taking Tips DVD**, email freedvd@studyguideteam.com with "FREE DVD" in the subject line and the following information in the body of the email:

  a. The title of your study guide.

  b. Your product rating on a scale of 1-5, with 5 being the highest rating.

  c. Your feedback about the study guide. What did you think of it?

  d. Your full name and shipping address to send your free DVD.

If you have any questions or concerns, please don't hesitate to contact us at freedvd@studyguideteam.com.

Thanks again!

CPSIA information can be obtained
at www.ICGtesting.com
Printed in the USA
BVHW011427230422
634833BV00004B/156